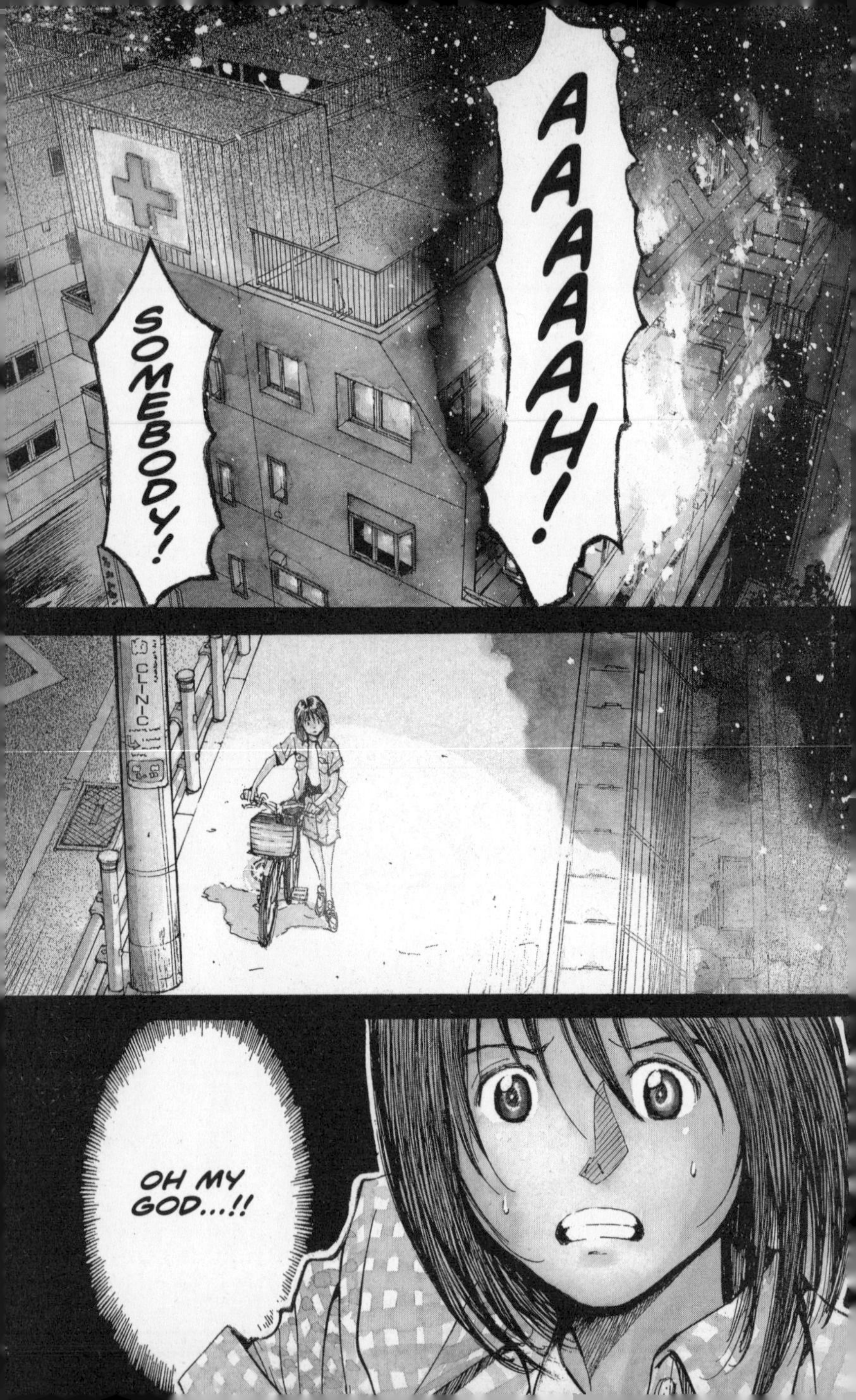
AAAAAH!
SOMEBODY!
CLINIC
OH MY GOD...!!

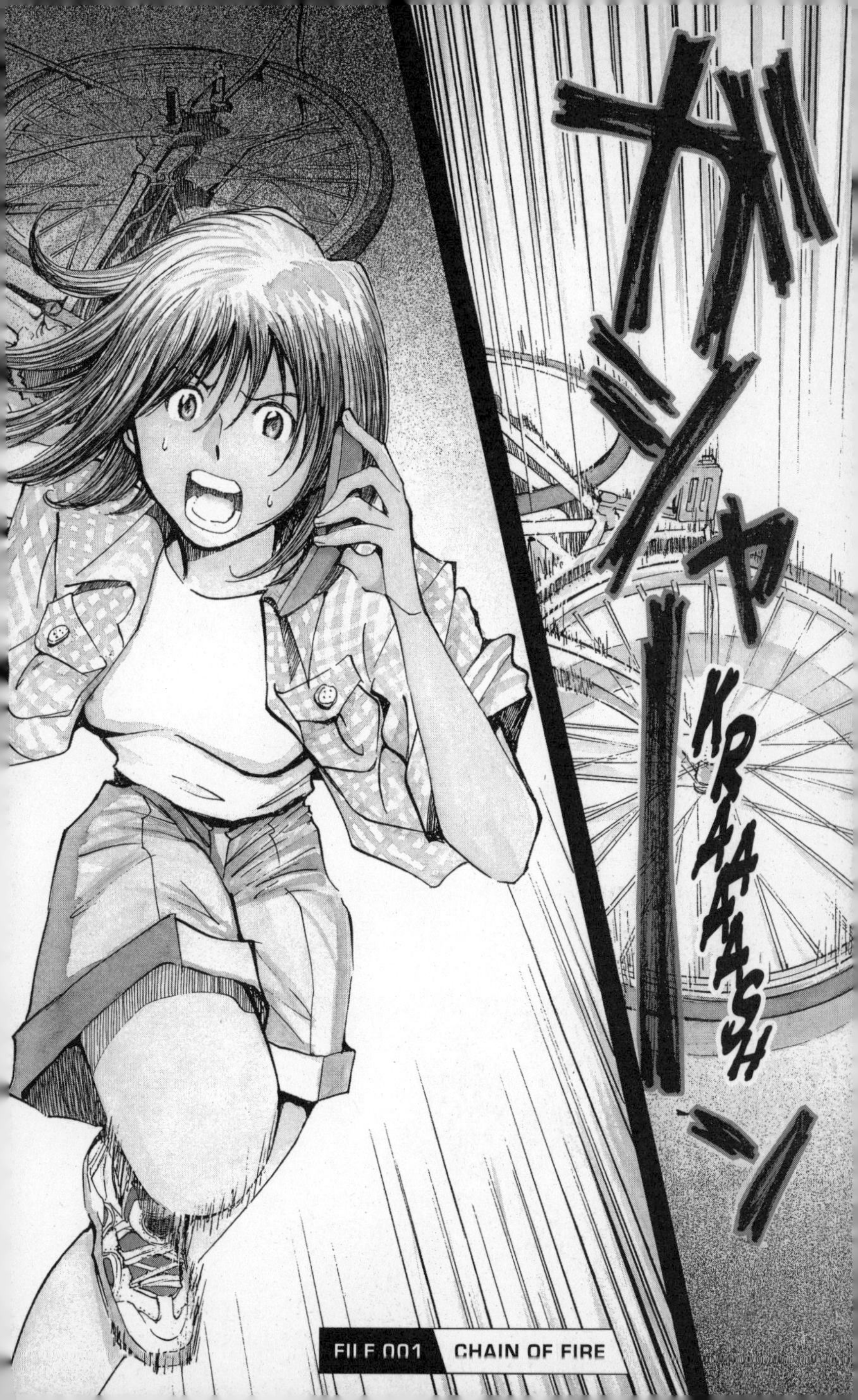
ガシャーン
KRAAAASH
FILE 001 CHAIN OF FIRE

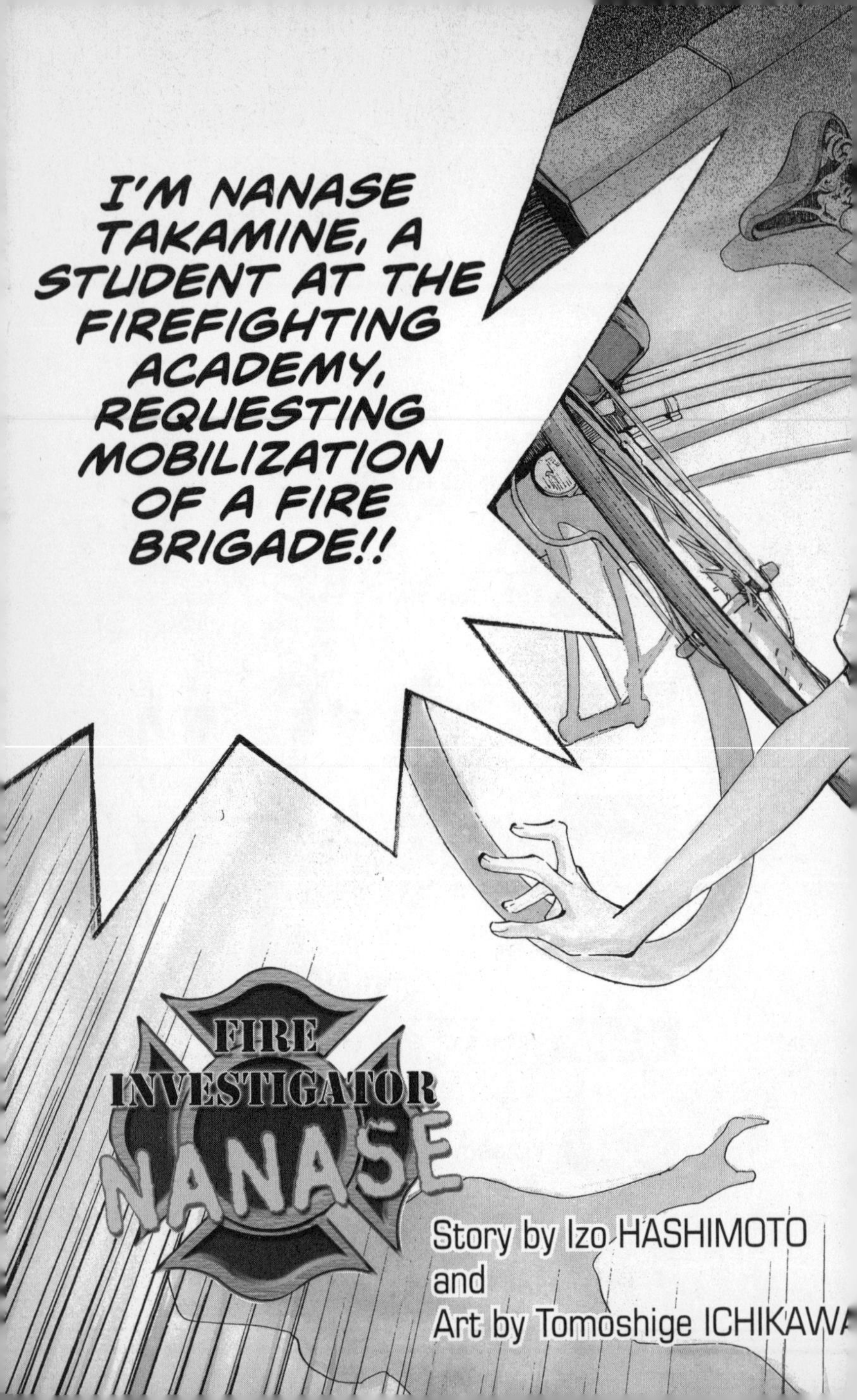
I'M NANASE TAKAMINE, A STUDENT AT THE FIREFIGHTING ACADEMY, REQUESTING MOBILIZATION OF A FIRE BRIGADE!!
FIRE INVESTIGATOR NANASE
Story by Izo HASHIMOTO
and
Art by Tomoshige ICHIKAWA

anase Fire Investigator

ONTENTS

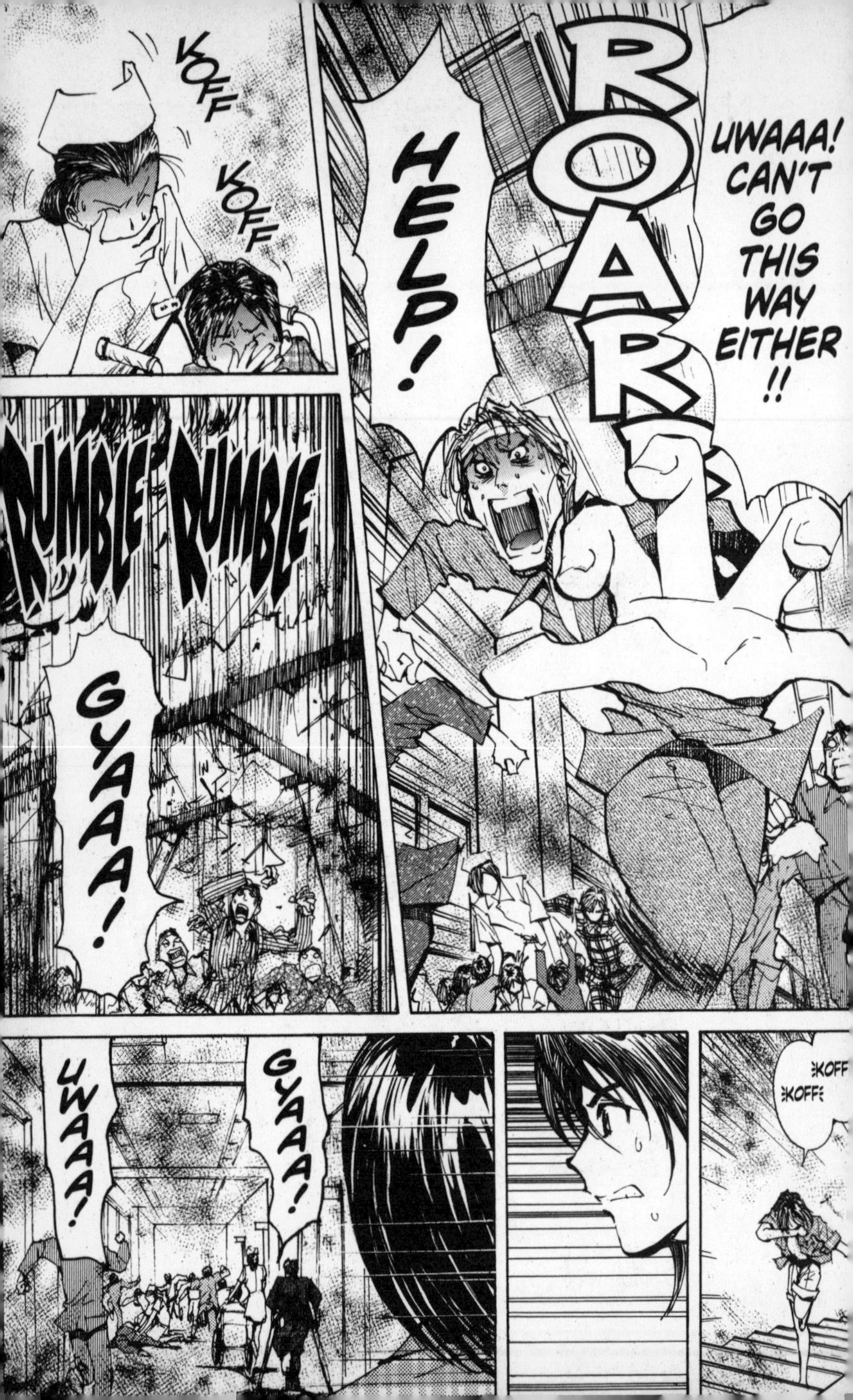
UWAAA! CAN'T GO THIS WAY EITHER!!
ROAR
HELP!
KOFF
KOFF
RUMBLE RUMBLE
GYAAAA!
KOFF
KOFF
GYAAAA!
UWAAAA!

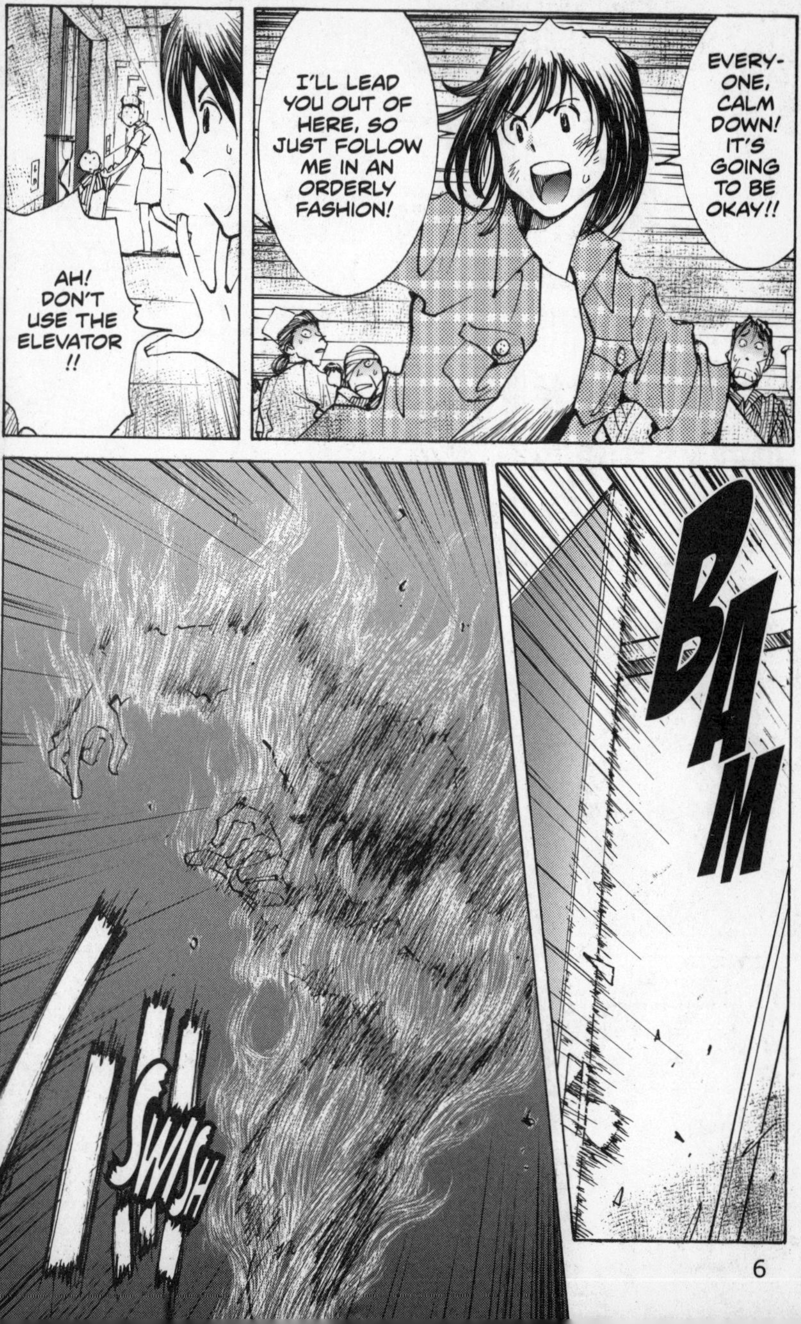
EVERY-ONE, CALM DOWN! IT'S GOING TO BE OKAY!!
I'LL LEAD YOU OUT OF HERE, SO JUST FOLLOW ME IN AN ORDERLY FASHION!
AH! DON'T USE THE ELEVATOR!!
BAM
SWISH

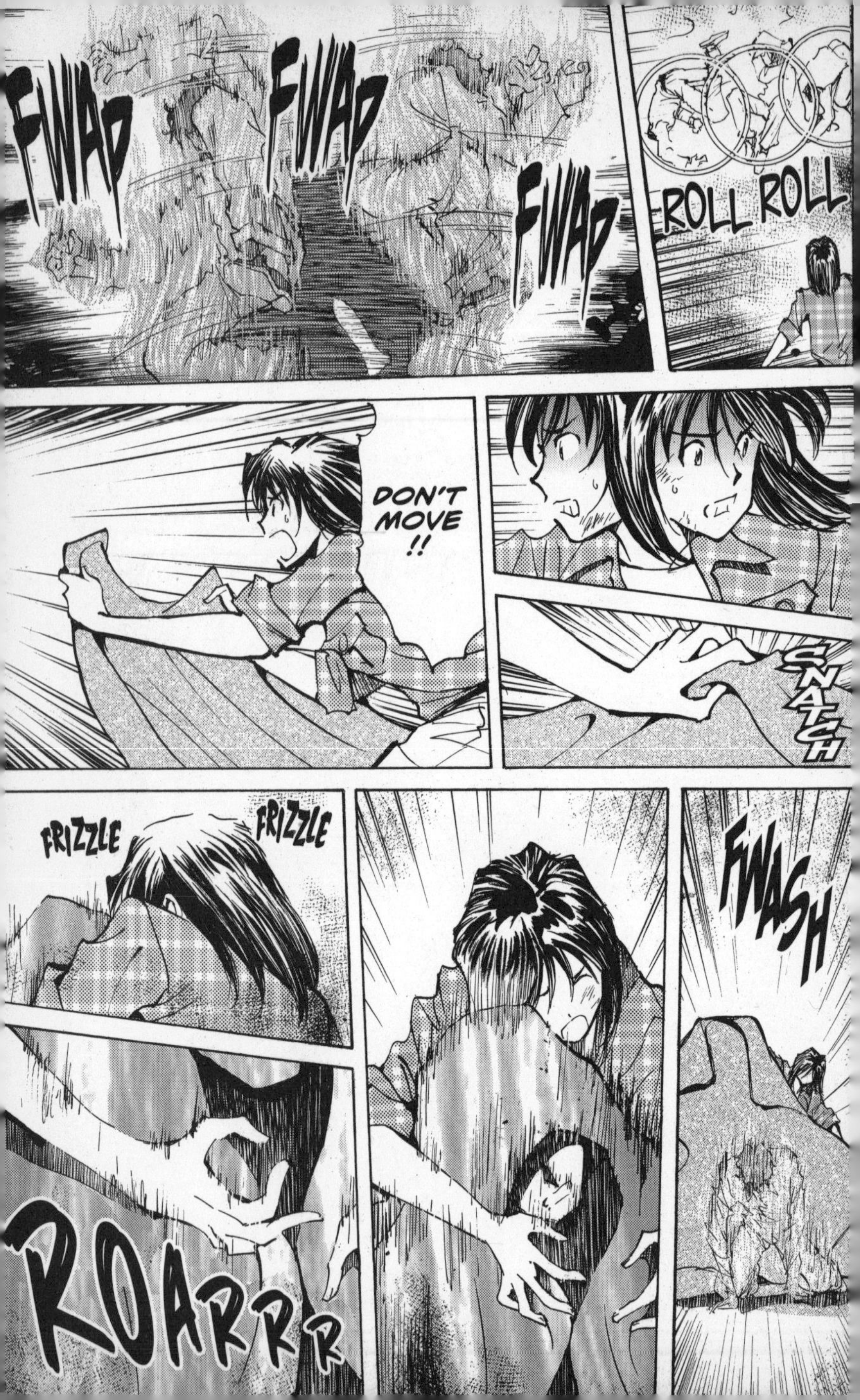
ROLL ROLL
FWAP
FWAP
FWAP
SNATCH
DON'T MOVE!!
FWASH
FRIZZLE
FRIZZLE
ROARRR

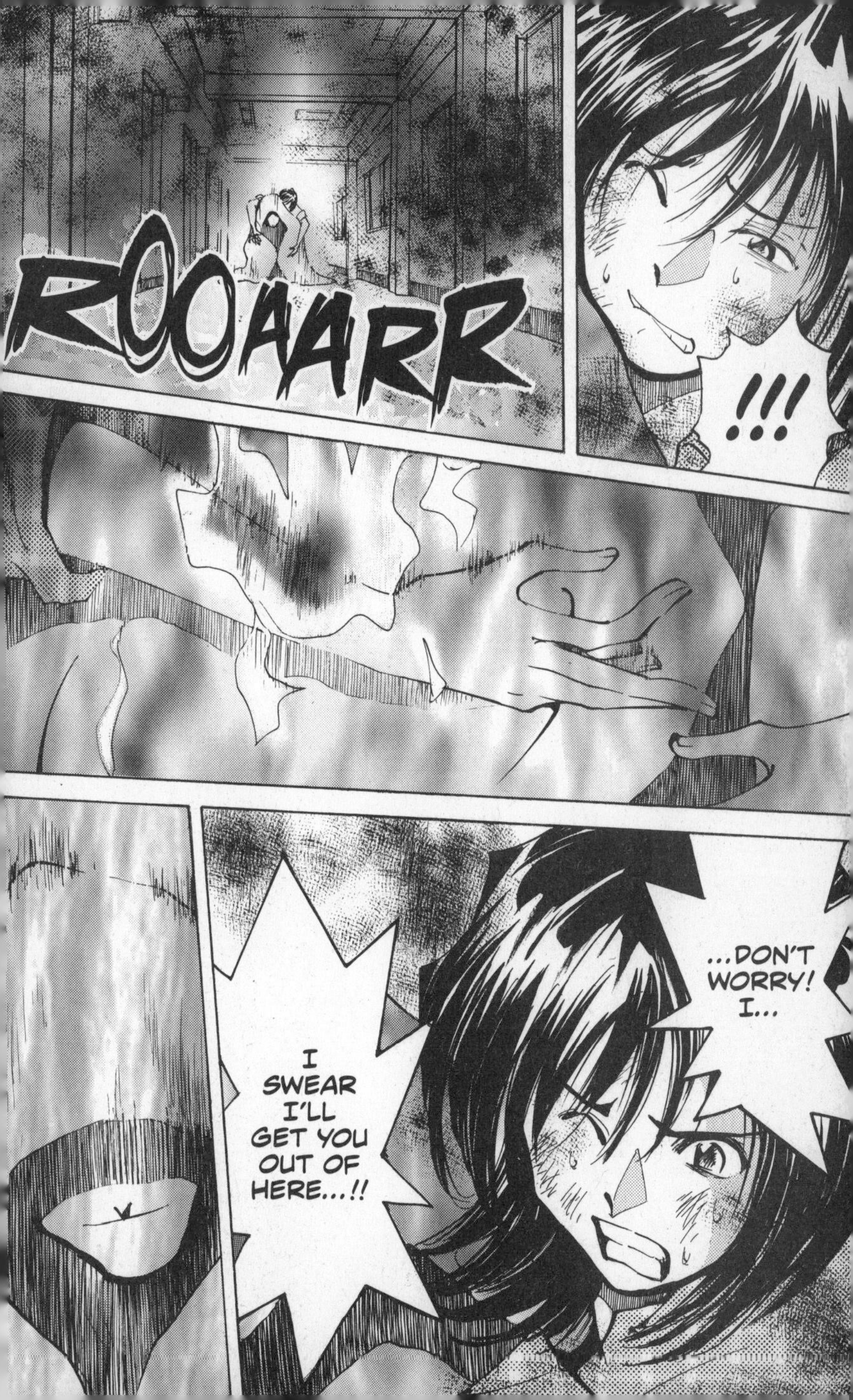
!!!
ROOAARR
...DON'T WORRY! I...
I SWEAR I'LL GET YOU OUT OF HERE...!!

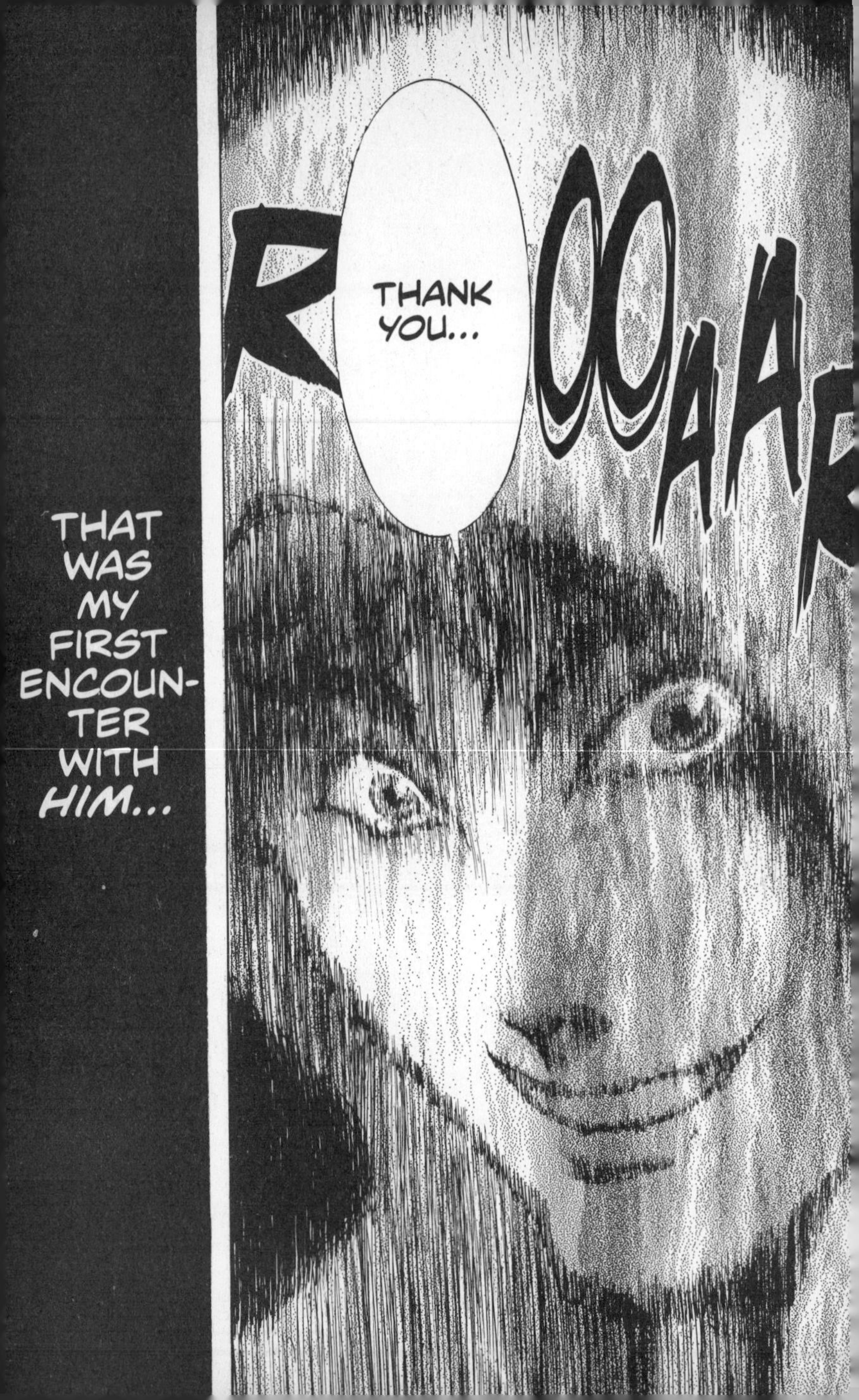
THANK YOU...
ROOAAR
THAT WAS MY FIRST ENCOUN-TER WITH *HIM*...

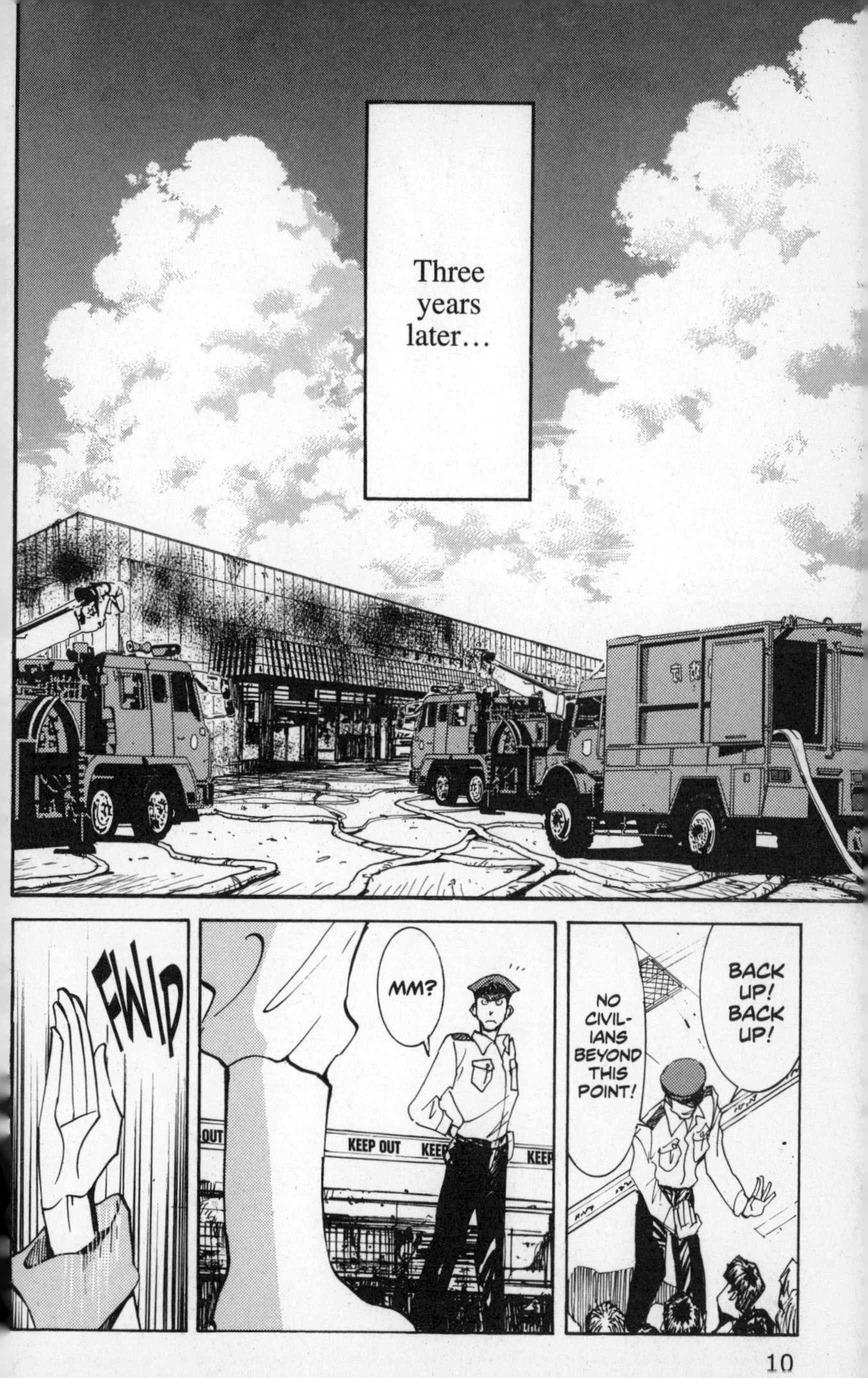
Three years later…
BACK UP! BACK UP!
NO CIVIL-IANS BEYOND THIS POINT!
KEEP OUT
MM?
FWIP

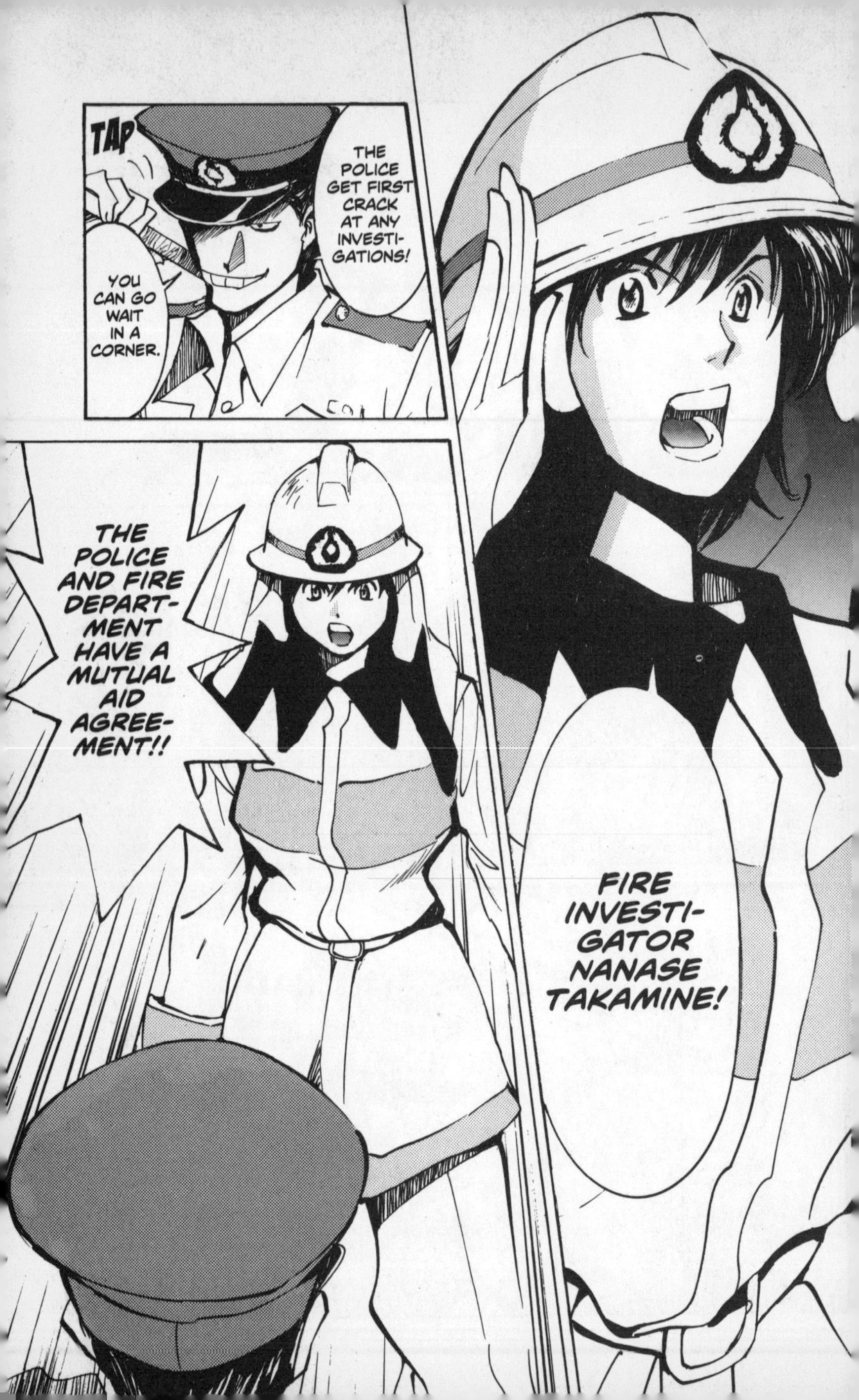
FIRE INVESTIGATOR NANASE TAKAMINE!
TAP
THE POLICE GET FIRST CRACK AT ANY INVESTIGATIONS!
YOU CAN GO WAIT IN A CORNER.
THE POLICE AND FIRE DEPARTMENT HAVE A MUTUAL AID AGREEMENT!!

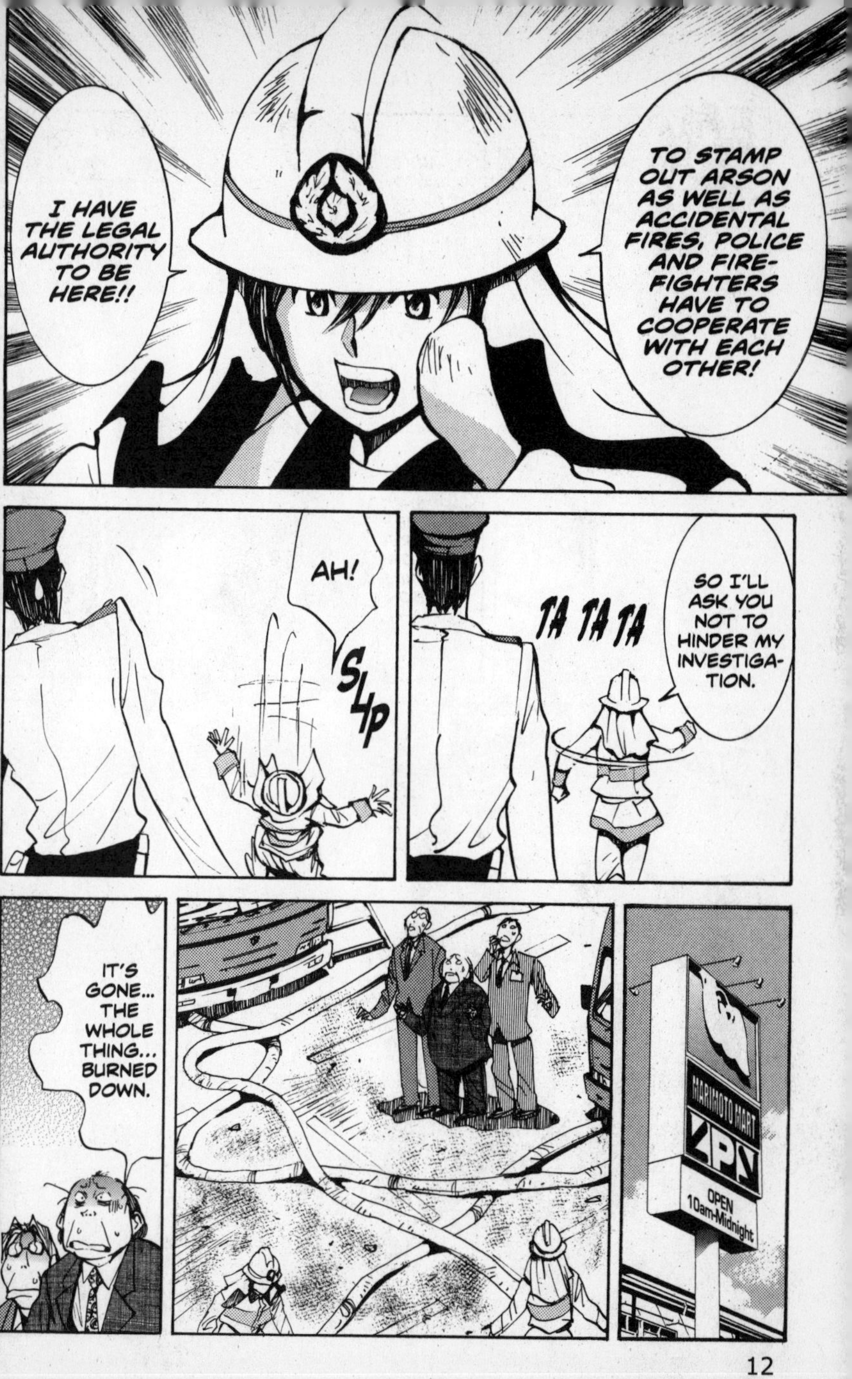
TO STAMP OUT ARSON AS WELL AS ACCIDENTAL FIRES, POLICE AND FIRE-FIGHTERS HAVE TO COOPERATE WITH EACH OTHER!
I HAVE THE LEGAL AUTHORITY TO BE HERE!!
SO I'LL ASK YOU NOT TO HINDER MY INVESTIGA-TION.
TA TA TA
AH!
SLIP
HARIMOTO MART
OPEN 10am-Midnight
IT'S GONE... THE WHOLE THING... BURNED DOWN.

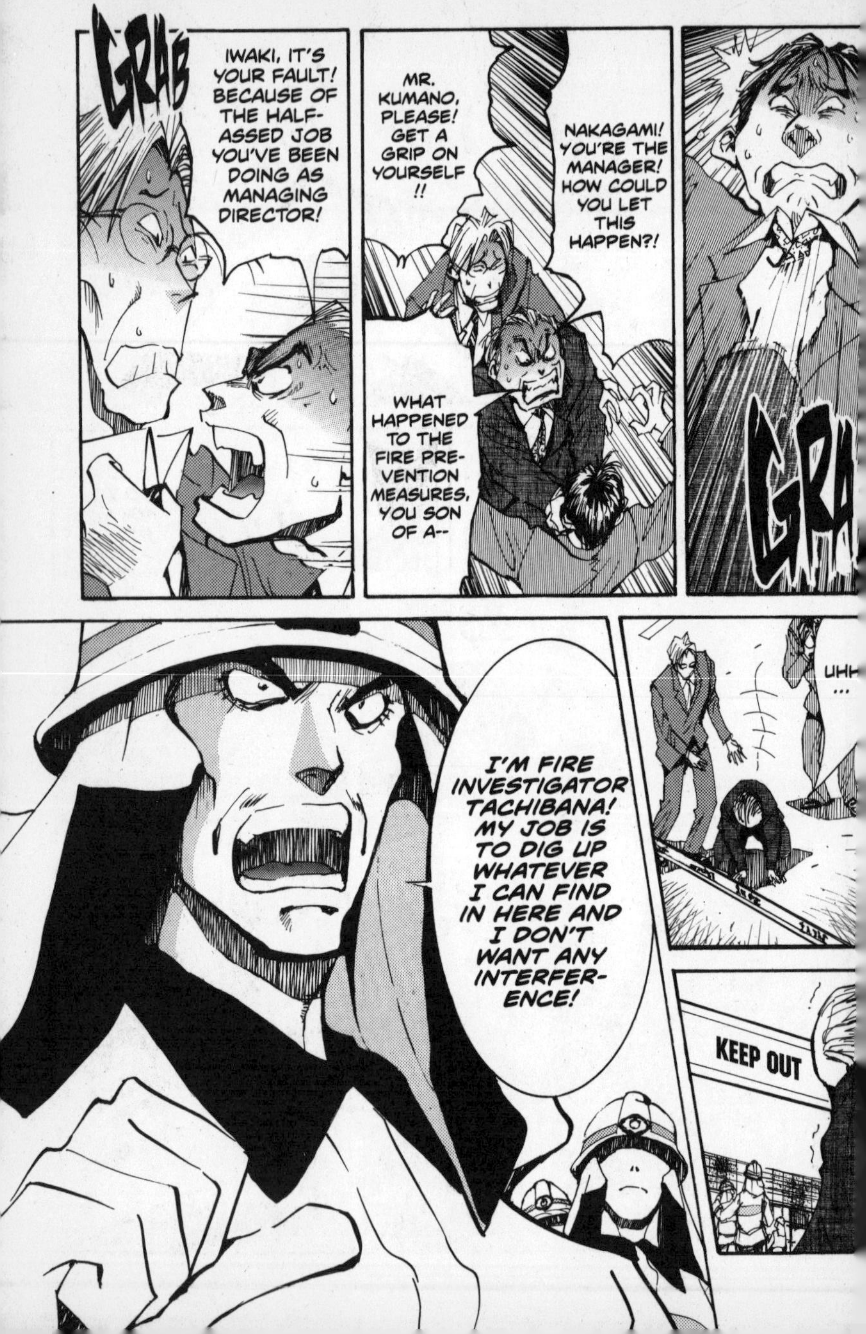
NAKAGAMI! YOU'RE THE MANAGER! HOW COULD YOU LET THIS HAPPEN?!
MR. KUMANO, PLEASE! GET A GRIP ON YOURSELF !!
WHAT HAPPENED TO THE FIRE PRE-VENTION MEASURES, YOU SON OF A--
GRAB
IWAKI, IT'S YOUR FAULT! BECAUSE OF THE HALF-ASSED JOB YOU'VE BEEN DOING AS MANAGING DIRECTOR!
UHH ...
KEEP OUT
I'M FIRE INVESTIGATOR TACHIBANA! MY JOB IS TO DIG UP WHATEVER I CAN FIND IN HERE AND I DON'T WANT ANY INTERFER-ENCE!

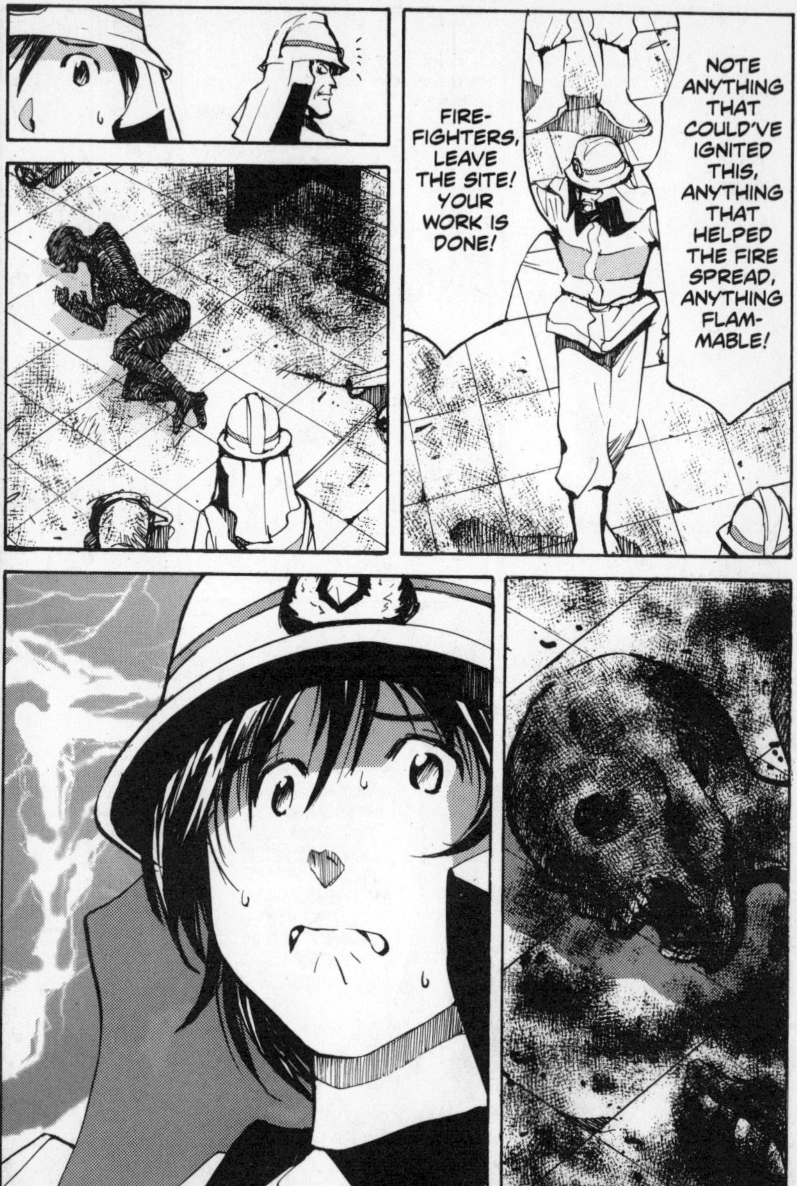
NOTE ANYTHING THAT COULD'VE IGNITED THIS, ANYTHING THAT HELPED THE FIRE SPREAD, ANYTHING FLAM-MABLE!
FIRE-FIGHTERS, LEAVE THE SITE! YOUR WORK IS DONE!

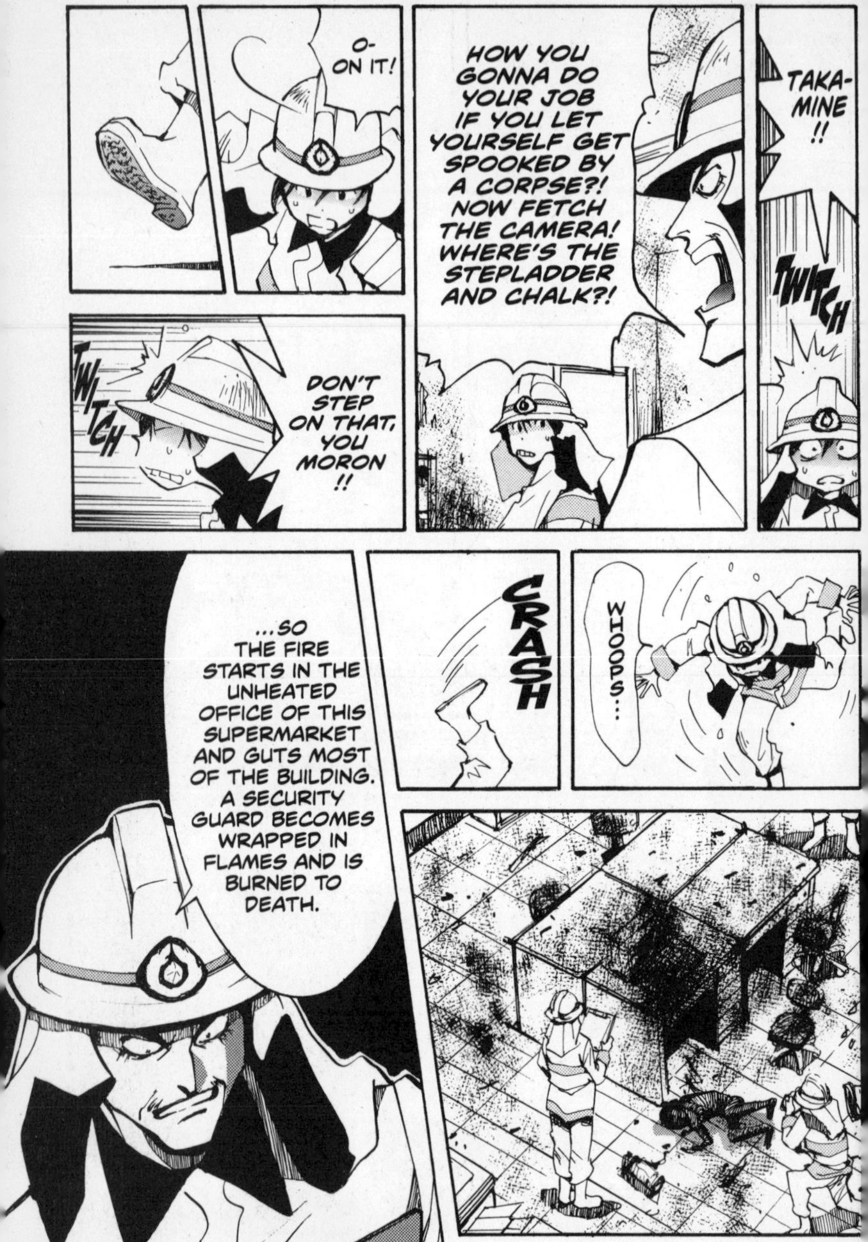
TAKA-MINE!!
TWITCH
HOW YOU GONNA DO YOUR JOB IF YOU LET YOURSELF GET SPOOKED BY A CORPSE?! NOW FETCH THE CAMERA! WHERE'S THE STEPLADDER AND CHALK?!
O- ON IT!
TWITCH
DON'T STEP ON THAT, YOU MORON!!
WHOOPS...
CRASH
...SO THE FIRE STARTS IN THE UNHEATED OFFICE OF THIS SUPERMARKET AND GUTS MOST OF THE BUILDING. A SECURITY GUARD BECOMES WRAPPED IN FLAMES AND IS BURNED TO DEATH.

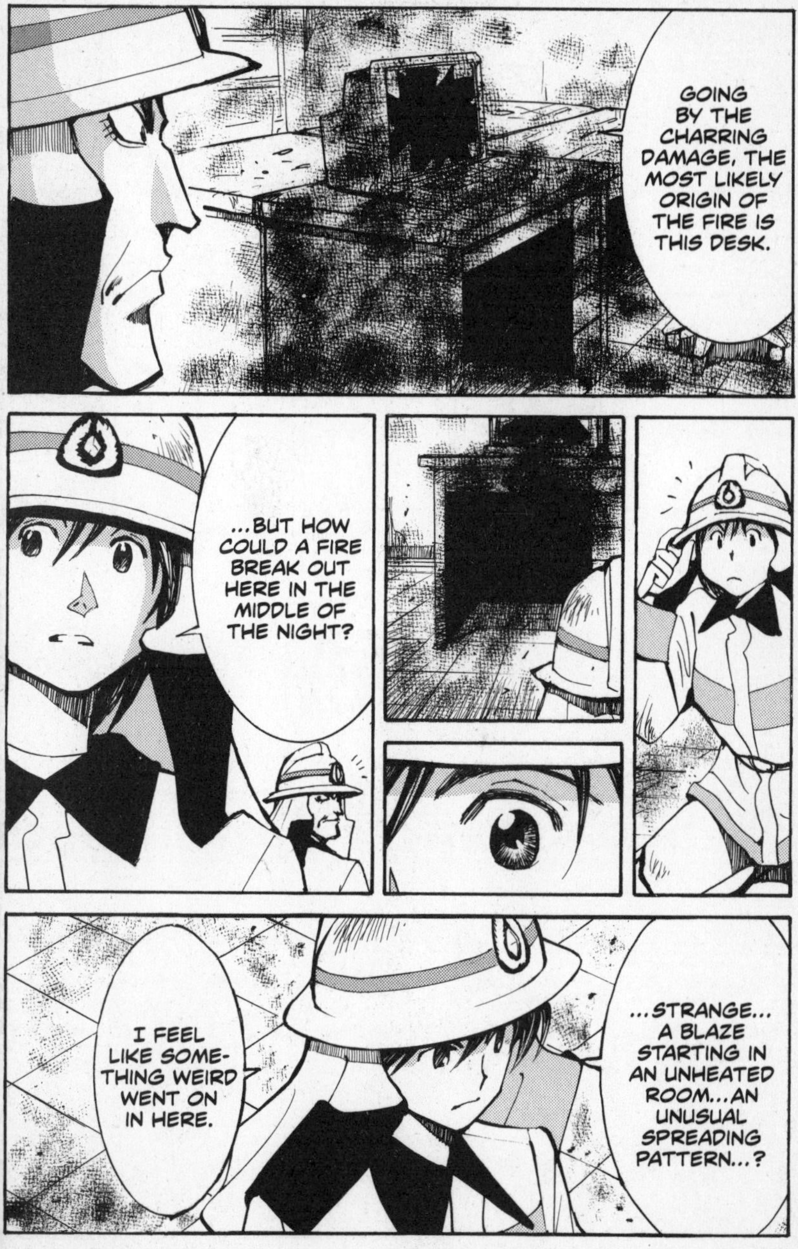
GOING BY THE CHARRING DAMAGE, THE MOST LIKELY ORIGIN OF THE FIRE IS THIS DESK.
...BUT HOW COULD A FIRE BREAK OUT HERE IN THE MIDDLE OF THE NIGHT?
...STRANGE... A BLAZE STARTING IN AN UNHEATED ROOM...AN UNUSUAL SPREADING PATTERN...?
I FEEL LIKE SOME-THING WEIRD WENT ON IN HERE.

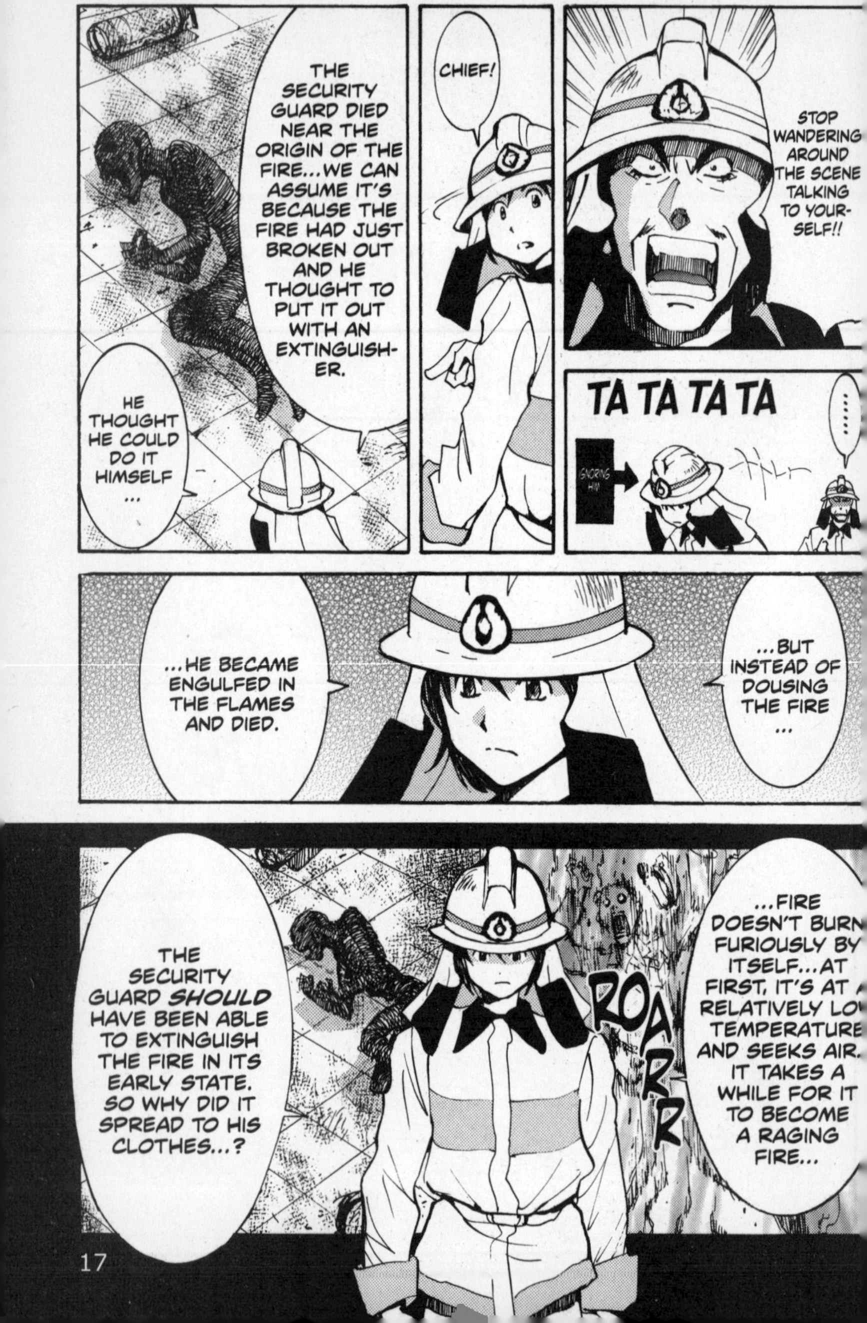

STOP WANDERING AROUND THE SCENE TALKING TO YOURSELF!!
TA TA TA TA
IGNORING HIM
......
CHIEF!
THE SECURITY GUARD DIED NEAR THE ORIGIN OF THE FIRE...WE CAN ASSUME IT'S BECAUSE THE FIRE HAD JUST BROKEN OUT AND HE THOUGHT TO PUT IT OUT WITH AN EXTINGUISH-ER.
HE THOUGHT HE COULD DO IT HIMSELF...
...BUT INSTEAD OF DOUSING THE FIRE...
...HE BECAME ENGULFED IN THE FLAMES AND DIED.
...FIRE DOESN'T BURN FURIOUSLY BY ITSELF...AT FIRST, IT'S AT A RELATIVELY LOW TEMPERATURE AND SEEKS AIR. IT TAKES A WHILE FOR IT TO BECOME A RAGING FIRE...
ROARR
THE SECURITY GUARD *SHOULD* HAVE BEEN ABLE TO EXTINGUISH THE FIRE IN ITS EARLY STATE. SO WHY DID IT SPREAD TO HIS CLOTHES...?

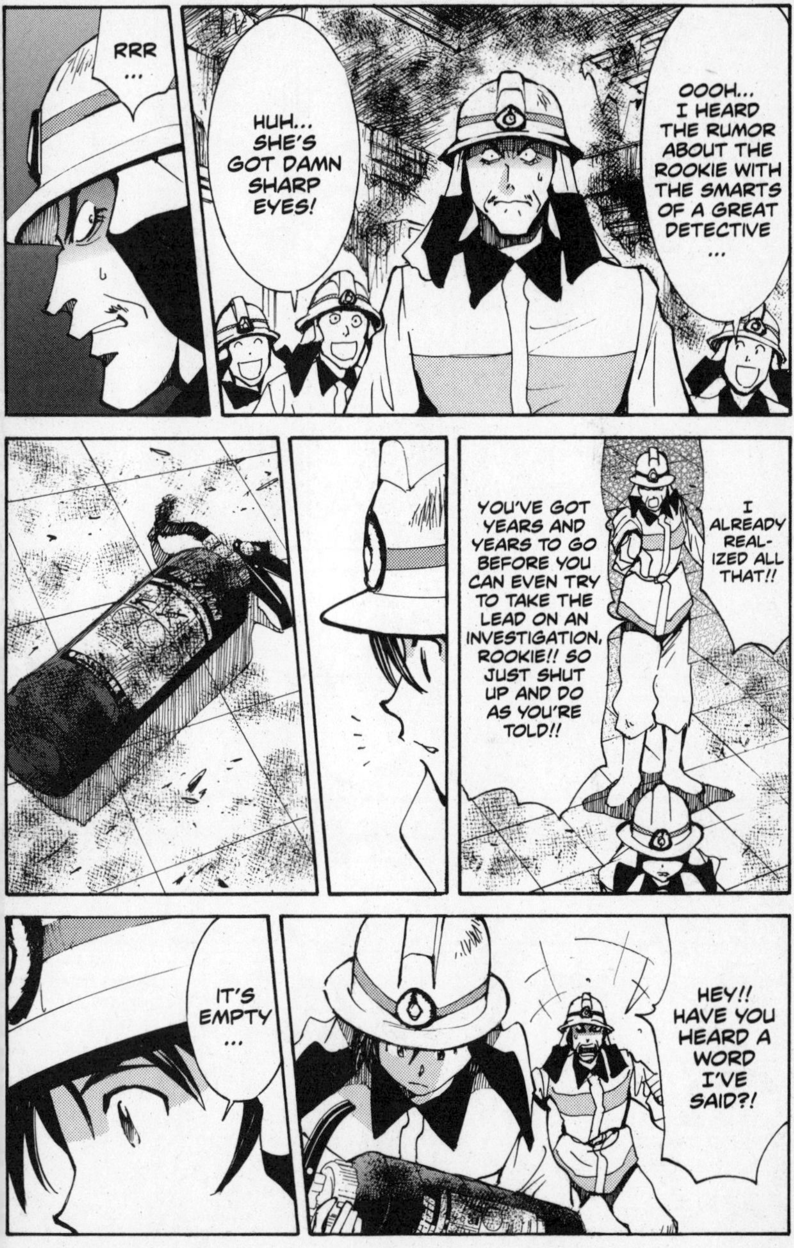
OOOH... I HEARD THE RUMOR ABOUT THE ROOKIE WITH THE SMARTS OF A GREAT DETECTIVE ...
HUH... SHE'S GOT DAMN SHARP EYES!
RRR ...
I ALREADY REAL-IZED ALL THAT!!
YOU'VE GOT YEARS AND YEARS TO GO BEFORE YOU CAN EVEN TRY TO TAKE THE LEAD ON AN INVESTIGATION, ROOKIE!! SO JUST SHUT UP AND DO AS YOU'RE TOLD!!
HEY!! HAVE YOU HEARD A WORD I'VE SAID?!
IT'S EMPTY ...

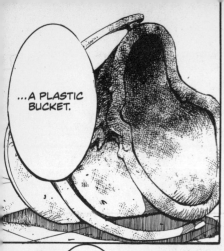

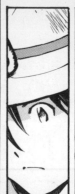

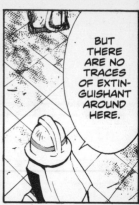

BUT THERE ARE NO TRACES OF EXTIN-GUISHANT AROUND HERE.
...A PLASTIC BUCKET.
WHY...?!
NOOO! MY HUS-BAND IS IN THERE!!
YOU CAN'T GO IN!!
LET GO OF ME!
PLEASE!

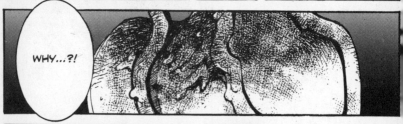

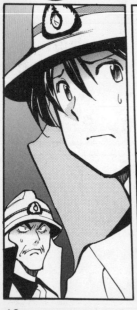

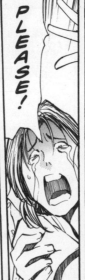

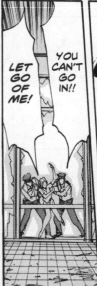

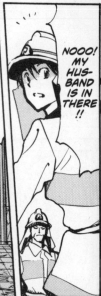

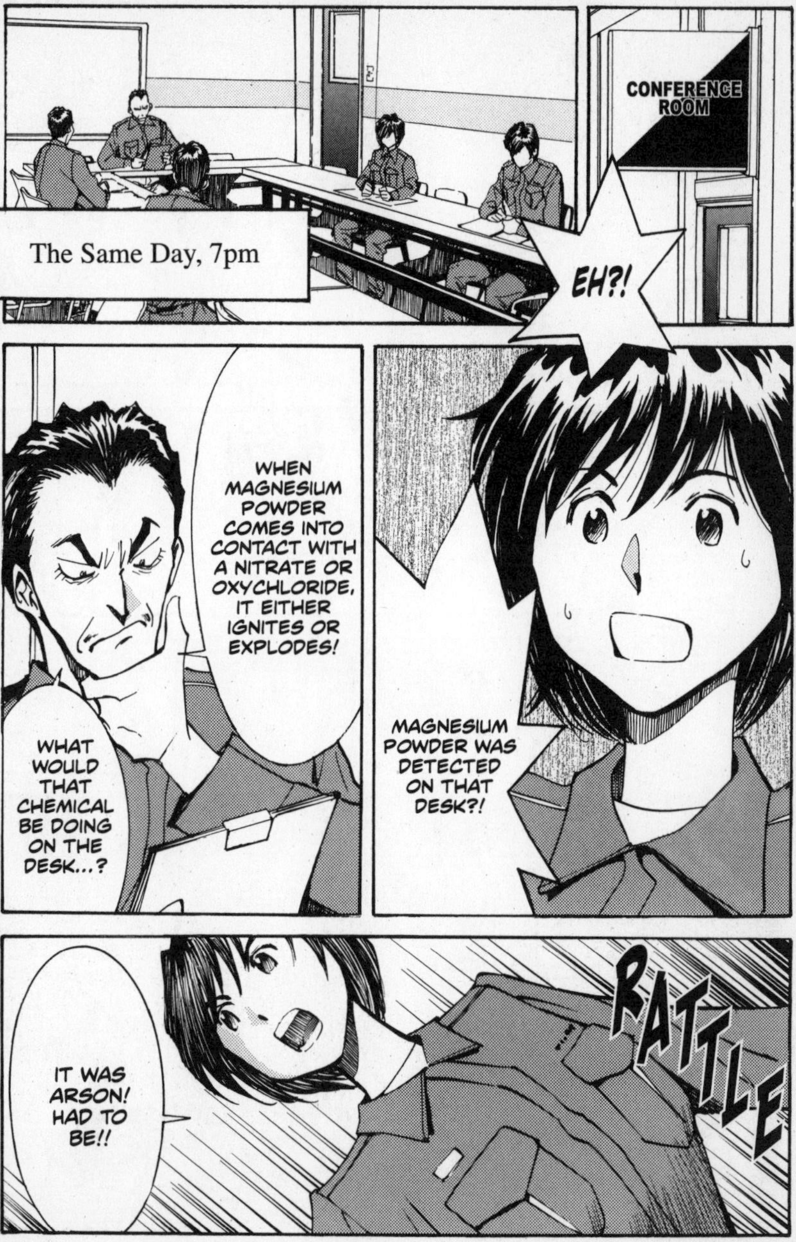
CONFERENCE ROOM
The Same Day, 7pm
EH?!
MAGNESIUM POWDER WAS DETECTED ON THAT DESK?!
WHEN MAGNESIUM POWDER COMES INTO CONTACT WITH A NITRATE OR OXYCHLORIDE, IT EITHER IGNITES OR EXPLODES!
WHAT WOULD THAT CHEMICAL BE DOING ON THE DESK...?
RATTLE
IT WAS ARSON! HAD TO BE!!

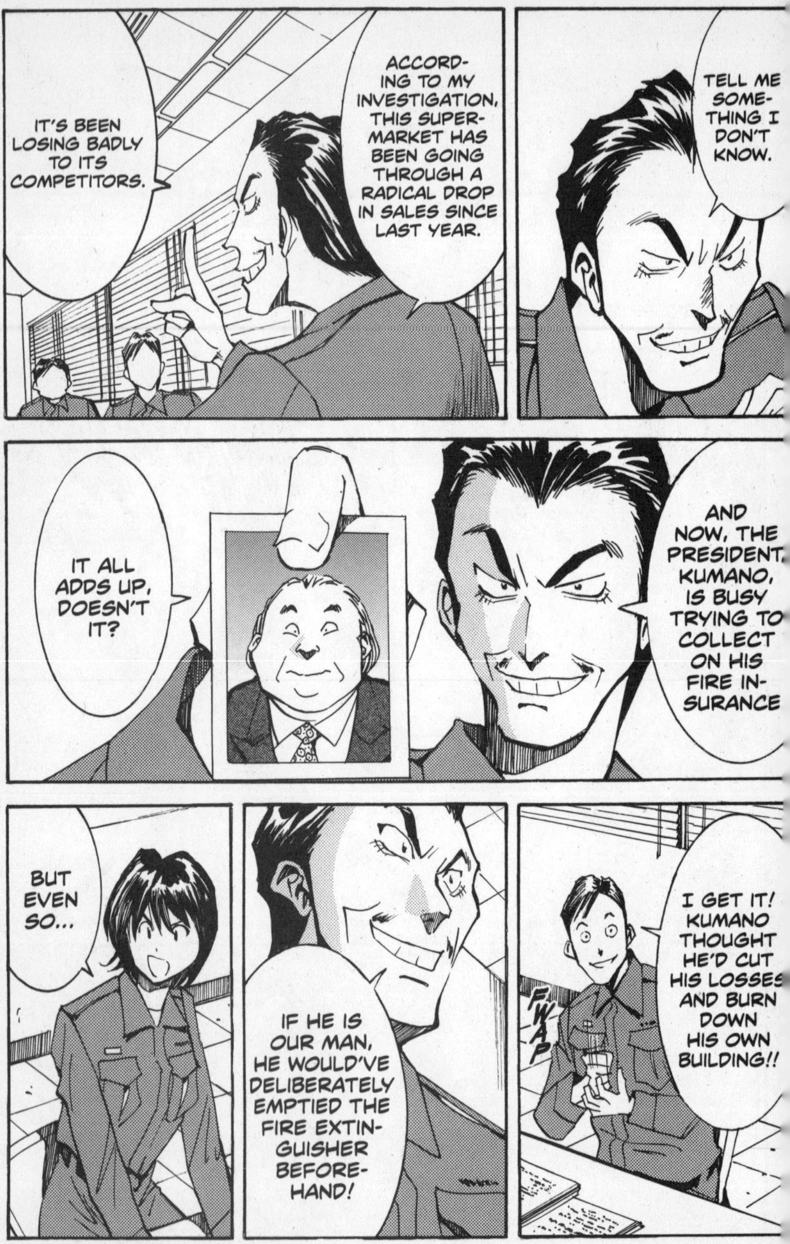
TELL ME SOMETHING I DON'T KNOW.
ACCORDING TO MY INVESTIGATION, THIS SUPERMARKET HAS BEEN GOING THROUGH A RADICAL DROP IN SALES SINCE LAST YEAR.
IT'S BEEN LOSING BADLY TO ITS COMPETITORS.
AND NOW, THE PRESIDENT, KUMANO, IS BUSY TRYING TO COLLECT ON HIS FIRE INSURANCE
IT ALL ADDS UP, DOESN'T IT?
I GET IT! KUMANO THOUGHT HE'D CUT HIS LOSSES AND BURN DOWN HIS OWN BUILDING!!
FWAP
IF HE IS OUR MAN, HE WOULD'VE DELIBERATELY EMPTIED THE FIRE EXTINGUISHER BEFOREHAND!
BUT EVEN SO...

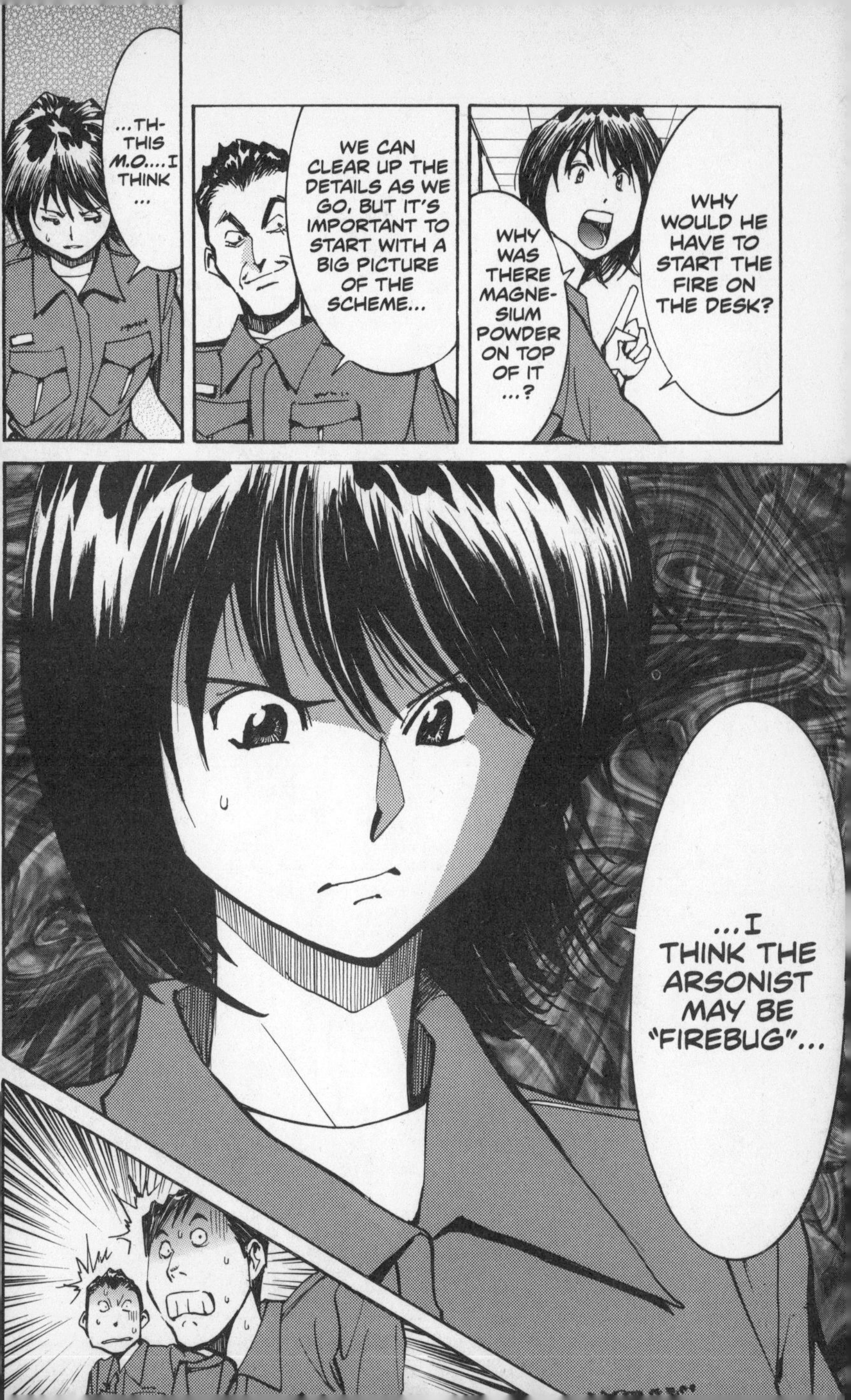
WHY WOULD HE HAVE TO START THE FIRE ON THE DESK?
WHY WAS THERE MAGNESIUM POWDER ON TOP OF IT ...?
WE CAN CLEAR UP THE DETAILS AS WE GO, BUT IT'S IMPORTANT TO START WITH A BIG PICTURE OF THE SCHEME...
...TH- THIS M.O.... I THINK ...
...I THINK THE ARSONIST MAY BE "FIREBUG"...

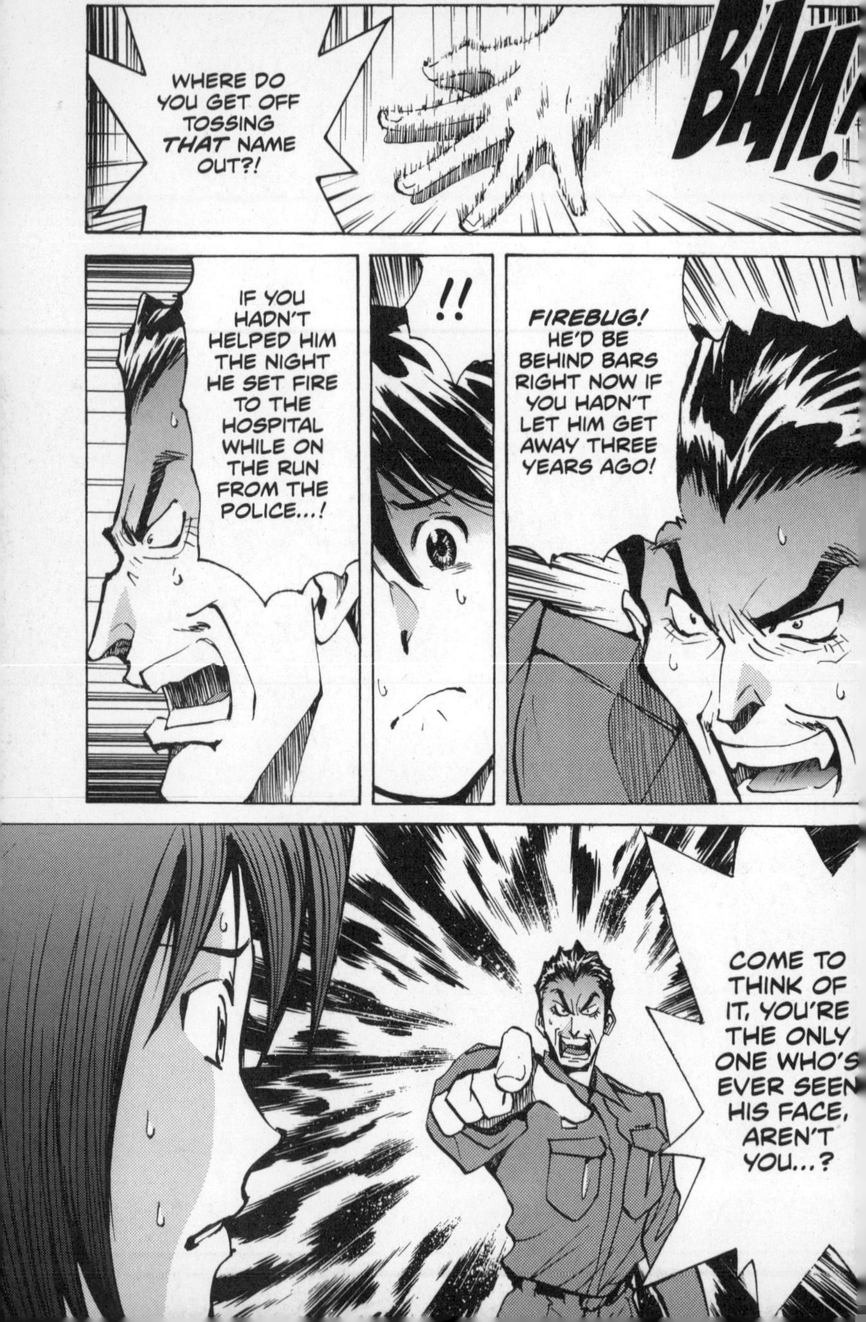
BAM!!
WHERE DO YOU GET OFF TOSSING *THAT* NAME OUT?!
FIREBUG! HE'D BE BEHIND BARS RIGHT NOW IF YOU HADN'T LET HIM GET AWAY THREE YEARS AGO!
!!
IF YOU HADN'T HELPED HIM THE NIGHT HE SET FIRE TO THE HOSPITAL WHILE ON THE RUN FROM THE POLICE...!
COME TO THINK OF IT, YOU'RE THE ONLY ONE WHO'S EVER SEEN HIS FACE, AREN'T YOU...?

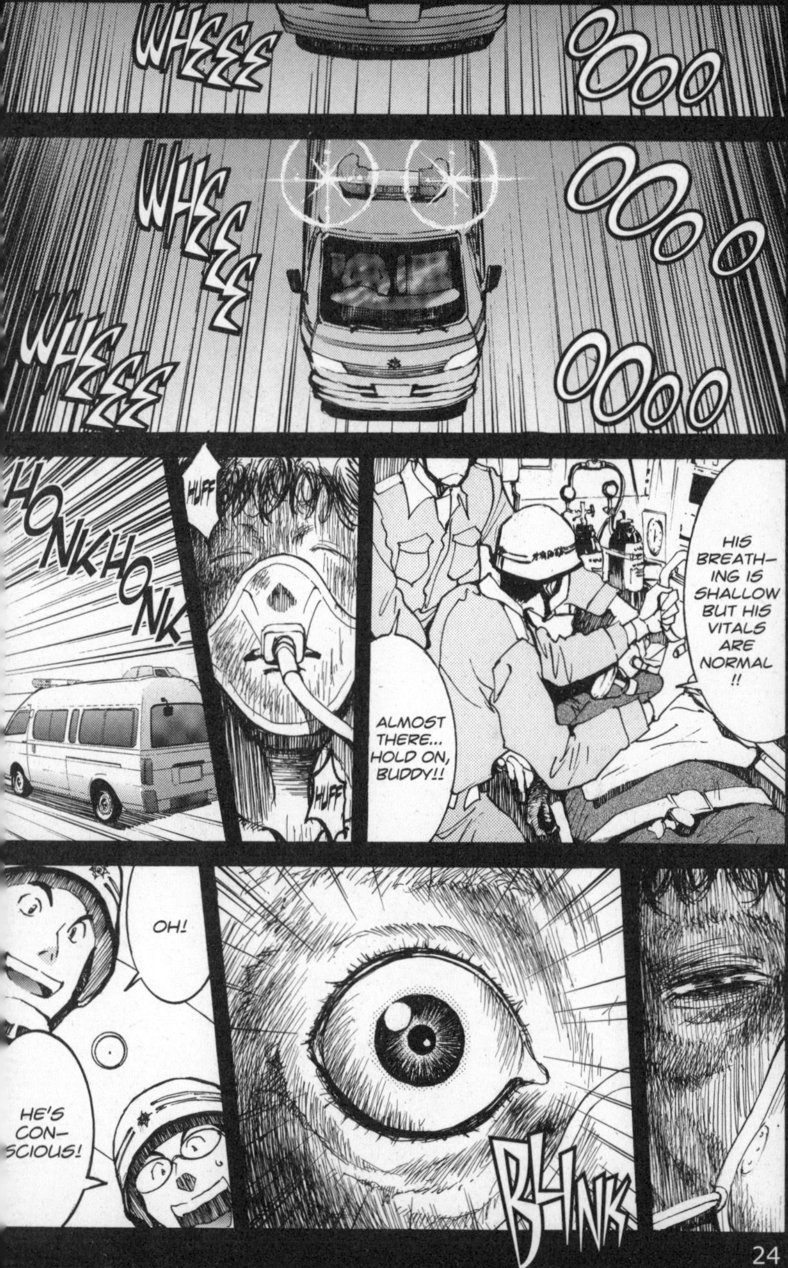
OOOO
WHEEE
OOOO O
WHEEE
WHEEE
OOOO
HIS BREATH-ING IS SHALLOW BUT HIS VITALS ARE NORMAL !!
ALMOST THERE... HOLD ON, BUDDY!!
HUFF
HUFF
HONK HONK
BLINK
OH!
HE'S CON-SCIOUS!

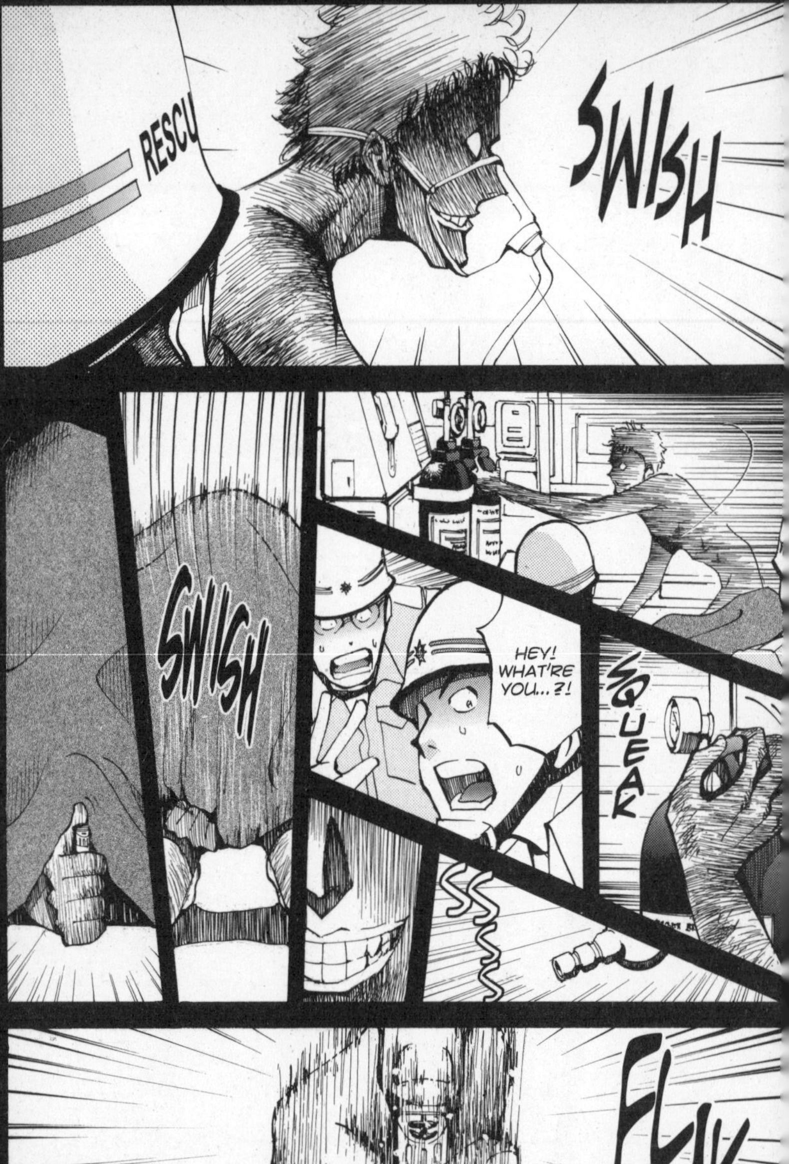
SWISH
RESCU
HEY! WHAT'RE YOU...?!
SQUEAK
SWISH
FLIK

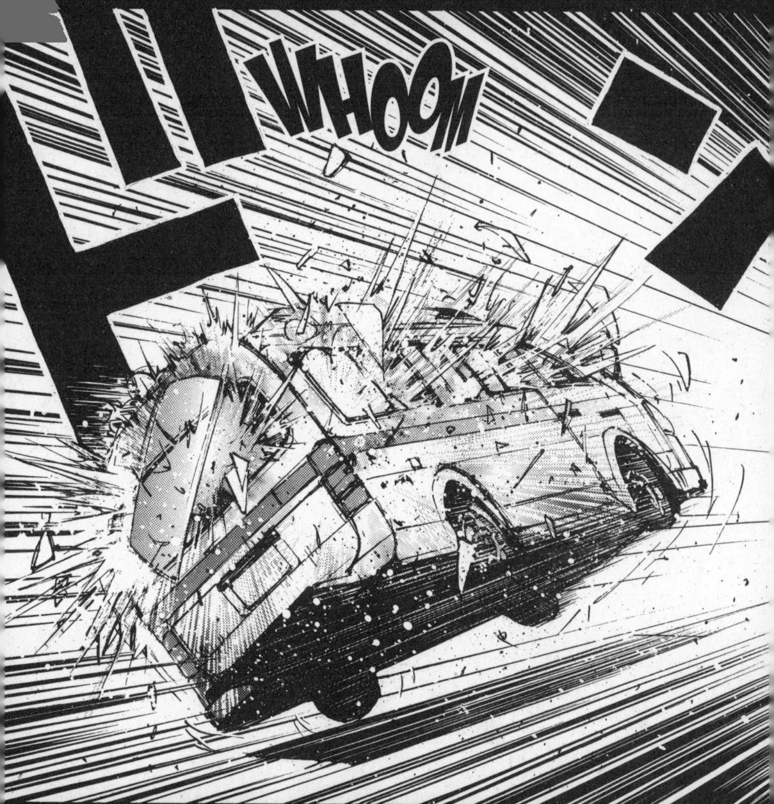
WHOOM
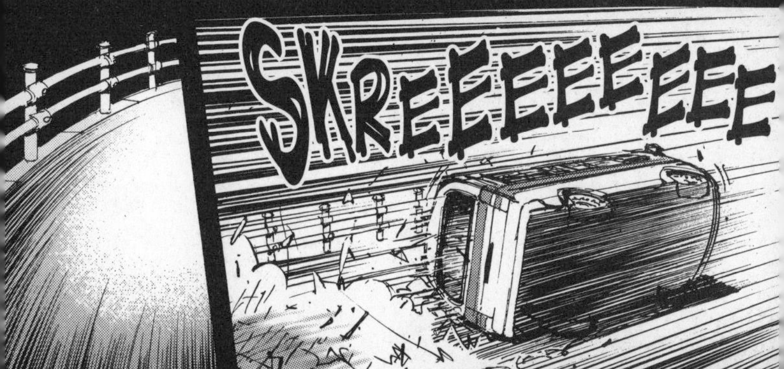
SKREEEEEEEE

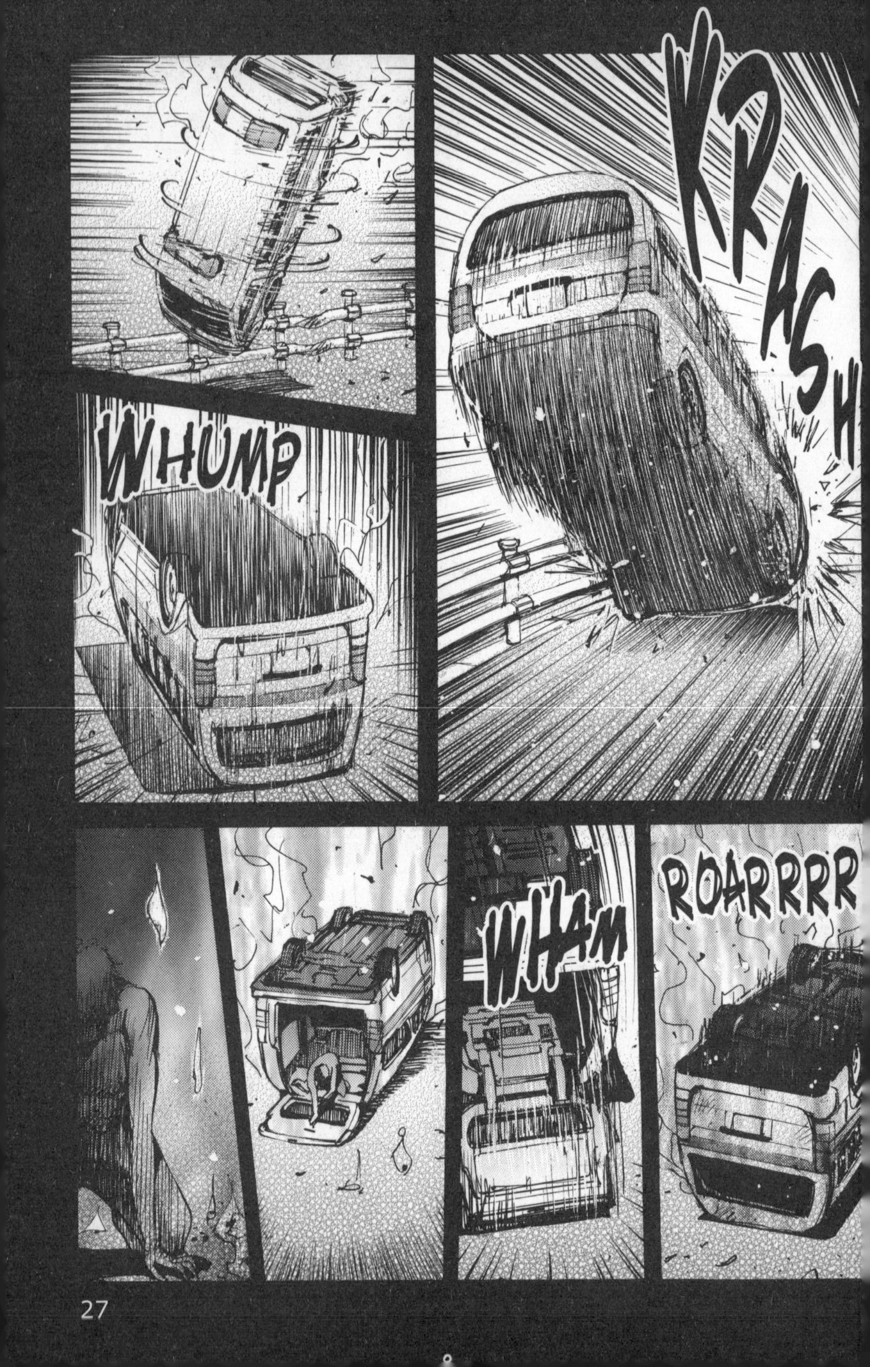
KRASH
WHUMP
ROARRRR
WHAM

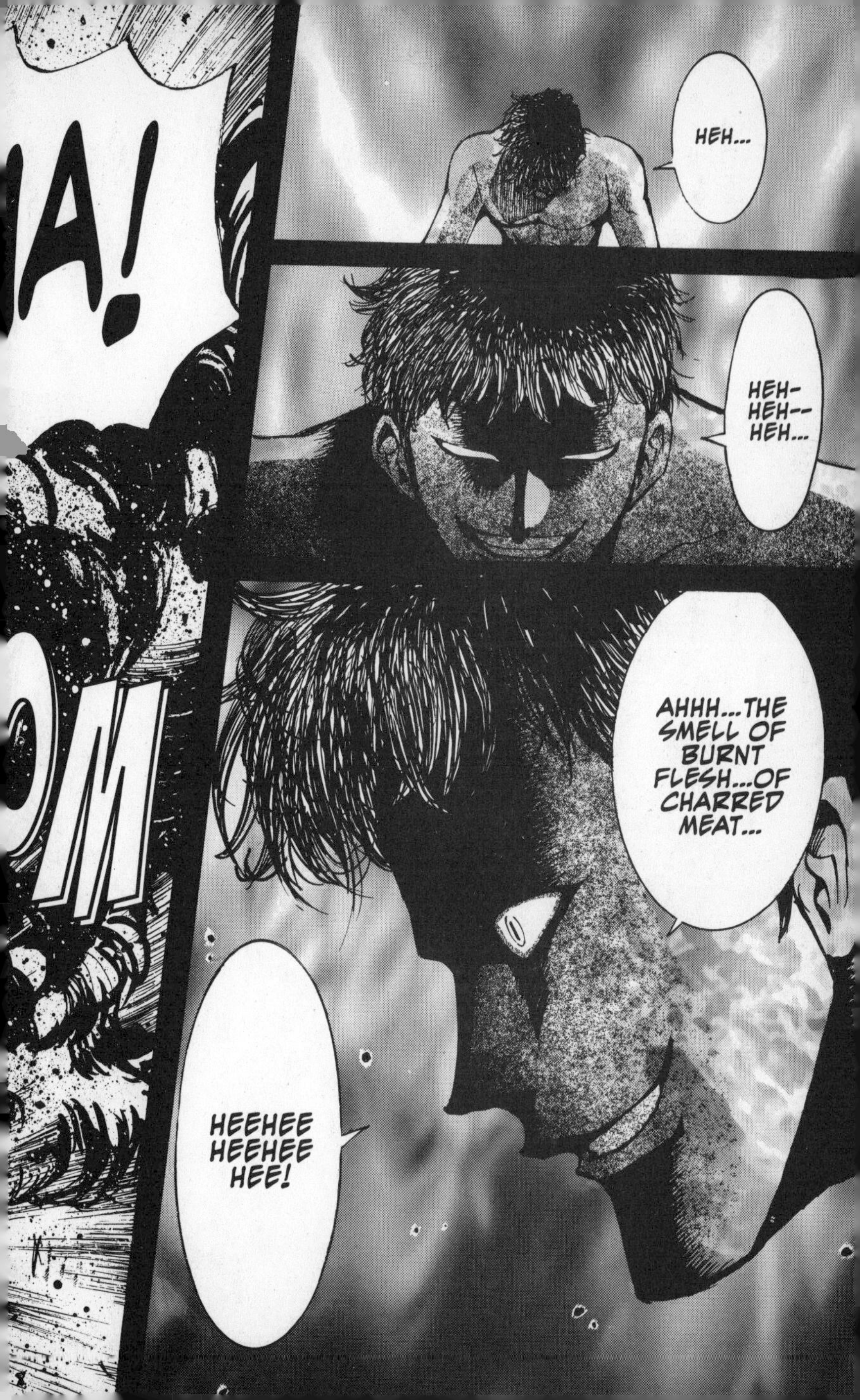
HEH...
HEH-HEH--HEH...
AHHH...THE SMELL OF BURNT FLESH...OF CHARRED MEAT...
HEEHEE HEEHEE HEE!

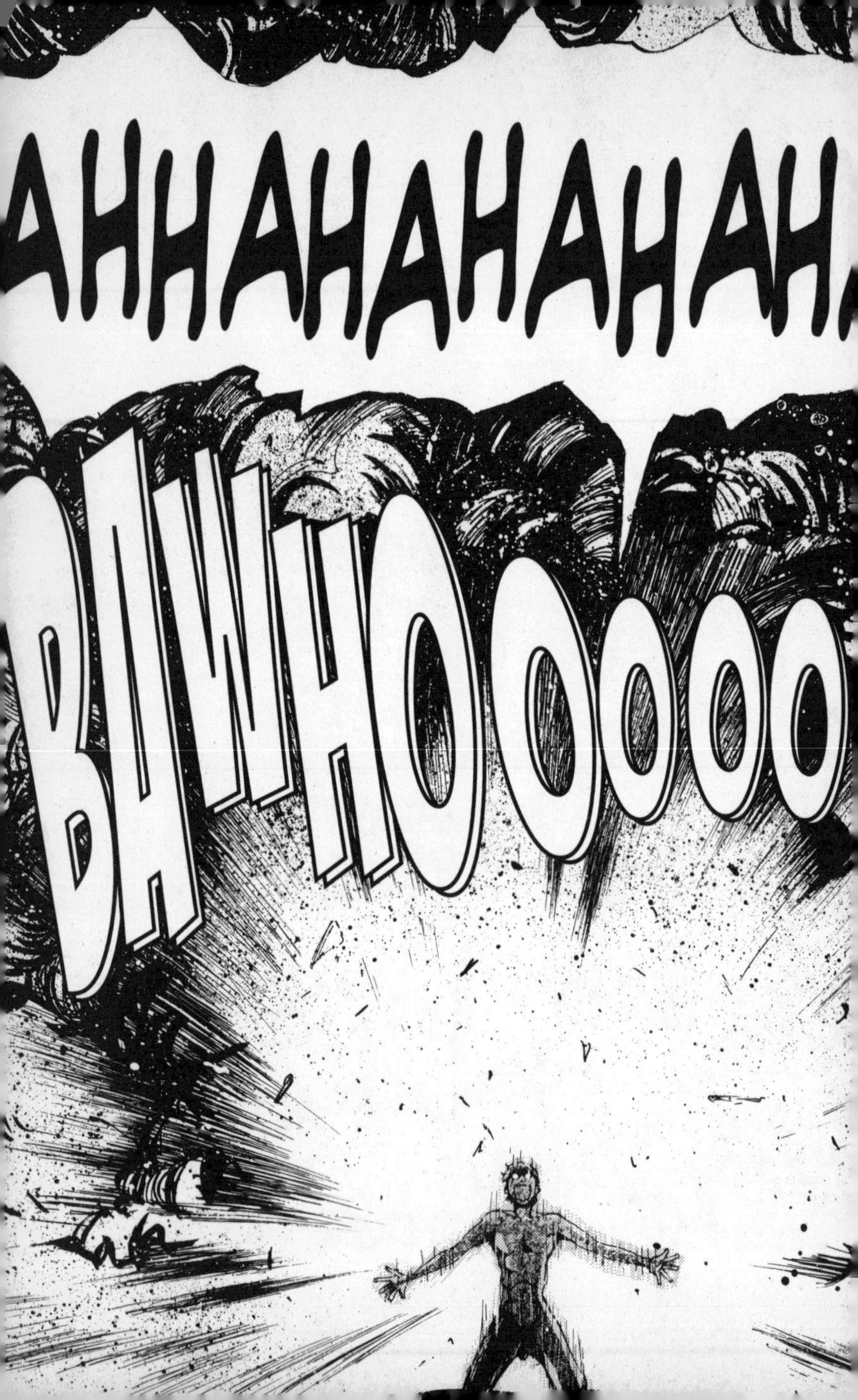
AHHAHAHAHAH
BWHOOOOO

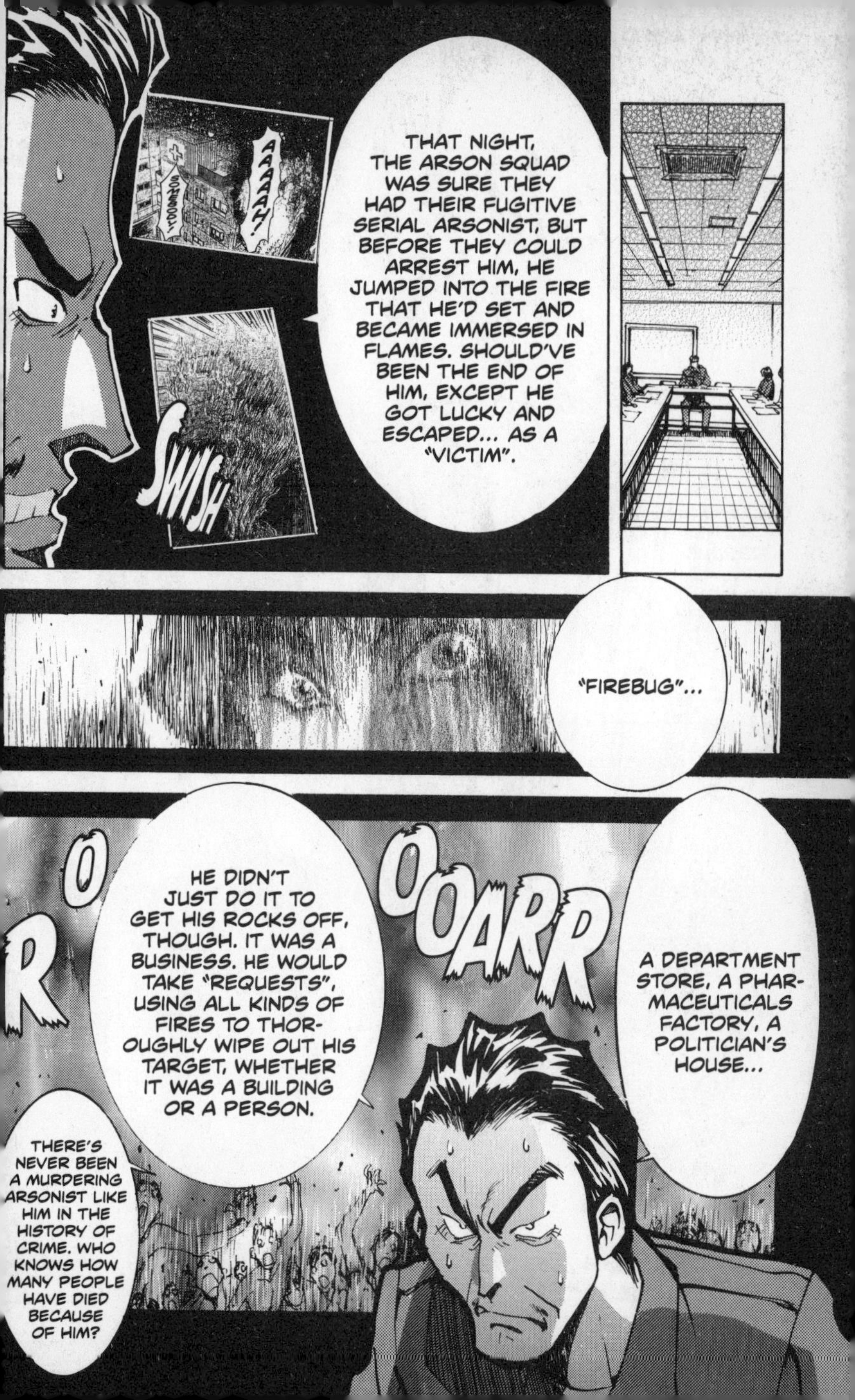
THAT NIGHT, THE ARSON SQUAD WAS SURE THEY HAD THEIR FUGITIVE SERIAL ARSONIST, BUT BEFORE THEY COULD ARREST HIM, HE JUMPED INTO THE FIRE THAT HE'D SET AND BECAME IMMERSED IN FLAMES. SHOULD'VE BEEN THE END OF HIM, EXCEPT HE GOT LUCKY AND ESCAPED... AS A "VICTIM".
AAAAAH!
SOMEBODY!
SWISH
"FIREBUG"...
A DEPARTMENT STORE, A PHAR-MACEUTICALS FACTORY, A POLITICIAN'S HOUSE...
OOARR
HE DIDN'T JUST DO IT TO GET HIS ROCKS OFF, THOUGH. IT WAS A BUSINESS. HE WOULD TAKE "REQUESTS", USING ALL KINDS OF FIRES TO THOR-OUGHLY WIPE OUT HIS TARGET, WHETHER IT WAS A BUILDING OR A PERSON.
O
R
THERE'S NEVER BEEN A MURDERING ARSONIST LIKE HIM IN THE HISTORY OF CRIME. WHO KNOWS HOW MANY PEOPLE HAVE DIED BECAUSE OF HIM?

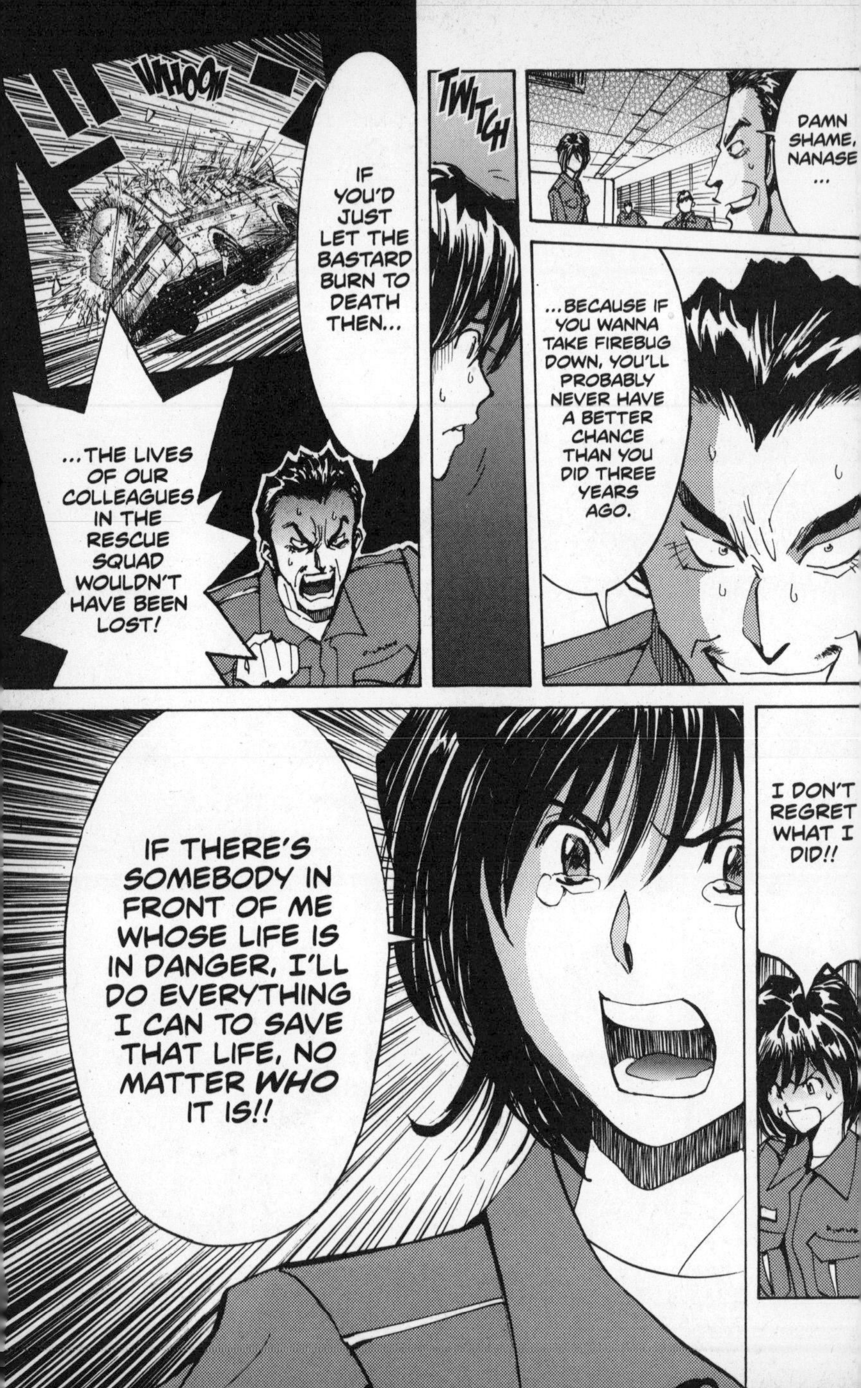
DAMN SHAME, NANASE ...
...BECAUSE IF YOU WANNA TAKE FIREBUG DOWN, YOU'LL PROBABLY NEVER HAVE A BETTER CHANCE THAN YOU DID THREE YEARS AGO.
TWITCH
IF YOU'D JUST LET THE BASTARD BURN TO DEATH THEN...
WHOOM
...THE LIVES OF OUR COLLEAGUES IN THE RESCUE SQUAD WOULDN'T HAVE BEEN LOST!
I DON'T REGRET WHAT I DID!!
IF THERE'S SOMEBODY IN FRONT OF ME WHOSE LIFE IS IN DANGER, I'LL DO EVERYTHING I CAN TO SAVE THAT LIFE, NO MATTER WHO IT IS!!

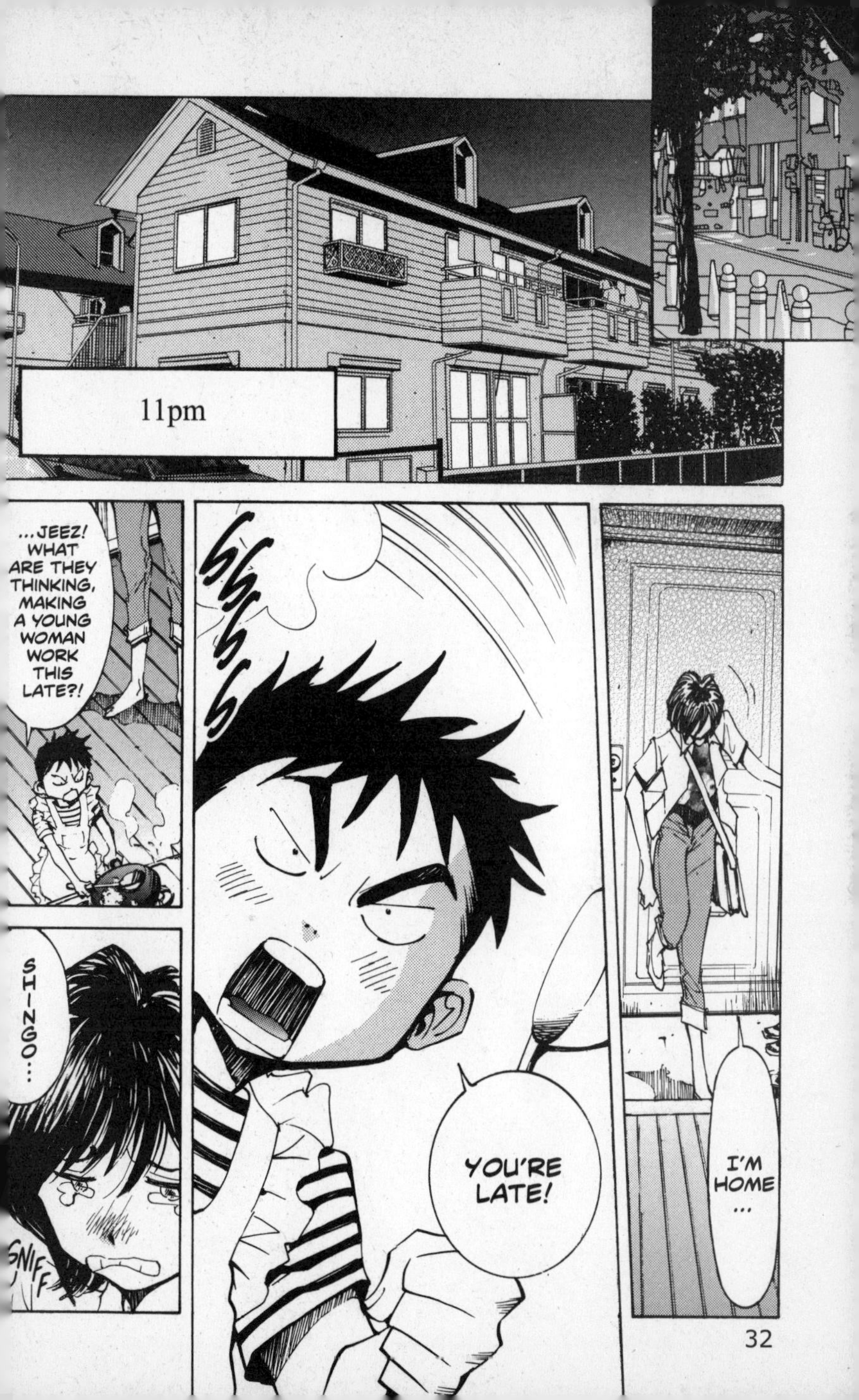
11pm
I'M HOME...
YOU'RE LATE!
...JEEZ! WHAT ARE THEY THINKING, MAKING A YOUNG WOMAN WORK THIS LATE?!
SHINGO...
SNIFF

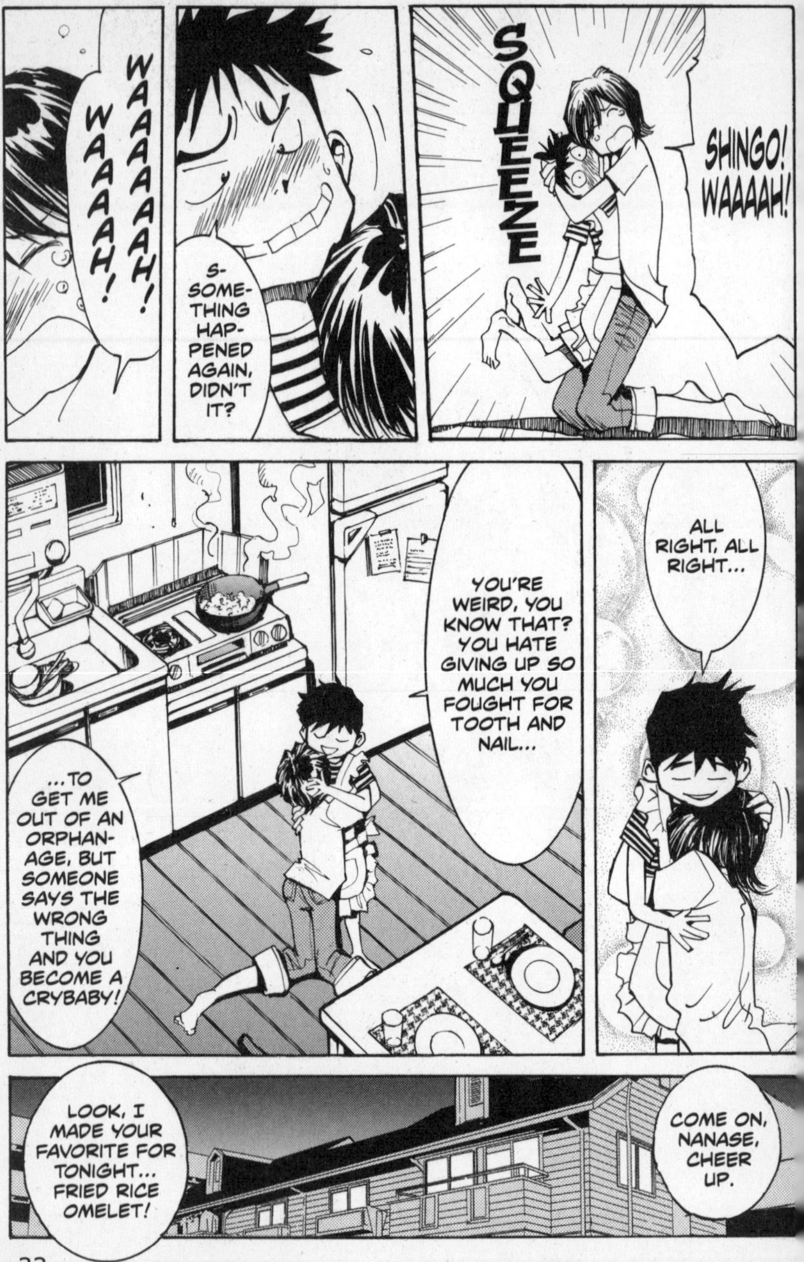
SHINGO! WAAAAH!
SQUEEZE
S-SOMETHING HAPPENED AGAIN, DIDN'T IT?
WAAAAAAAH! WAAAAAH!
ALL RIGHT, ALL RIGHT...
YOU'RE WEIRD, YOU KNOW THAT? YOU HATE GIVING UP SO MUCH YOU FOUGHT FOR TOOTH AND NAIL...
...TO GET ME OUT OF AN ORPHANAGE, BUT SOMEONE SAYS THE WRONG THING AND YOU BECOME A CRYBABY!
COME ON, NANASE, CHEER UP.
LOOK, I MADE YOUR FAVORITE FOR TONIGHT... FRIED RICE OMELET!

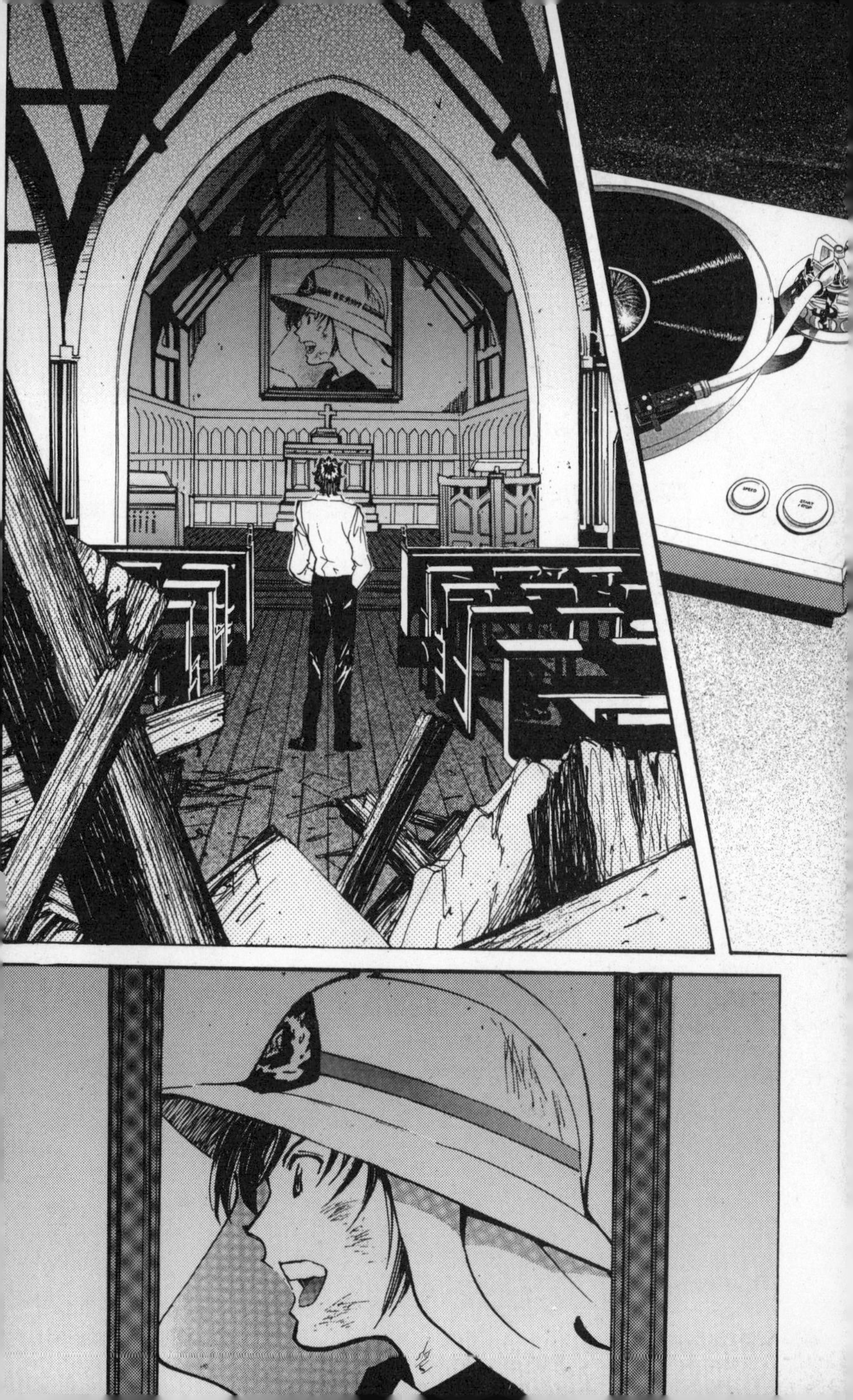
SPEED
START / STOP

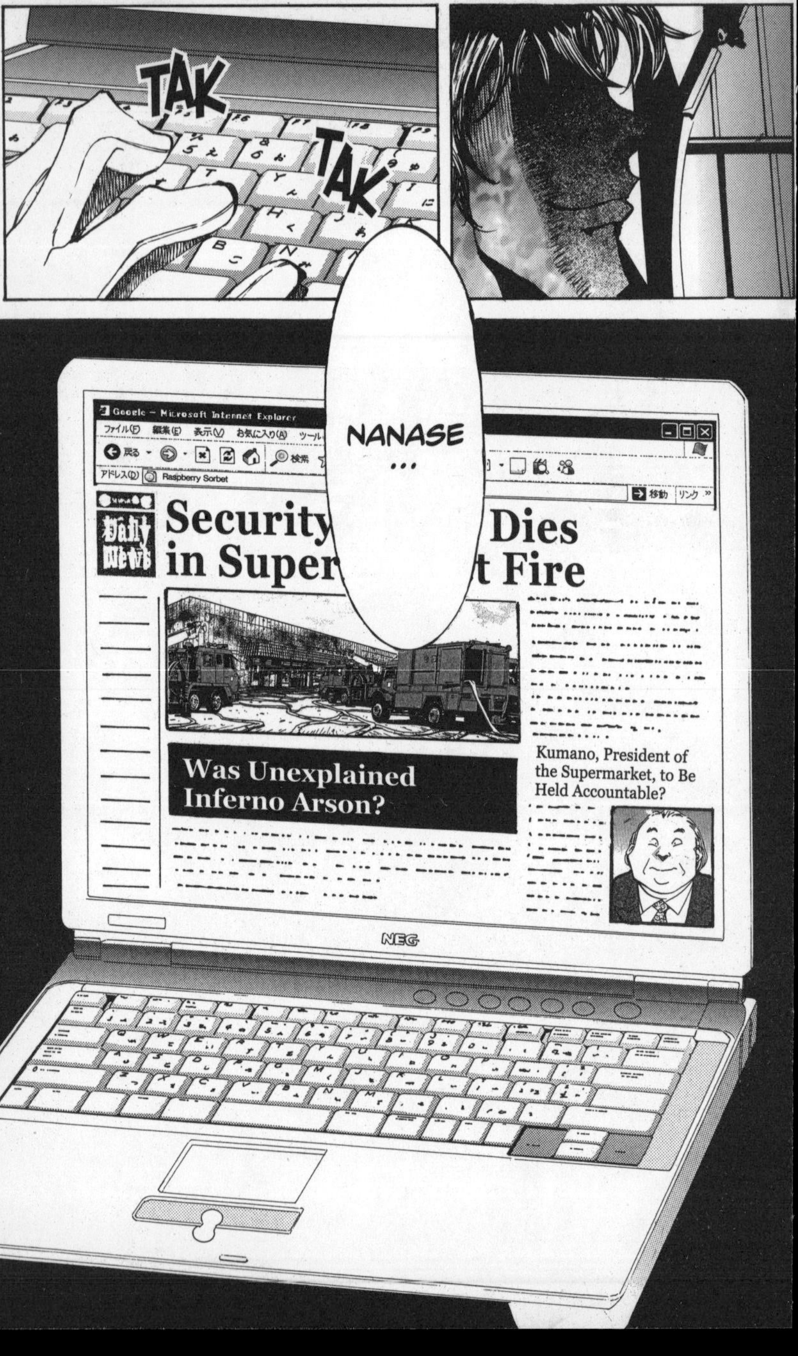
TAK
TAK
NANASE ...
Google - Microsoft Internet Explorer
ファイル(F) 編集(E) 表示(V) お気に入り(A) ツール
戻る 検索
アドレス(D) Raspberry Sorbet
移動 リンク
Daily News
Security Dies
in Super t Fire
Was Unexplained Inferno Arson?
Kumano, President of the Supermarket, to Be Held Accountable?
NEG

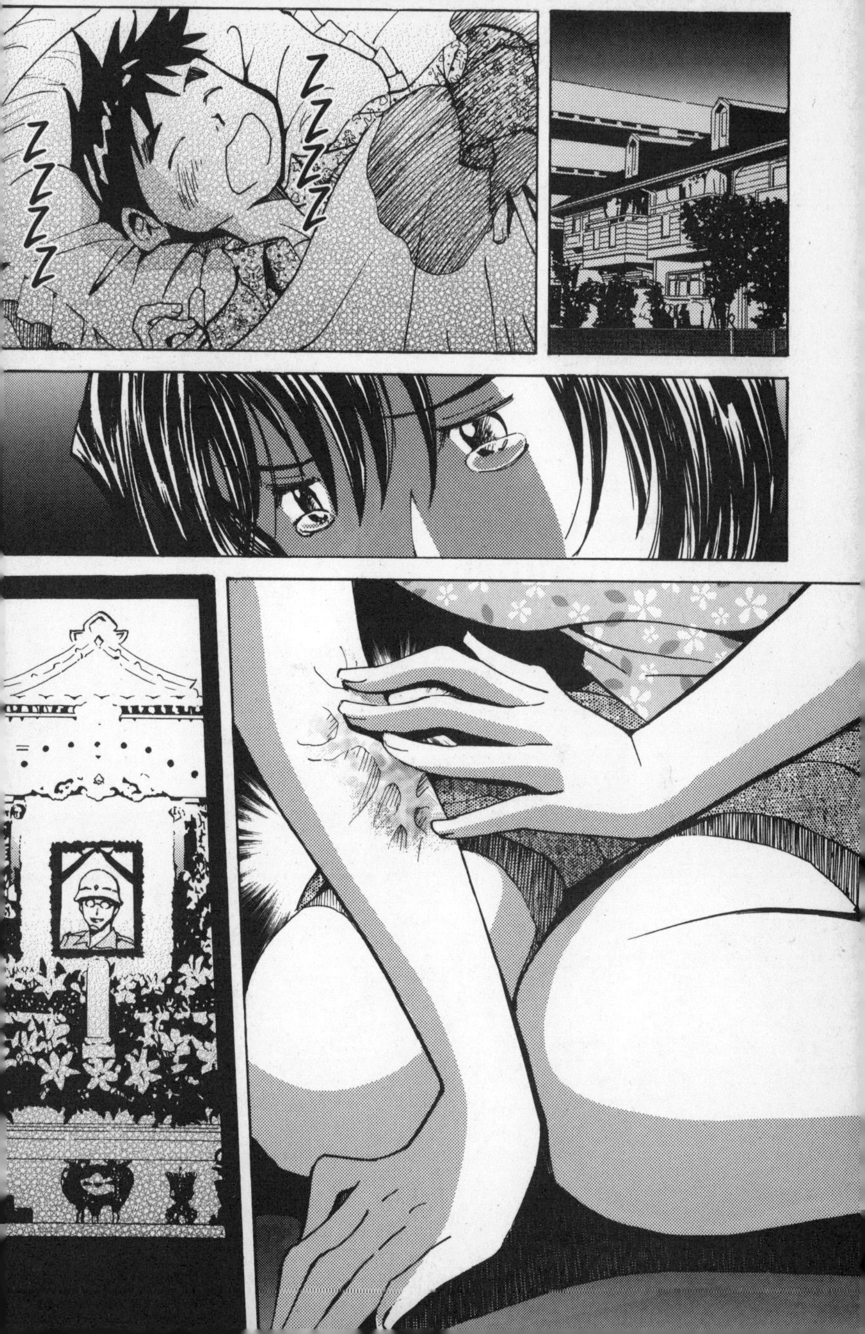
ZZZZZ
ZZZZZ

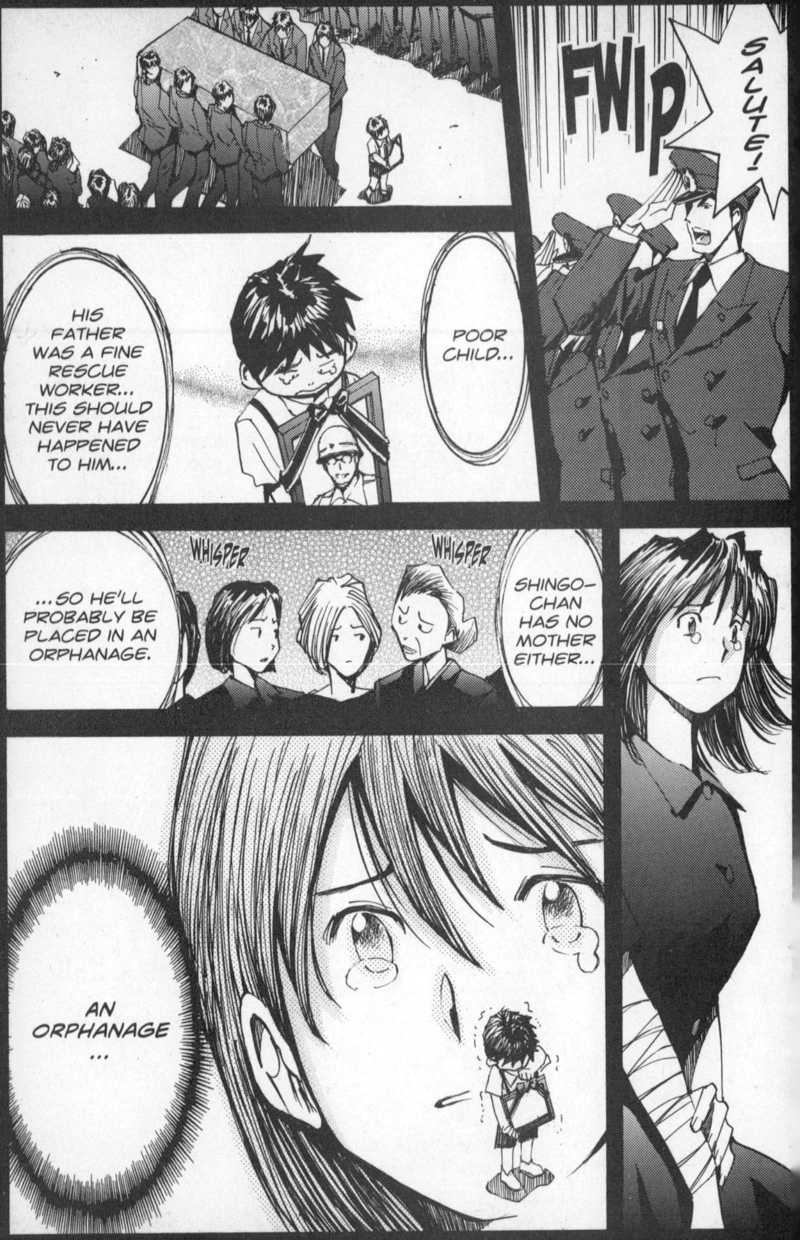
SALUTE!
FWIP
POOR CHILD...
HIS FATHER WAS A FINE RESCUE WORKER... THIS SHOULD NEVER HAVE HAPPENED TO HIM...
WHISPER
SHINGO-CHAN HAS NO MOTHER EITHER...
WHISPER
...SO HE'LL PROBABLY BE PLACED IN AN ORPHANAGE.
AN ORPHANAGE...

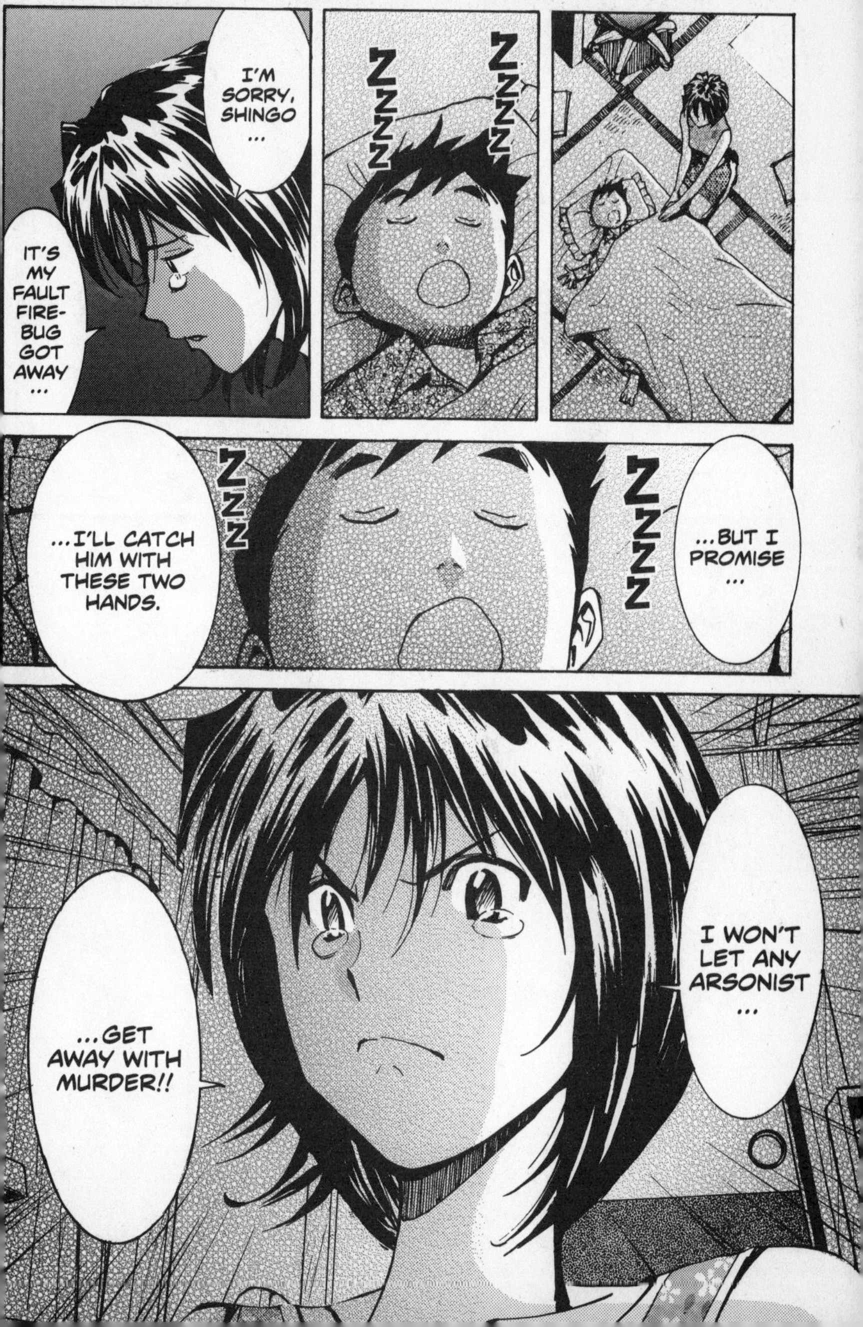
ZZZZ
ZZZZ
I'M SORRY, SHINGO ...
IT'S MY FAULT FIRE-BUG GOT AWAY ...
ZZZZ
...BUT I PROMISE ...
ZZZ
...I'LL CATCH HIM WITH THESE TWO HANDS.
I WON'T LET ANY ARSONIST ...
...GET AWAY WITH MURDER!!

3am

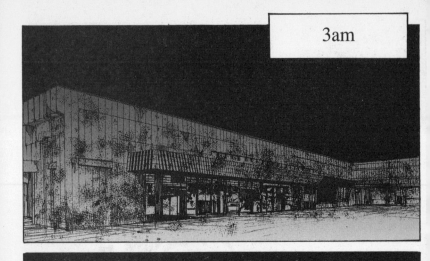

P OUT **KEEP OUT** KEEP

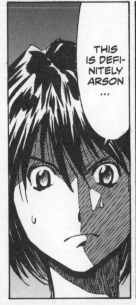

THIS IS DEFINITELY ARSON...

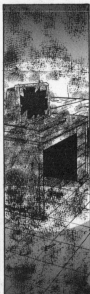

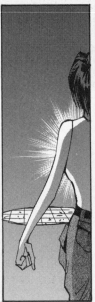

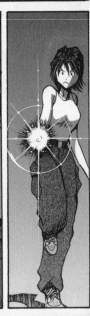

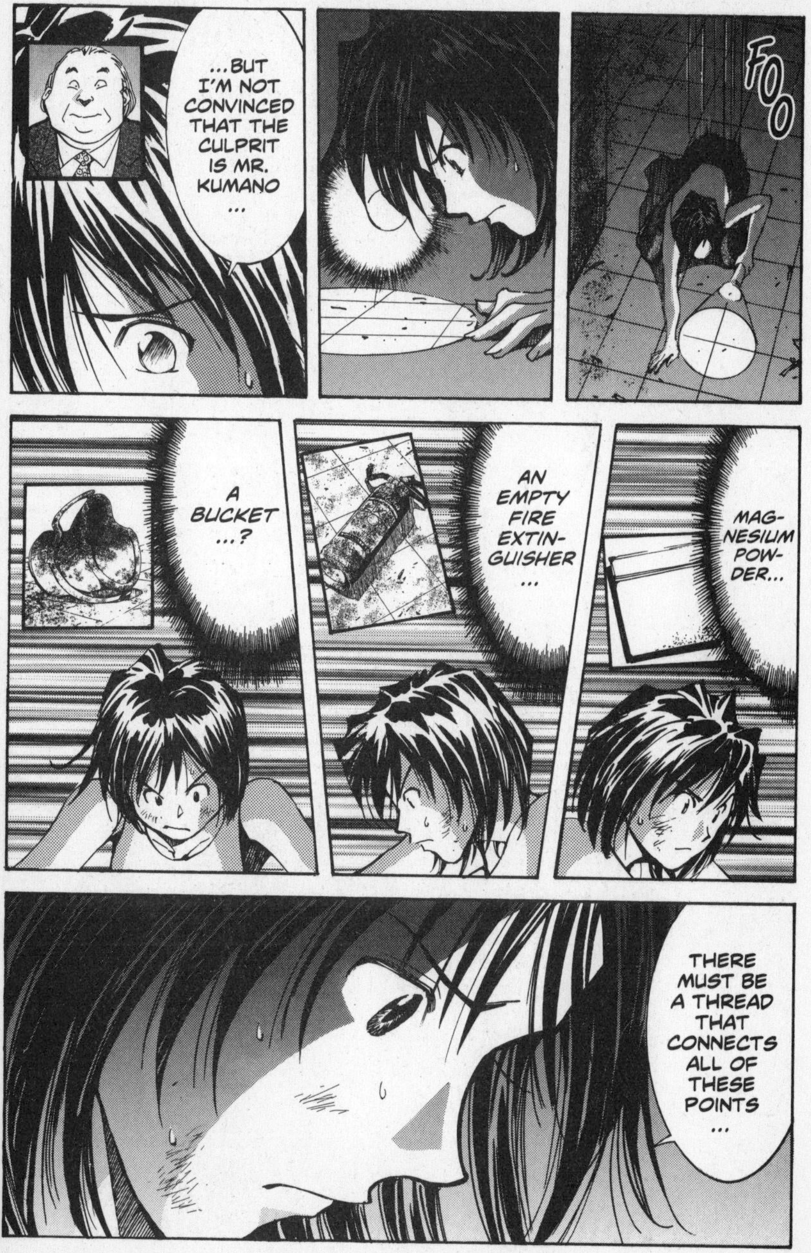
FOO
...BUT I'M NOT CONVINCED THAT THE CULPRIT IS MR. KUMANO ...
MAG- NESIUM POW- DER...
AN EMPTY FIRE EXTIN- GUISHER ...
A BUCKET ...?
THERE MUST BE A THREAD THAT CONNECTS ALL OF THESE POINTS ...

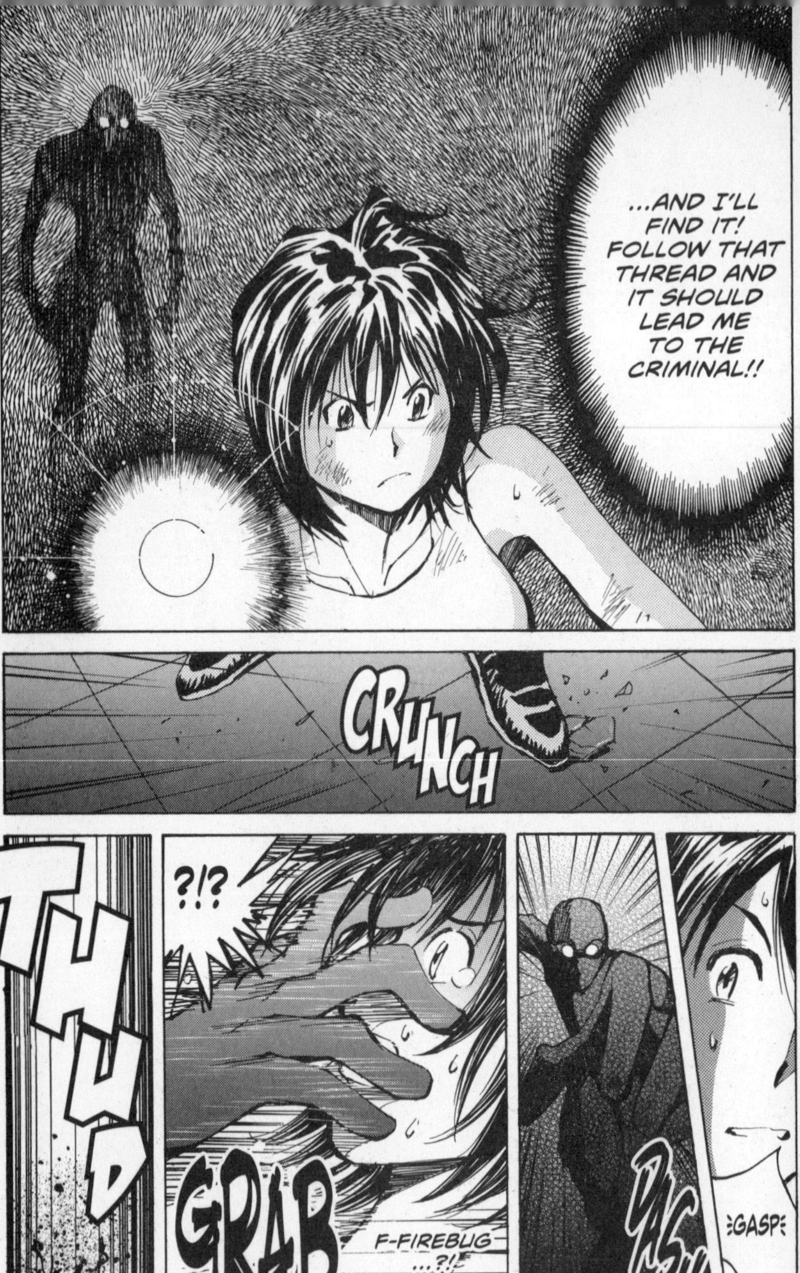
...AND I'LL FIND IT! FOLLOW THAT THREAD AND IT SHOULD LEAD ME TO THE CRIMINAL!!
CRUNCH
GASP
DASH
?!?
F-FIREBUG ...?!
GRAB
THUD

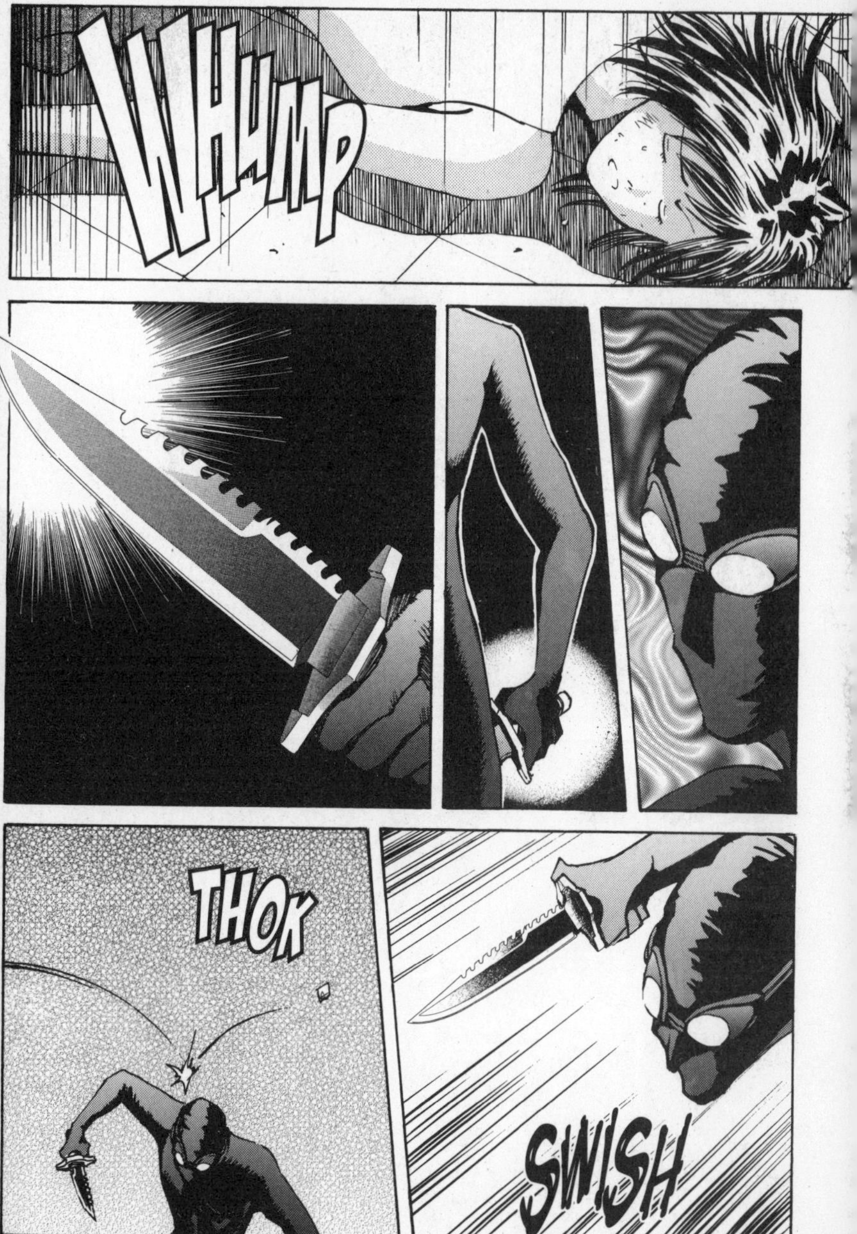
WHUMP
SWISH
THOK

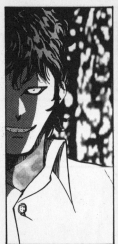

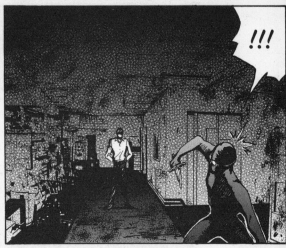

!!!

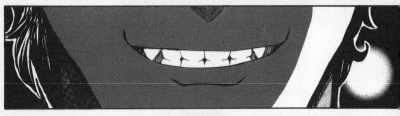

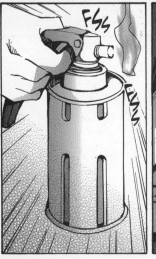

FSS

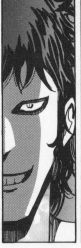

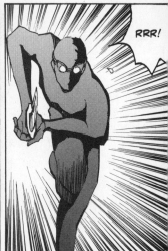

RRR!

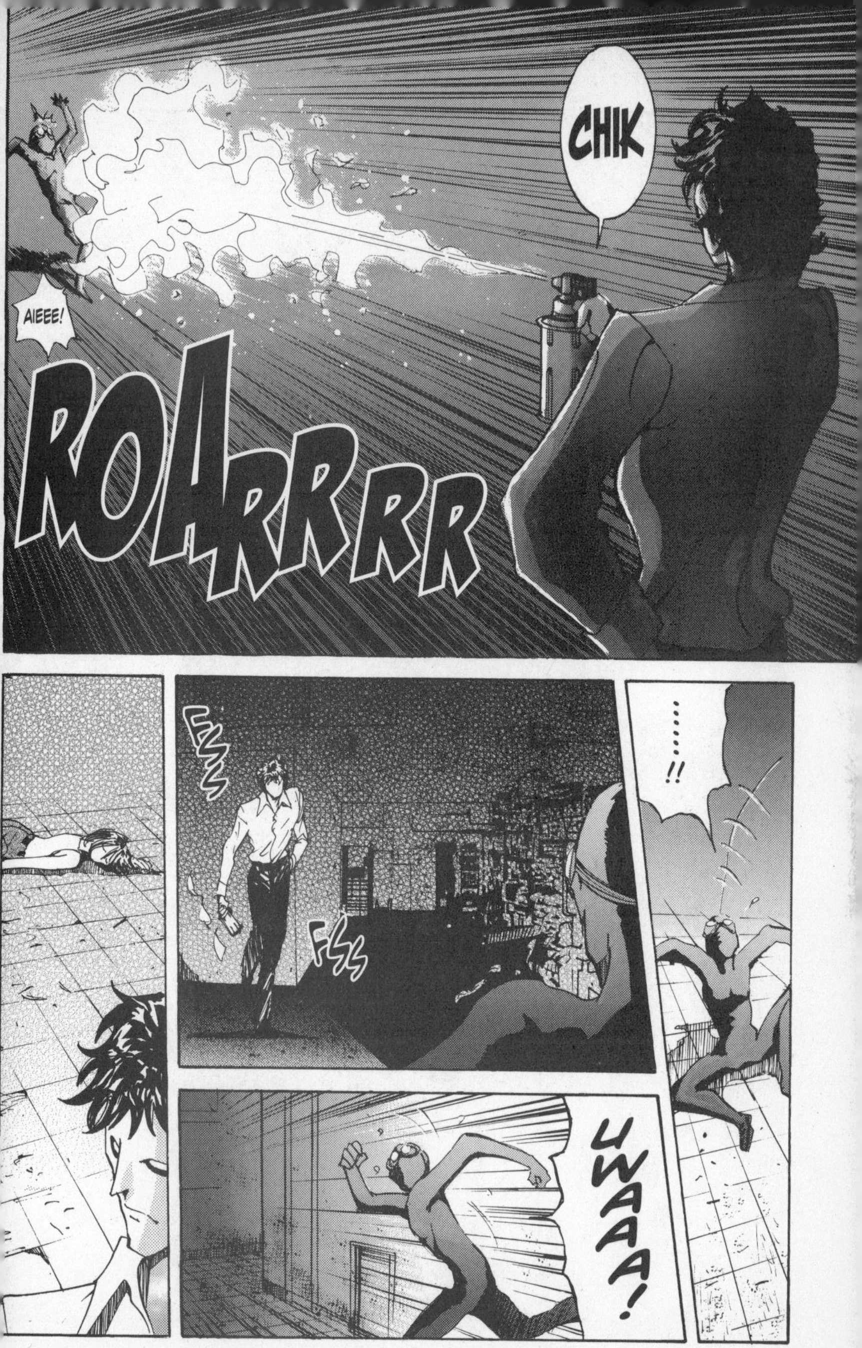
CHIK
AIEEE!
ROARRRRR
......!!
FSSS
FSS
UWAAA!

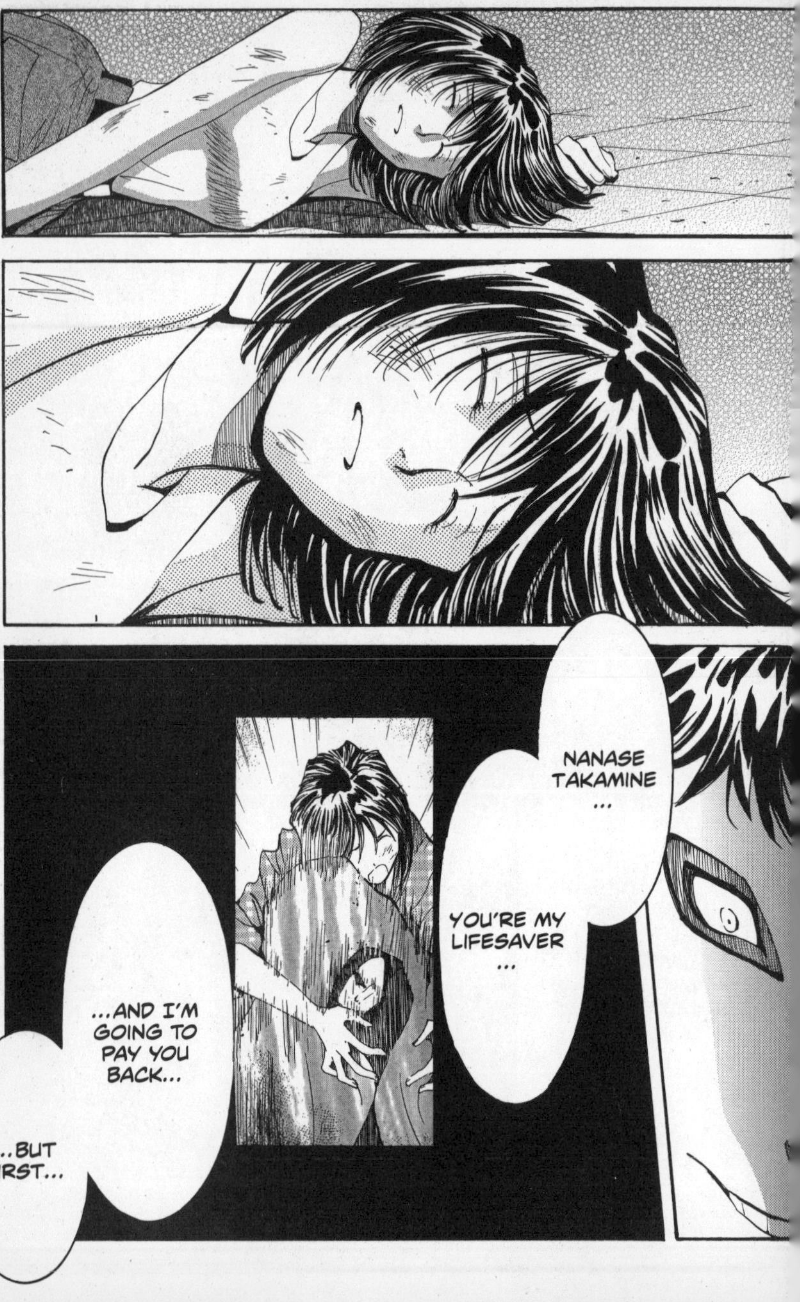
NANASE TAKAMINE ...
YOU'RE MY LIFESAVER ...
...AND I'M GOING TO PAY YOU BACK...
...BUT FIRST...

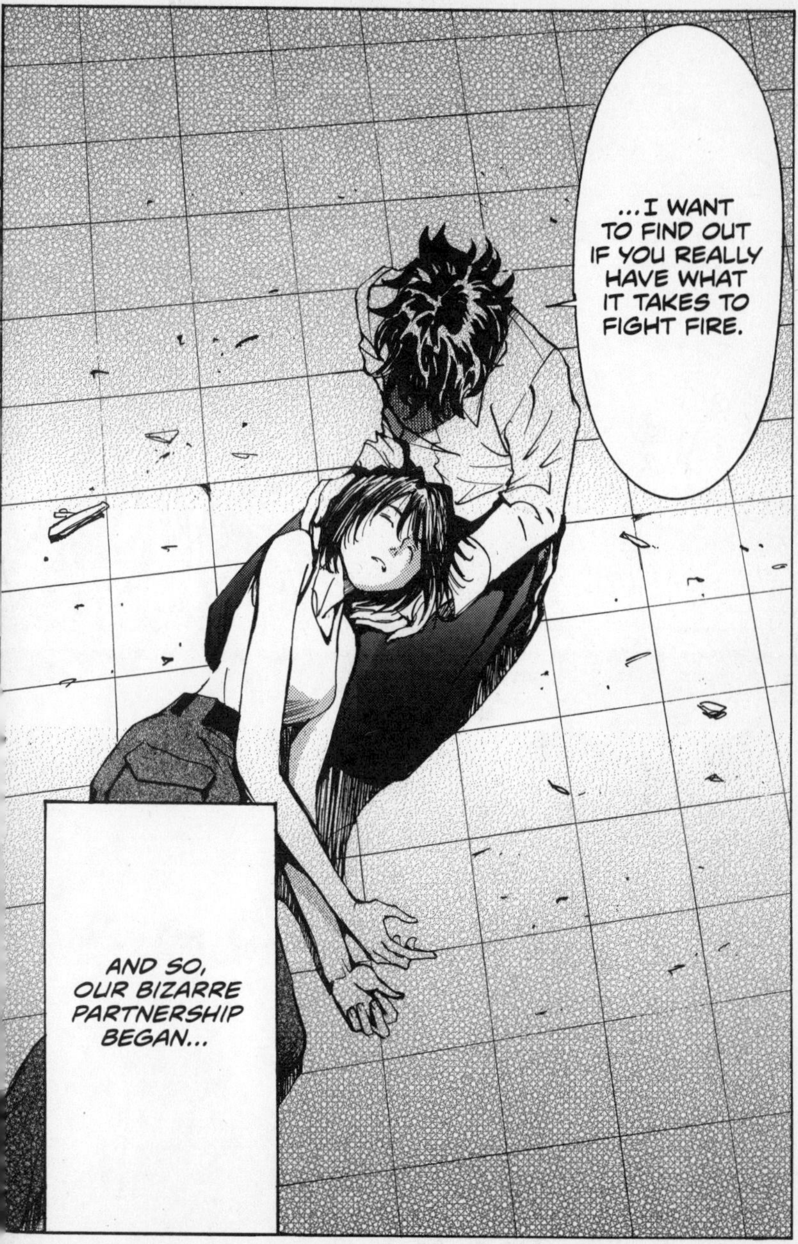
...I WANT TO FIND OUT IF YOU REALLY HAVE WHAT IT TAKES TO FIGHT FIRE.
AND SO, OUR BIZARRE PARTNERSHIP BEGAN...

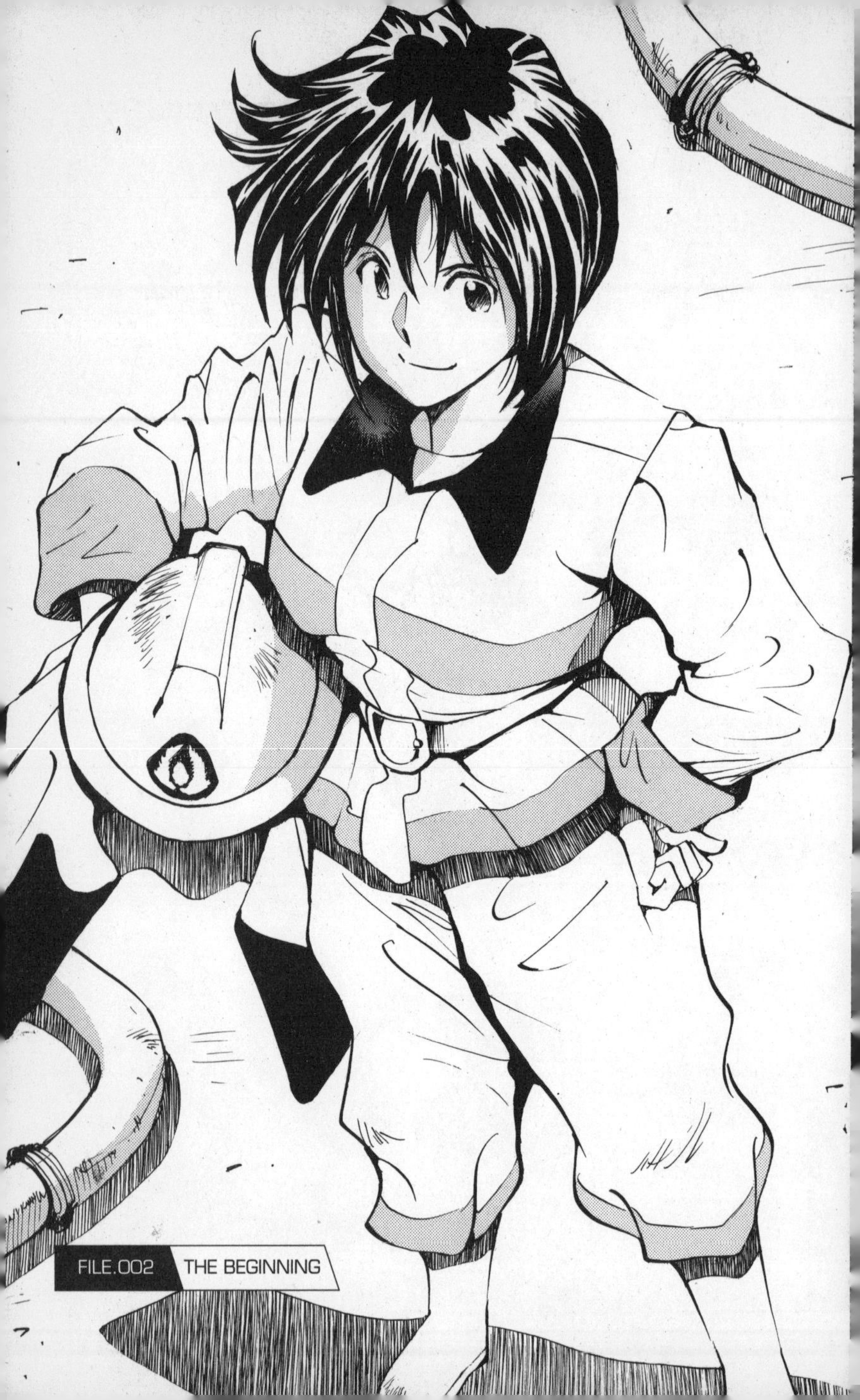
FILE.002
THE BEGINNING

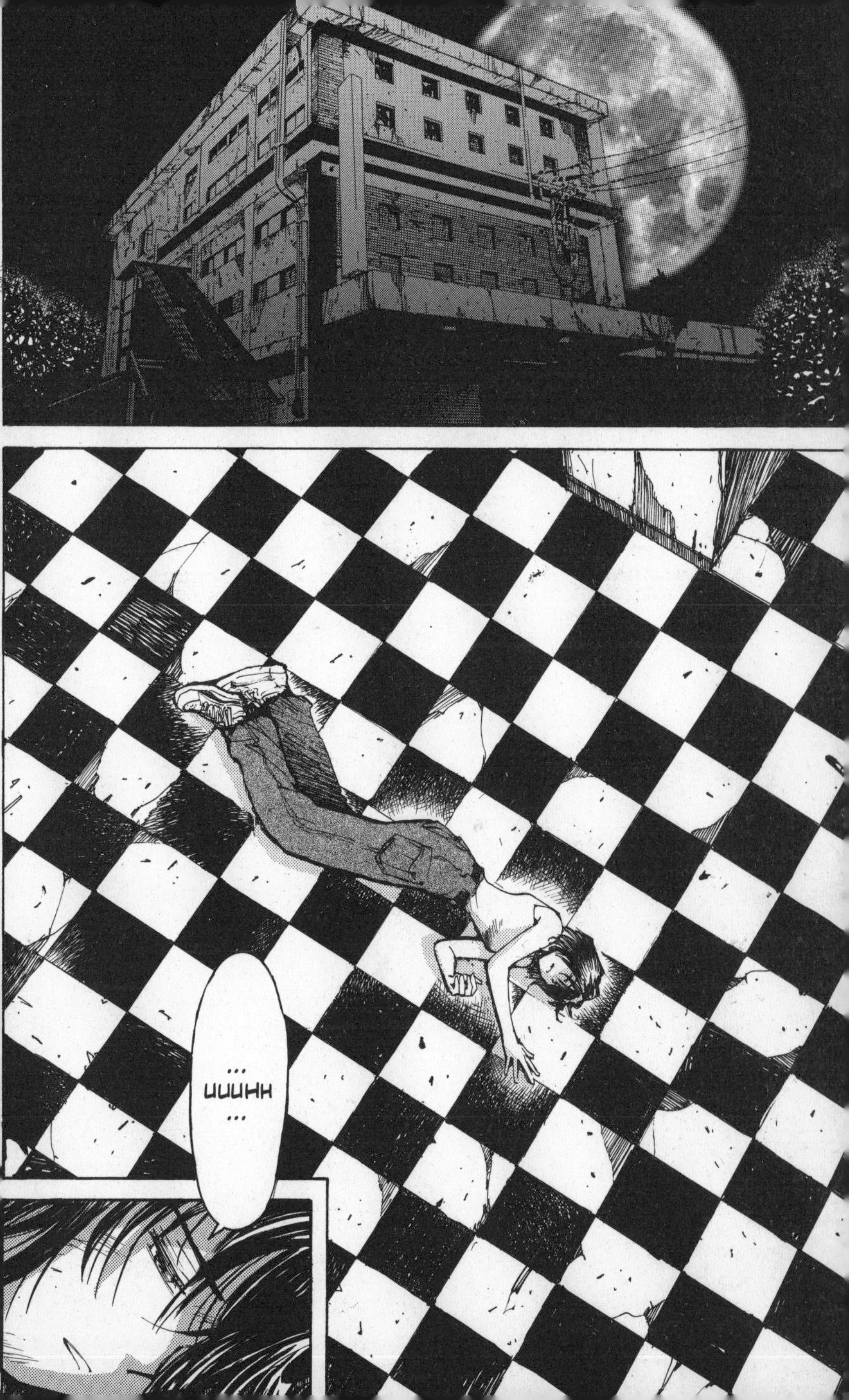
...UUUHH...

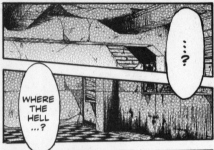

... ?

WHERE THE HELL ...?

THAT'S RIGHT... I WENT TO INVESTIGATE THE FIRE BY MYSELF...

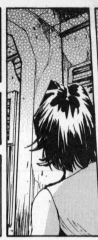
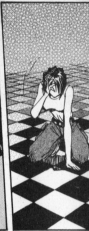
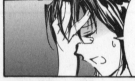

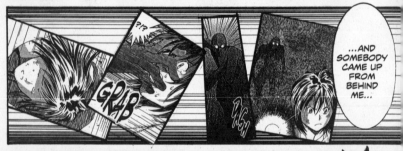

GRAB

...AND SOMEBODY CAME UP FROM BEHIND ME...

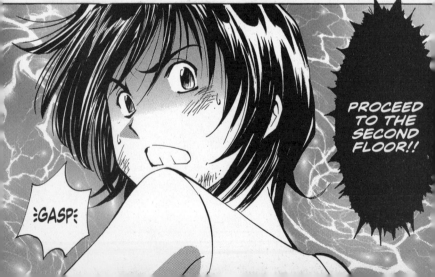

PROCEED TO THE SECOND FLOOR!!

≈GASP≈

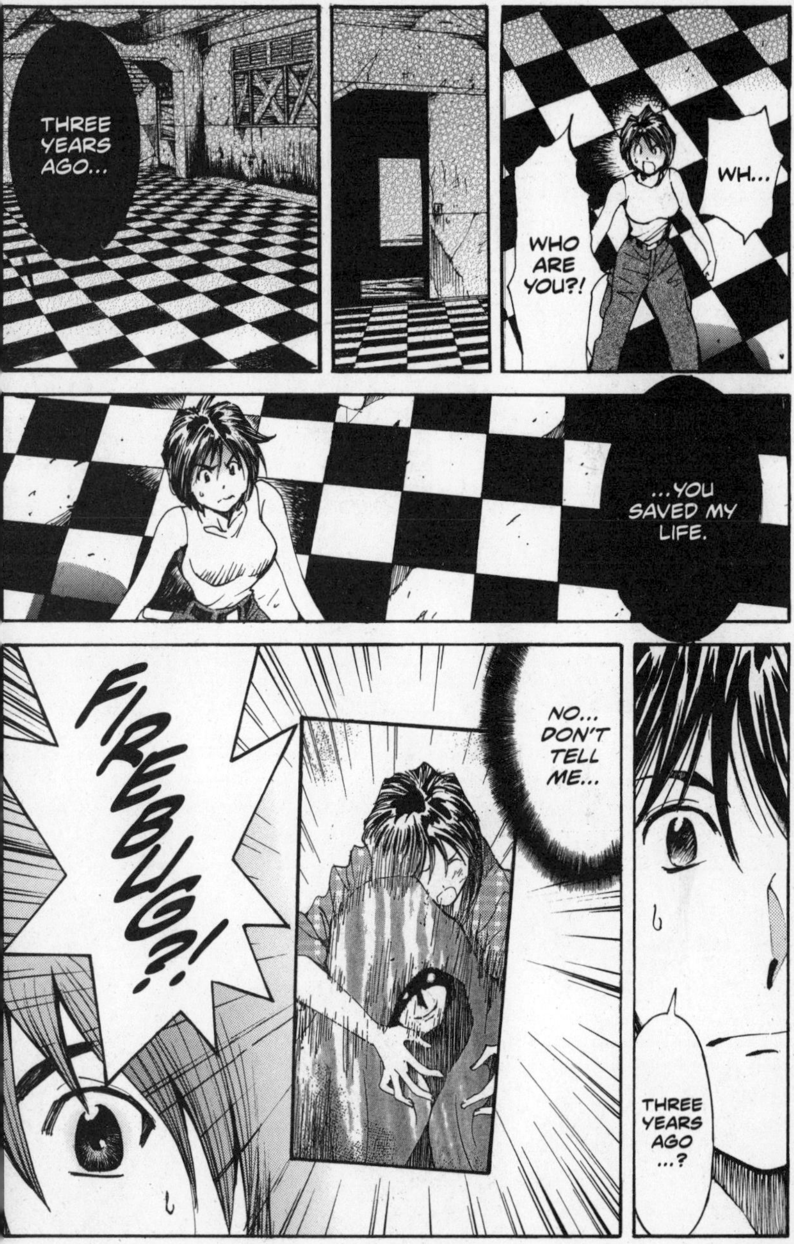
WH...
WHO ARE YOU?!
THREE YEARS AGO...
...YOU SAVED MY LIFE.
THREE YEARS AGO ...?
NO... DON'T TELL ME...
FIREBUG?!

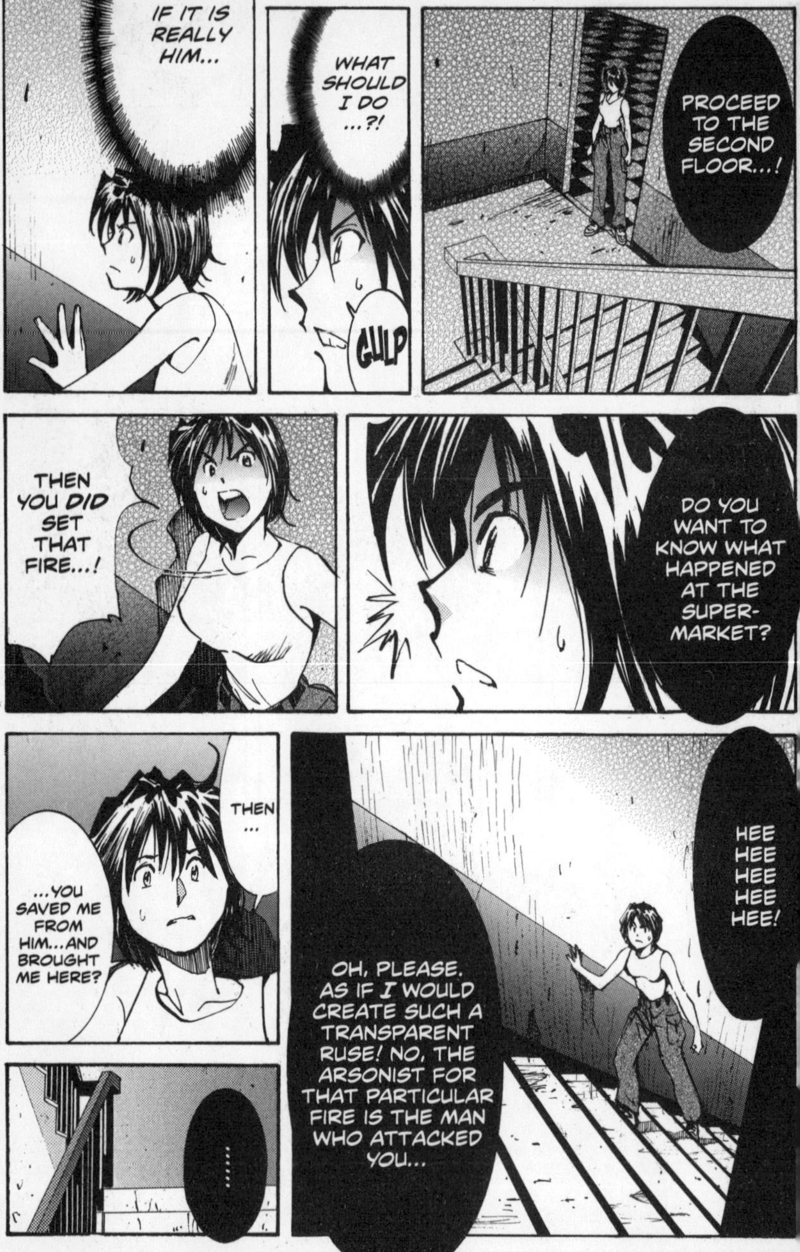
PROCEED TO THE SECOND FLOOR...!
WHAT SHOULD I DO ...?!
GULP
IF IT IS REALLY HIM...
DO YOU WANT TO KNOW WHAT HAPPENED AT THE SUPER-MARKET?
THEN YOU DID SET THAT FIRE...!
HEE HEE HEE HEE HEE!
OH, PLEASE. AS IF I WOULD CREATE SUCH A TRANSPARENT RUSE! NO, THE ARSONIST FOR THAT PARTICULAR FIRE IS THE MAN WHO ATTACKED YOU...
THEN ...
...YOU SAVED ME FROM HIM...AND BROUGHT ME HERE?
......

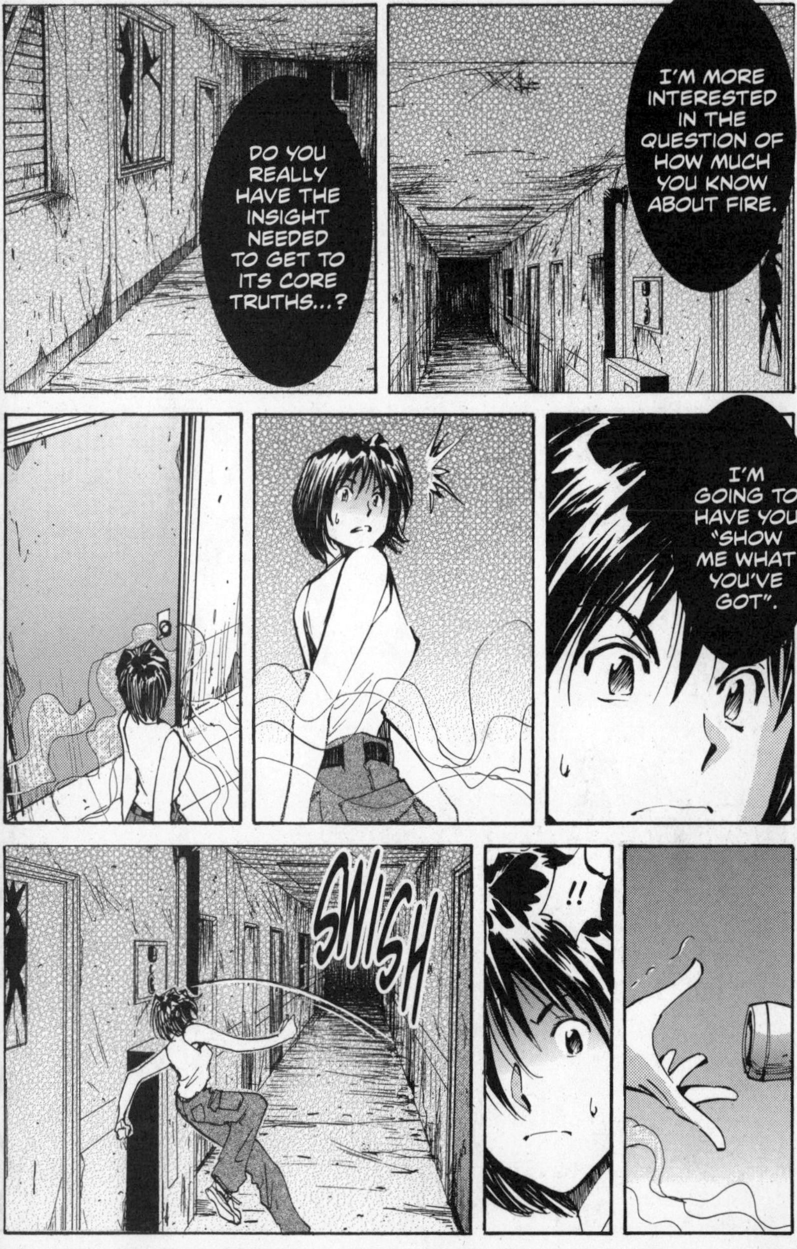
I'M MORE INTERESTED IN THE QUESTION OF HOW MUCH YOU KNOW ABOUT FIRE.
DO YOU REALLY HAVE THE INSIGHT NEEDED TO GET TO ITS CORE TRUTHS...?
I'M GOING TO HAVE YOU "SHOW ME WHAT YOU'VE GOT".
!!
SWISH

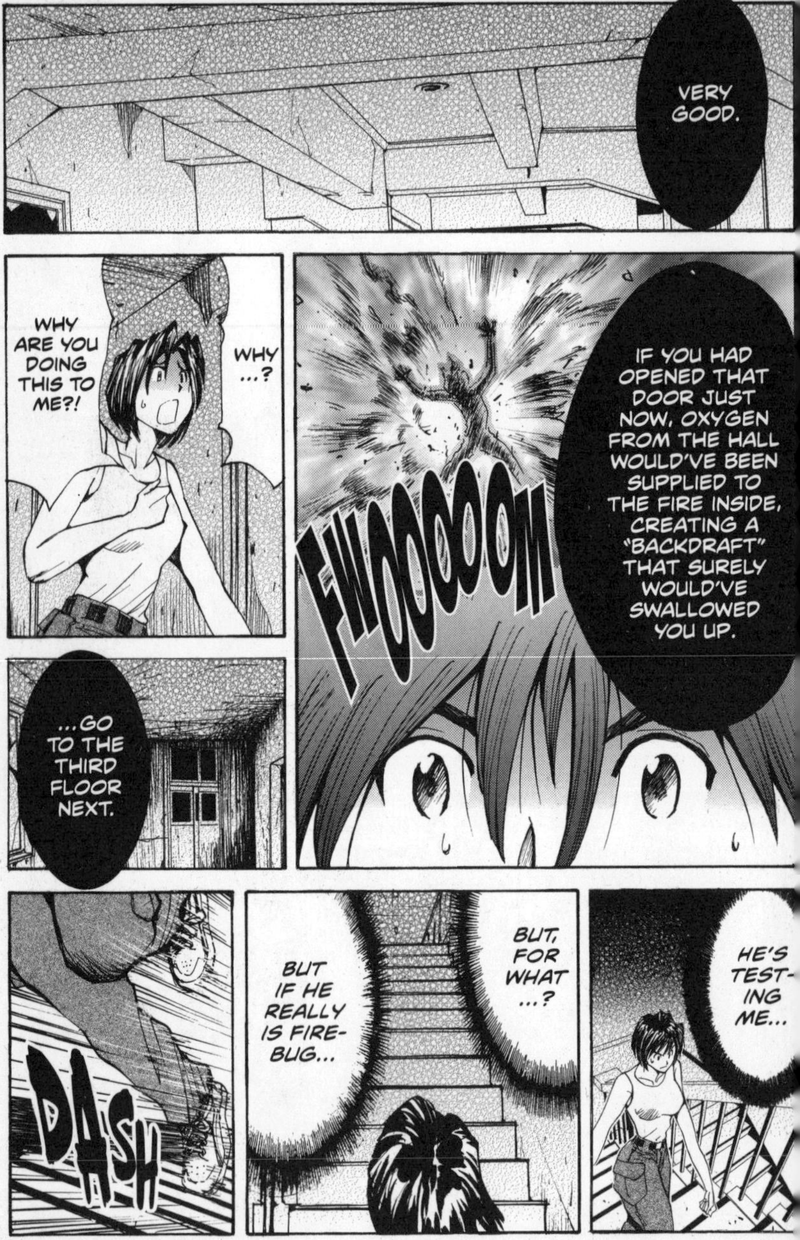

VERY GOOD.
IF YOU HAD OPENED THAT DOOR JUST NOW, OXYGEN FROM THE HALL WOULD'VE BEEN SUPPLIED TO THE FIRE INSIDE, CREATING A "BACKDRAFT" THAT SURELY WOULD'VE SWALLOWED YOU UP.
FWOOOOOM
WHY ...?
WHY ARE YOU DOING THIS TO ME?!
...GO TO THE THIRD FLOOR NEXT.
HE'S TEST-ING ME...
BUT, FOR WHAT ...?
BUT IF HE REALLY IS FIRE-BUG...
DASH

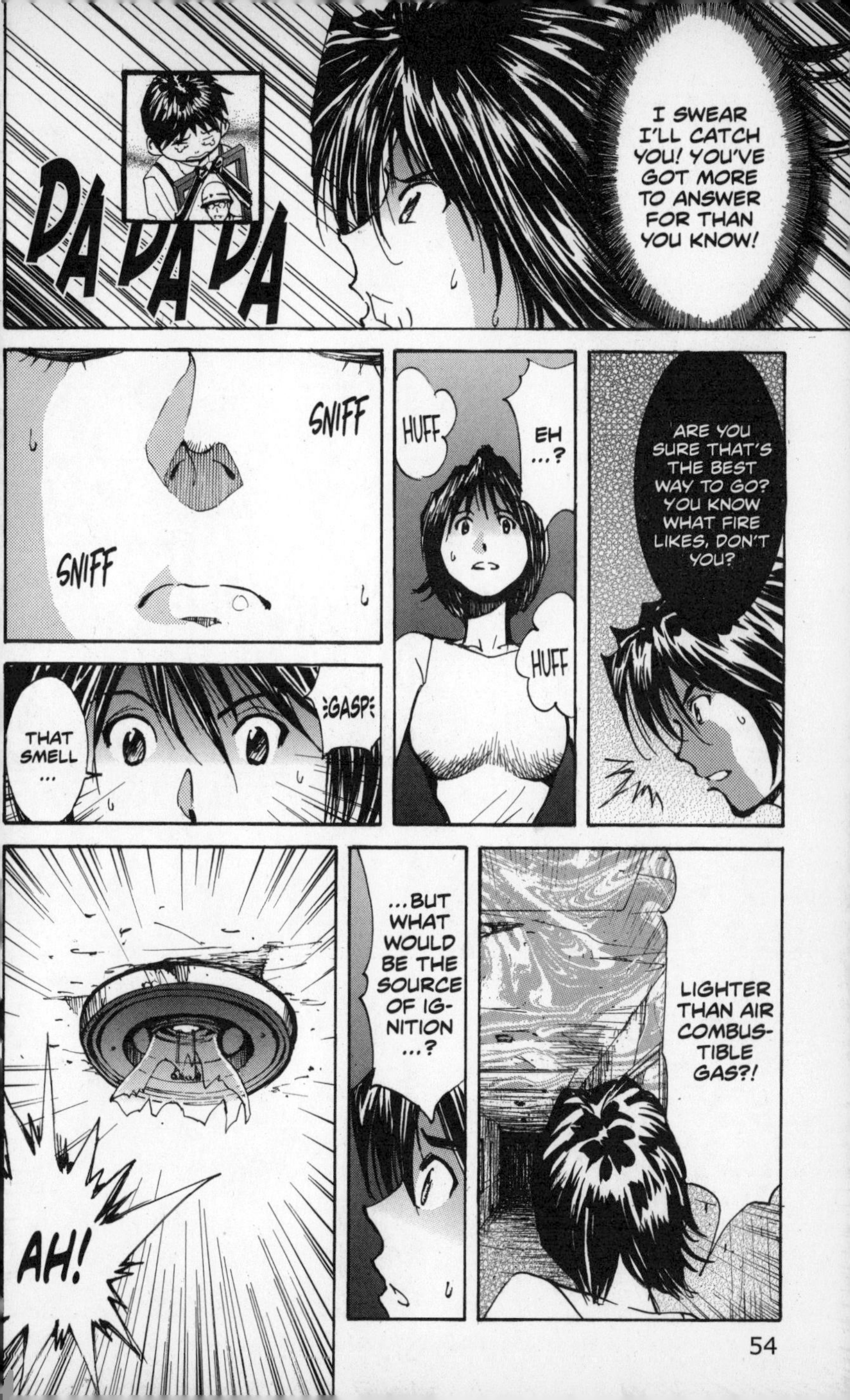
I SWEAR I'LL CATCH YOU! YOU'VE GOT MORE TO ANSWER FOR THAN YOU KNOW!
DA DA DA
ARE YOU SURE THAT'S THE BEST WAY TO GO? YOU KNOW WHAT FIRE LIKES, DON'T YOU?
EH ...?
HUFF
HUFF
SNIFF
SNIFF
GASP
THAT SMELL ...
LIGHTER THAN AIR COMBUSTIBLE GAS?!
...BUT WHAT WOULD BE THE SOURCE OF IGNITION ...?
AH!

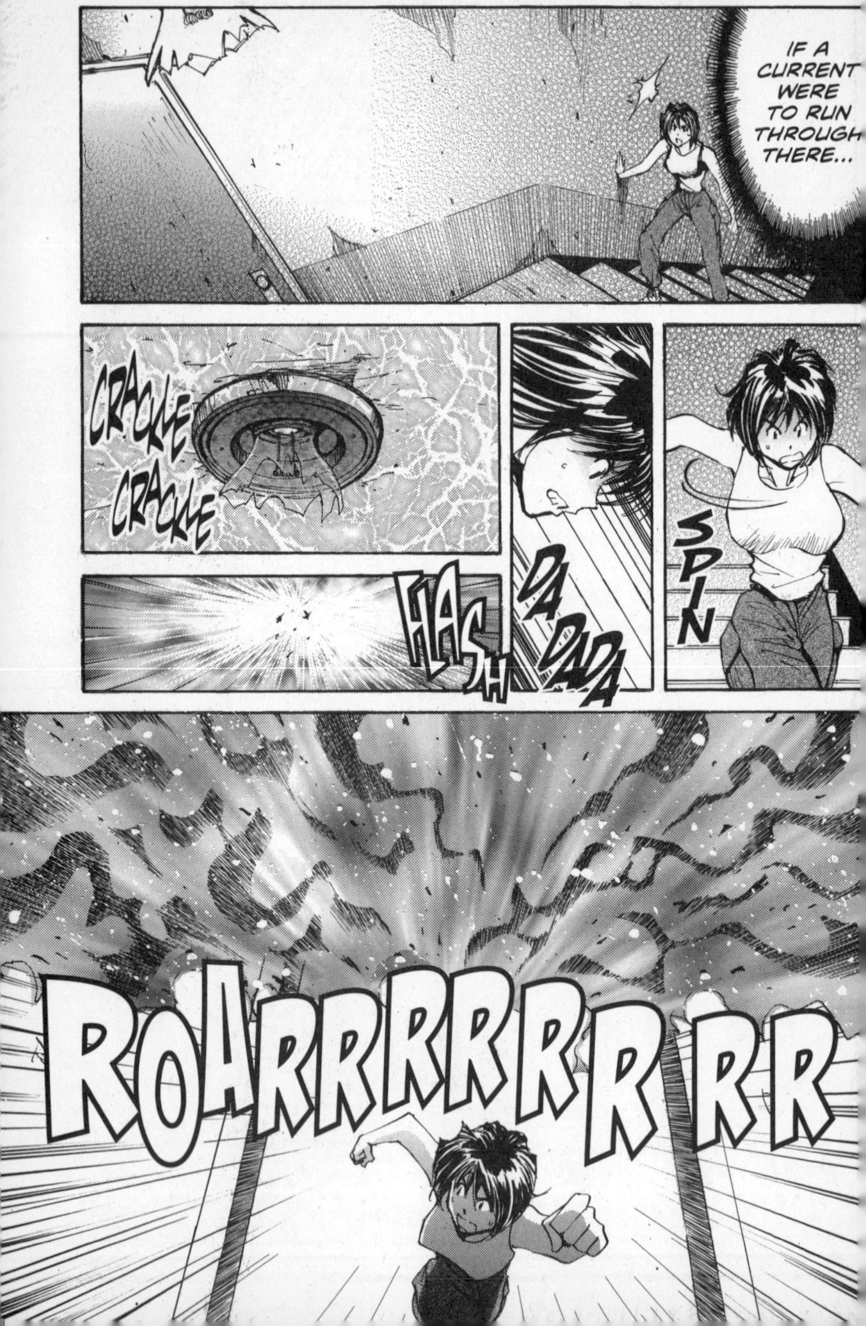
IF A CURRENT WERE TO RUN THROUGH THERE...
SPIN
DADADA
CRACKLE CRACKLE
FLASH
ROARRRRRRRRR

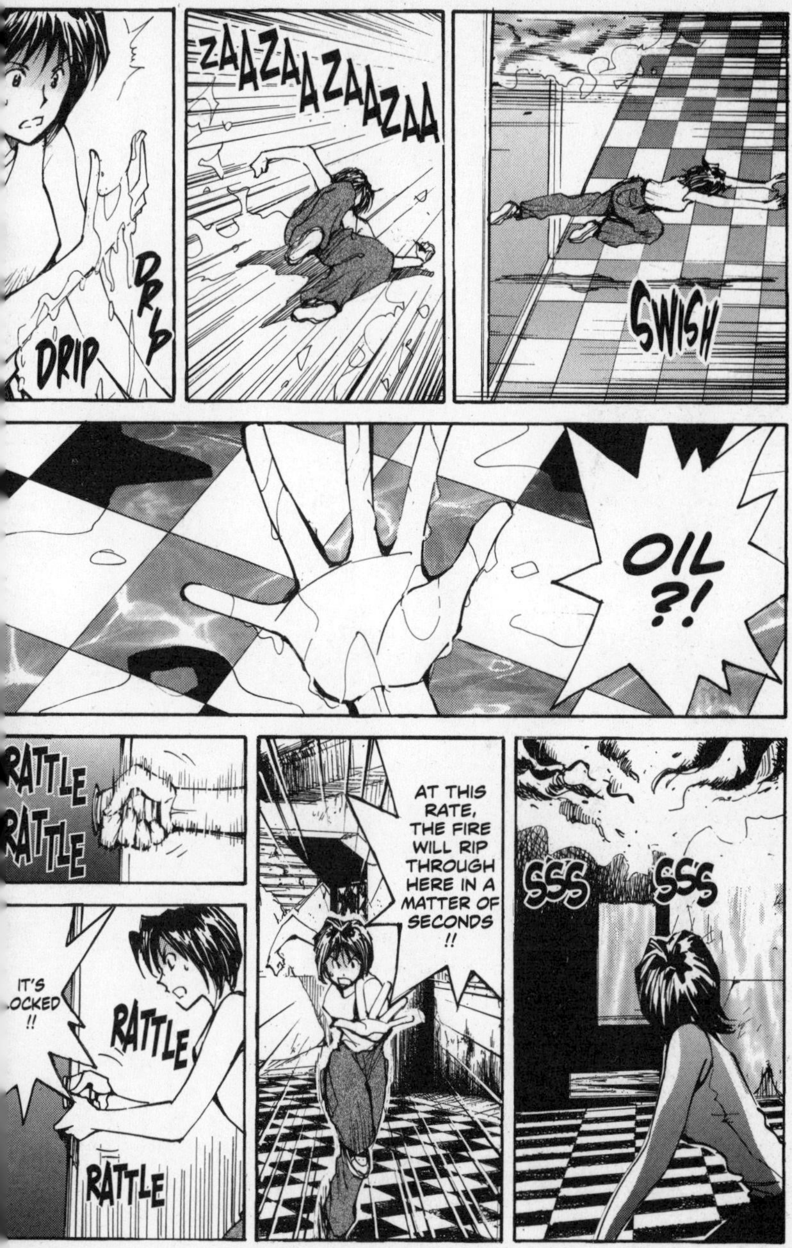
SWISH
ZAAZAAZAAZAA
DRIP
DRIP
OIL?!
SSS SSS
AT THIS RATE, THE FIRE WILL RIP THROUGH HERE IN A MATTER OF SECONDS!!
RATTLE RATTLE
IT'S LOCKED!!
RATTLE
RATTLE

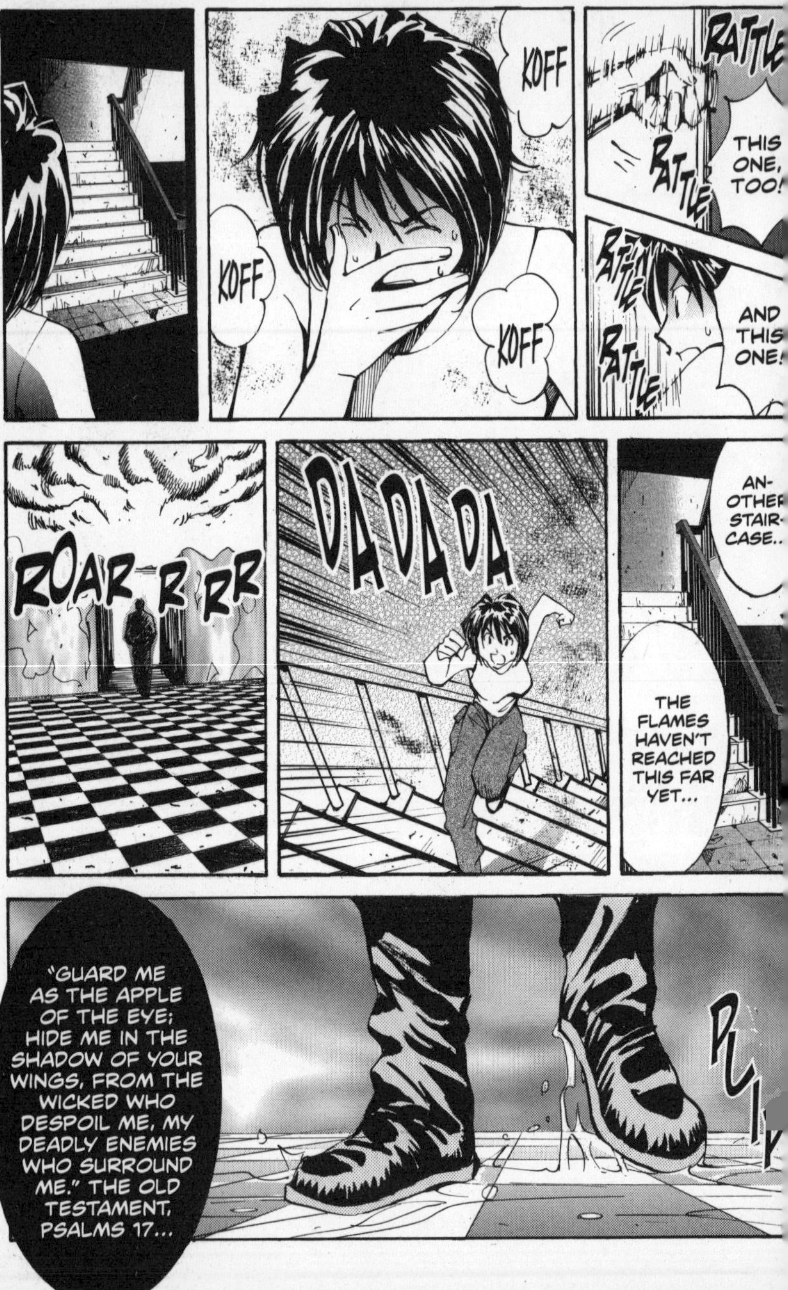
RATTLE
RATTLE
THIS ONE, TOO!
RATTLE
RATTLE
AND THIS ONE!
KOFF
KOFF
KOFF
AN-OTHER STAIR-CASE...
THE FLAMES HAVEN'T REACHED THIS FAR YET...
DA DA DA
ROAR R RR
"GUARD ME AS THE APPLE OF THE EYE; HIDE ME IN THE SHADOW OF YOUR WINGS, FROM THE WICKED WHO DESPOIL ME, MY DEADLY ENEMIES WHO SURROUND ME." THE OLD TESTAMENT, PSALMS 17...

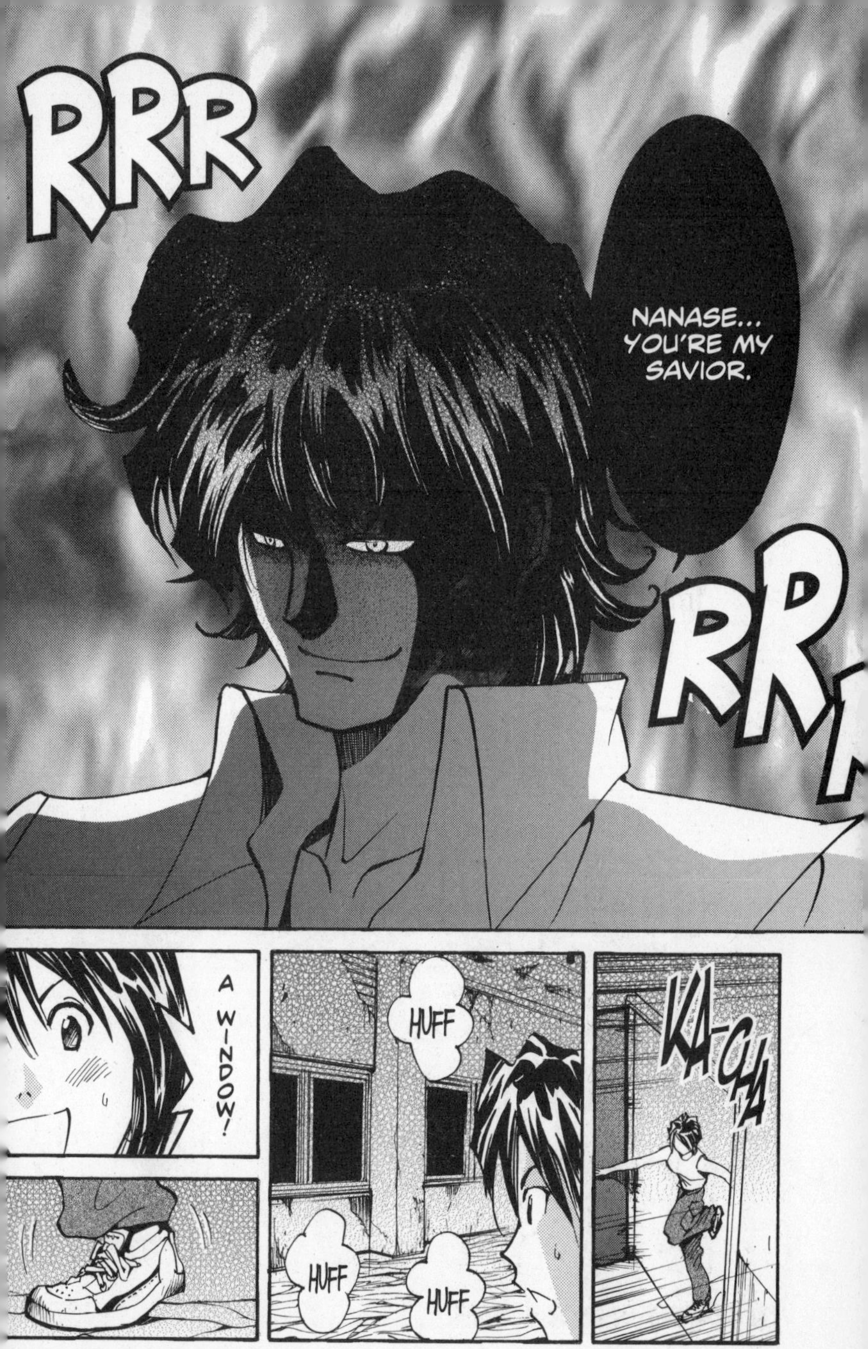
RRR
NANASE... YOU'RE MY SAVIOR.
RR
KA-CHA
HUFF
HUFF
HUFF
A WINDOW!

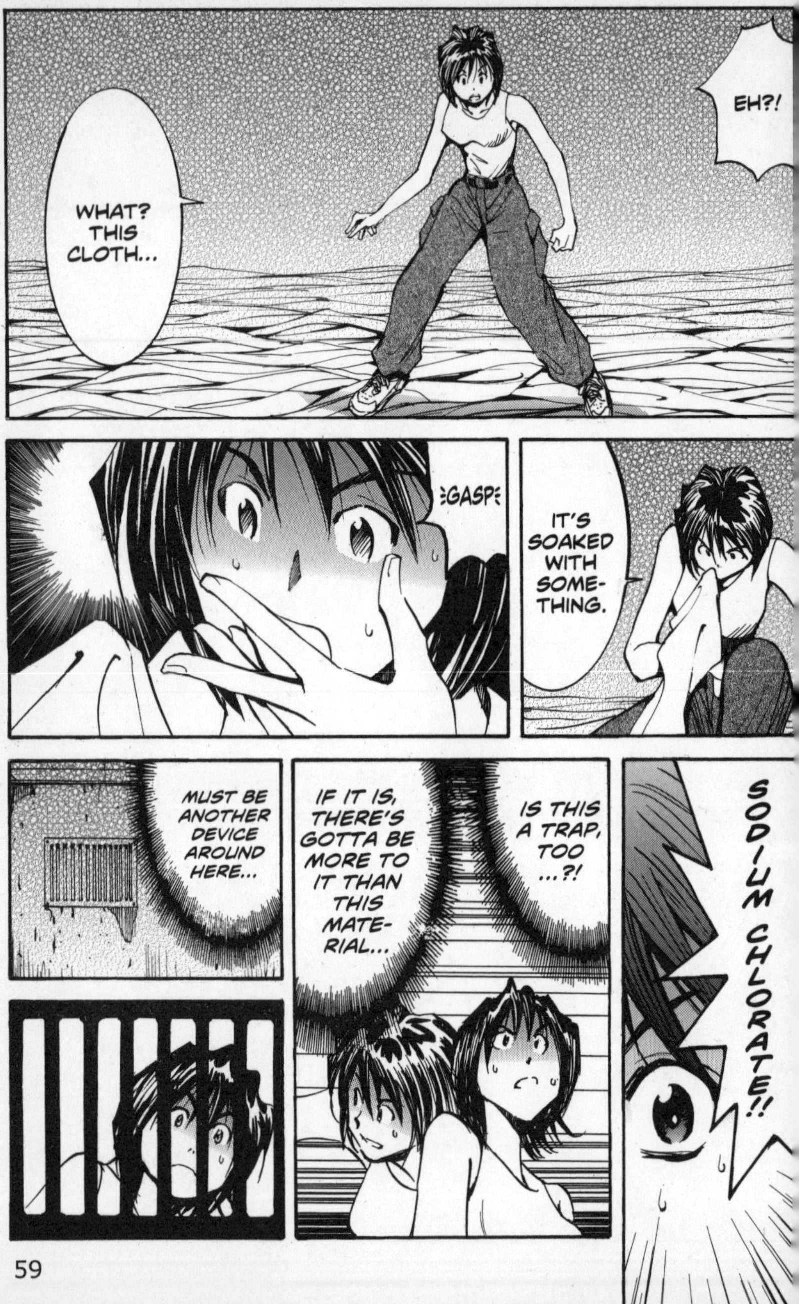
EH?!
WHAT? THIS CLOTH...
IT'S SOAKED WITH SOME-THING.
GASP
SODIUM CHLORATE!!
IS THIS A TRAP, TOO ...?!
IF IT IS, THERE'S GOTTA BE MORE TO IT THAN THIS MATE-RIAL...
MUST BE ANOTHER DEVICE AROUND HERE...

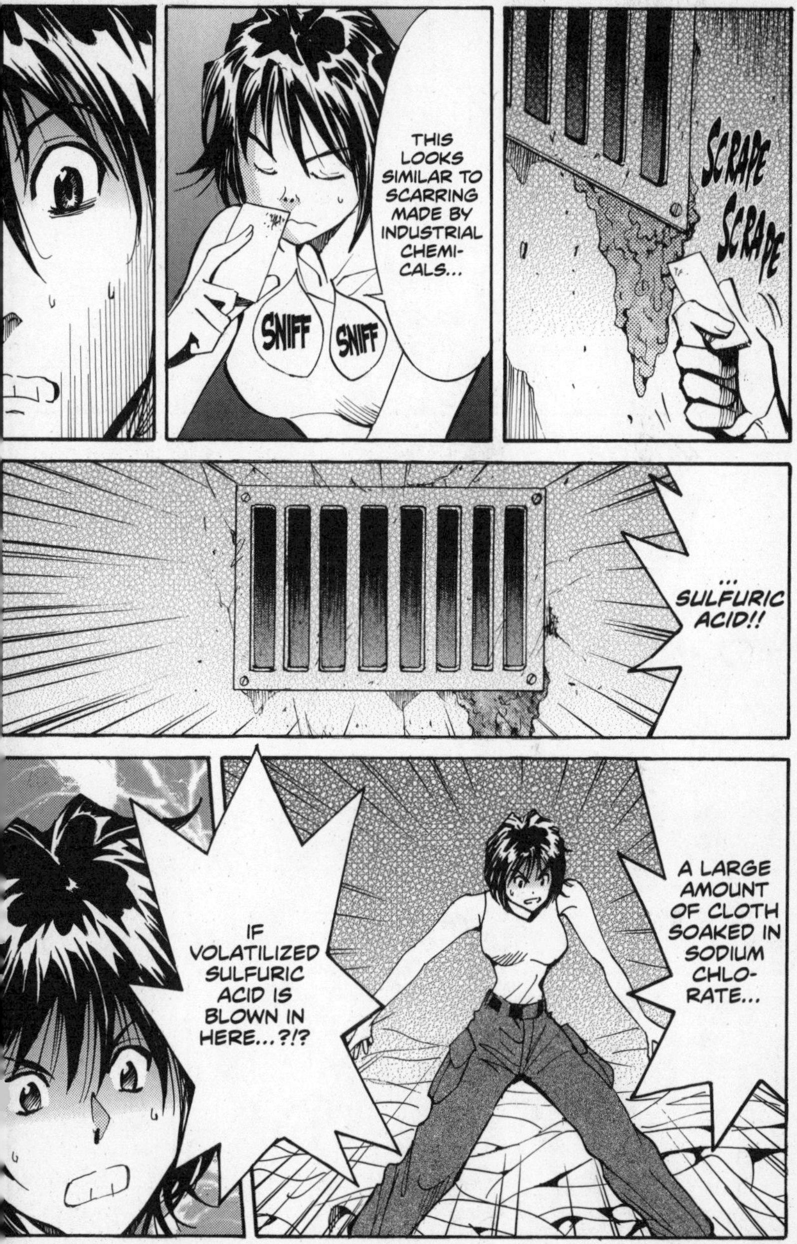
SCRAPE
SCRAPE
THIS LOOKS SIMILAR TO SCARRING MADE BY INDUSTRIAL CHEMI-CALS...
SNIFF
SNIFF
... SULFURIC ACID!!
A LARGE AMOUNT OF CLOTH SOAKED IN SODIUM CHLO-RATE...
IF VOLATILIZED SULFURIC ACID IS BLOWN IN HERE...?!?

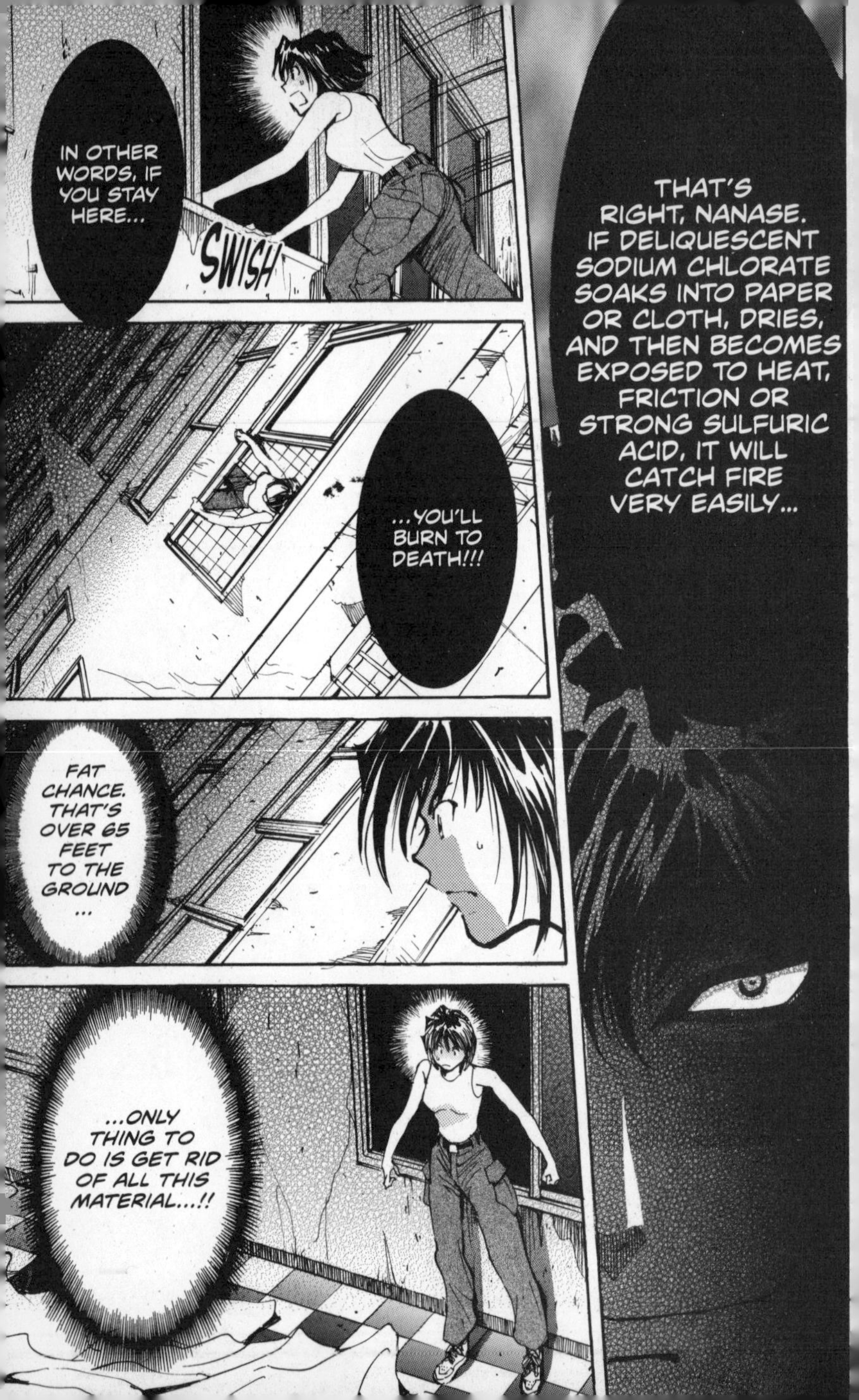
THAT'S RIGHT, NANASE. IF DELIQUESCENT SODIUM CHLORATE SOAKS INTO PAPER OR CLOTH, DRIES, AND THEN BECOMES EXPOSED TO HEAT, FRICTION OR STRONG SULFURIC ACID, IT WILL CATCH FIRE VERY EASILY...
IN OTHER WORDS, IF YOU STAY HERE...
SWISH
...YOU'LL BURN TO DEATH!!!
FAT CHANCE. THAT'S OVER 65 FEET TO THE GROUND ...
...ONLY THING TO DO IS GET RID OF ALL THIS MATERIAL...!!

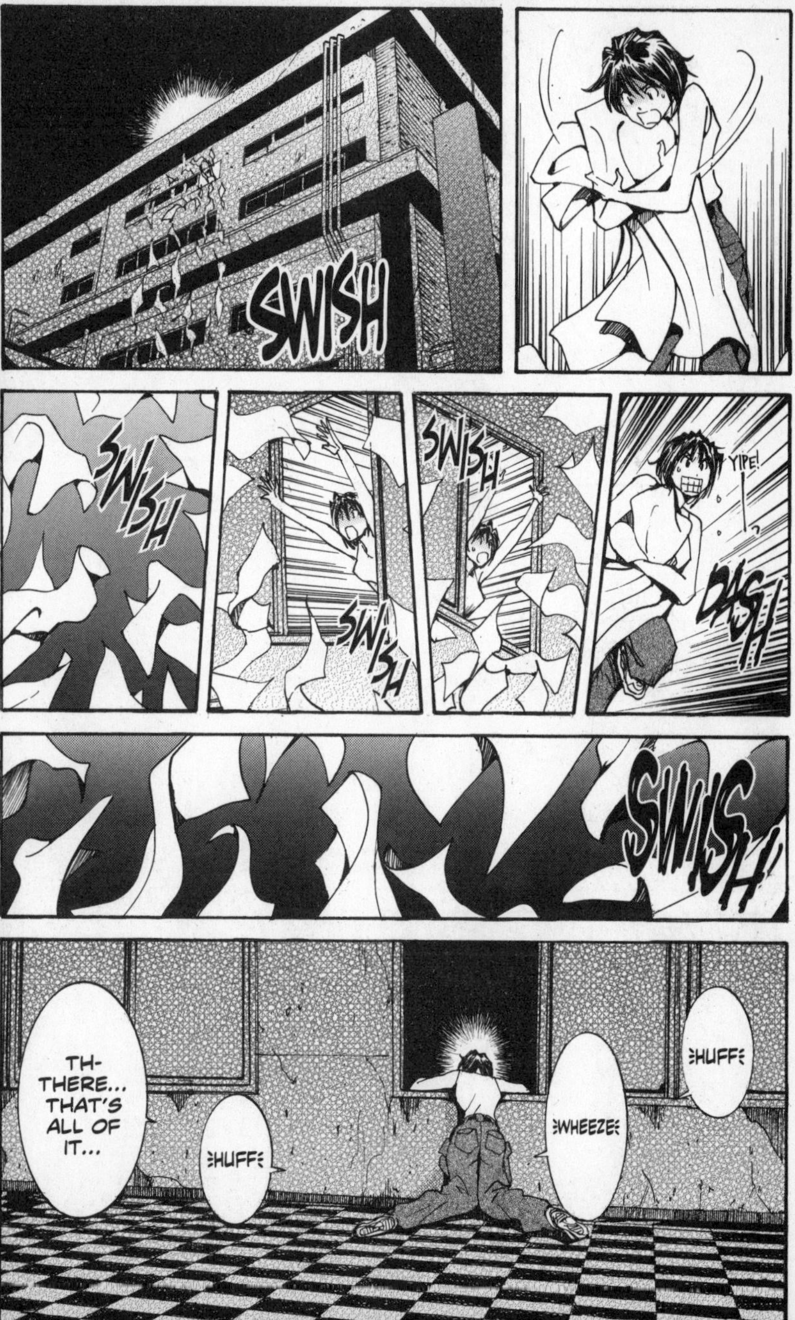

SWISH
YIPE!
DASH
SWISH
SWISH
SWISH
SWISH
HUFF
WHEEZE
HUFF
TH-THERE... THAT'S ALL OF IT...

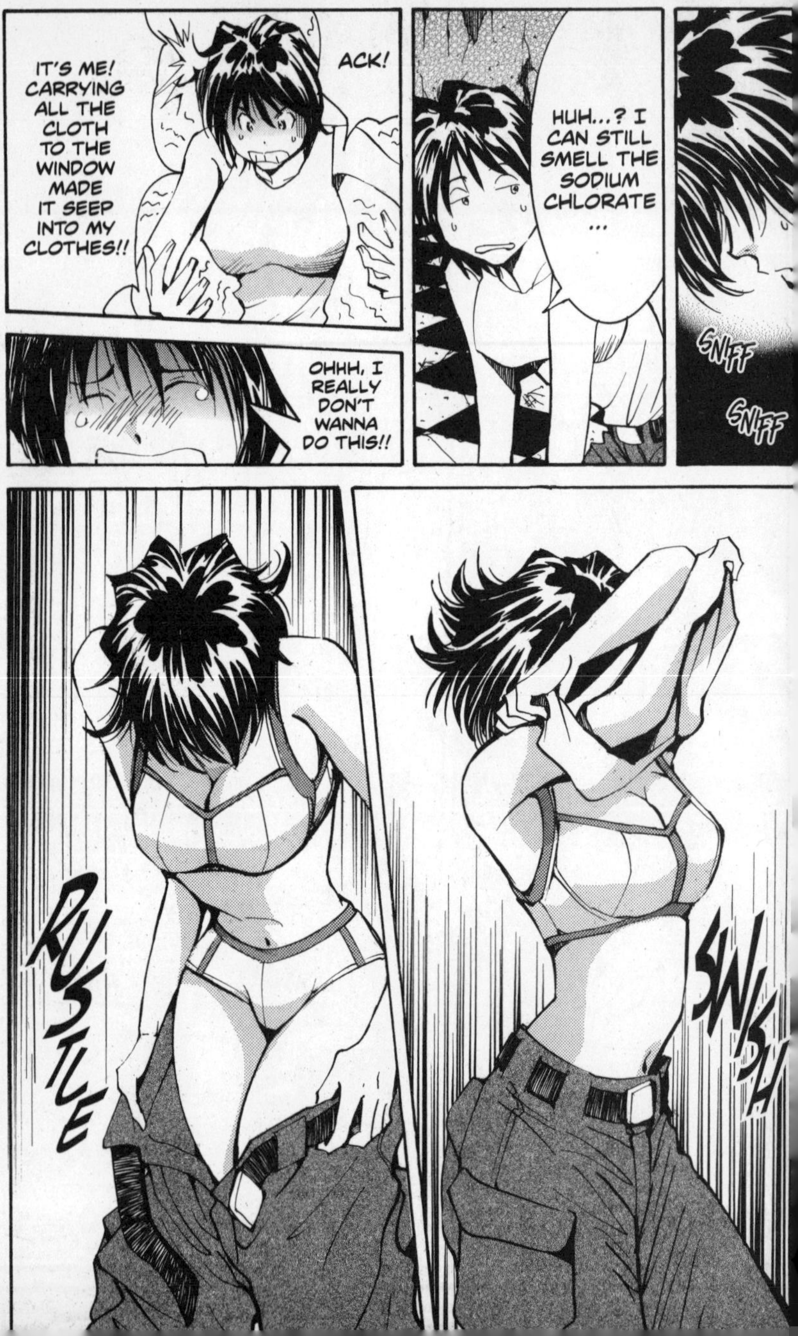
SNIFF
SNIFF
HUH...? I CAN STILL SMELL THE SODIUM CHLORATE ...
ACK!
IT'S ME! CARRYING ALL THE CLOTH TO THE WINDOW MADE IT SEEP INTO MY CLOTHES!!
OHHH, I REALLY DON'T WANNA DO THIS!!
SWISH
RUSTLE

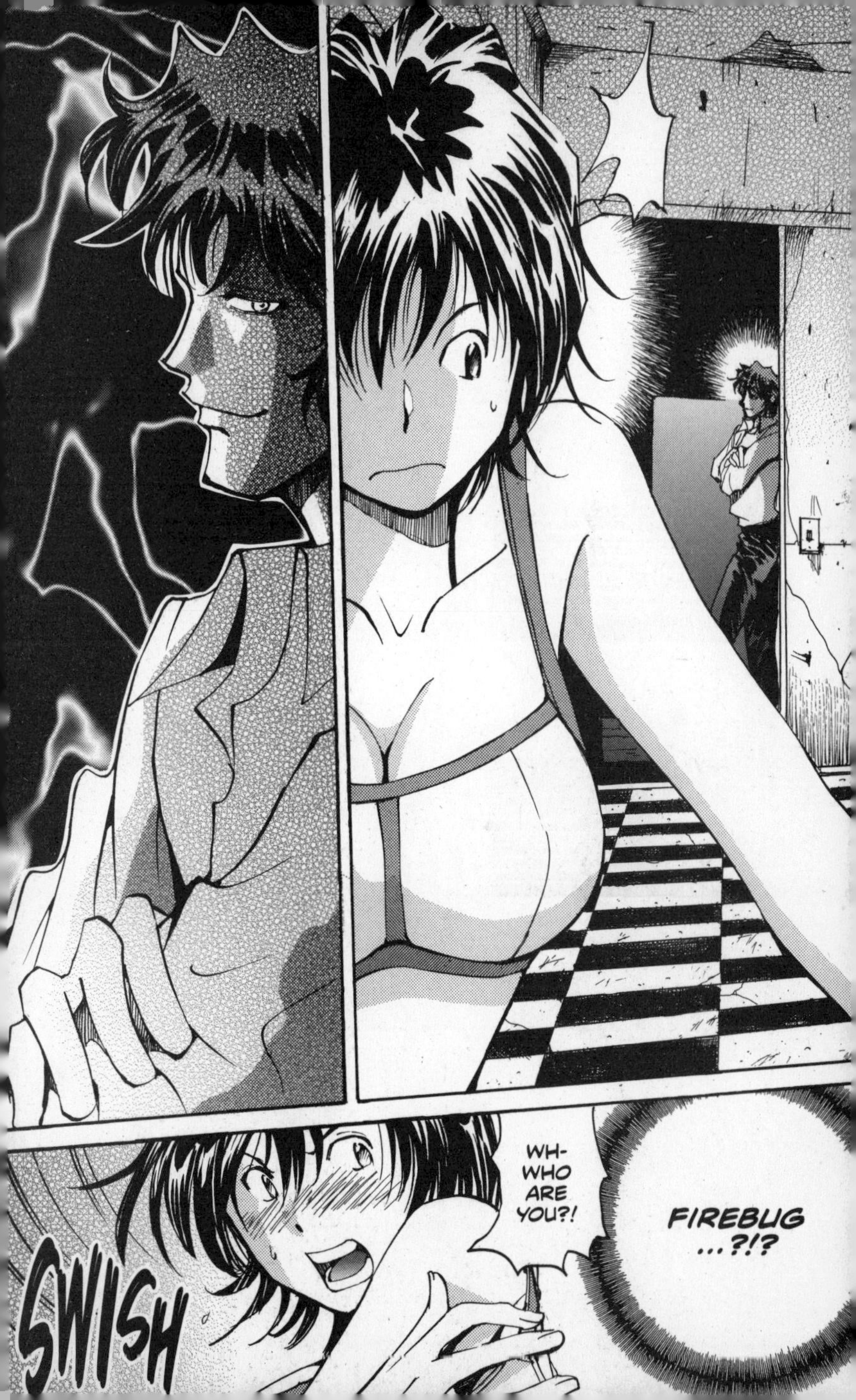
FIREBUG ...?!?
WH- WHO ARE YOU?!
SWISH

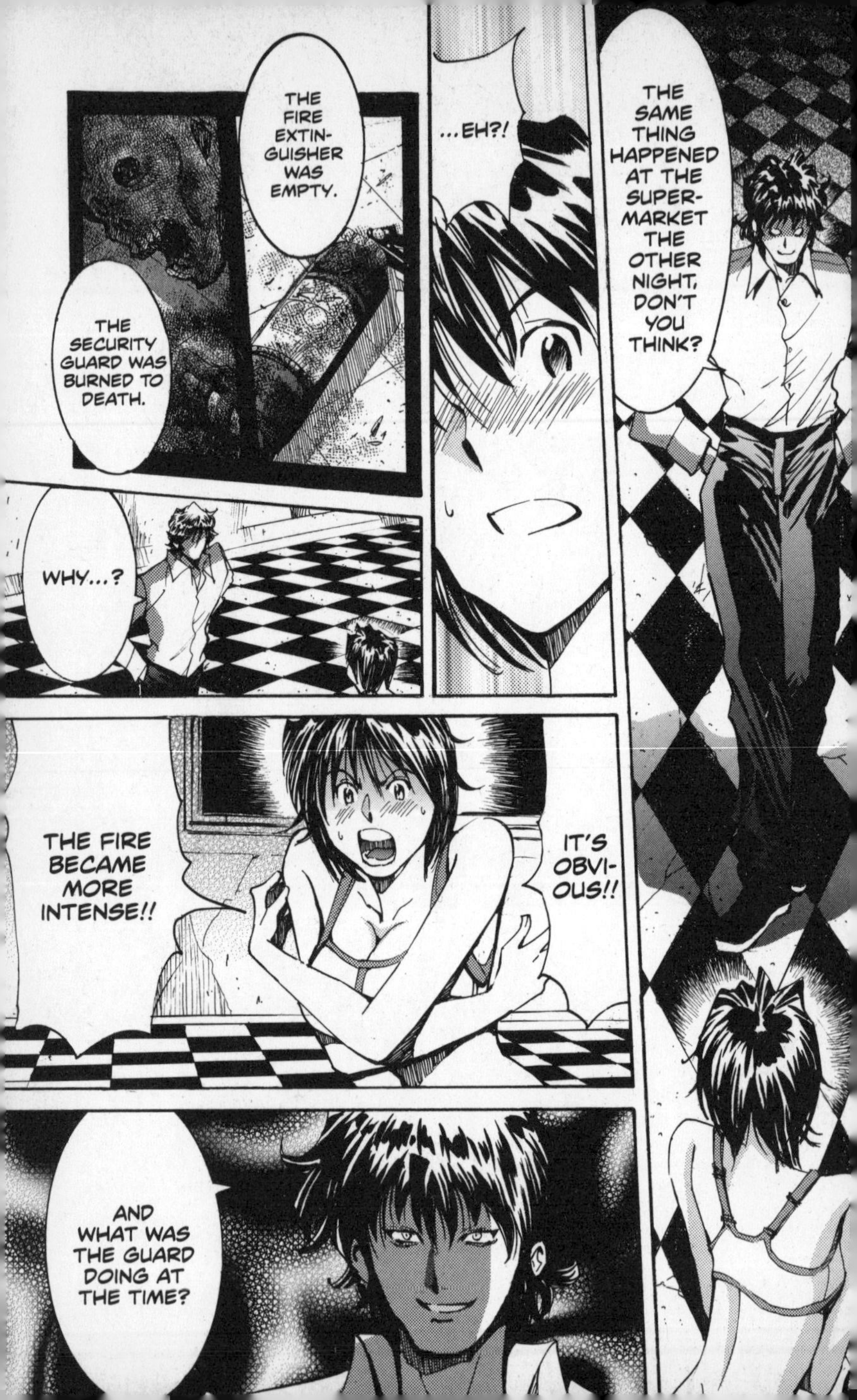
THE SAME THING HAPPENED AT THE SUPER-MARKET THE OTHER NIGHT, DON'T YOU THINK?
...EH?!
THE FIRE EXTIN-GUISHER WAS EMPTY.
THE SECURITY GUARD WAS BURNED TO DEATH.
WHY...?
IT'S OBVI-OUS!!
THE FIRE BECAME MORE INTENSE!!
AND WHAT WAS THE GUARD DOING AT THE TIME?

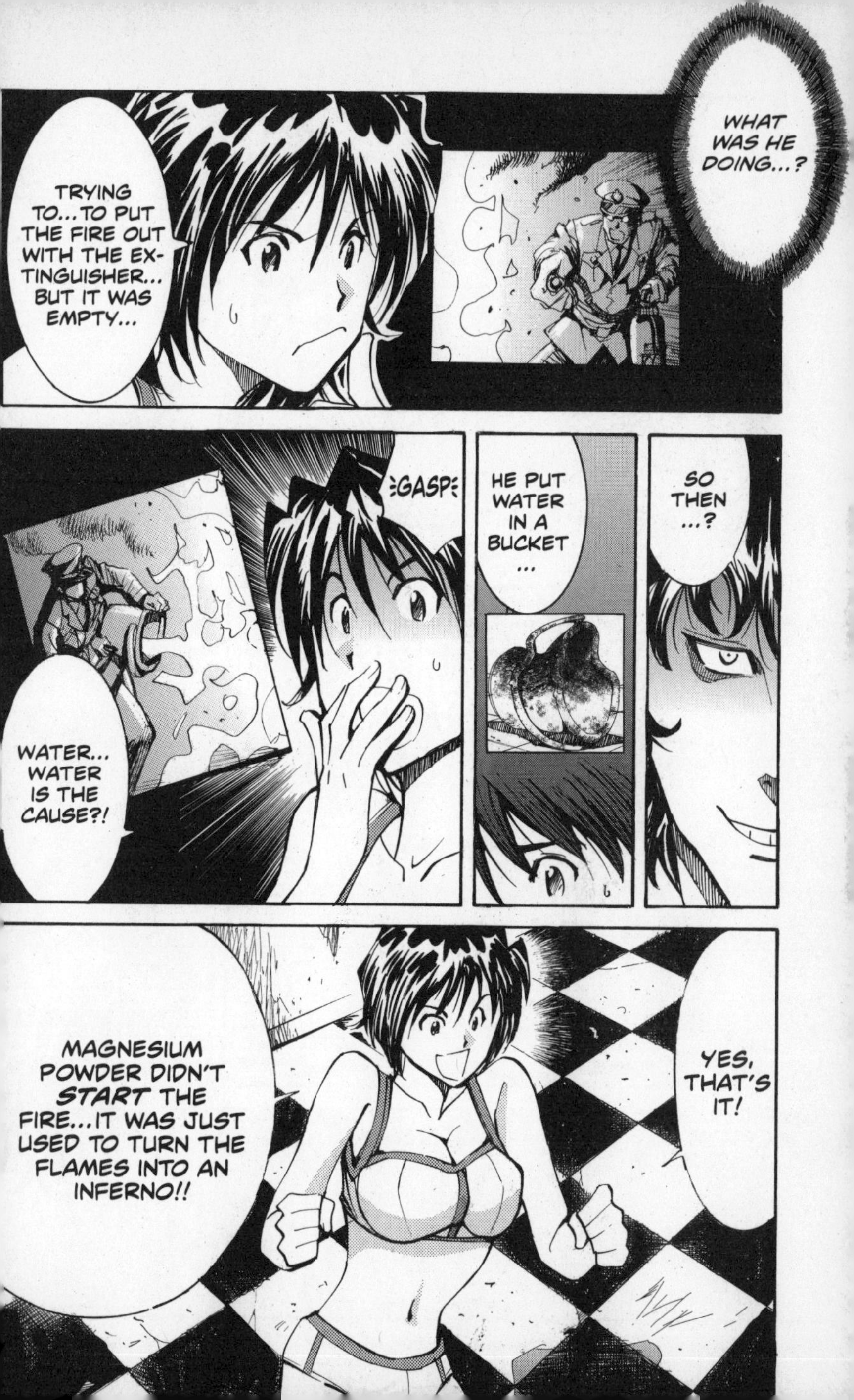
WHAT WAS HE DOING...?
TRYING TO...TO PUT THE FIRE OUT WITH THE EXTINGUISHER... BUT IT WAS EMPTY...
SO THEN ...?
HE PUT WATER IN A BUCKET ...
GASP
WATER... WATER IS THE CAUSE?!
YES, THAT'S IT!
MAGNESIUM POWDER DIDN'T *START* THE FIRE...IT WAS JUST USED TO TURN THE FLAMES INTO AN INFERNO!!

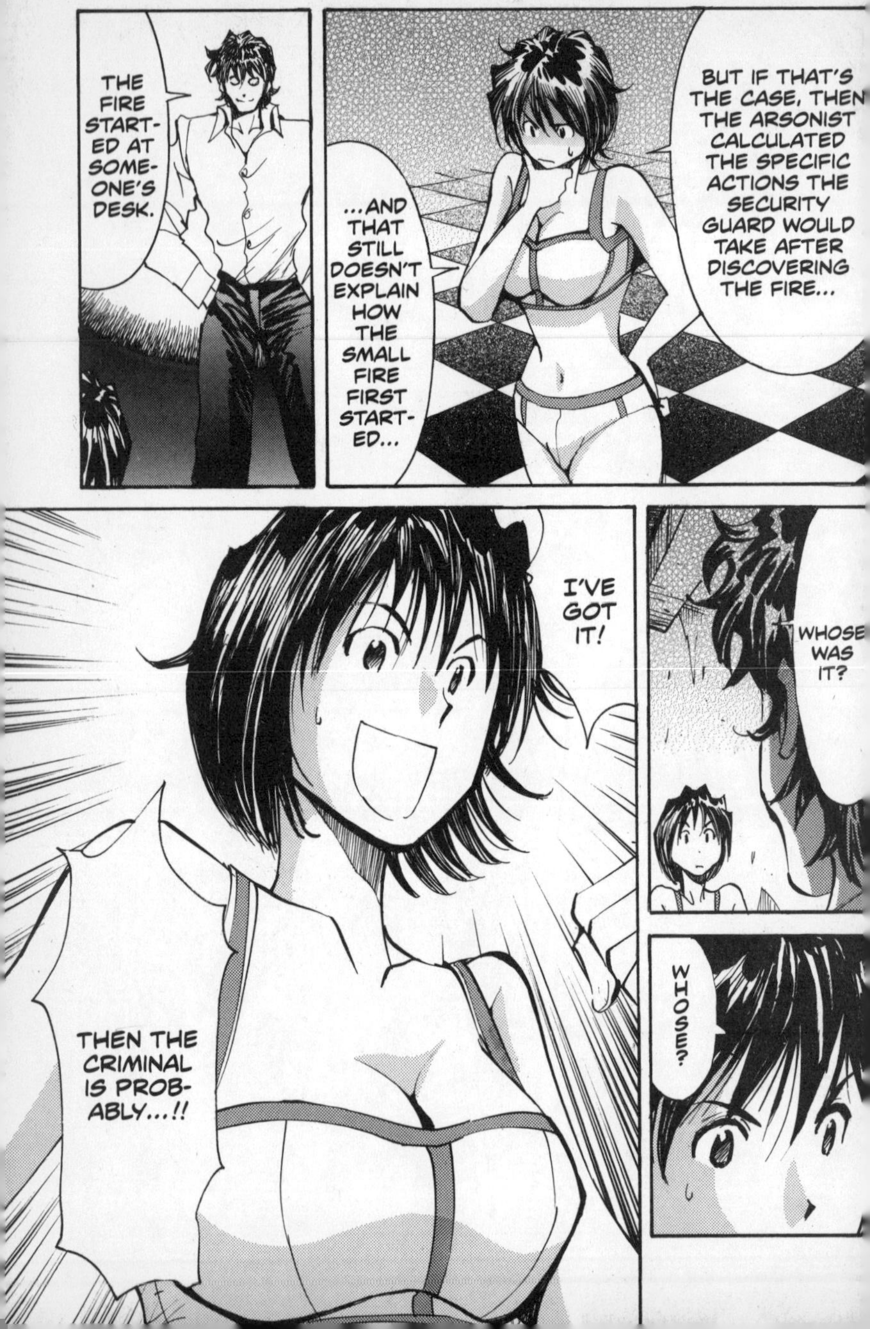
BUT IF THAT'S THE CASE, THEN THE ARSONIST CALCULATED THE SPECIFIC ACTIONS THE SECURITY GUARD WOULD TAKE AFTER DISCOVERING THE FIRE...
...AND THAT STILL DOESN'T EXPLAIN HOW THE SMALL FIRE FIRST STARTED...
THE FIRE STARTED AT SOMEONE'S DESK.
WHOSE WAS IT?
WHOSE?
I'VE GOT IT!
THEN THE CRIMINAL IS PROBABLY...!!

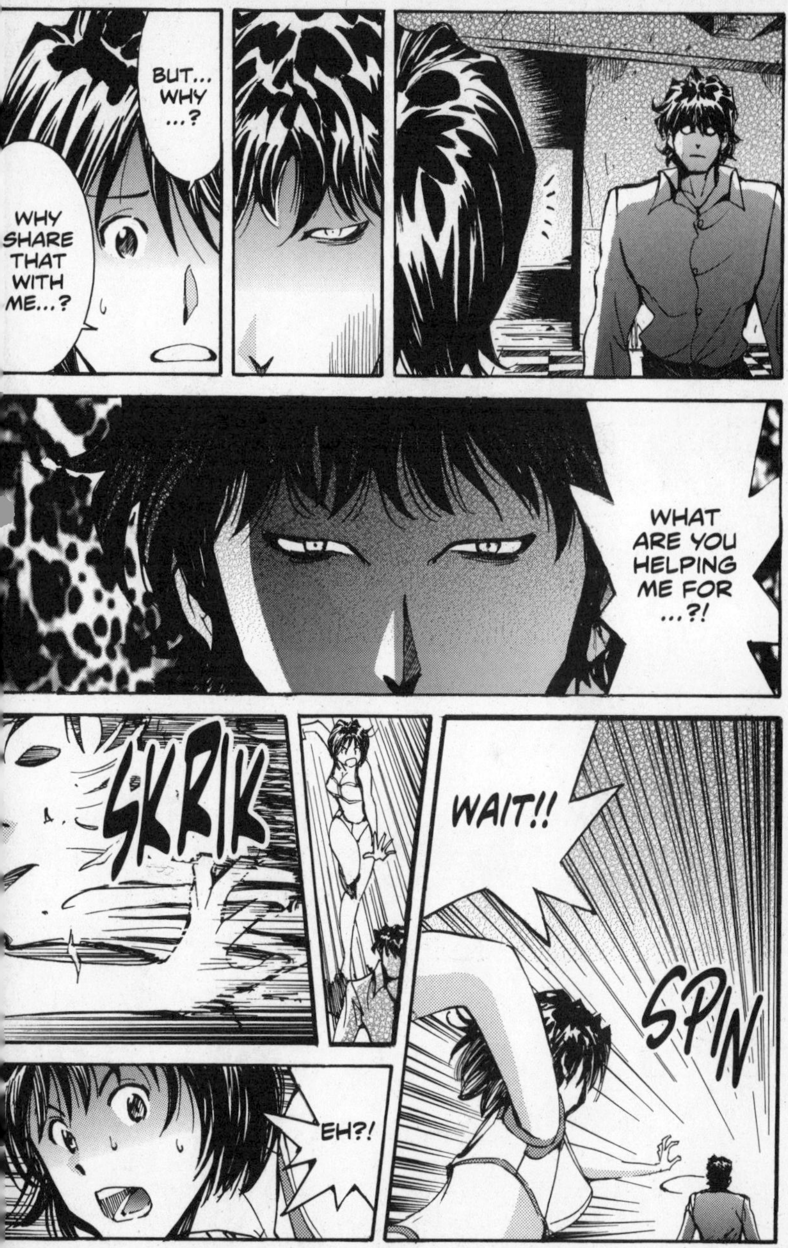
BUT... WHY ...?
WHY SHARE THAT WITH ME...?
WHAT ARE YOU HELPING ME FOR ...?!
WAIT!!
SPIN
SKRIK
EH?!

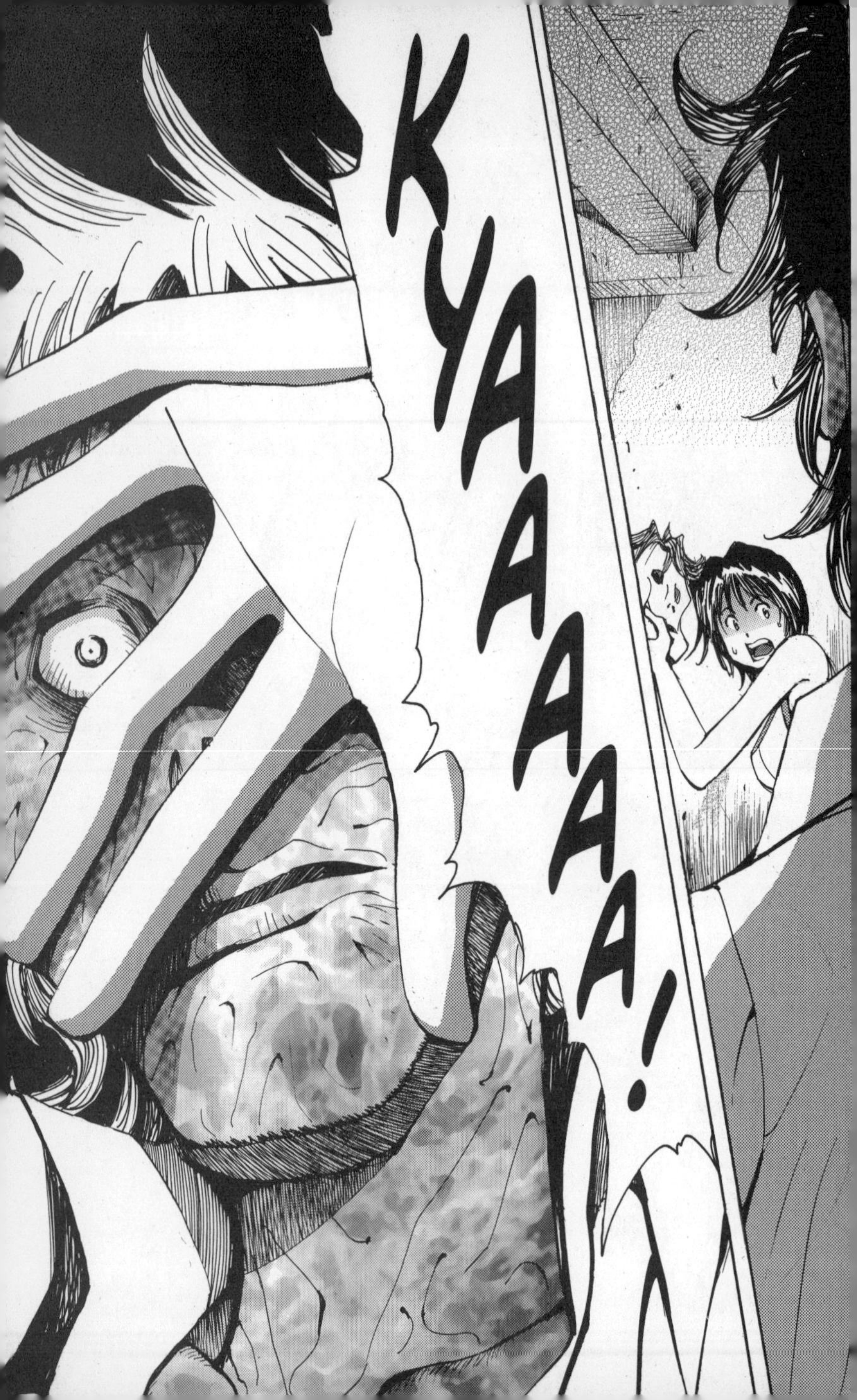
KYAAAAAAA!

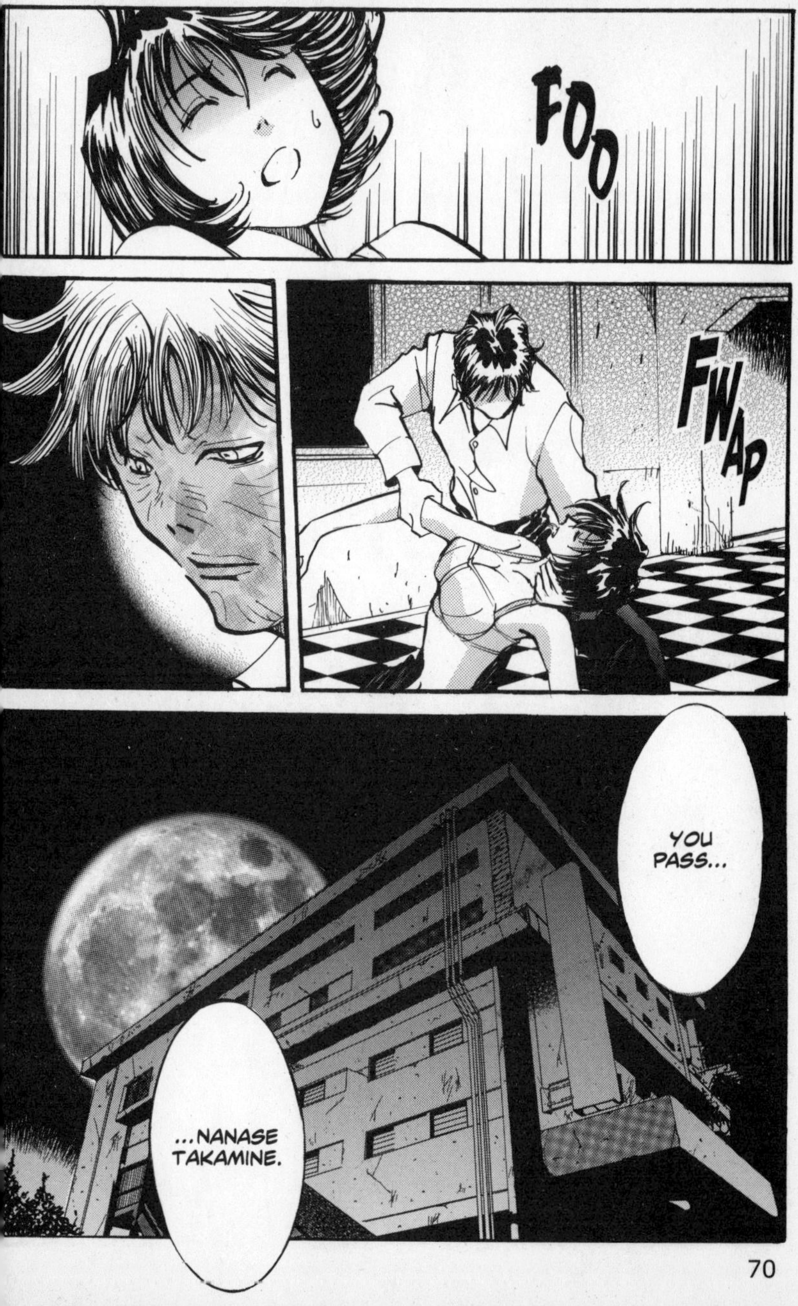
FOO
FWAP
YOU PASS...
...NANASE TAKAMINE.

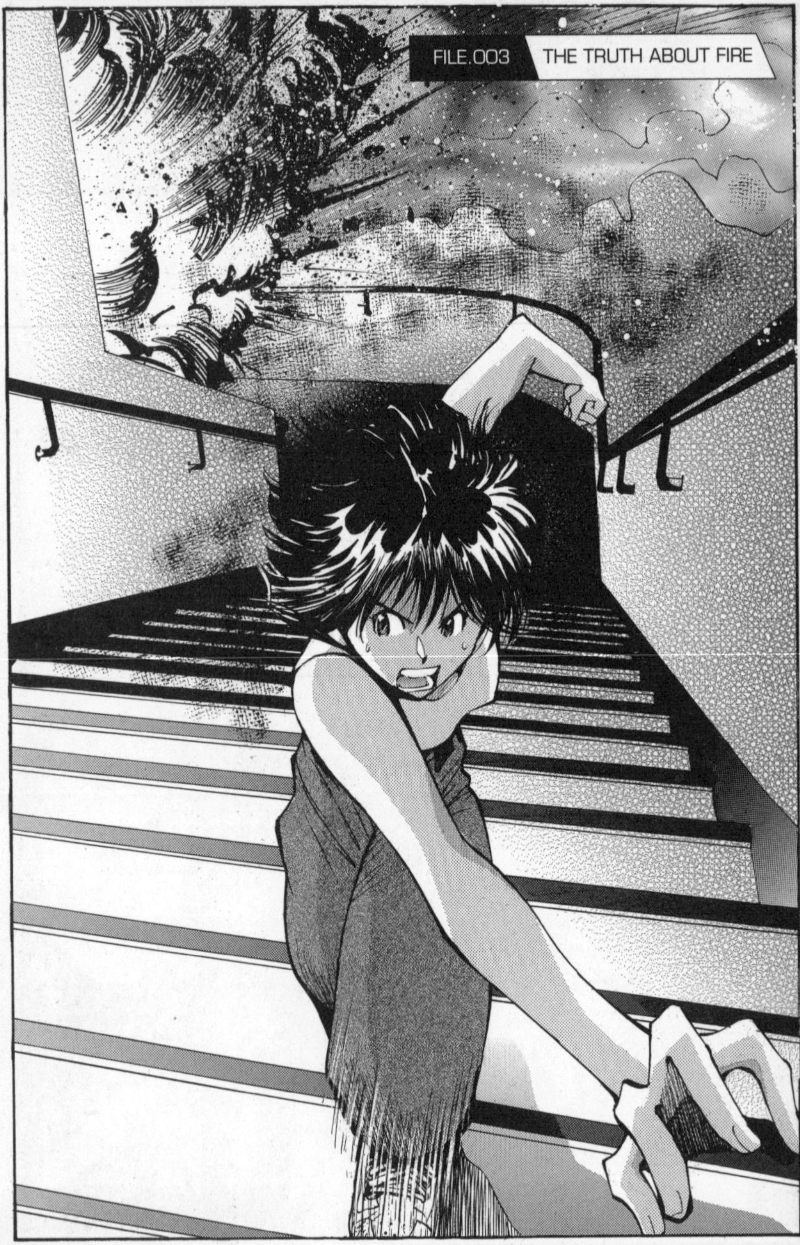
FILE.003
THE TRUTH ABOUT FIRE

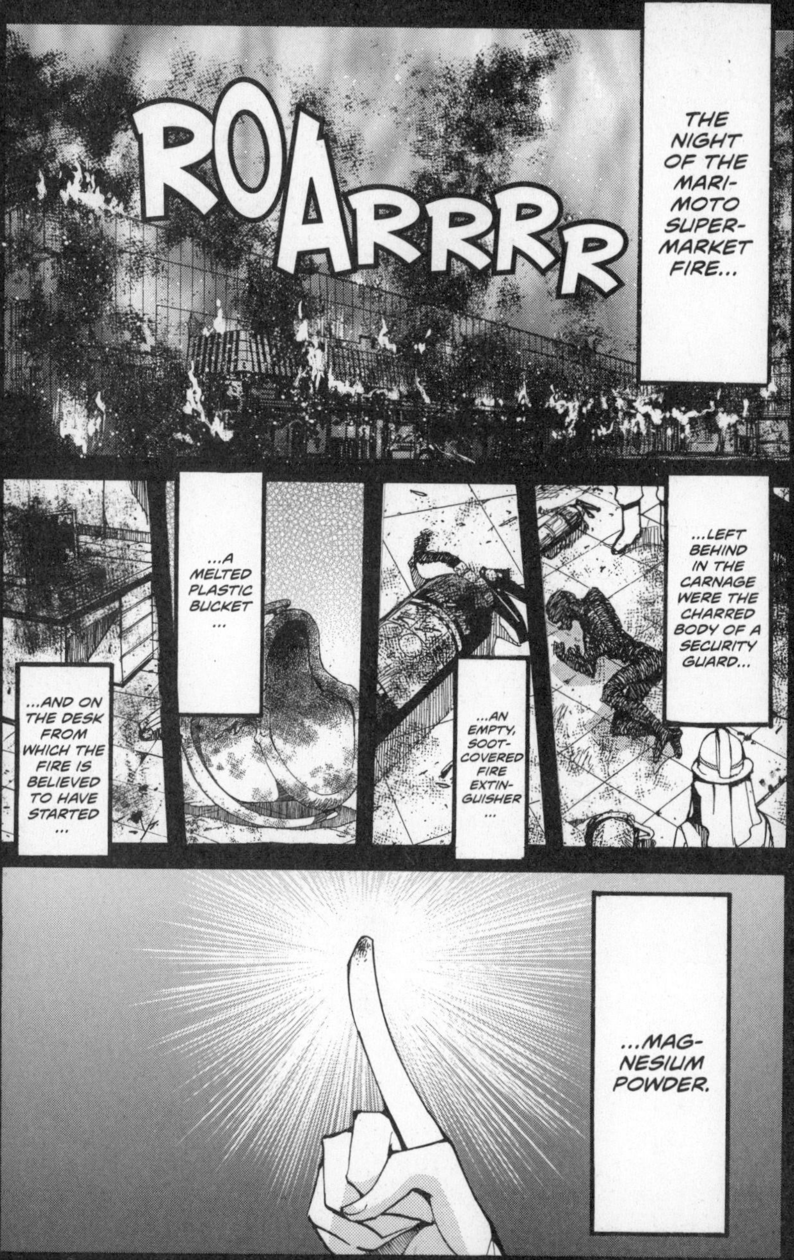
THE NIGHT OF THE MARI-MOTO SUPER-MARKET FIRE...
ROAARRRR
...LEFT BEHIND IN THE CARNAGE WERE THE CHARRED BODY OF A SECURITY GUARD...
...AN EMPTY, SOOT-COVERED FIRE EXTIN-GUISHER ...
...A MELTED PLASTIC BUCKET ...
...AND ON THE DESK FROM WHICH THE FIRE IS BELIEVED TO HAVE STARTED ...
...MAG-NESIUM POWDER.

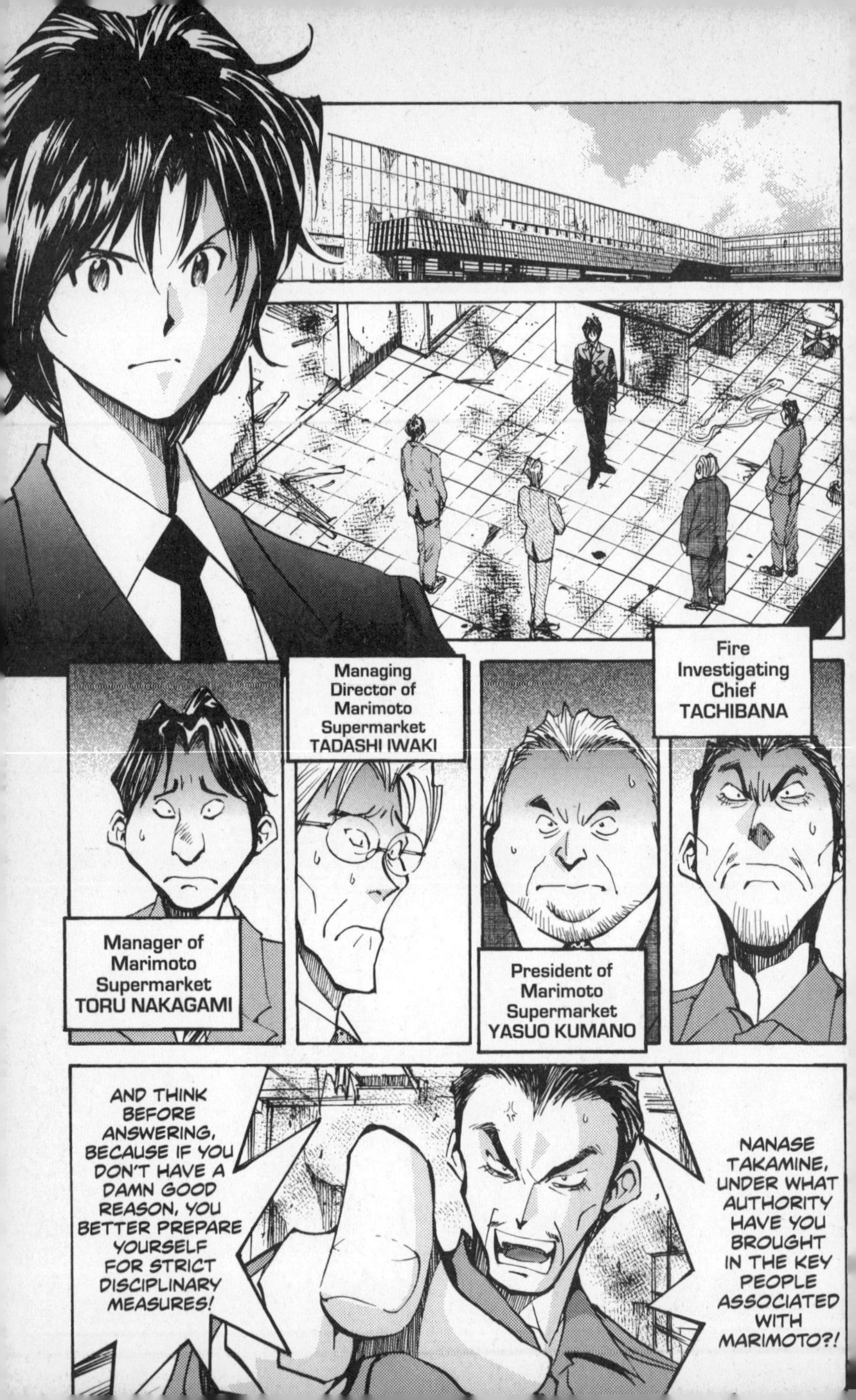
Fire Investigating Chief TACHIBANA
President of Marimoto Supermarket YASUO KUMANO
Managing Director of Marimoto Supermarket TADASHI IWAKI
Manager of Marimoto Supermarket TORU NAKAGAMI
NANASE TAKAMINE, UNDER WHAT AUTHORITY HAVE YOU BROUGHT IN THE KEY PEOPLE ASSOCIATED WITH MARIMOTO?!
AND THINK BEFORE ANSWERING, BECAUSE IF YOU DON'T HAVE A DAMN GOOD REASON, YOU BETTER PREPARE YOURSELF FOR STRICT DISCIPLINARY MEASURES!

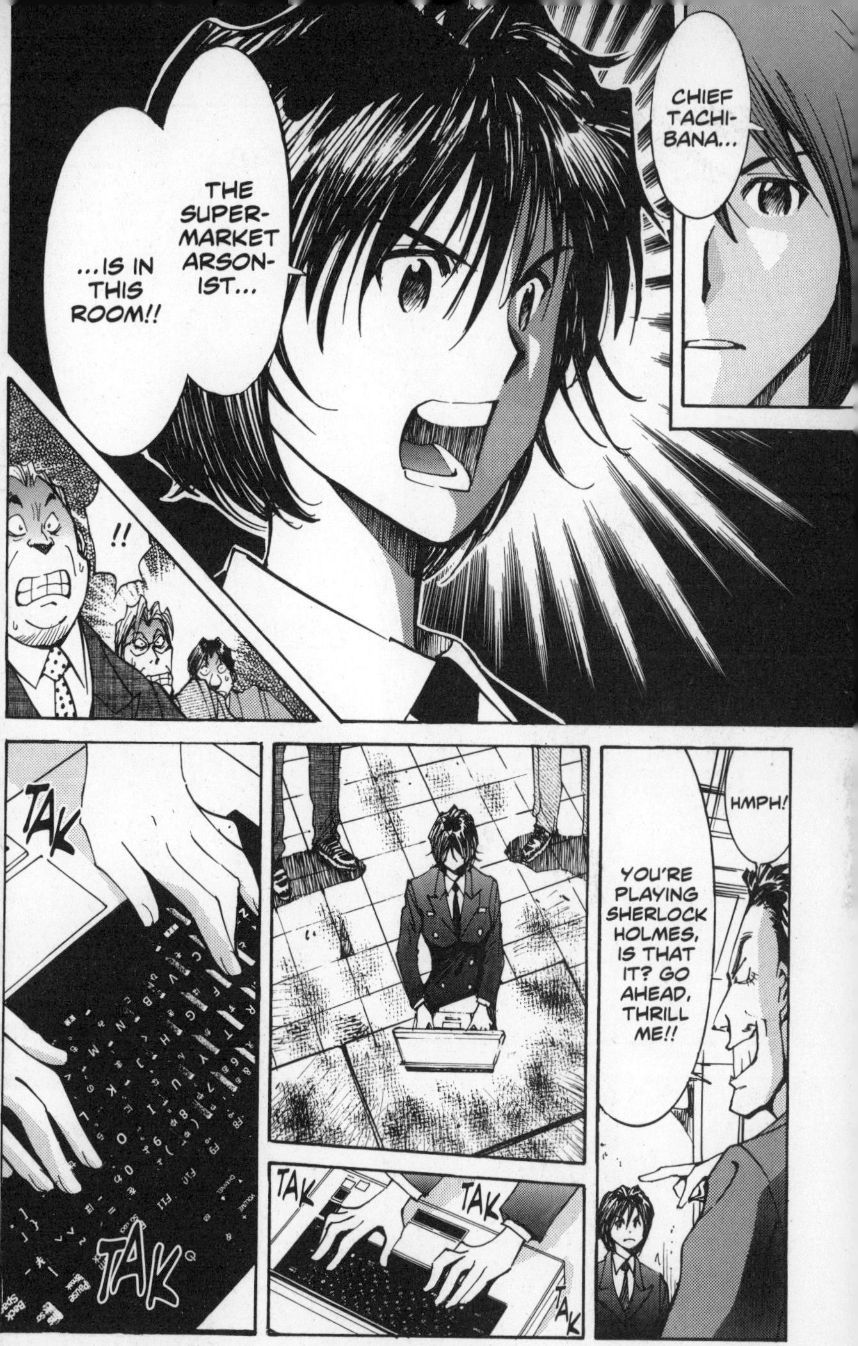
CHIEF TACHI-BANA...
THE SUPER-MARKET ARSON-IST...
...IS IN THIS ROOM!!
!!
HMPH!
YOU'RE PLAYING SHERLOCK HOLMES, IS THAT IT? GO AHEAD, THRILL ME!!
TAK
TAK
TAK
TAK
TAK

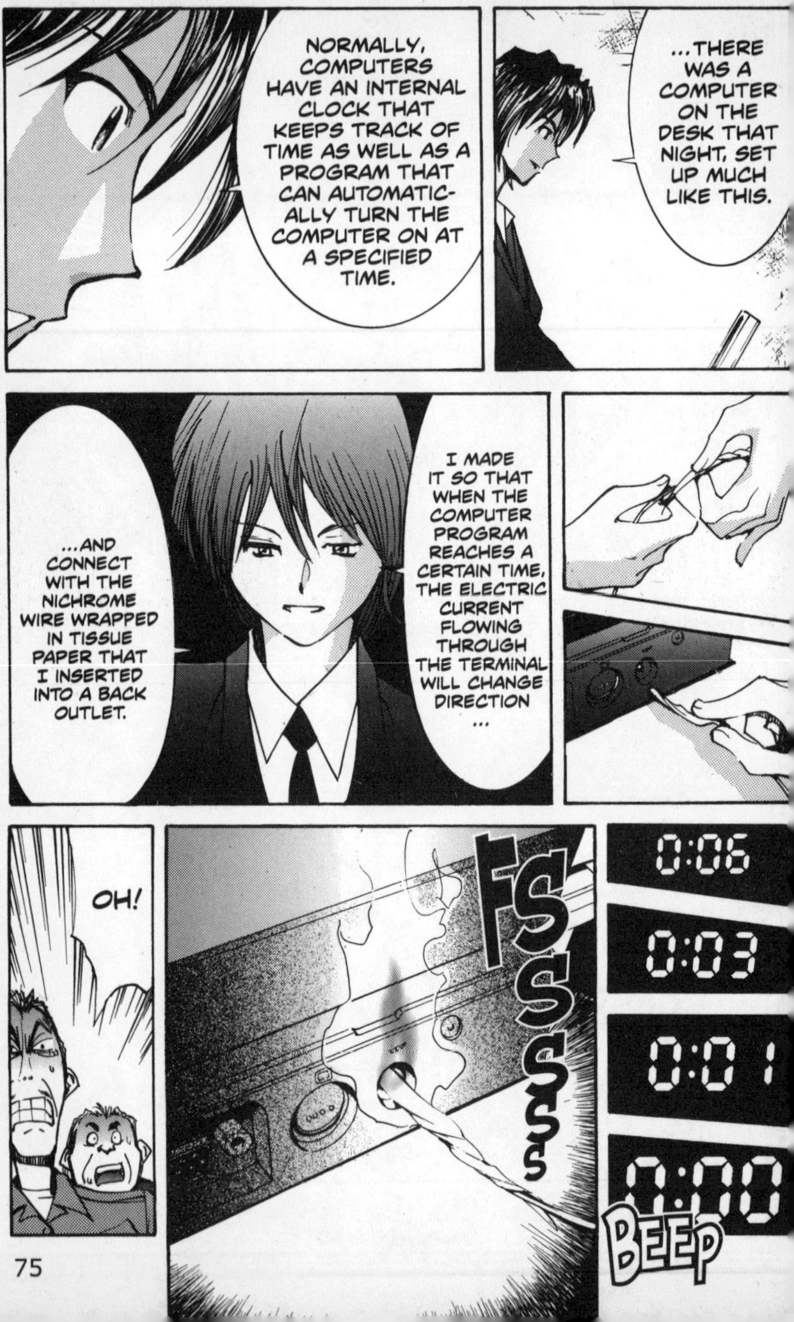
...THERE WAS A COMPUTER ON THE DESK THAT NIGHT, SET UP MUCH LIKE THIS.
NORMALLY, COMPUTERS HAVE AN INTERNAL CLOCK THAT KEEPS TRACK OF TIME AS WELL AS A PROGRAM THAT CAN AUTOMATIC-ALLY TURN THE COMPUTER ON AT A SPECIFIED TIME.
I MADE IT SO THAT WHEN THE COMPUTER PROGRAM REACHES A CERTAIN TIME, THE ELECTRIC CURRENT FLOWING THROUGH THE TERMINAL WILL CHANGE DIRECTION ...
...AND CONNECT WITH THE NICHROME WIRE WRAPPED IN TISSUE PAPER THAT I INSERTED INTO A BACK OUTLET.
0:06
0:03
0:01
0:00
BEEP
FSSSSSS
OH!

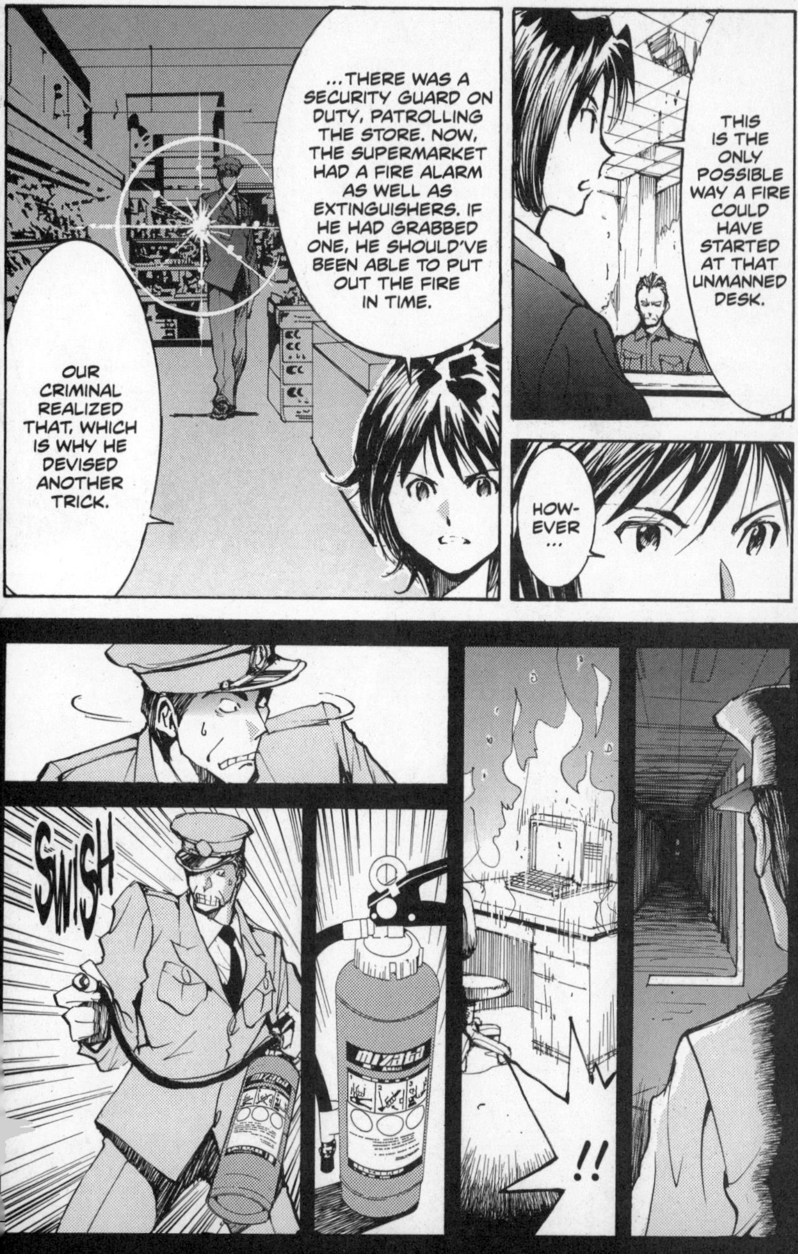
THIS IS THE ONLY POSSIBLE WAY A FIRE COULD HAVE STARTED AT THAT UNMANNED DESK.
HOW-EVER...
...THERE WAS A SECURITY GUARD ON DUTY, PATROLLING THE STORE. NOW, THE SUPERMARKET HAD A FIRE ALARM AS WELL AS EXTINGUISHERS. IF HE HAD GRABBED ONE, HE SHOULD'VE BEEN ABLE TO PUT OUT THE FIRE IN TIME.
OUR CRIMINAL REALIZED THAT, WHICH IS WHY HE DEVISED ANOTHER TRICK.
!!
SWISH

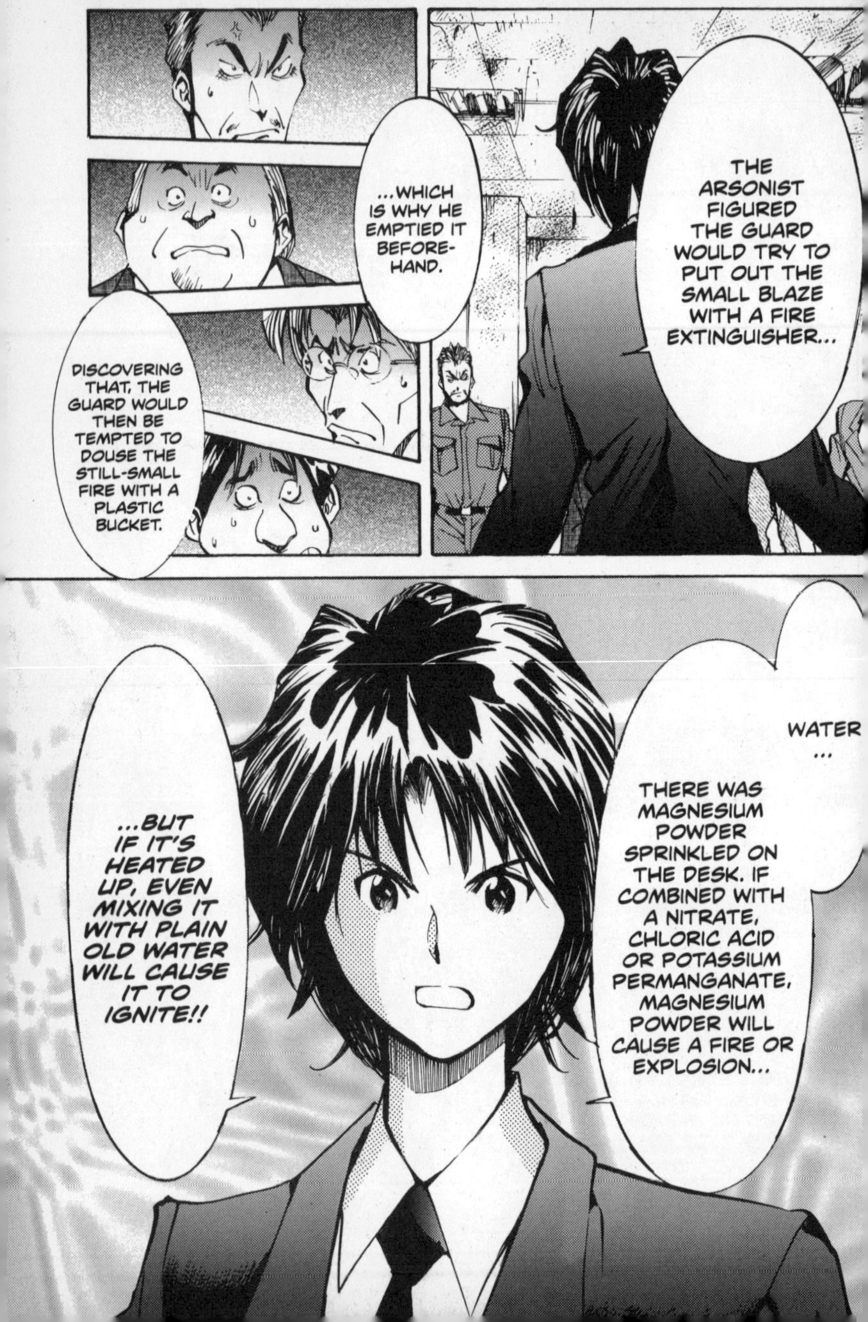
THE ARSONIST FIGURED THE GUARD WOULD TRY TO PUT OUT THE SMALL BLAZE WITH A FIRE EXTINGUISHER...
...WHICH IS WHY HE EMPTIED IT BEFORE-HAND.
DISCOVERING THAT, THE GUARD WOULD THEN BE TEMPTED TO DOUSE THE STILL-SMALL FIRE WITH A PLASTIC BUCKET.
WATER ...
THERE WAS MAGNESIUM POWDER SPRINKLED ON THE DESK. IF COMBINED WITH A NITRATE, CHLORIC ACID OR POTASSIUM PERMANGANATE, MAGNESIUM POWDER WILL CAUSE A FIRE OR EXPLOSION...
...BUT IF IT'S HEATED UP, EVEN MIXING IT WITH PLAIN OLD WATER WILL CAUSE IT TO IGNITE!!

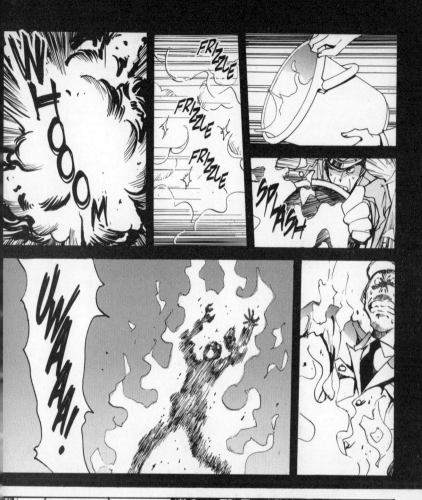

WHOOOOM

FRIZZLE

FRIZZLE

FRIZZLE

SPLASH

UWAAA!

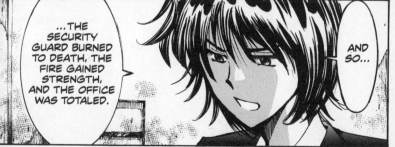

...THE SECURITY GUARD BURNED TO DEATH, THE FIRE GAINED STRENGTH, AND THE OFFICE WAS TOTALED.

AND SO...

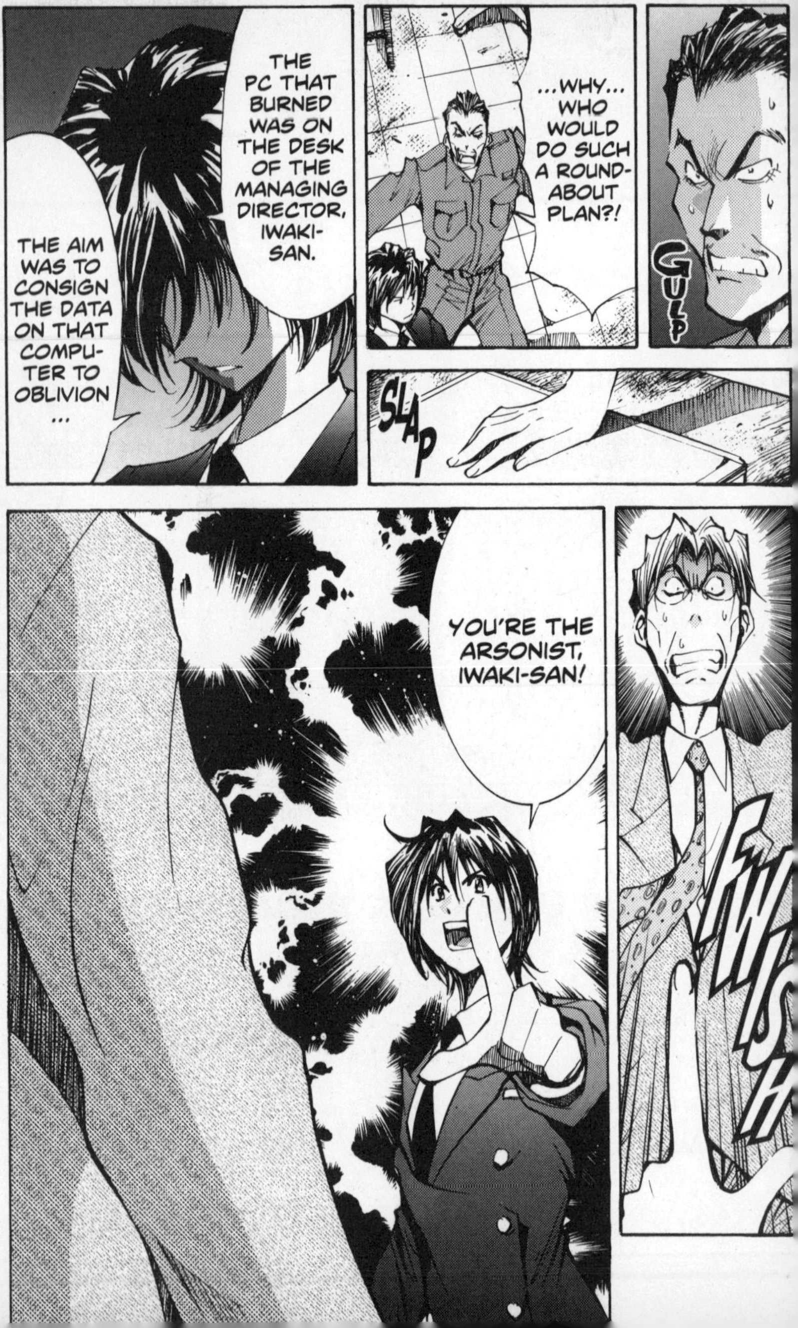
GULP
...WHY... WHO WOULD DO SUCH A ROUND-ABOUT PLAN?!
SLAP
THE PC THAT BURNED WAS ON THE DESK OF THE MANAGING DIRECTOR, IWAKI-SAN.
THE AIM WAS TO CONSIGN THE DATA ON THAT COMPUTER TO OBLIVION ...
FWISH
YOU'RE THE ARSONIST, IWAKI-SAN!

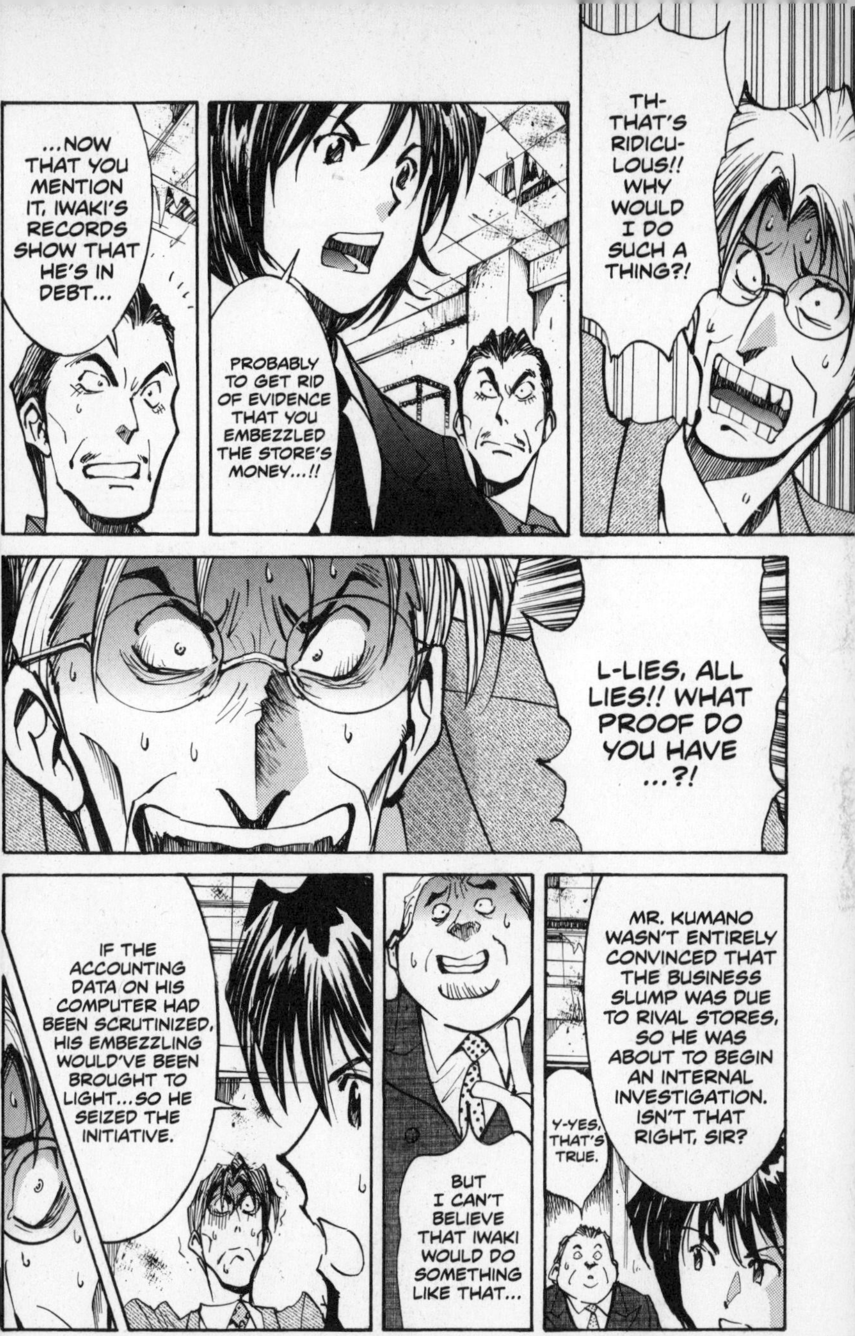
TH-THAT'S RIDICULOUS!! WHY WOULD I DO SUCH A THING?!
PROBABLY TO GET RID OF EVIDENCE THAT YOU EMBEZZLED THE STORE'S MONEY...!!
...NOW THAT YOU MENTION IT, IWAKI'S RECORDS SHOW THAT HE'S IN DEBT...
L-LIES, ALL LIES!! WHAT PROOF DO YOU HAVE ...?!
MR. KUMANO WASN'T ENTIRELY CONVINCED THAT THE BUSINESS SLUMP WAS DUE TO RIVAL STORES, SO HE WAS ABOUT TO BEGIN AN INTERNAL INVESTIGATION. ISN'T THAT RIGHT, SIR?
Y-YES, THAT'S TRUE.
BUT I CAN'T BELIEVE THAT IWAKI WOULD DO SOMETHING LIKE THAT...
IF THE ACCOUNTING DATA ON HIS COMPUTER HAD BEEN SCRUTINIZED, HIS EMBEZZLING WOULD'VE BEEN BROUGHT TO LIGHT...SO HE SEIZED THE INITIATIVE.

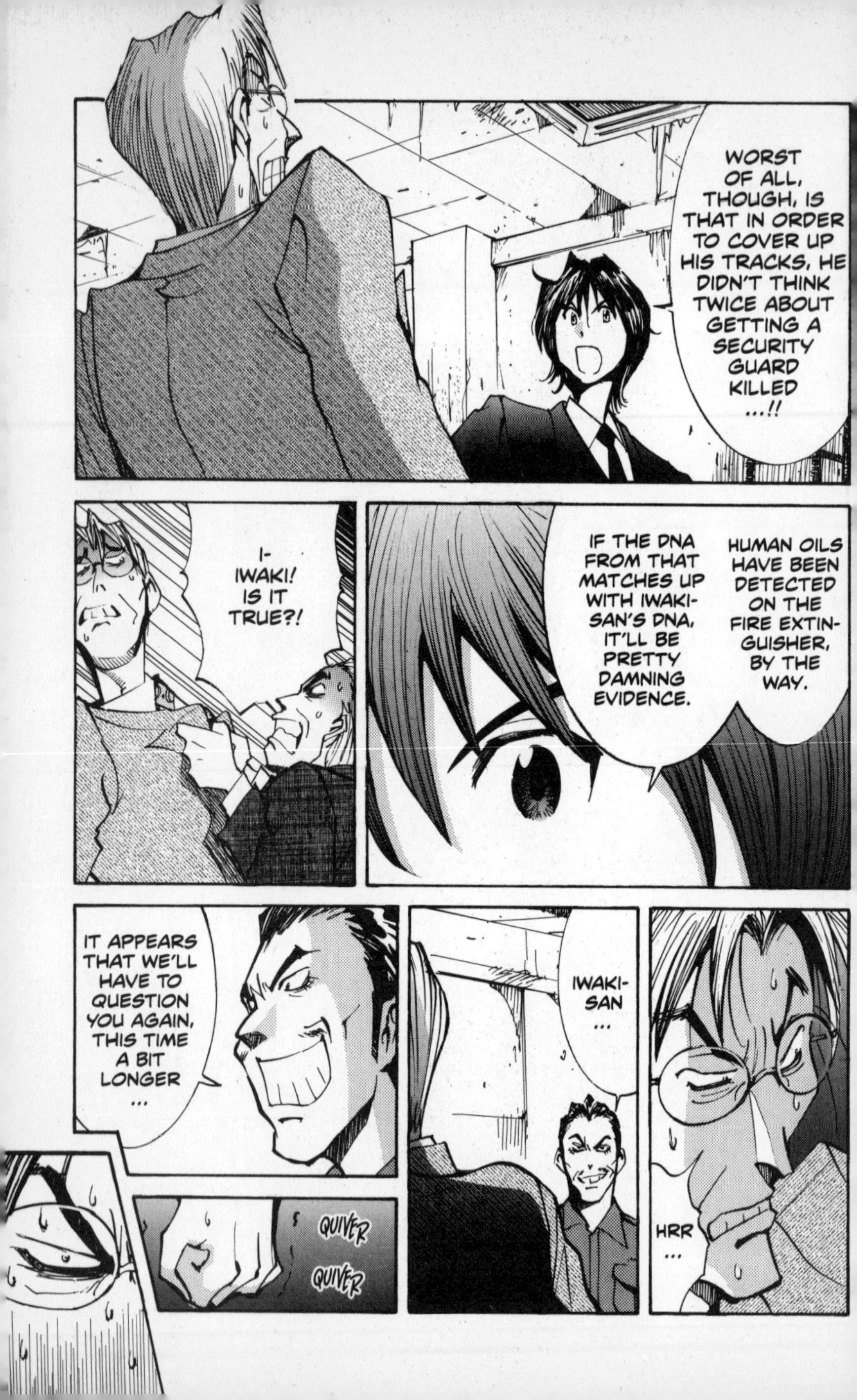
WORST OF ALL, THOUGH, IS THAT IN ORDER TO COVER UP HIS TRACKS, HE DIDN'T THINK TWICE ABOUT GETTING A SECURITY GUARD KILLED ...!!
HUMAN OILS HAVE BEEN DETECTED ON THE FIRE EXTIN-GUISHER, BY THE WAY.
IF THE DNA FROM THAT MATCHES UP WITH IWAKI-SAN'S DNA, IT'LL BE PRETTY DAMNING EVIDENCE.
I- IWAKI! IS IT TRUE?!
HRR ...
IWAKI-SAN ...
IT APPEARS THAT WE'LL HAVE TO QUESTION YOU AGAIN, THIS TIME A BIT LONGER ...
QUIVER
QUIVER

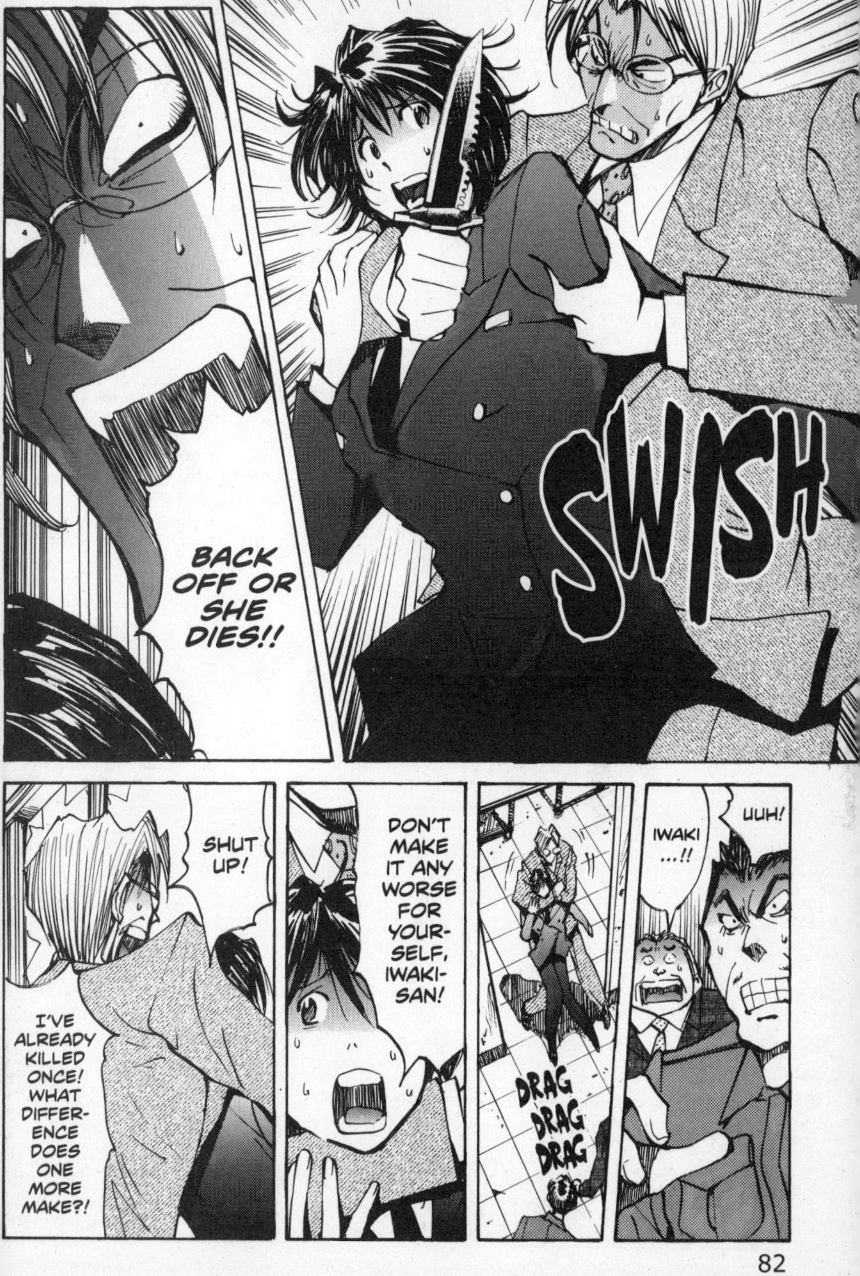
SWISH
BACK OFF OR SHE DIES!!
UUH!
IWAKI ...!!
DRAG DRAG DRAG
DON'T MAKE IT ANY WORSE FOR YOURSELF, IWAKI-SAN!
SHUT UP!
I'VE ALREADY KILLED ONCE! WHAT DIFFERENCE DOES ONE MORE MAKE?!

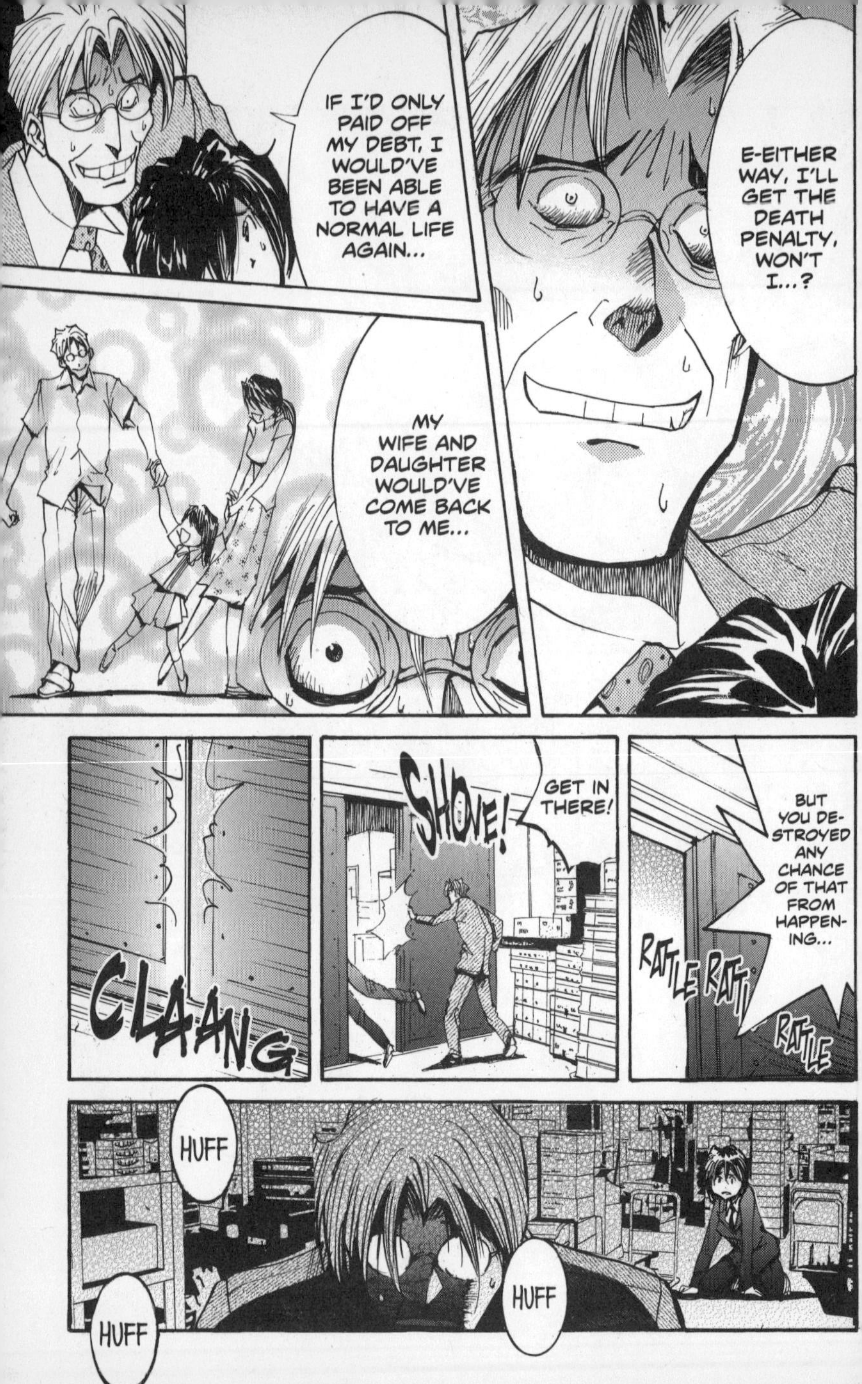
E-EITHER WAY, I'LL GET THE DEATH PENALTY, WON'T I...?
IF I'D ONLY PAID OFF MY DEBT, I WOULD'VE BEEN ABLE TO HAVE A NORMAL LIFE AGAIN...
MY WIFE AND DAUGHTER WOULD'VE COME BACK TO ME...
BUT YOU DE-STROYED ANY CHANCE OF THAT FROM HAPPEN-ING...
RATTLE RATTL
RATTLE
GET IN THERE!
SHOVE!
CLAANG
HUFF
HUFF
HUFF

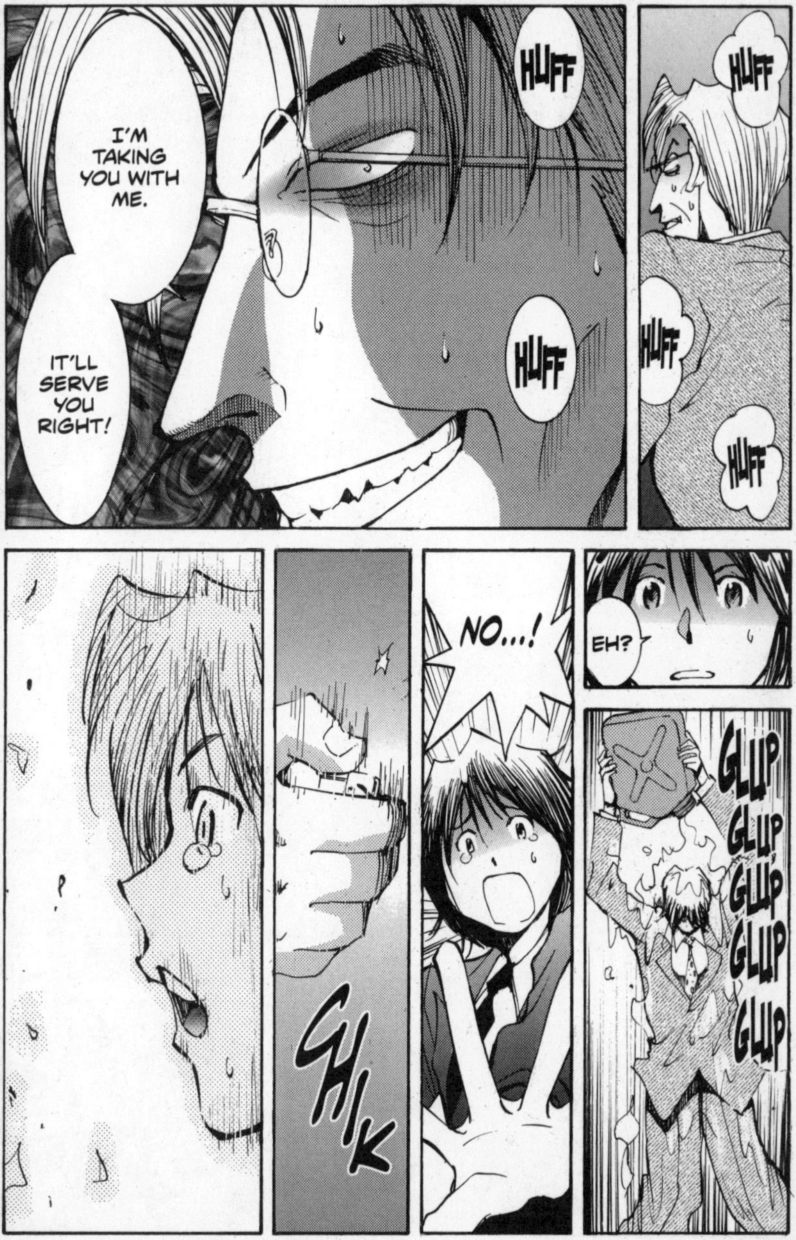
HUFF
HUFF
HUFF
HUFF
I'M TAKING YOU WITH ME.
HUFF
IT'LL SERVE YOU RIGHT!
EH?
GLUP GLUP GLUP GLUP GLUP
NO...!
CHIK

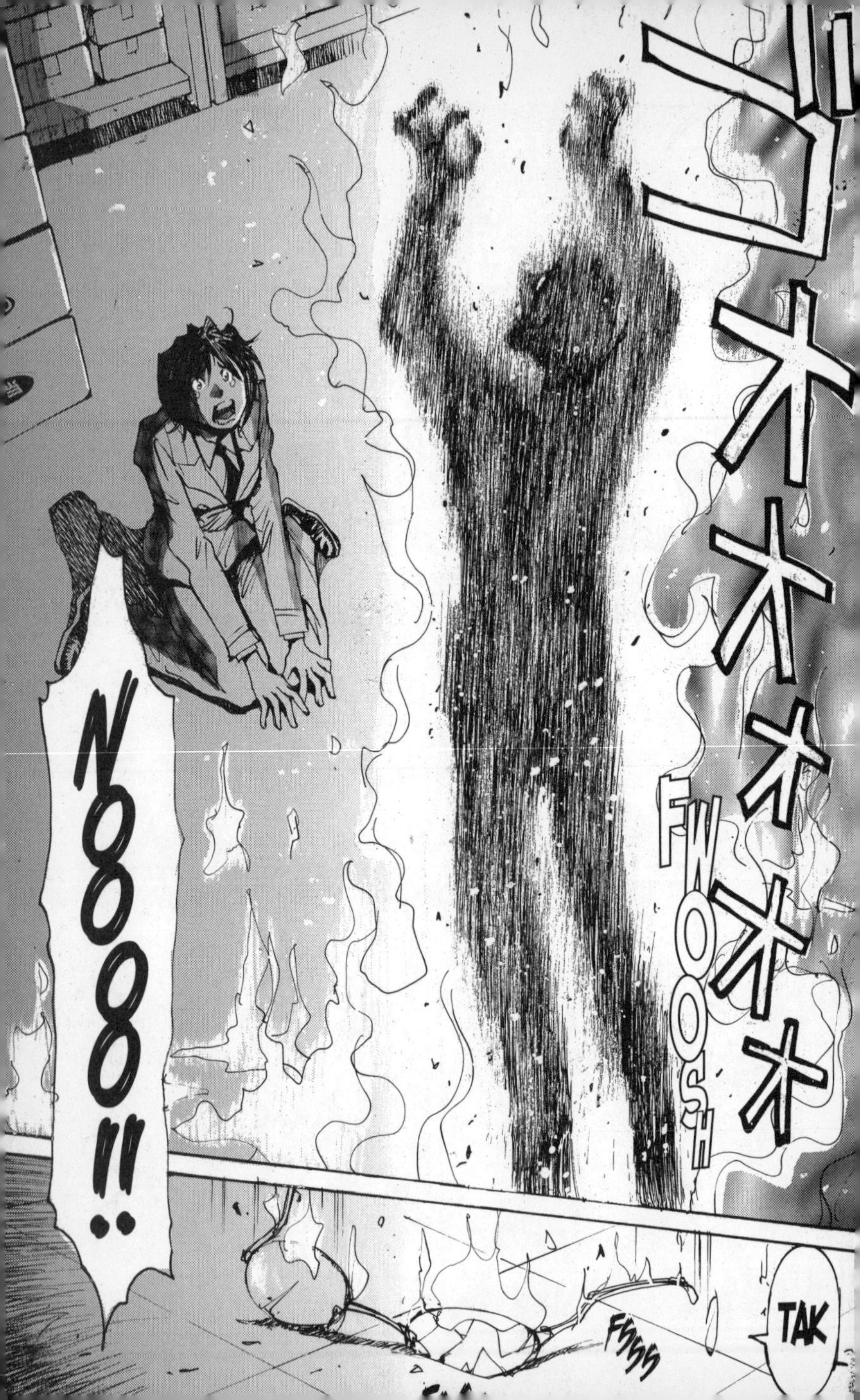
ゴオオオオオ
FWOOSH
NOOOO!!
TAK
FSSSS

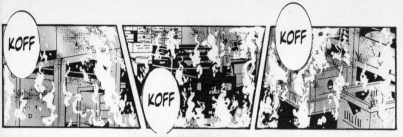

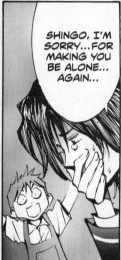

SHINGO, I'M SORRY...FOR MAKING YOU BE ALONE... AGAIN...

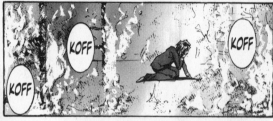

HE WAS RIGHT...AT THIS RATE, I WILL BE JOINING HIM...

FLAMES ARE SPREADING...

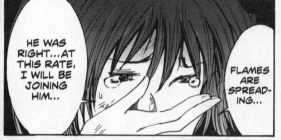

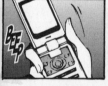

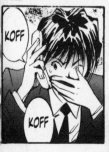

KOFF

KOFF

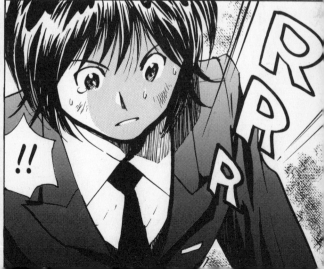

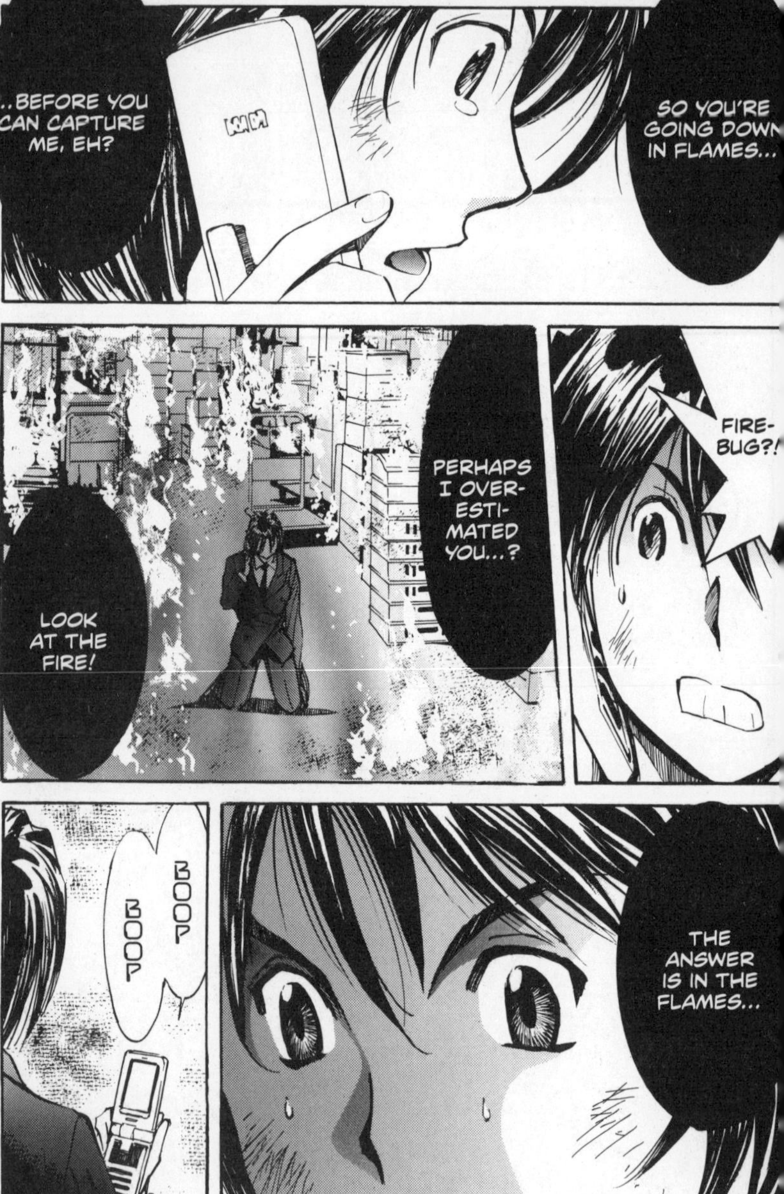
SO YOU'RE GOING DOWN IN FLAMES...
...BEFORE YOU CAN CAPTURE ME, EH?
FIRE-BUG?!
PERHAPS I OVER-ESTI-MATED YOU...?
LOOK AT THE FIRE!
THE ANSWER IS IN THE FLAMES...
BOOP BOOP

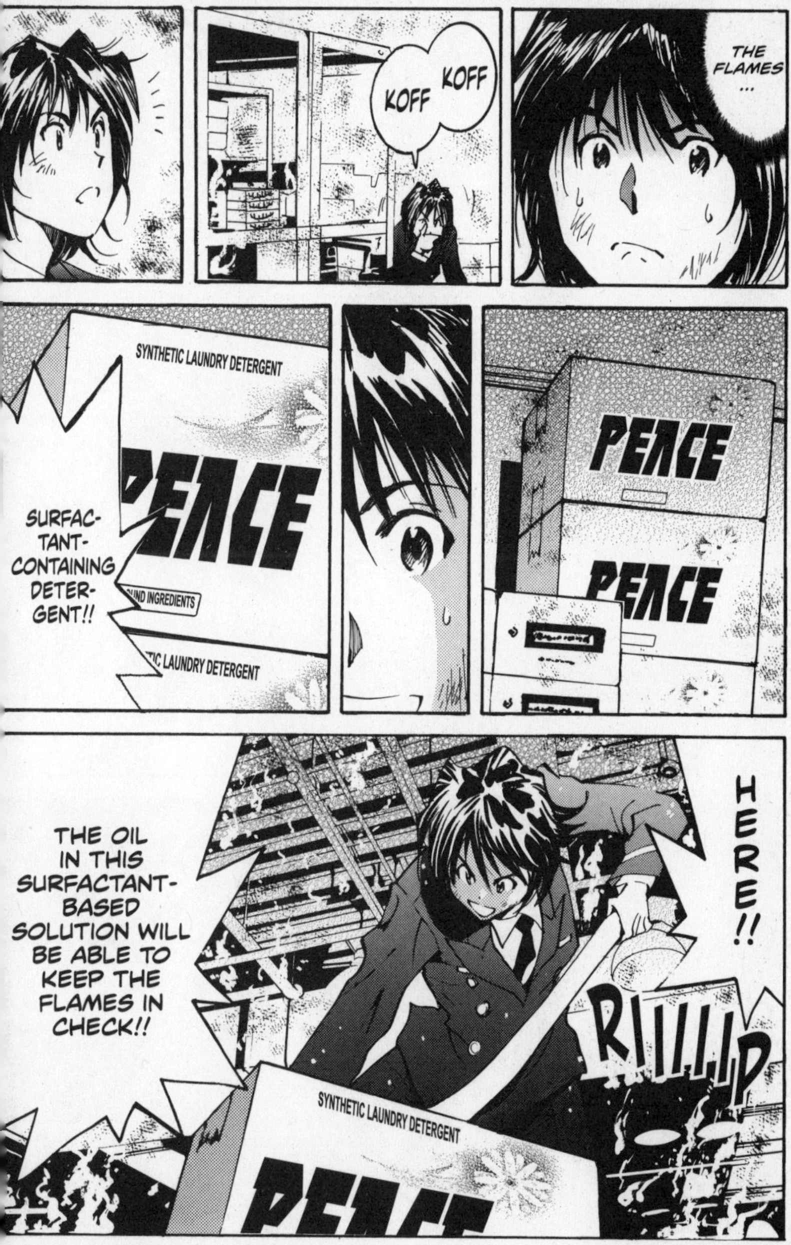
THE FLAMES ...
KOFF KOFF
PEACE
PEACE
SYNTHETIC LAUNDRY DETERGENT
PEACE
SURFACTANT-CONTAINING DETERGENT!!
HERE!!
THE OIL IN THIS SURFACTANT-BASED SOLUTION WILL BE ABLE TO KEEP THE FLAMES IN CHECK!!
RIIIIIP
SYNTHETIC LAUNDRY DETERGENT

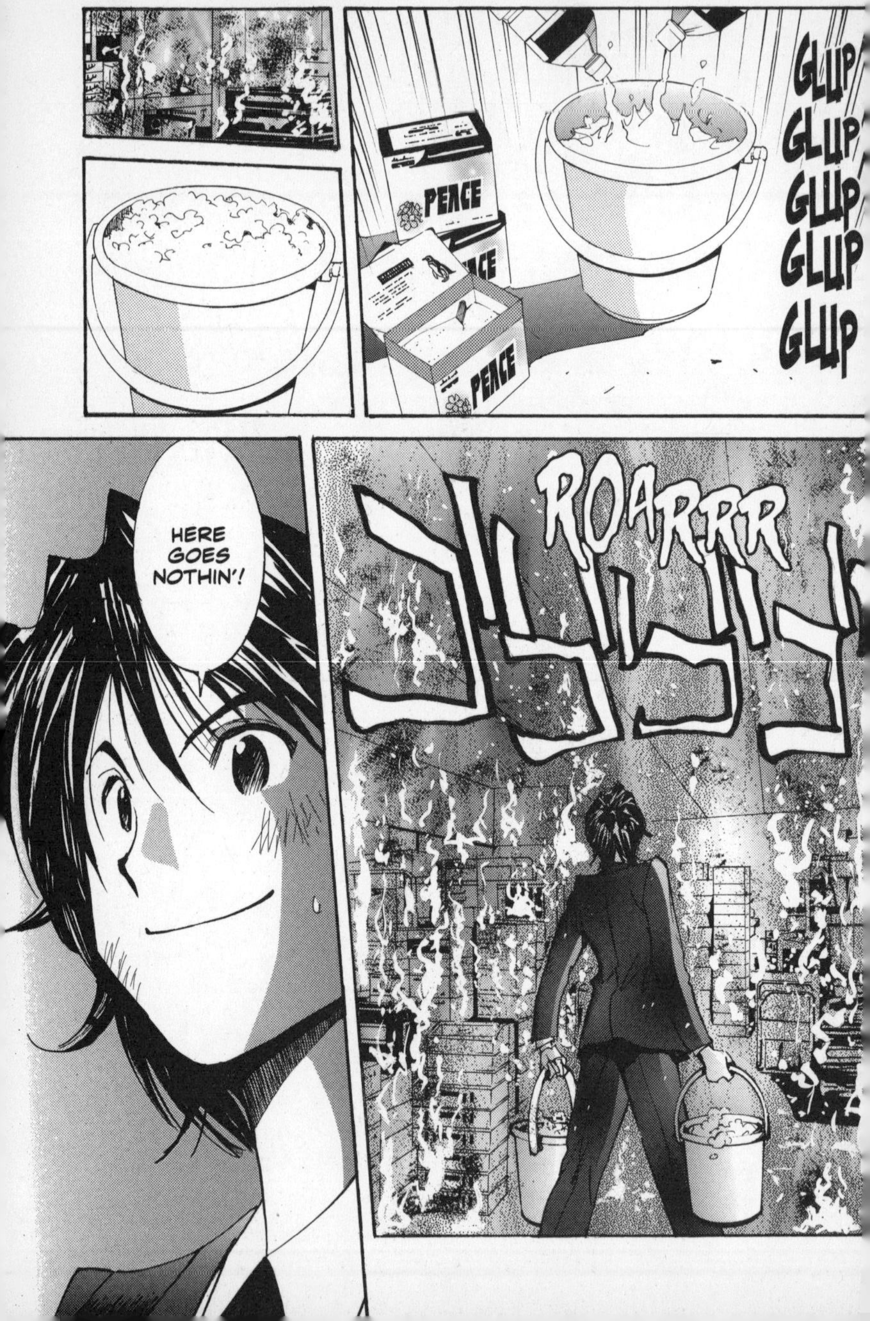
GLUP GLUP GLUP GLUP GLUP
PEACE
PEACE
ROARRR
HERE GOES NOTHIN'!

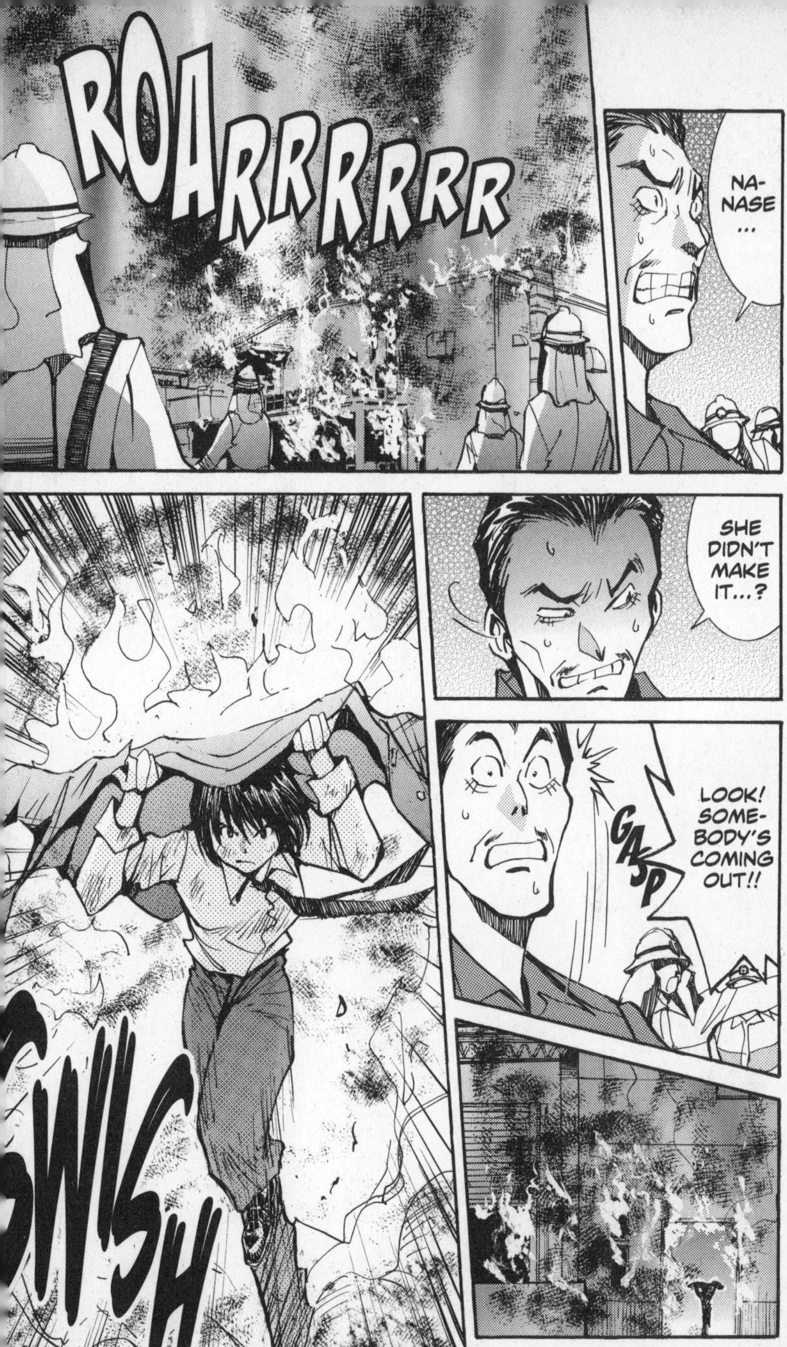
NA-NASE...
ROARRRRRRR
SHE DIDN'T MAKE IT...?
GASP
LOOK! SOME-BODY'S COMING OUT!!
SWISH

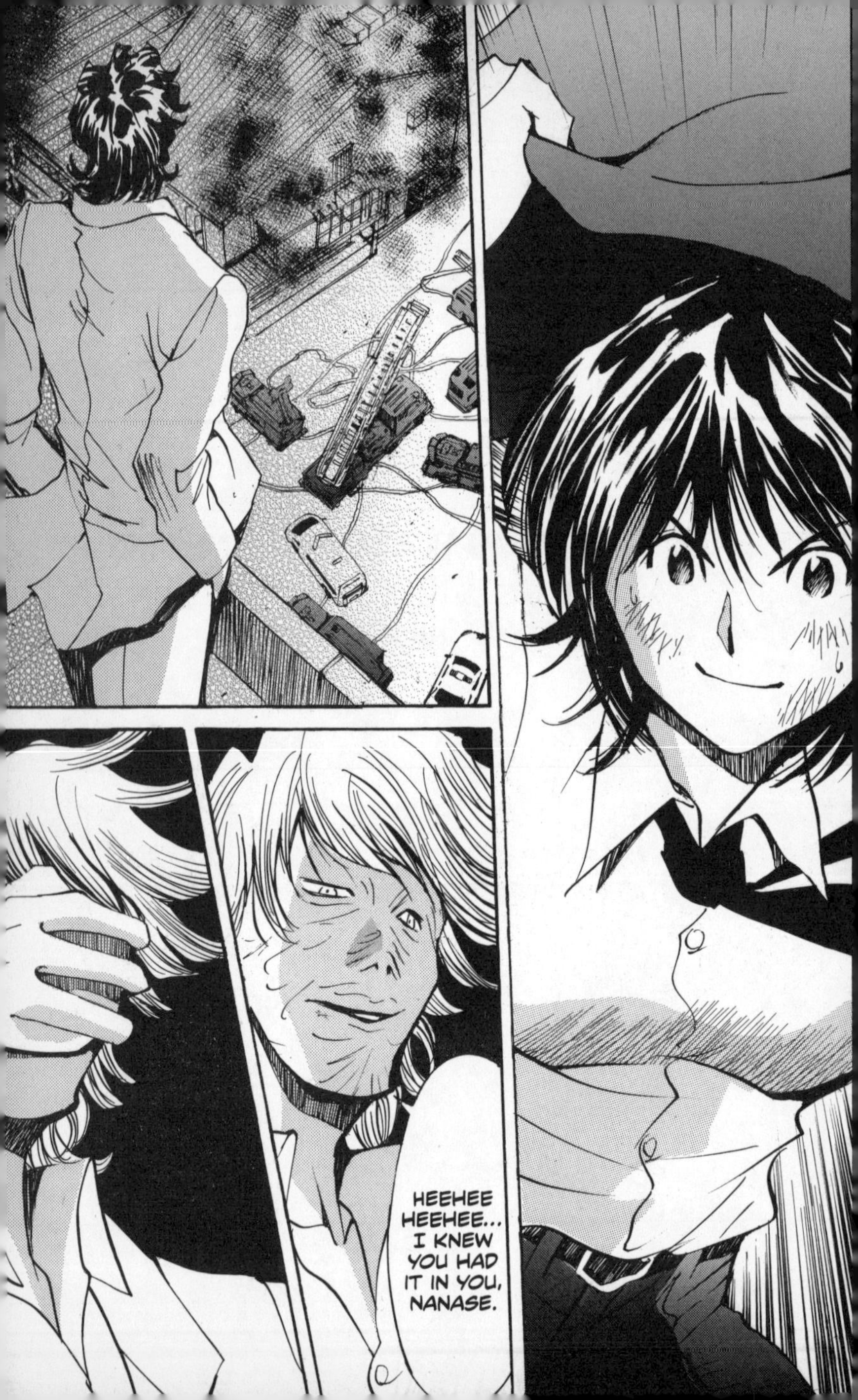
HEEHEE HEEHEE... I KNEW YOU HAD IT IN YOU, NANASE.

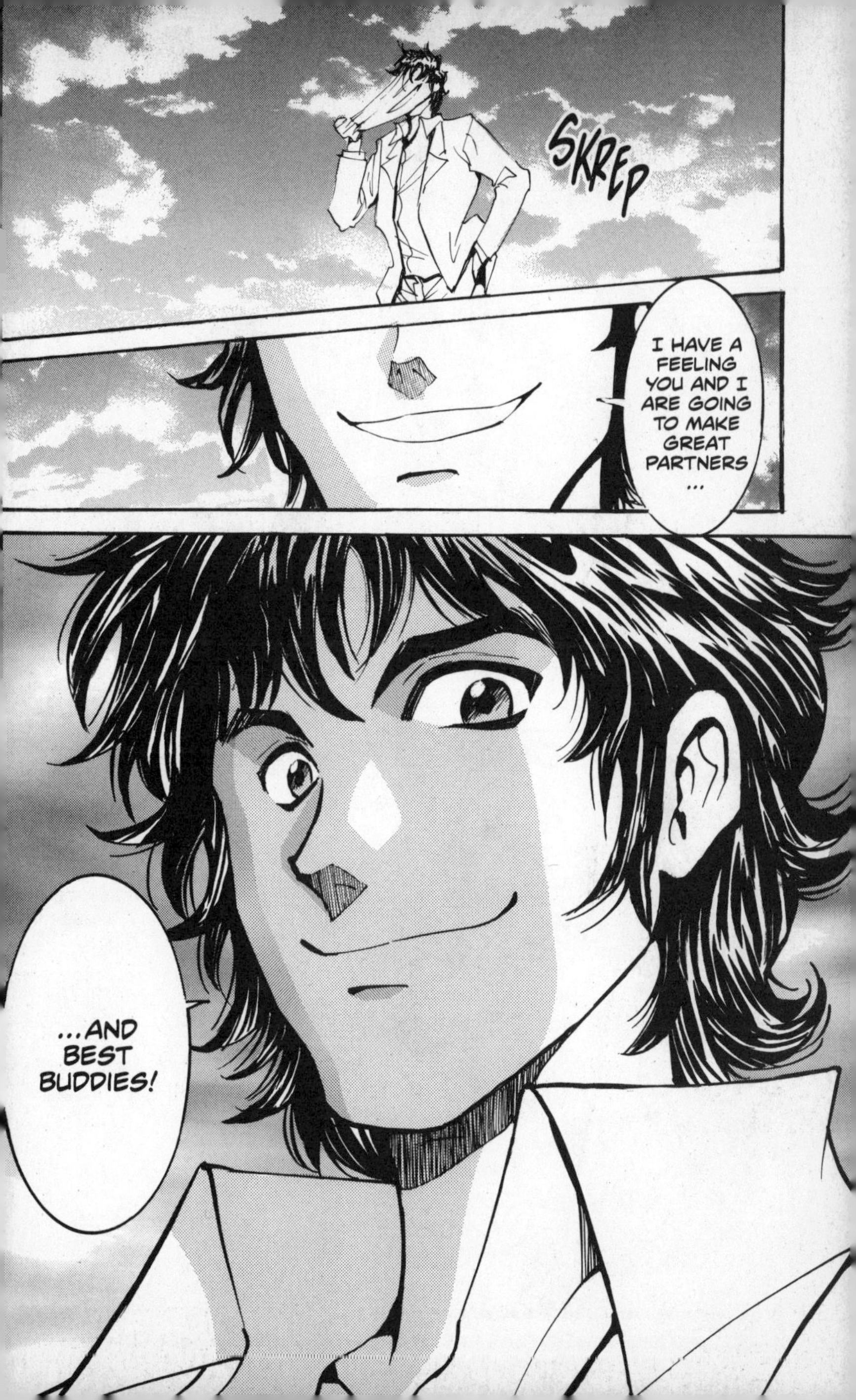
SKREP
I HAVE A FEELING YOU AND I ARE GOING TO MAKE GREAT PARTNERS ...
...AND BEST BUDDIES!

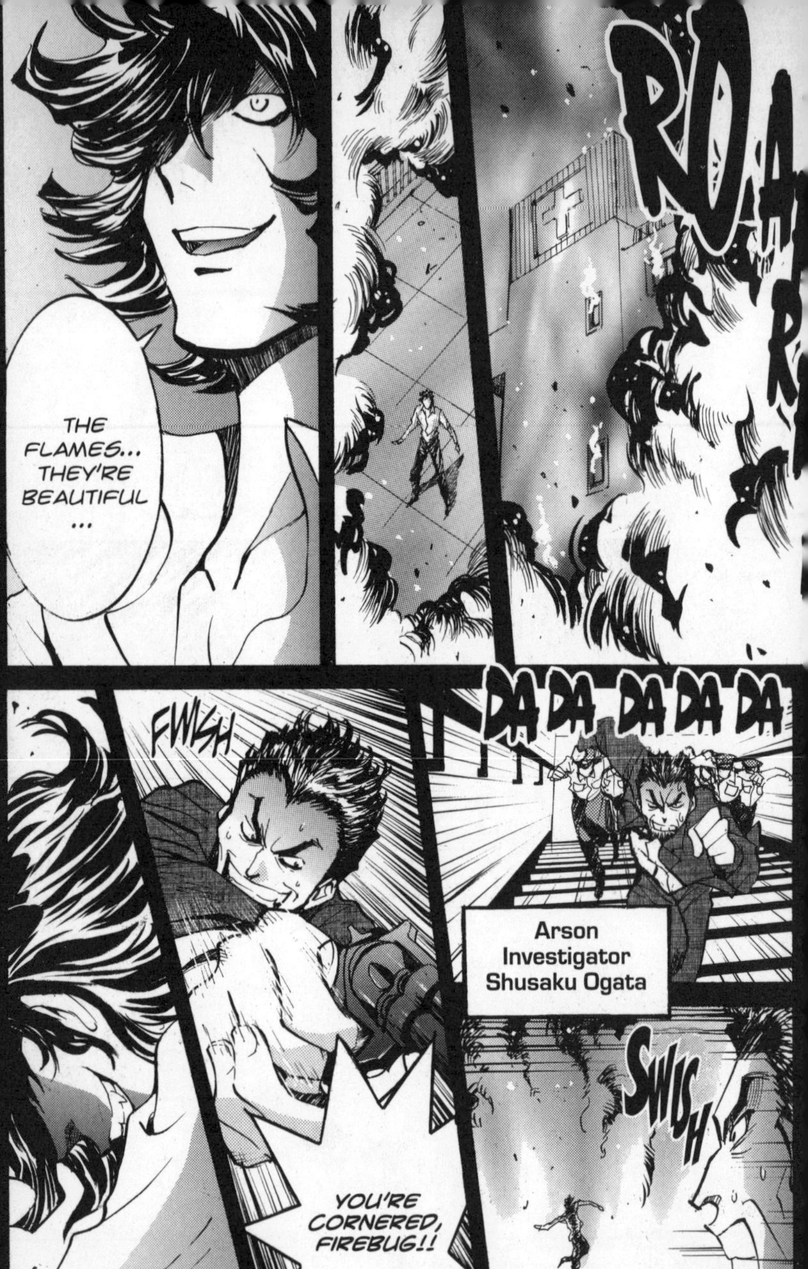
ROAR
THE FLAMES... THEY'RE BEAUTIFUL...
DA DA DA DA DA
Arson Investigator Shusaku Ogata
SWISH
FWISH
YOU'RE CORNERED, FIREBUG!!

FILE.004 PETALS OF ENVY (part one)

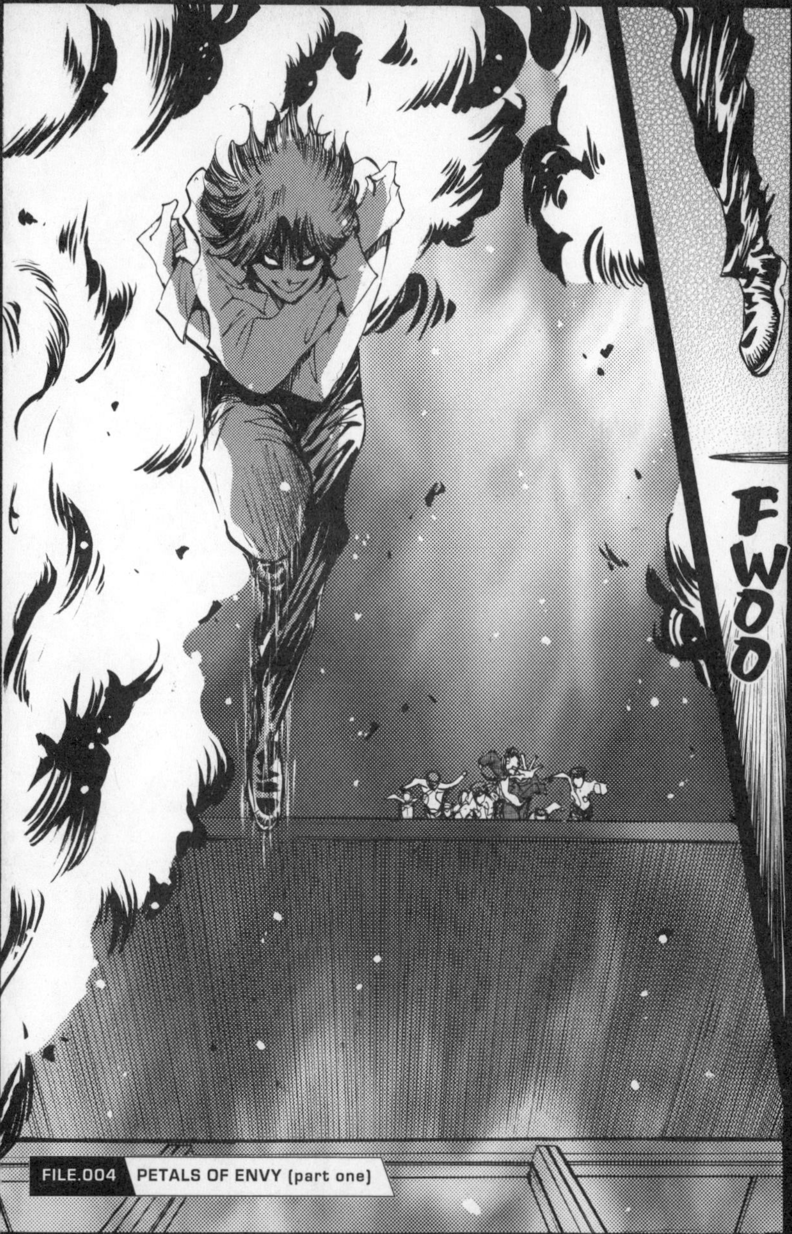
FWOO
FILE.004 PETALS OF ENVY (part one)

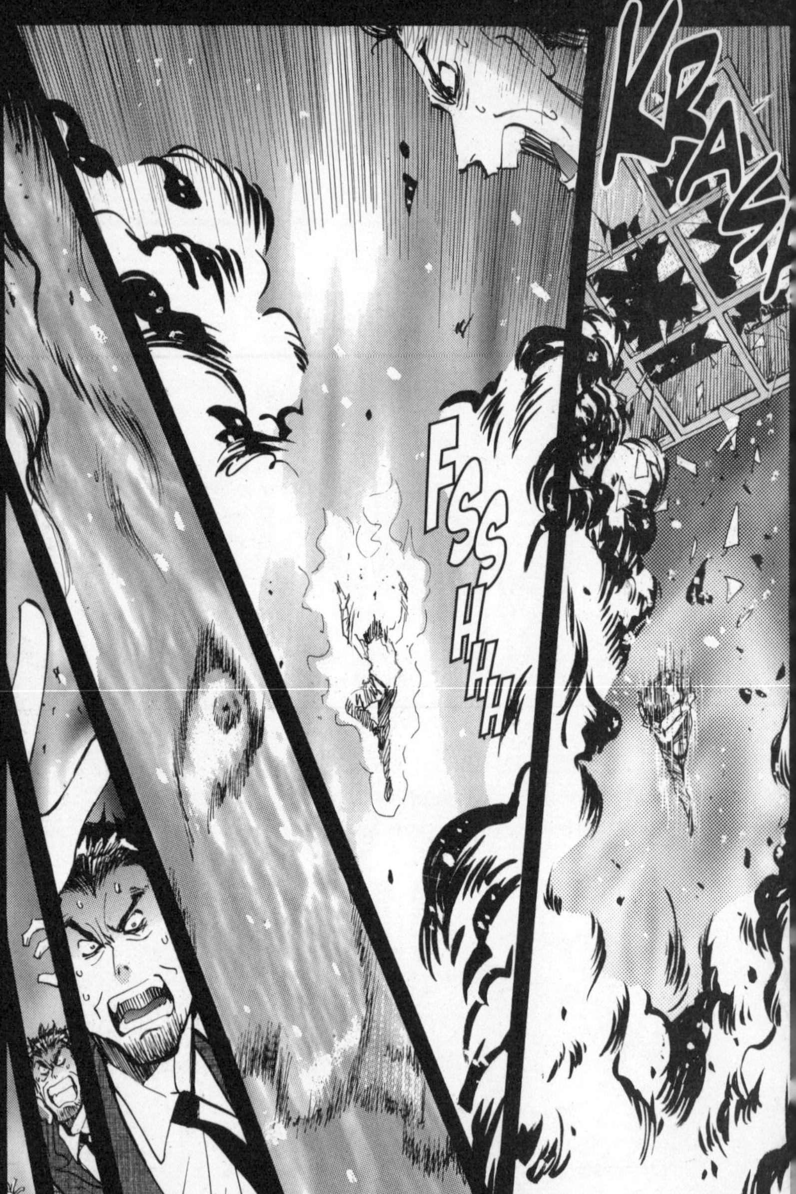
KRASH
FSSHHHH

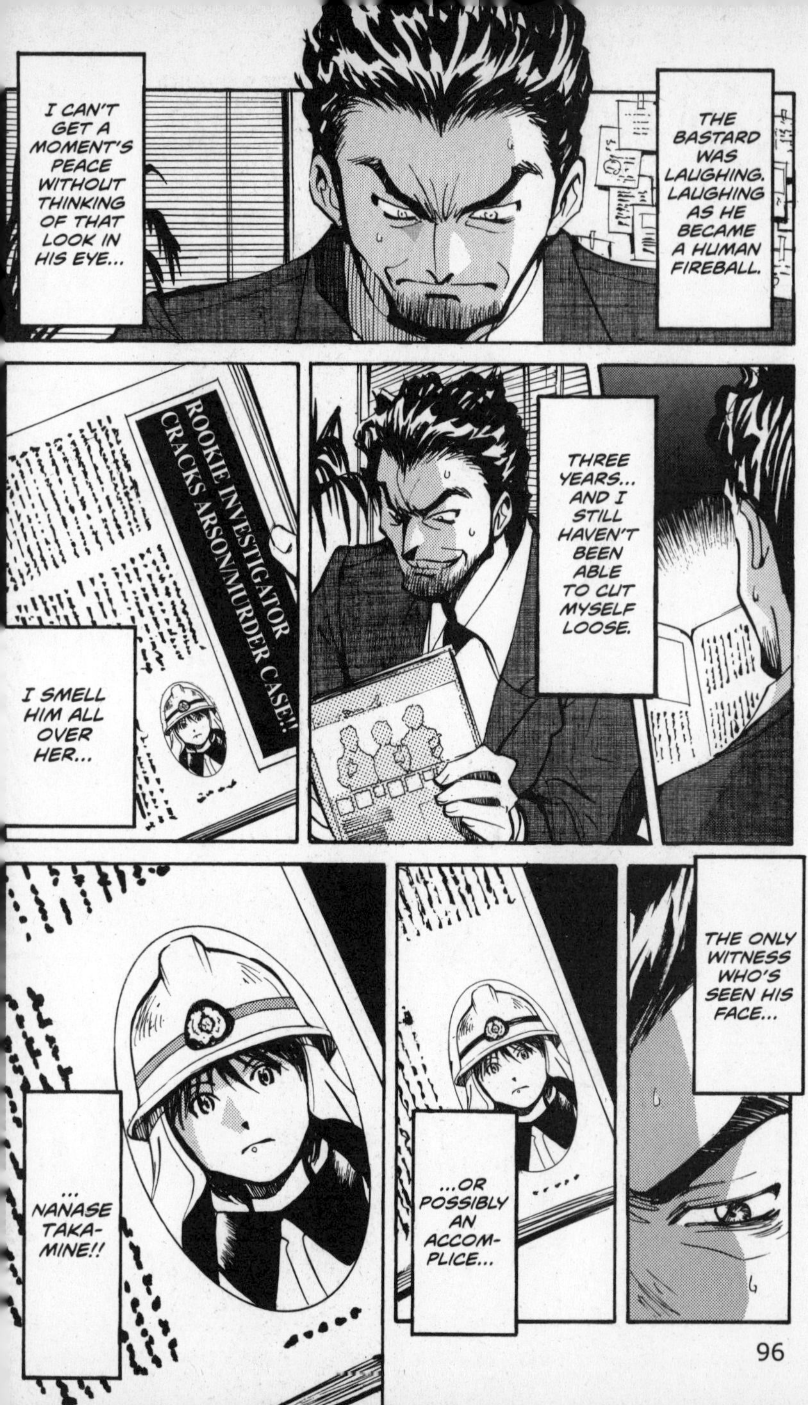
THE BASTARD WAS LAUGHING. LAUGHING AS HE BECAME A HUMAN FIREBALL.
I CAN'T GET A MOMENT'S PEACE WITHOUT THINKING OF THAT LOOK IN HIS EYE...
THREE YEARS... AND I STILL HAVEN'T BEEN ABLE TO CUT MYSELF LOOSE.
ROOKIE INVESTIGATOR CRACKS ARSONMURDER CASE!!
I SMELL HIM ALL OVER HER...
THE ONLY WITNESS WHO'S SEEN HIS FACE...
...OR POSSIBLY AN ACCOMPLICE...
...NANASE TAKAMINE!!

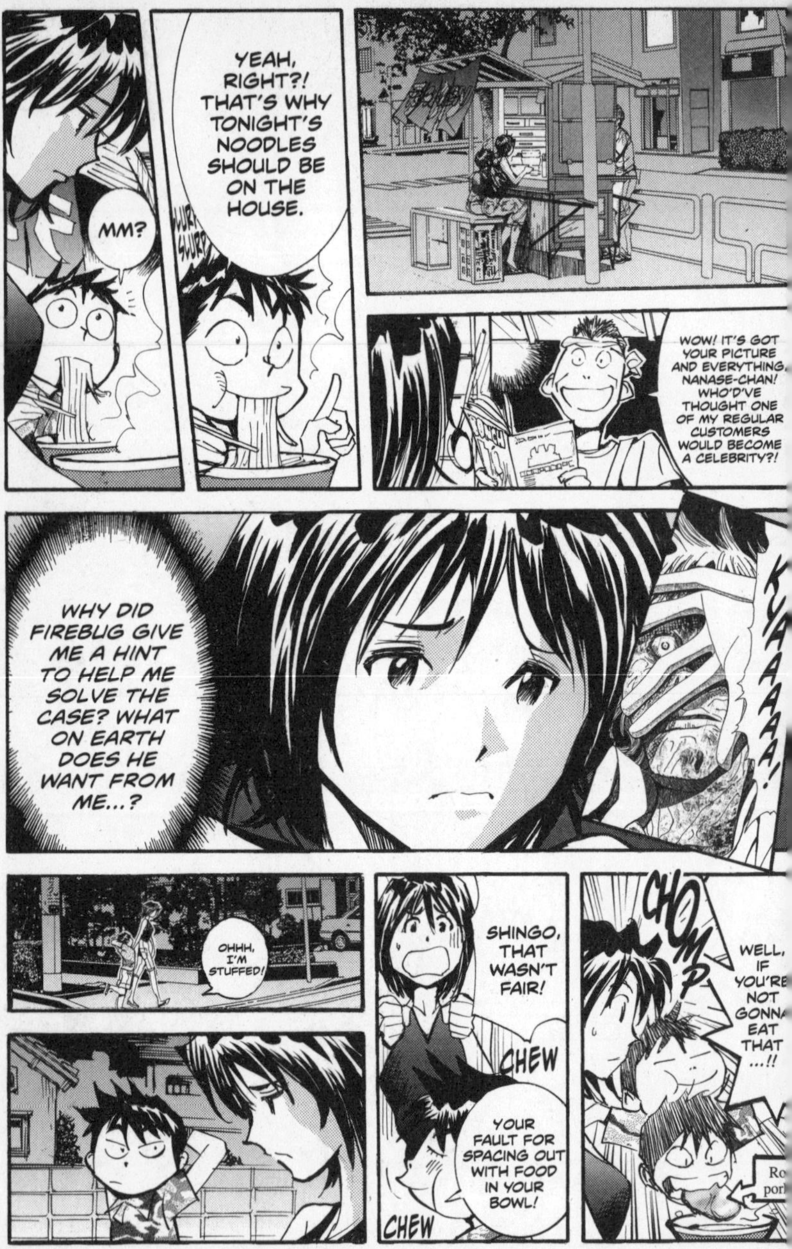
WOW! IT'S GOT YOUR PICTURE AND EVERYTHING, NANASE-CHAN! WHO'D'VE THOUGHT ONE OF MY REGULAR CUSTOMERS WOULD BECOME A CELEBRITY?!
YEAH, RIGHT?! THAT'S WHY TONIGHT'S NOODLES SHOULD BE ON THE HOUSE.
SLURP SLURP
MM?
KYAAAAAA!
WHY DID FIREBUG GIVE ME A HINT TO HELP ME SOLVE THE CASE? WHAT ON EARTH DOES HE WANT FROM ME...?
CHOMP
WELL, IF YOU'RE NOT GONNA EAT THAT ...!!
SHINGO, THAT WASN'T FAIR!
CHEW
YOUR FAULT FOR SPACING OUT WITH FOOD IN YOUR BOWL!
CHEW
OHHH, I'M STUFFED!

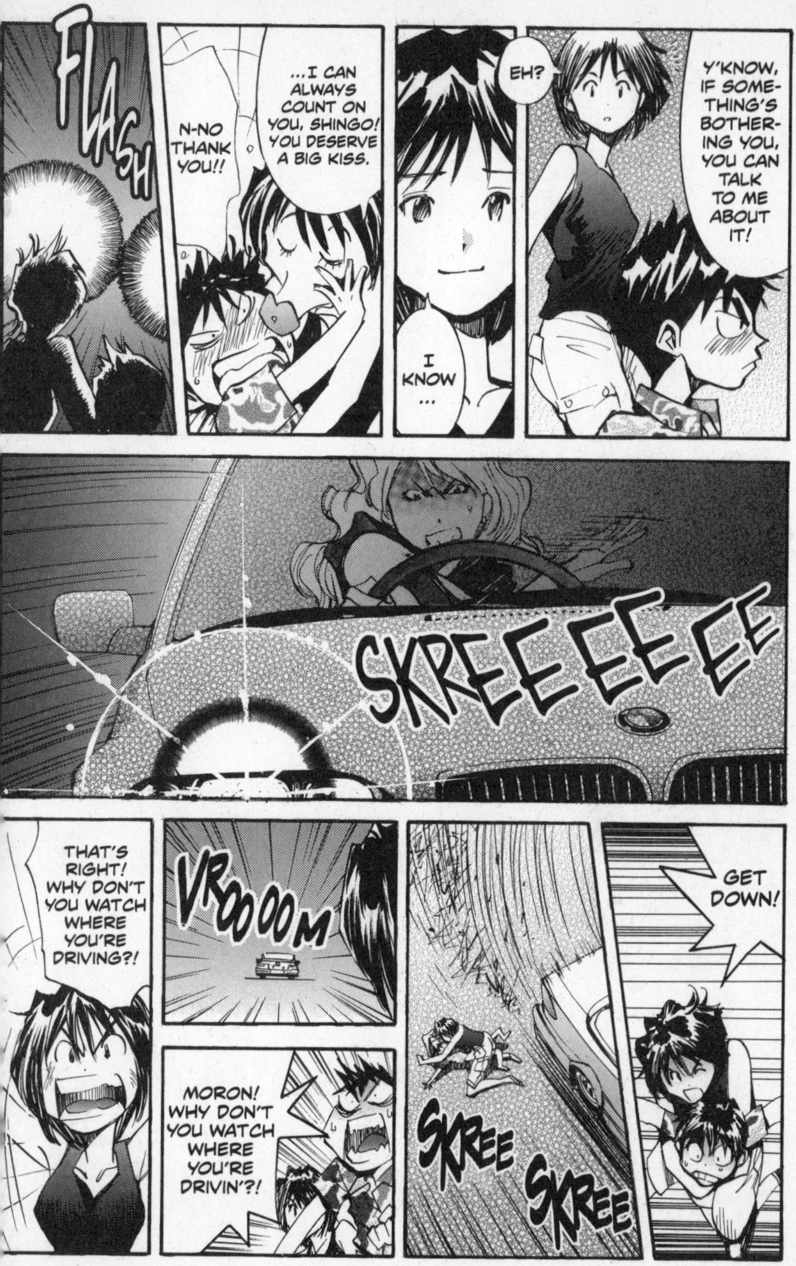

Y'KNOW, IF SOMETHING'S BOTHERING YOU, YOU CAN TALK TO ME ABOUT IT!
EH?
I KNOW ...
...I CAN ALWAYS COUNT ON YOU, SHINGO! YOU DESERVE A BIG KISS.
N-NO THANK YOU!!
FLASH
SKREEEEEEE
GET DOWN!
SKREE
SKREE
VROOOOM
MORON! WHY DON'T YOU WATCH WHERE YOU'RE DRIVIN'?!
THAT'S RIGHT! WHY DON'T YOU WATCH WHERE YOU'RE DRIVING?!

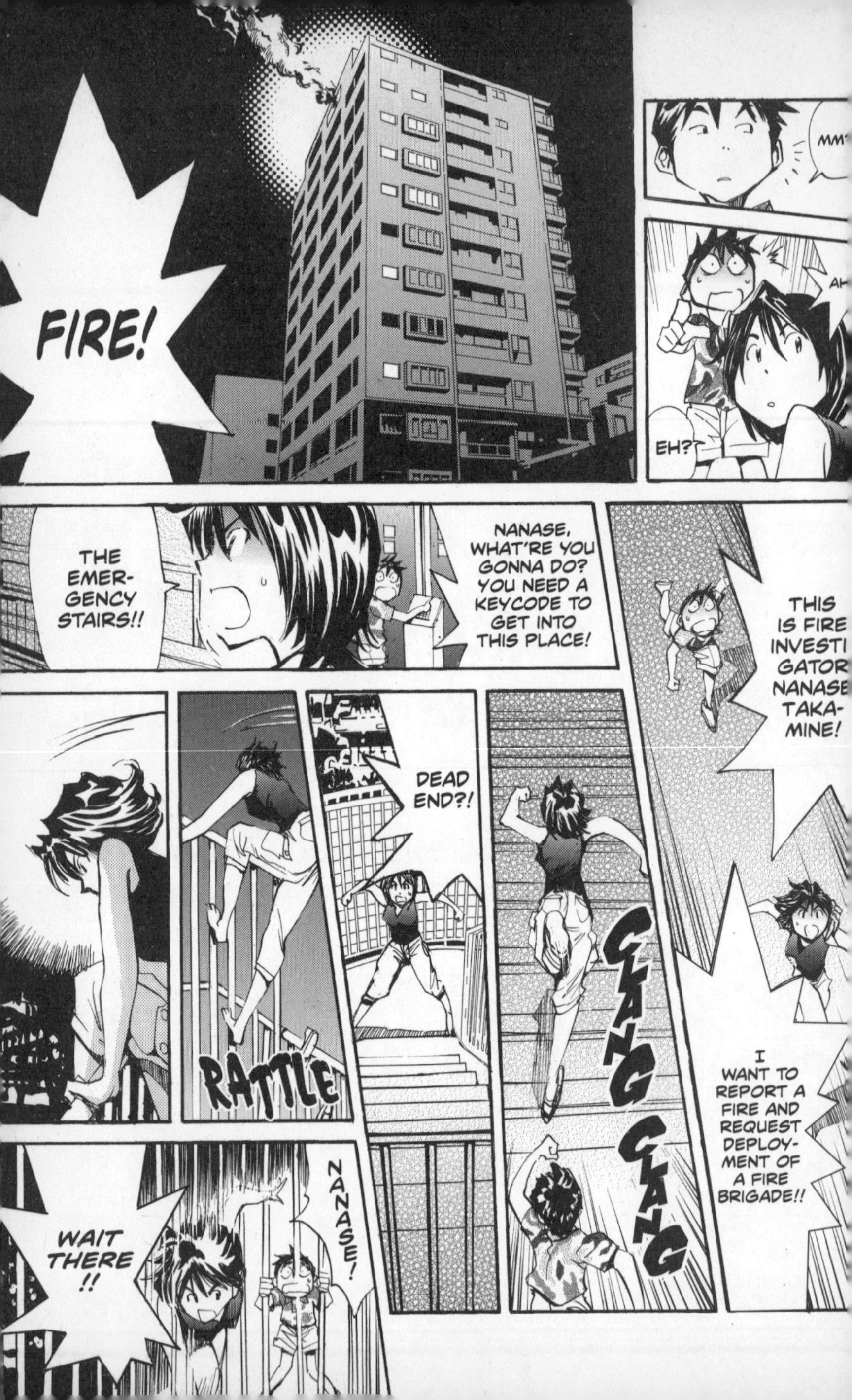
MM?
AH
EH?
FIRE!
THIS IS FIRE INVESTI GATOR NANASE TAKA-MINE!
I WANT TO REPORT A FIRE AND REQUEST DEPLOY-MENT OF A FIRE BRIGADE!!
NANASE, WHAT'RE YOU GONNA DO? YOU NEED A KEYCODE TO GET INTO THIS PLACE!
THE EMER-GENCY STAIRS!!
CLANG CLANG
DEAD END?!
RATTLE
NANASE!
WAIT THERE!!

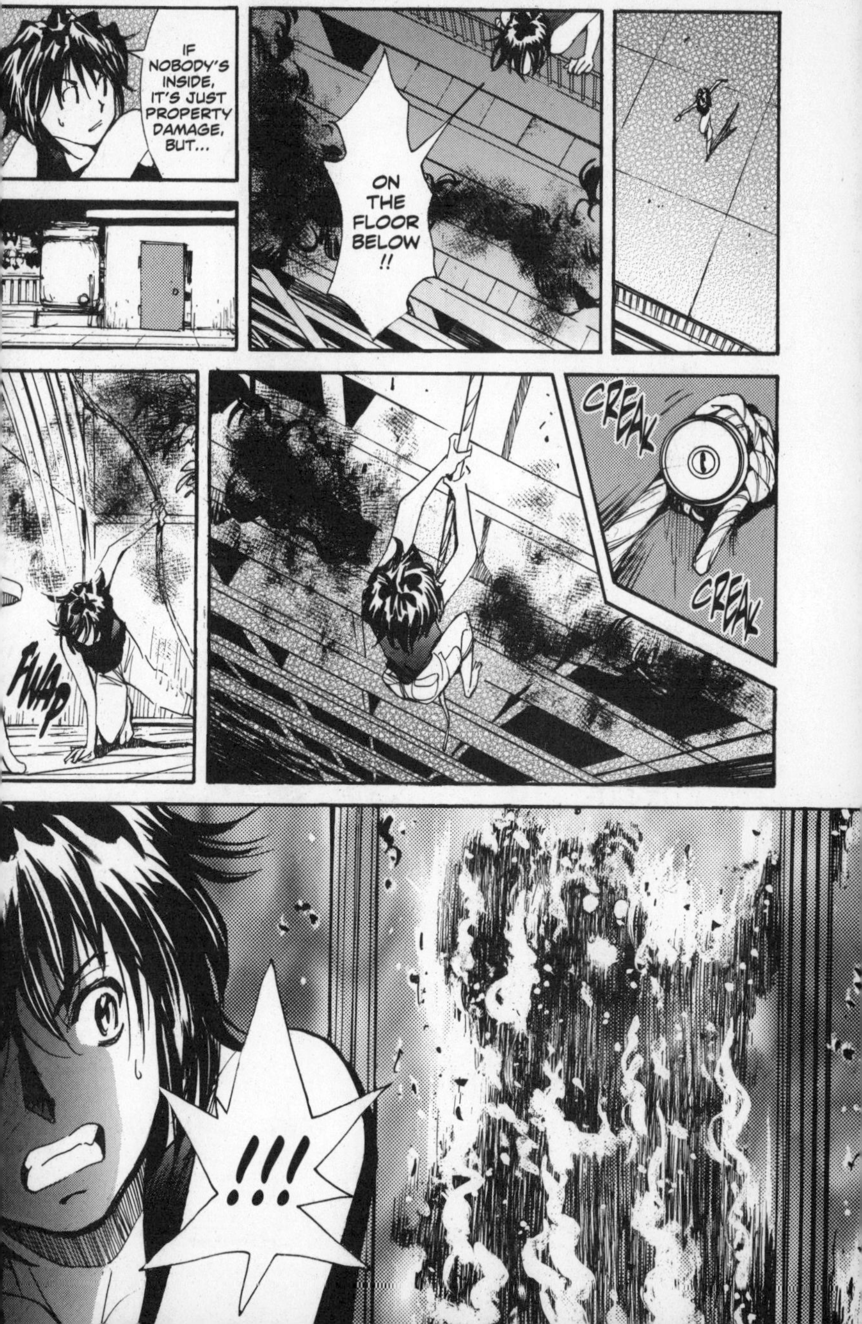
ON THE FLOOR BELOW !!
IF NOBODY'S INSIDE, IT'S JUST PROPERTY DAMAGE, BUT...
CREAK
CREAK
FWAP
!!!

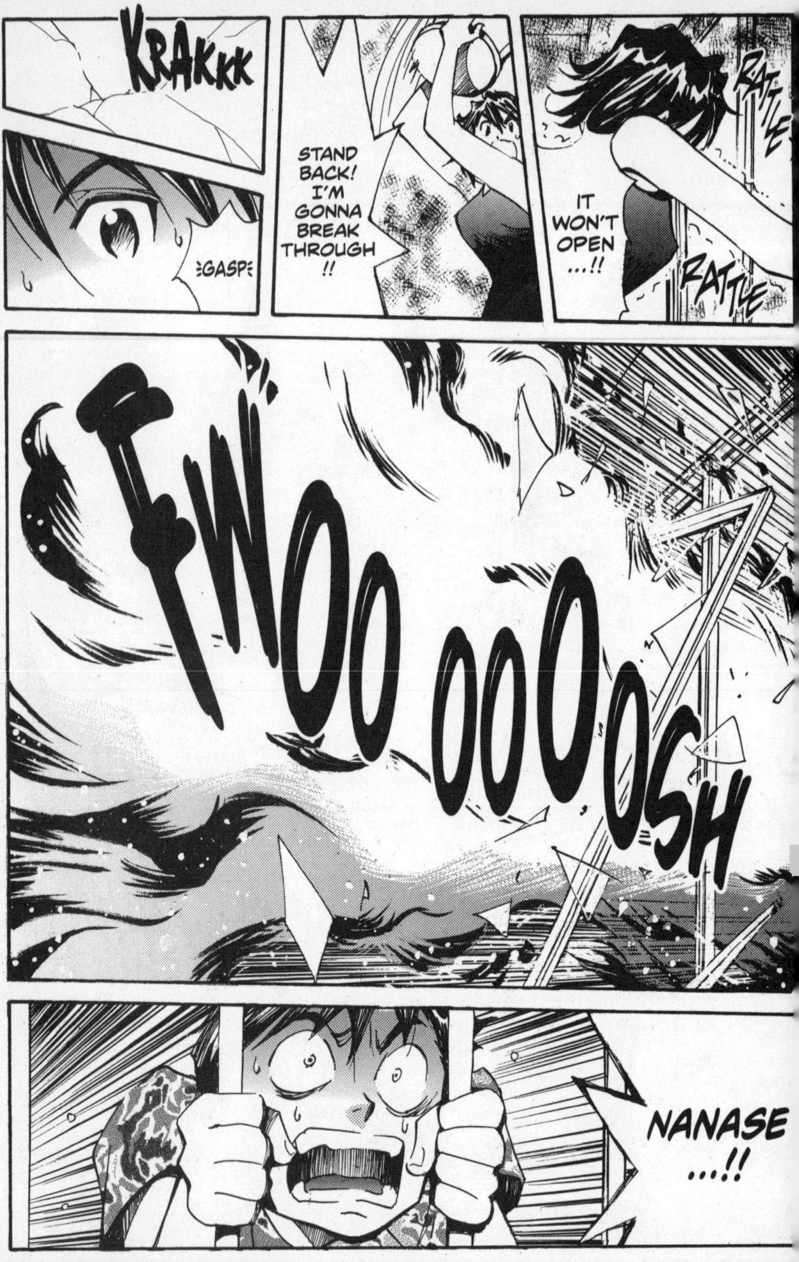
RATTLE
IT WON'T OPEN ...!!
RATTLE
STAND BACK! I'M GONNA BREAK THROUGH !!
KRAKKK
GASP
FWOOOOOOOSH
NANASE ...!!

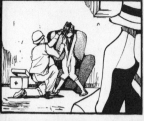

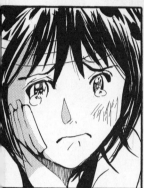

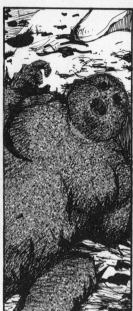

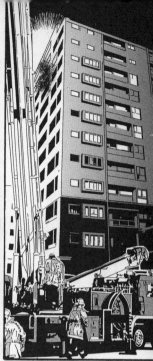

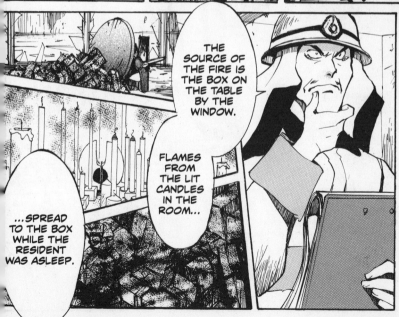

THE SOURCE OF THE FIRE IS THE BOX ON THE TABLE BY THE WINDOW.

FLAMES FROM THE LIT CANDLES IN THE ROOM...

...SPREAD TO THE BOX WHILE THE RESIDENT WAS ASLEEP.

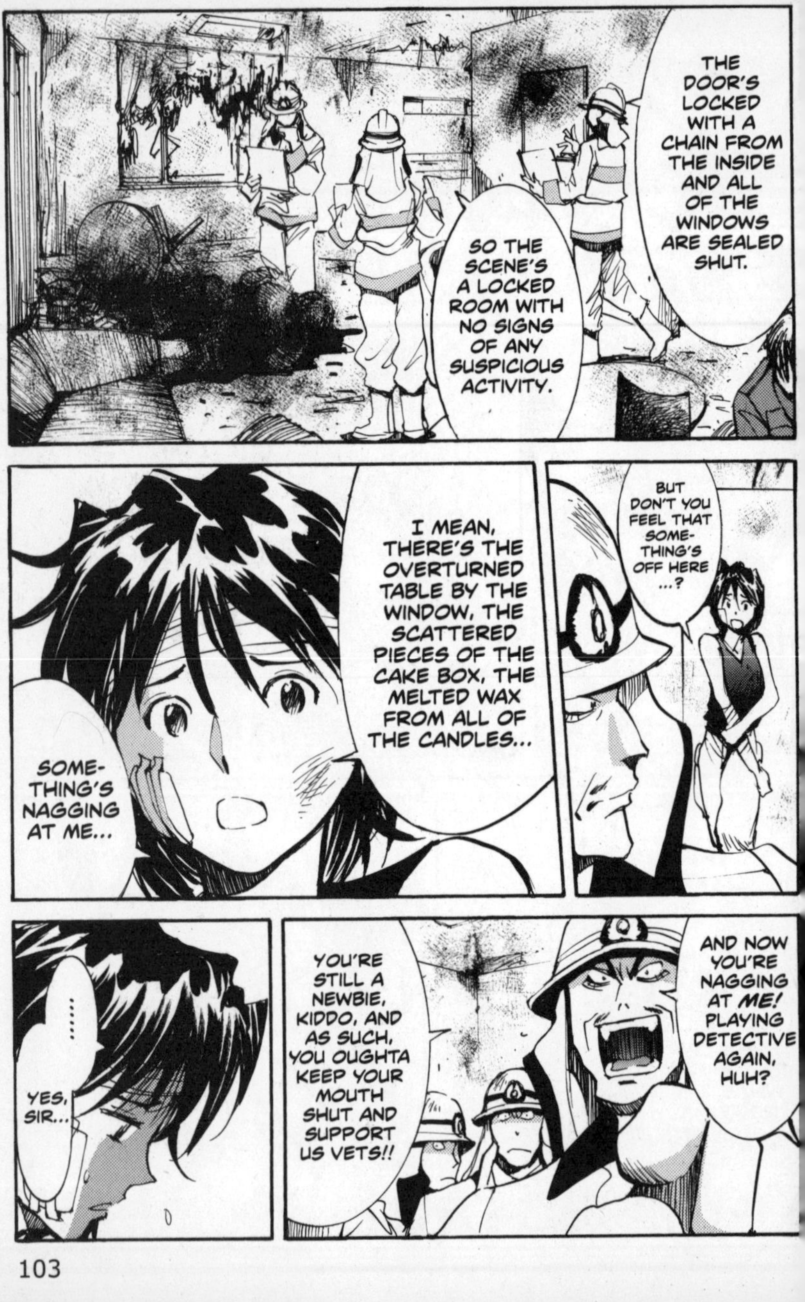
THE DOOR'S LOCKED WITH A CHAIN FROM THE INSIDE AND ALL OF THE WINDOWS ARE SEALED SHUT.
SO THE SCENE'S A LOCKED ROOM WITH NO SIGNS OF ANY SUSPICIOUS ACTIVITY.
BUT DON'T YOU FEEL THAT SOME-THING'S OFF HERE ...?
I MEAN, THERE'S THE OVERTURNED TABLE BY THE WINDOW, THE SCATTERED PIECES OF THE CAKE BOX, THE MELTED WAX FROM ALL OF THE CANDLES...
SOME-THING'S NAGGING AT ME...
AND NOW YOU'RE NAGGING AT *ME!* PLAYING DETECTIVE AGAIN, HUH?
YOU'RE STILL A NEWBIE, KIDDO, AND AS SUCH, YOU OUGHTA KEEP YOUR MOUTH SHUT AND SUPPORT US VETS!!
......
YES, SIR...

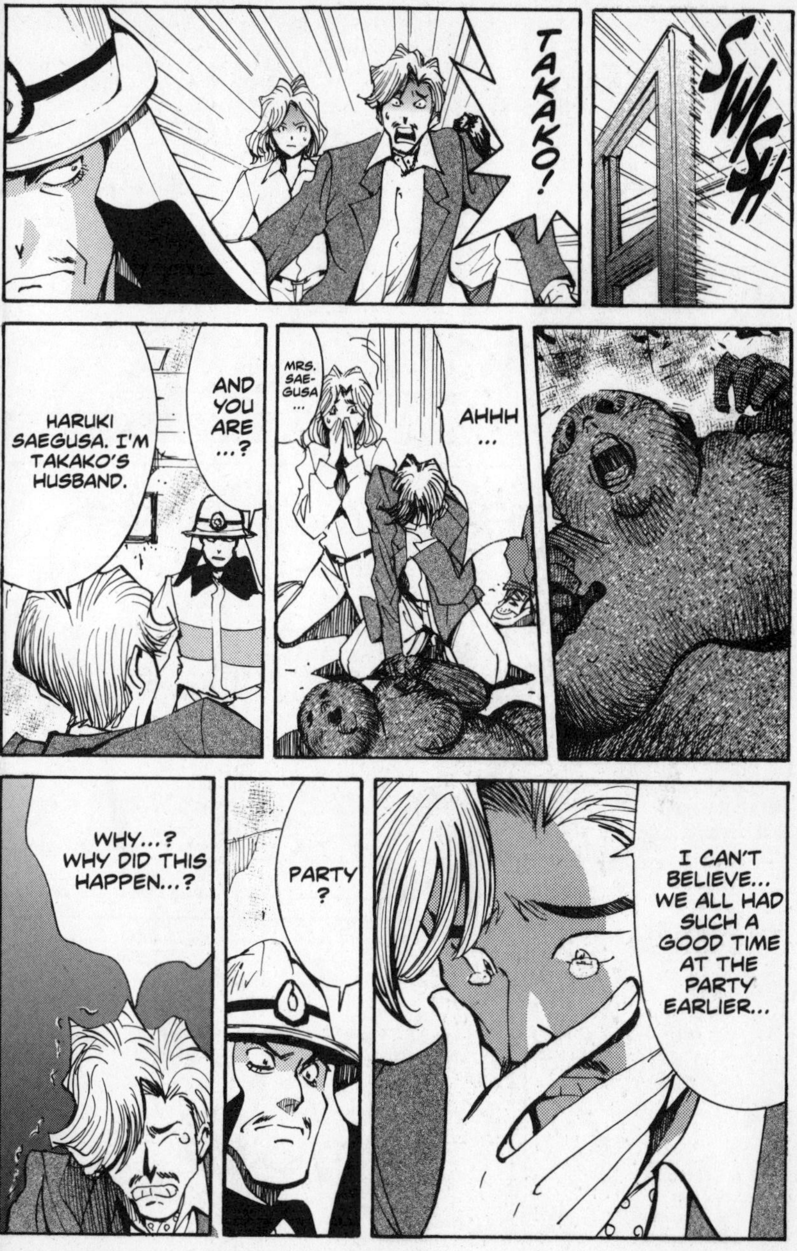
SWISH
TAKAKO!
AHHH ...
MRS. SAE-GUSA ...
AND YOU ARE ...?
HARUKI SAEGUSA. I'M TAKAKO'S HUSBAND.
I CAN'T BELIEVE... WE ALL HAD SUCH A GOOD TIME AT THE PARTY EARLIER...
PARTY ?
WHY...? WHY DID THIS HAPPEN...?

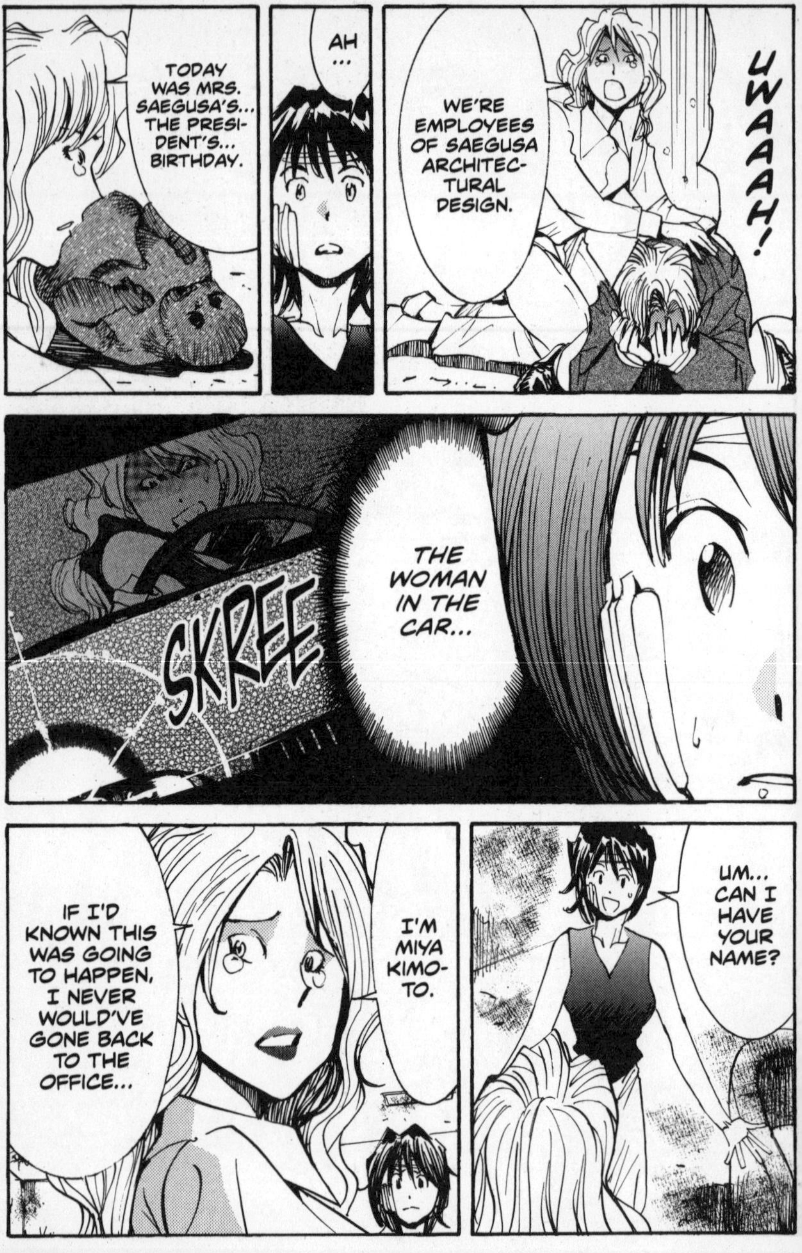
UWAAAAH!
WE'RE EMPLOYEES OF SAEGUSA ARCHITEC-TURAL DESIGN.
AH ...
TODAY WAS MRS. SAEGUSA'S... THE PRESI-DENT'S... BIRTHDAY.
THE WOMAN IN THE CAR...
SKREE
UM... CAN I HAVE YOUR NAME?
I'M MIYA KIMO-TO.
IF I'D KNOWN THIS WAS GOING TO HAPPEN, I NEVER WOULD'VE GONE BACK TO THE OFFICE...

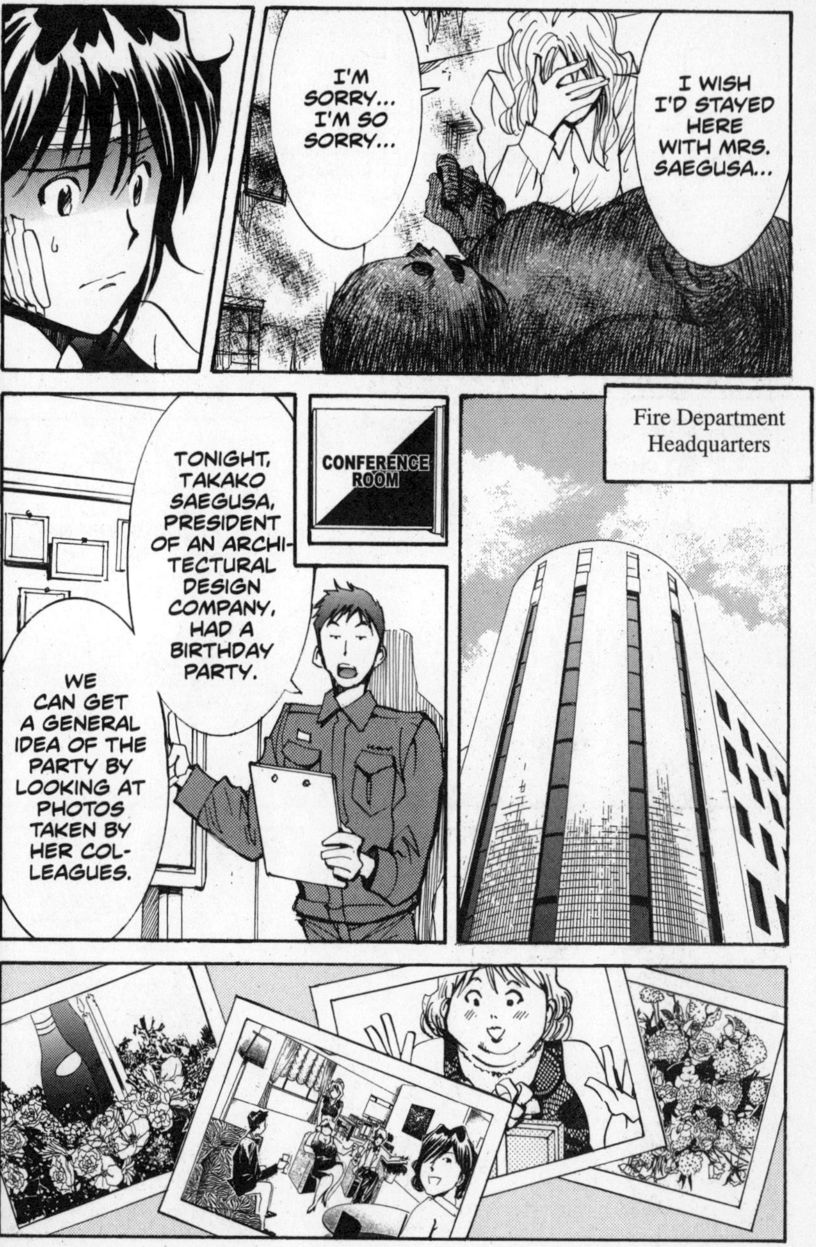
I WISH I'D STAYED HERE WITH MRS. SAEGUSA...
I'M SORRY... I'M SO SORRY...
Fire Department Headquarters
CONFERENCE ROOM
TONIGHT, TAKAKO SAEGUSA, PRESIDENT OF AN ARCHI-TECTURAL DESIGN COMPANY, HAD A BIRTHDAY PARTY.
WE CAN GET A GENERAL IDEA OF THE PARTY BY LOOKING AT PHOTOS TAKEN BY HER COL-LEAGUES.

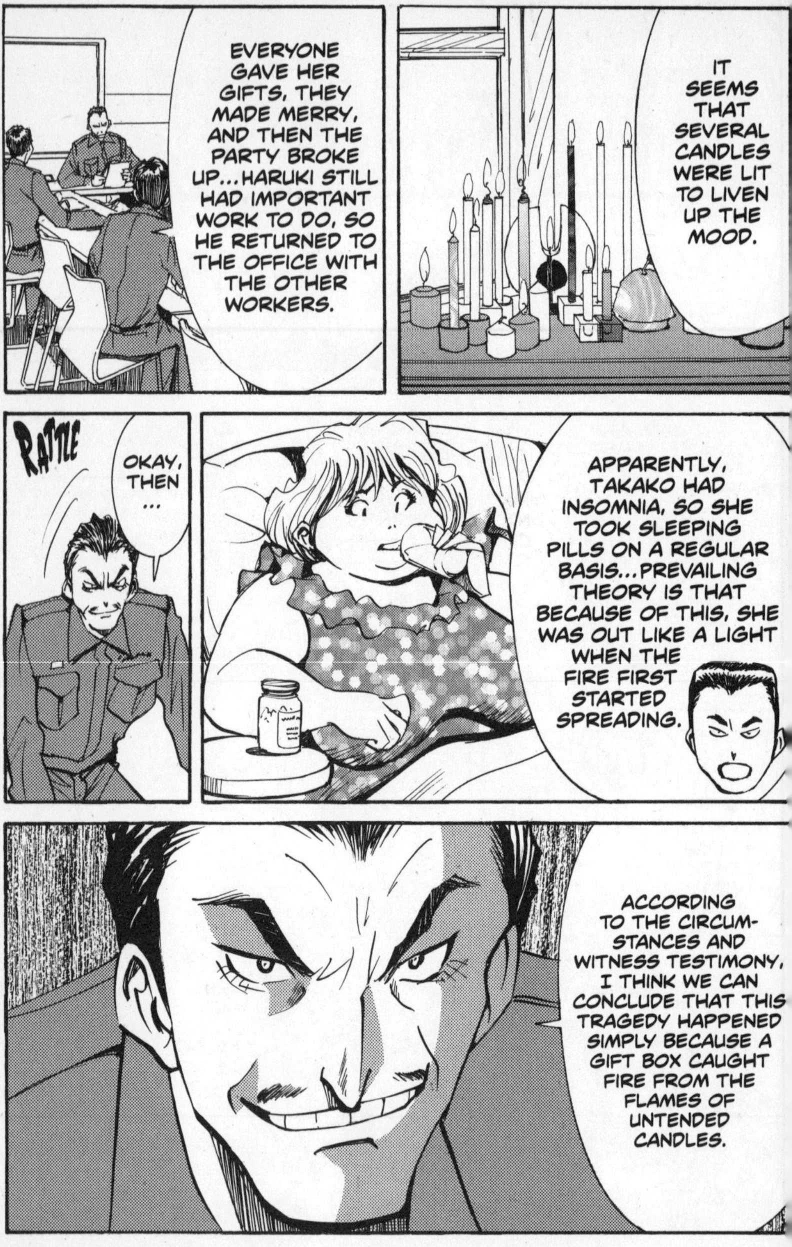
IT SEEMS THAT SEVERAL CANDLES WERE LIT TO LIVEN UP THE MOOD.
EVERYONE GAVE HER GIFTS, THEY MADE MERRY, AND THEN THE PARTY BROKE UP...HARUKI STILL HAD IMPORTANT WORK TO DO, SO HE RETURNED TO THE OFFICE WITH THE OTHER WORKERS.
APPARENTLY, TAKAKO HAD INSOMNIA, SO SHE TOOK SLEEPING PILLS ON A REGULAR BASIS...PREVAILING THEORY IS THAT BECAUSE OF THIS, SHE WAS OUT LIKE A LIGHT WHEN THE FIRE FIRST STARTED SPREADING.
RATTLE
OKAY, THEN ...
ACCORDING TO THE CIRCUM-STANCES AND WITNESS TESTIMONY, I THINK WE CAN CONCLUDE THAT THIS TRAGEDY HAPPENED SIMPLY BECAUSE A GIFT BOX CAUGHT FIRE FROM THE FLAMES OF UNTENDED CANDLES.

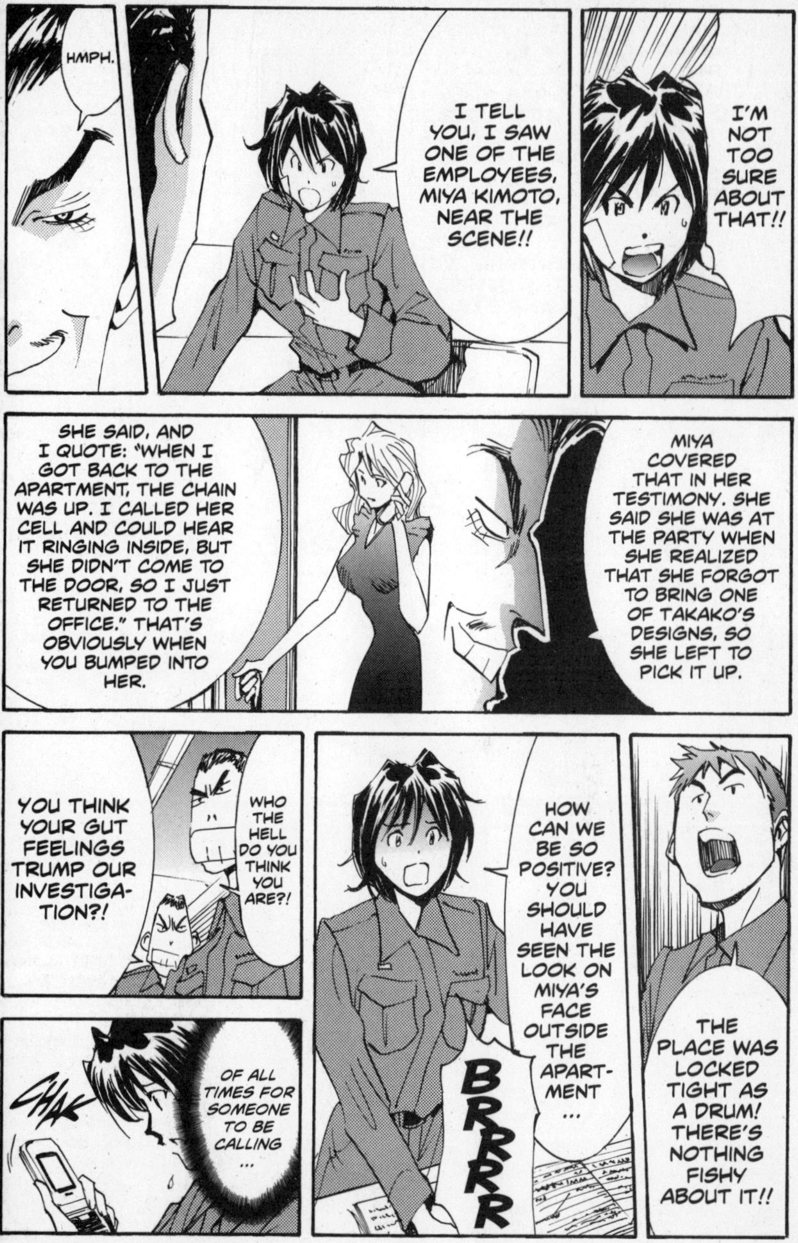
I'M NOT TOO SURE ABOUT THAT!!
I TELL YOU, I SAW ONE OF THE EMPLOYEES, MIYA KIMOTO, NEAR THE SCENE!!
HMPH.
MIYA COVERED THAT IN HER TESTIMONY. SHE SAID SHE WAS AT THE PARTY WHEN SHE REALIZED THAT SHE FORGOT TO BRING ONE OF TAKAKO'S DESIGNS, SO SHE LEFT TO PICK IT UP.
SHE SAID, AND I QUOTE: "WHEN I GOT BACK TO THE APARTMENT, THE CHAIN WAS UP. I CALLED HER CELL AND COULD HEAR IT RINGING INSIDE, BUT SHE DIDN'T COME TO THE DOOR, SO I JUST RETURNED TO THE OFFICE." THAT'S OBVIOUSLY WHEN YOU BUMPED INTO HER.
THE PLACE WAS LOCKED TIGHT AS A DRUM! THERE'S NOTHING FISHY ABOUT IT!!
HOW CAN WE BE SO POSITIVE? YOU SHOULD HAVE SEEN THE LOOK ON MIYA'S FACE OUTSIDE THE APARTMENT ...
BRRRR
WHO THE HELL DO YOU THINK YOU ARE?!
YOU THINK YOUR GUT FEELINGS TRUMP OUR INVESTIGATION?!
OF ALL TIMES FOR SOMEONE TO BE CALLING ...
CHAK

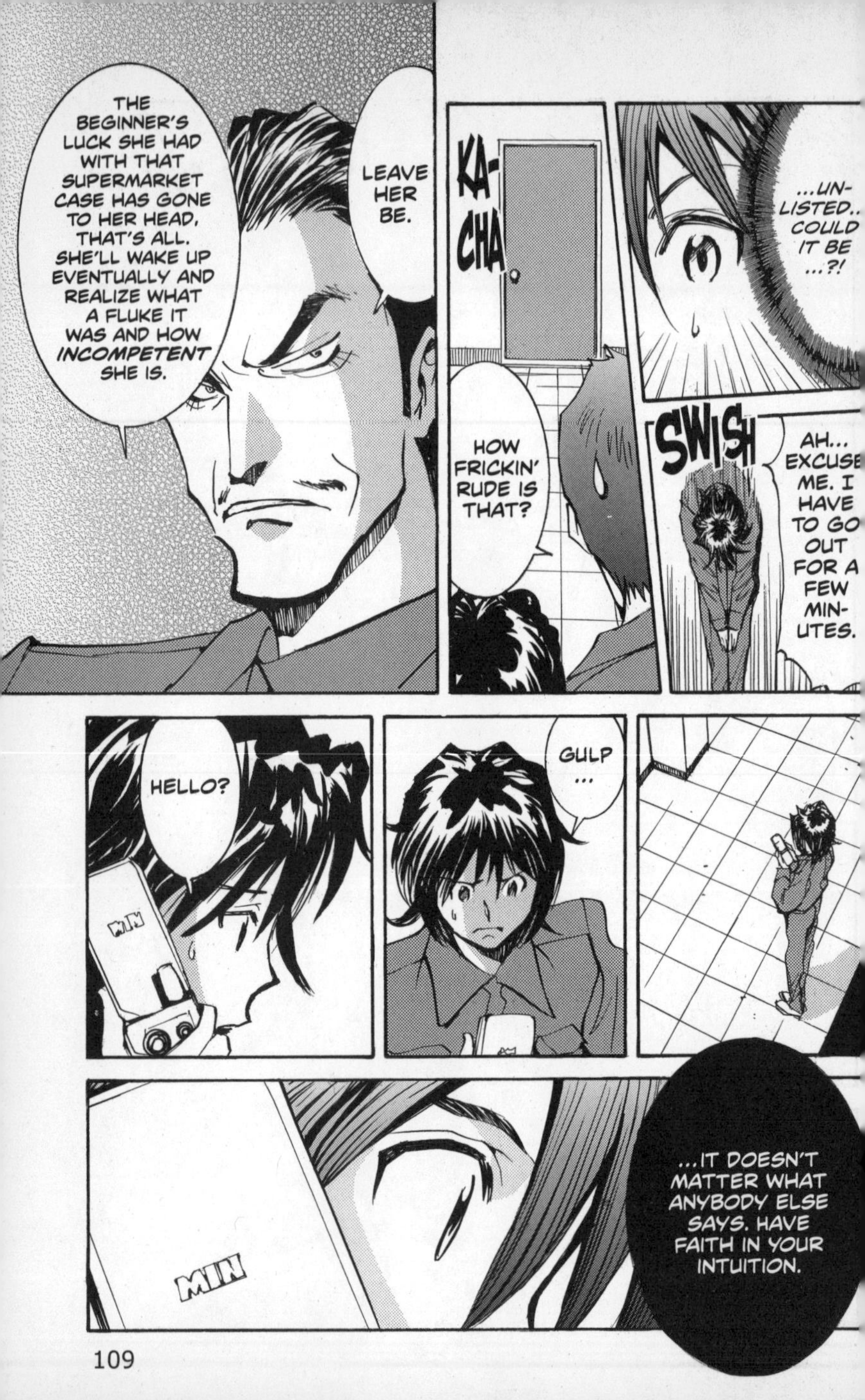
...UN-LISTED.. COULD IT BE ...?!
KA-CHA
SWISH
AH... EXCUSE ME. I HAVE TO GO OUT FOR A FEW MIN-UTES.
HOW FRICKIN' RUDE IS THAT?
LEAVE HER BE.
THE BEGINNER'S LUCK SHE HAD WITH THAT SUPERMARKET CASE HAS GONE TO HER HEAD, THAT'S ALL. SHE'LL WAKE UP EVENTUALLY AND REALIZE WHAT A FLUKE IT WAS AND HOW *INCOMPETENT* SHE IS.
GULP ...
HELLO?
MIN
...IT DOESN'T MATTER WHAT ANYBODY ELSE SAYS. HAVE FAITH IN YOUR INTUITION.
MIN

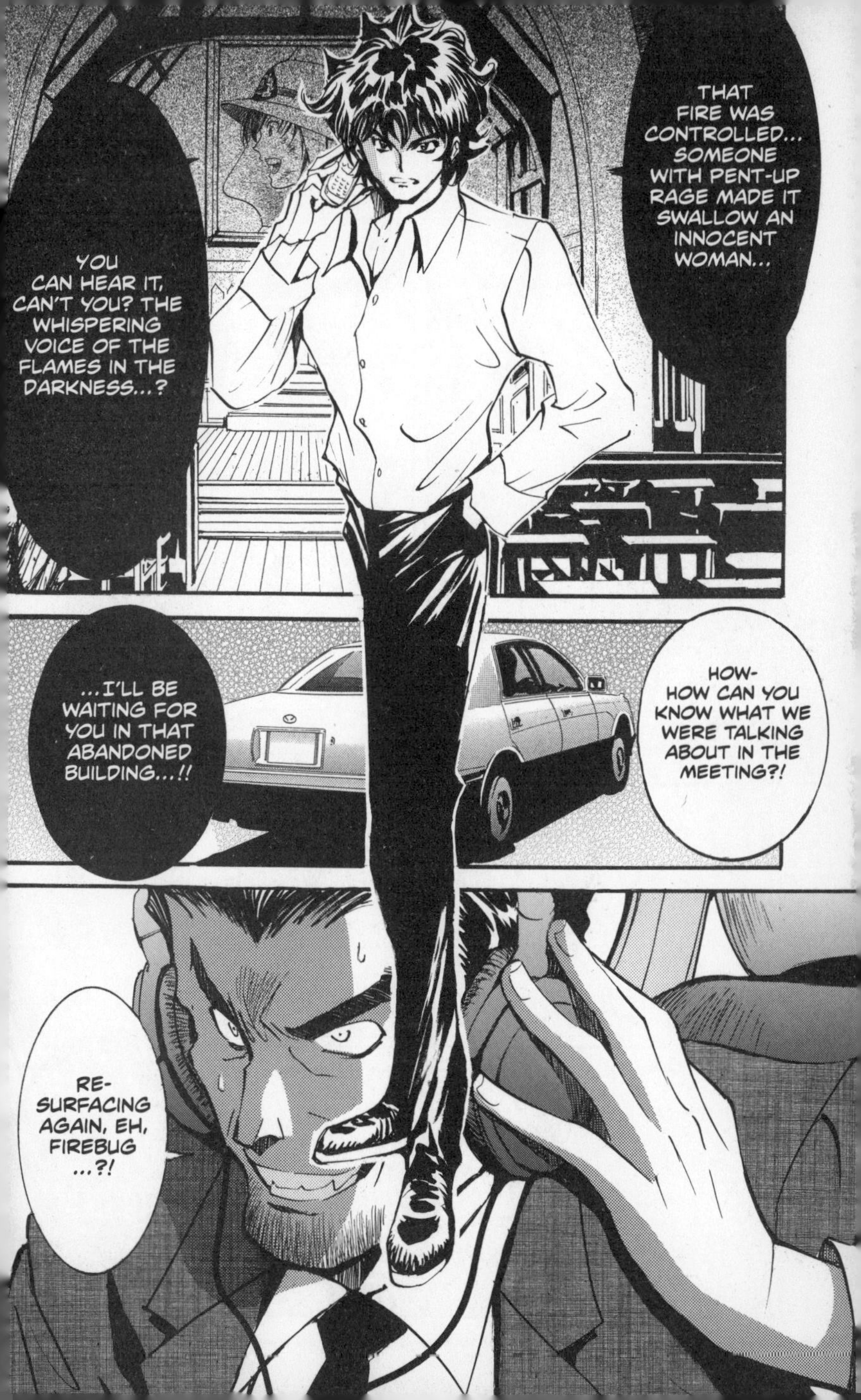
THAT FIRE WAS CONTROLLED... SOMEONE WITH PENT-UP RAGE MADE IT SWALLOW AN INNOCENT WOMAN...
YOU CAN HEAR IT, CAN'T YOU? THE WHISPERING VOICE OF THE FLAMES IN THE DARKNESS...?
HOW- HOW CAN YOU KNOW WHAT WE WERE TALKING ABOUT IN THE MEETING?!
...I'LL BE WAITING FOR YOU IN THAT ABANDONED BUILDING...!!
RE-SURFACING AGAIN, EH, FIREBUG ...?!

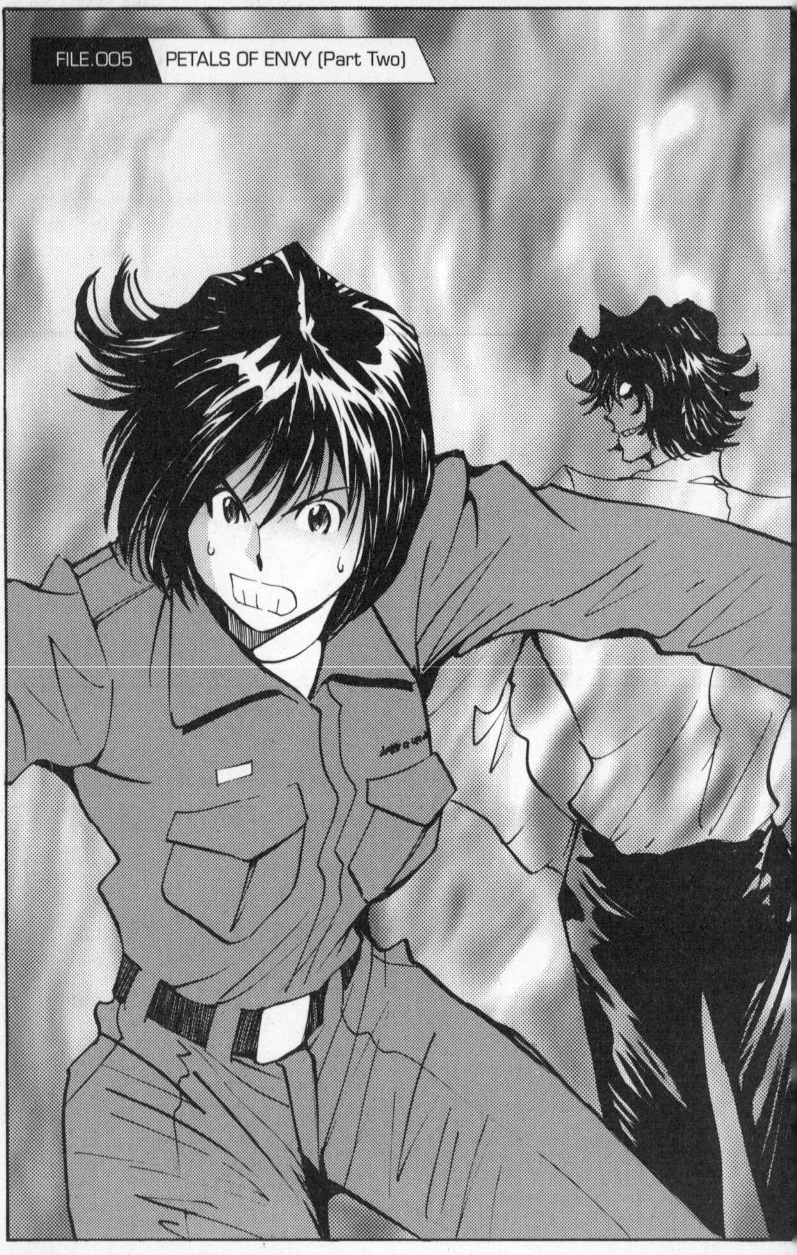
FILE.005
PETALS OF ENVY (Part Two)

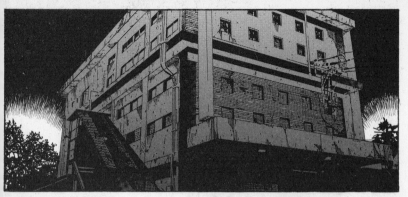

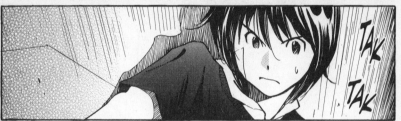

TAK
TAK

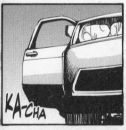

KA-CHA

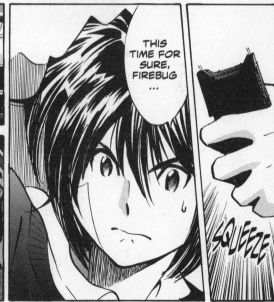

THIS TIME FOR SURE, FIREBUG...

SQUEEZE

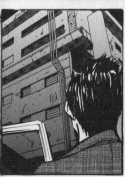

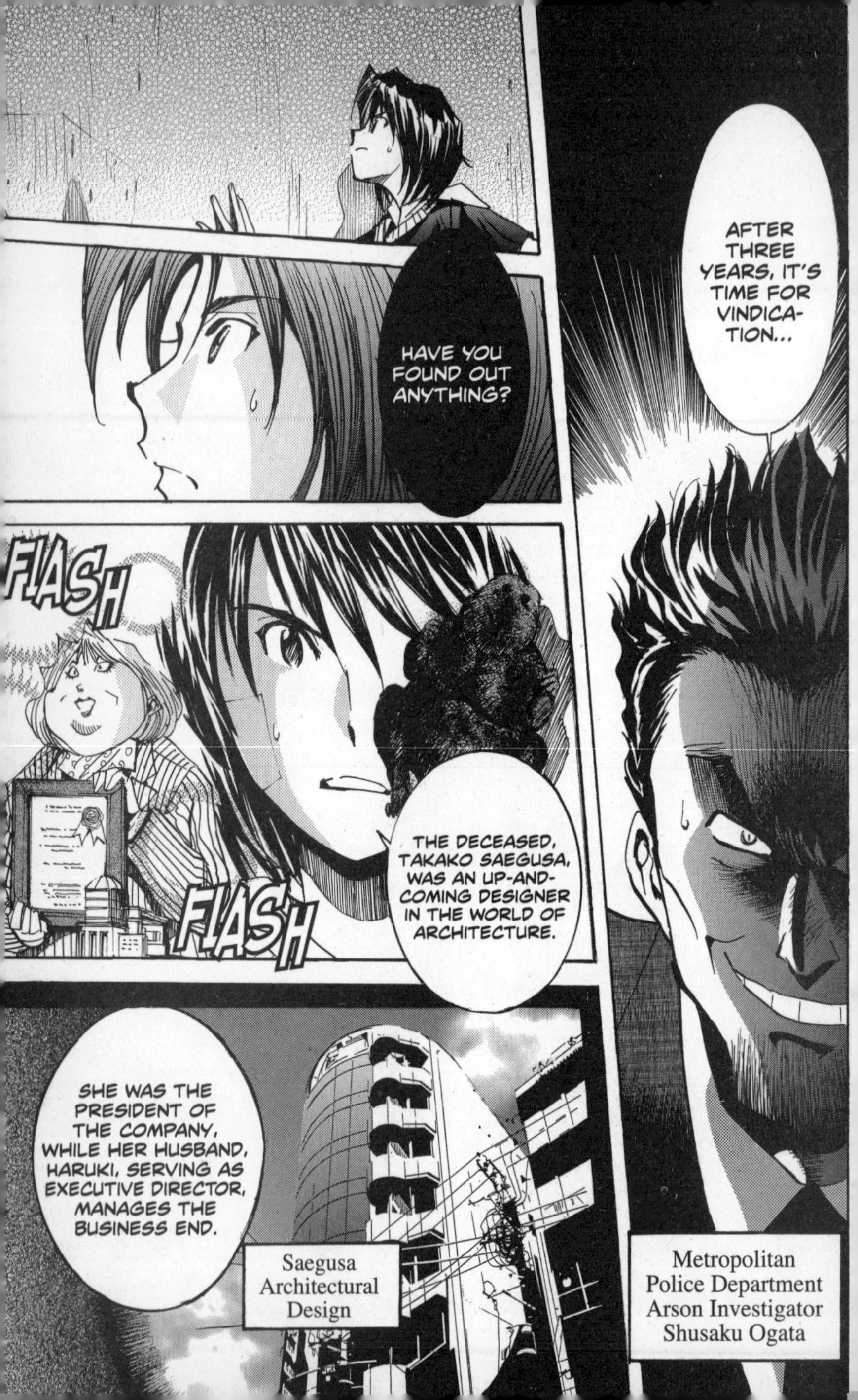
AFTER THREE YEARS, IT'S TIME FOR VINDICATION...
Metropolitan Police Department Arson Investigator Shusaku Ogata
HAVE YOU FOUND OUT ANYTHING?
FLASH
THE DECEASED, TAKAKO SAEGUSA, WAS AN UP-AND-COMING DESIGNER IN THE WORLD OF ARCHITECTURE.
FLASH
SHE WAS THE PRESIDENT OF THE COMPANY, WHILE HER HUSBAND, HARUKI, SERVING AS EXECUTIVE DIRECTOR, MANAGES THE BUSINESS END.
Saegusa Architectural Design

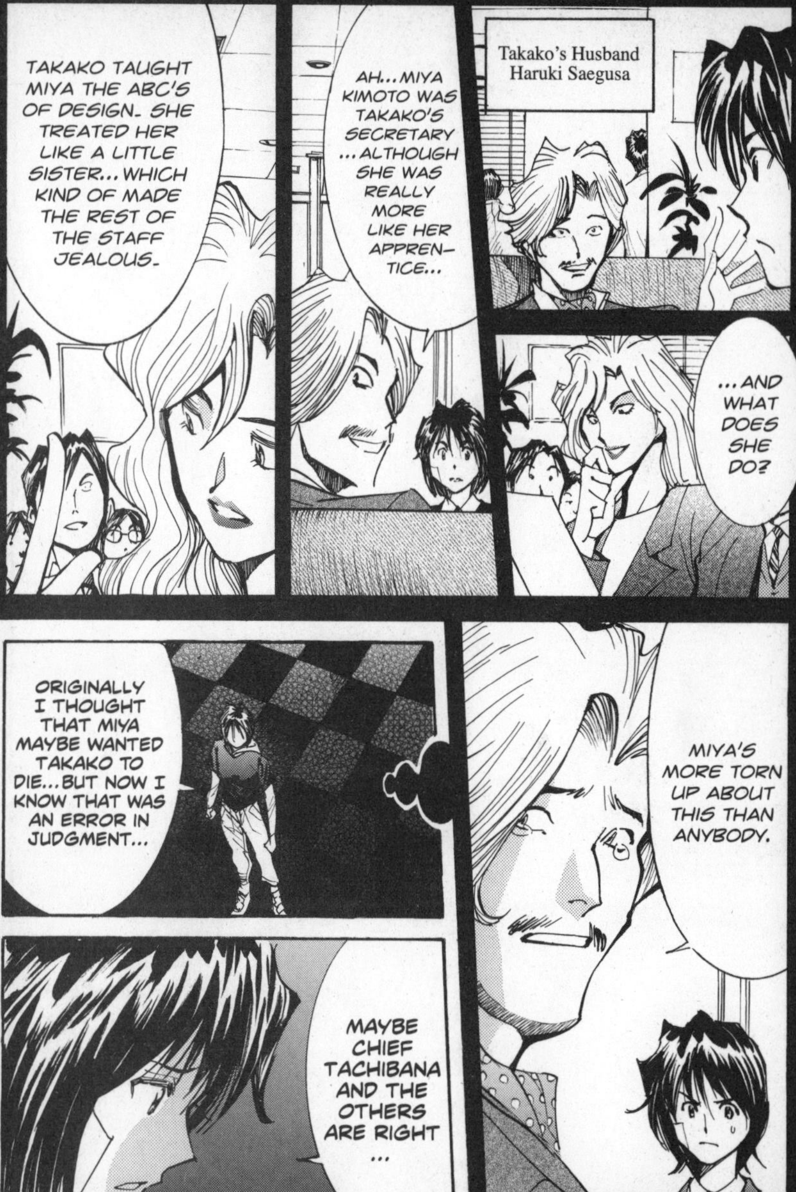
Takako's Husband Haruki Saegusa
...AND WHAT DOES SHE DO?
AH...MIYA KIMOTO WAS TAKAKO'S SECRETARY ...ALTHOUGH SHE WAS REALLY MORE LIKE HER APPREN-TICE...
TAKAKO TAUGHT MIYA THE ABC'S OF DESIGN. SHE TREATED HER LIKE A LITTLE SISTER...WHICH KIND OF MADE THE REST OF THE STAFF JEALOUS.
MIYA'S MORE TORN UP ABOUT THIS THAN ANYBODY.
ORIGINALLY I THOUGHT THAT MIYA MAYBE WANTED TAKAKO TO DIE...BUT NOW I KNOW THAT WAS AN ERROR IN JUDGMENT...
MAYBE CHIEF TACHIBANA AND THE OTHERS ARE RIGHT ...

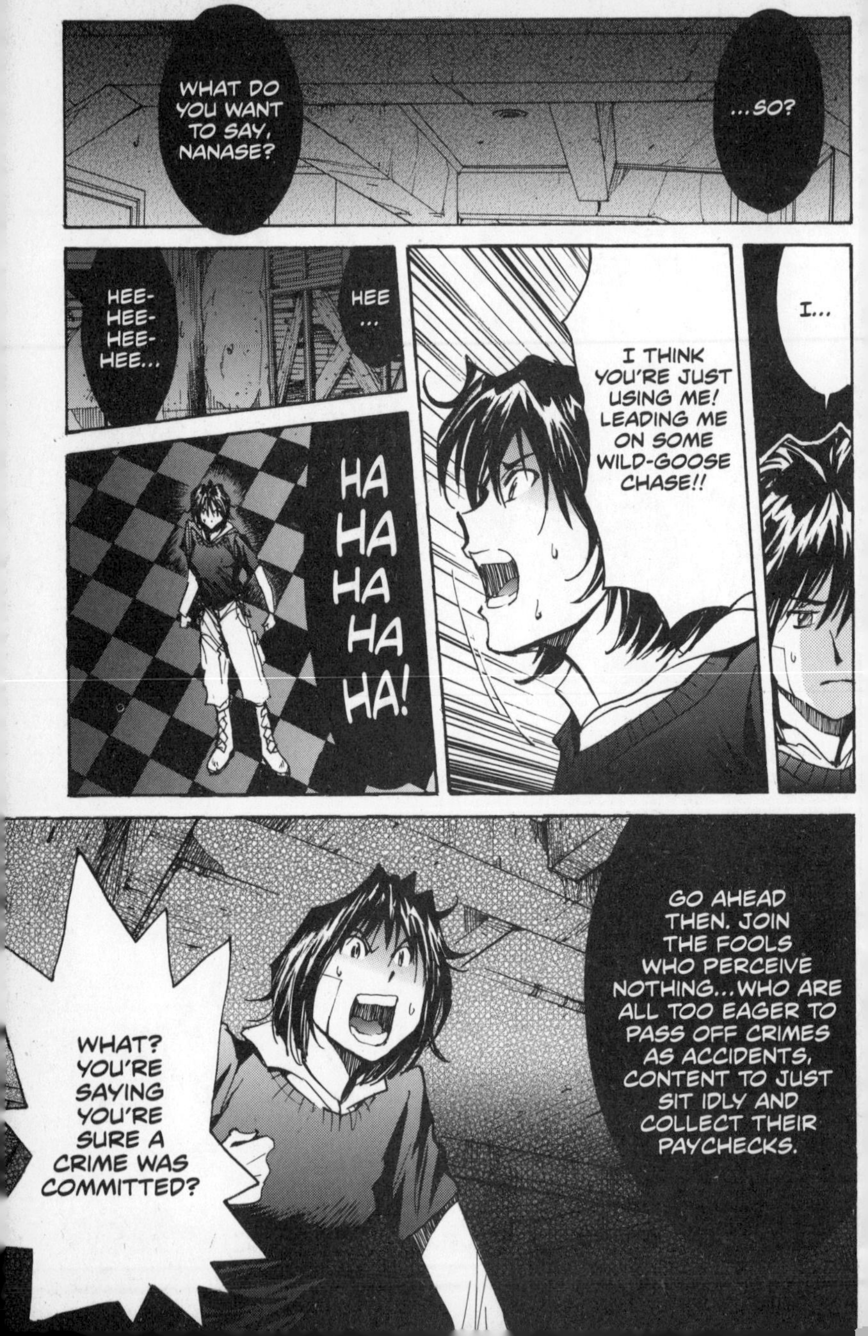
...SO?
WHAT DO YOU WANT TO SAY, NANASE?
I...
I THINK YOU'RE JUST USING ME! LEADING ME ON SOME WILD-GOOSE CHASE!!
HEE ...
HEE-HEE-HEE-HEE...
HA HA HA HA HA!
GO AHEAD THEN. JOIN THE FOOLS WHO PERCEIVE NOTHING...WHO ARE ALL TOO EAGER TO PASS OFF CRIMES AS ACCIDENTS, CONTENT TO JUST SIT IDLY AND COLLECT THEIR PAYCHECKS.
WHAT? YOU'RE SAYING YOU'RE SURE A CRIME WAS COMMITTED?

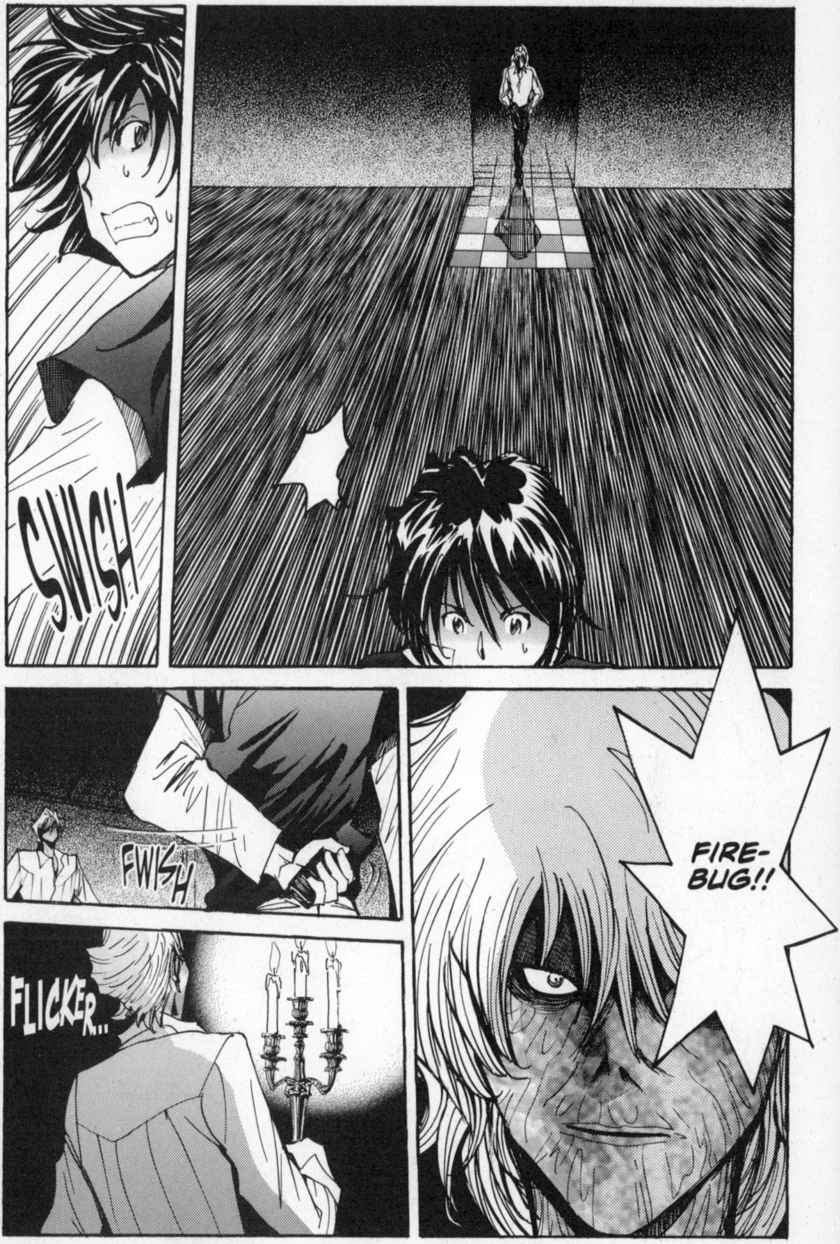
SWISH
FIRE-BUG!!
FWISH
FLICKER...

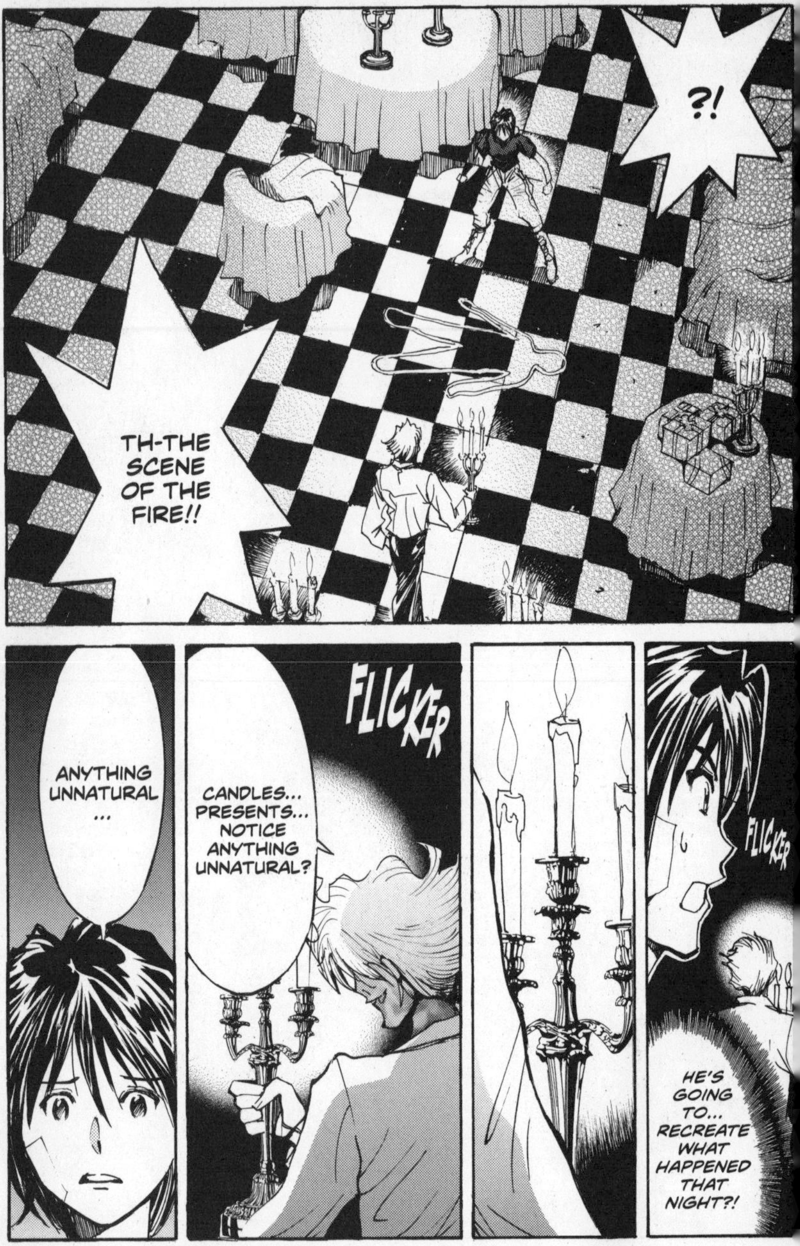
?!
TH-THE SCENE OF THE FIRE!!
FLICKER
HE'S GOING TO... RECREATE WHAT HAPPENED THAT NIGHT?!
FLICKER
CANDLES... PRESENTS... NOTICE ANYTHING UNNATURAL?
ANYTHING UNNATURAL ...

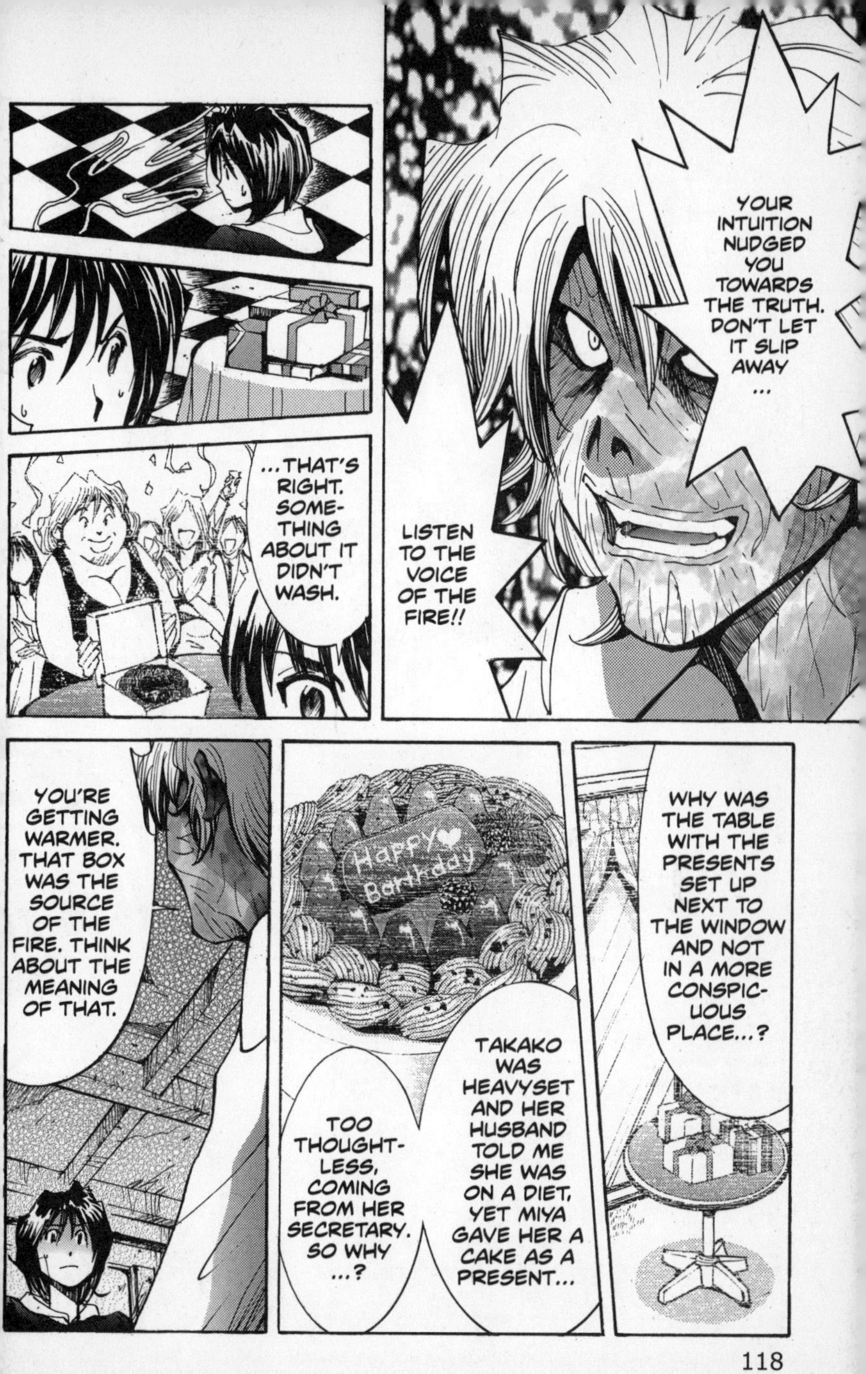
YOUR INTUITION NUDGED YOU TOWARDS THE TRUTH. DON'T LET IT SLIP AWAY ...
LISTEN TO THE VOICE OF THE FIRE!!
...THAT'S RIGHT. SOME-THING ABOUT IT DIDN'T WASH.
WHY WAS THE TABLE WITH THE PRESENTS SET UP NEXT TO THE WINDOW AND NOT IN A MORE CONSPIC-UOUS PLACE...?
Happy♥ Birthday
TAKAKO WAS HEAVYSET AND HER HUSBAND TOLD ME SHE WAS ON A DIET, YET MIYA GAVE HER A CAKE AS A PRESENT...
TOO THOUGHT-LESS, COMING FROM HER SECRETARY. SO WHY ...?
YOU'RE GETTING WARMER. THAT BOX WAS THE SOURCE OF THE FIRE. THINK ABOUT THE MEANING OF THAT.

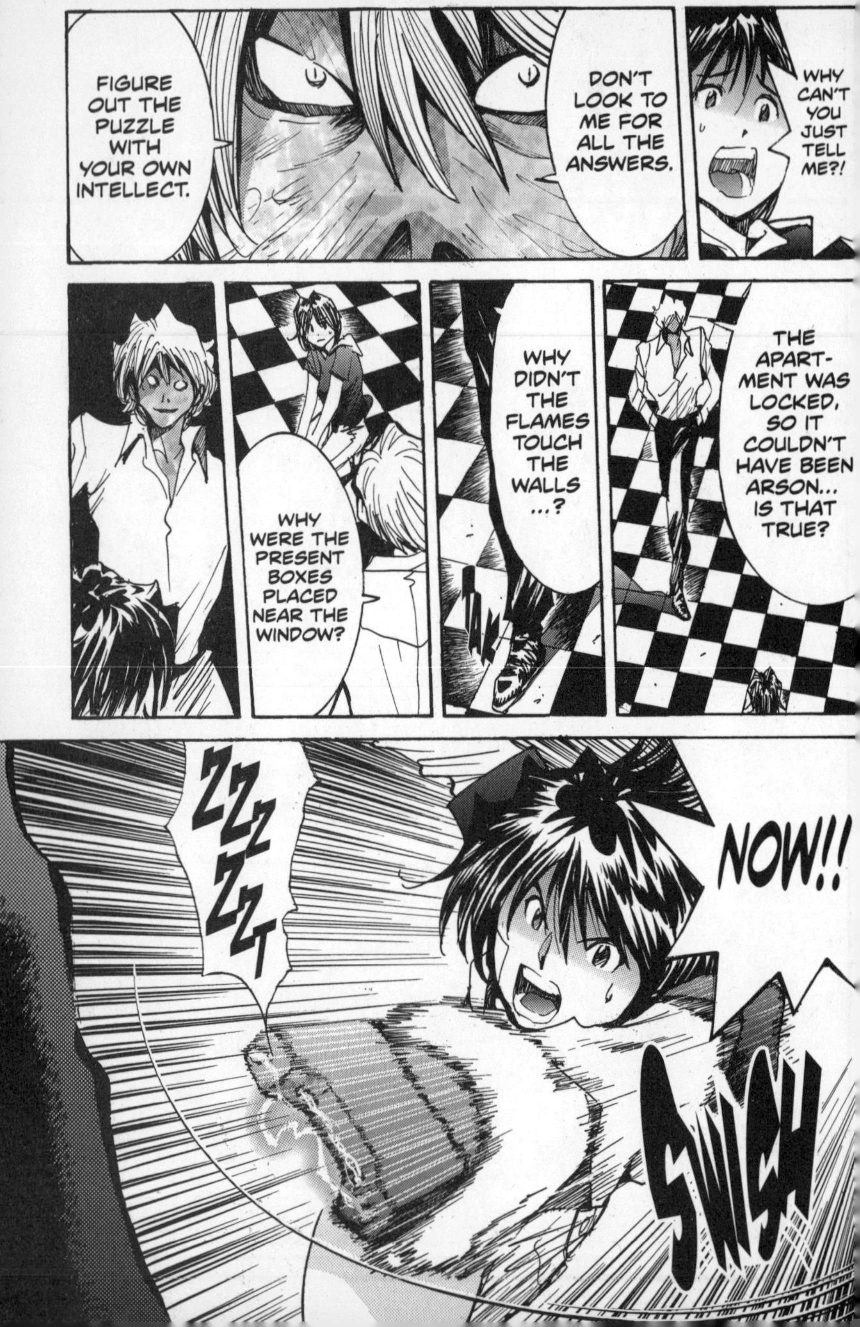
WHY CAN'T YOU JUST TELL ME?!
DON'T LOOK TO ME FOR ALL THE ANSWERS.
FIGURE OUT THE PUZZLE WITH YOUR OWN INTELLECT.
THE APART-MENT WAS LOCKED, SO IT COULDN'T HAVE BEEN ARSON... IS THAT TRUE?
WHY DIDN'T THE FLAMES TOUCH THE WALLS ...?
TAK
WHY WERE THE PRESENT BOXES PLACED NEAR THE WINDOW?
NOW!!
ZZZZT
SWISH

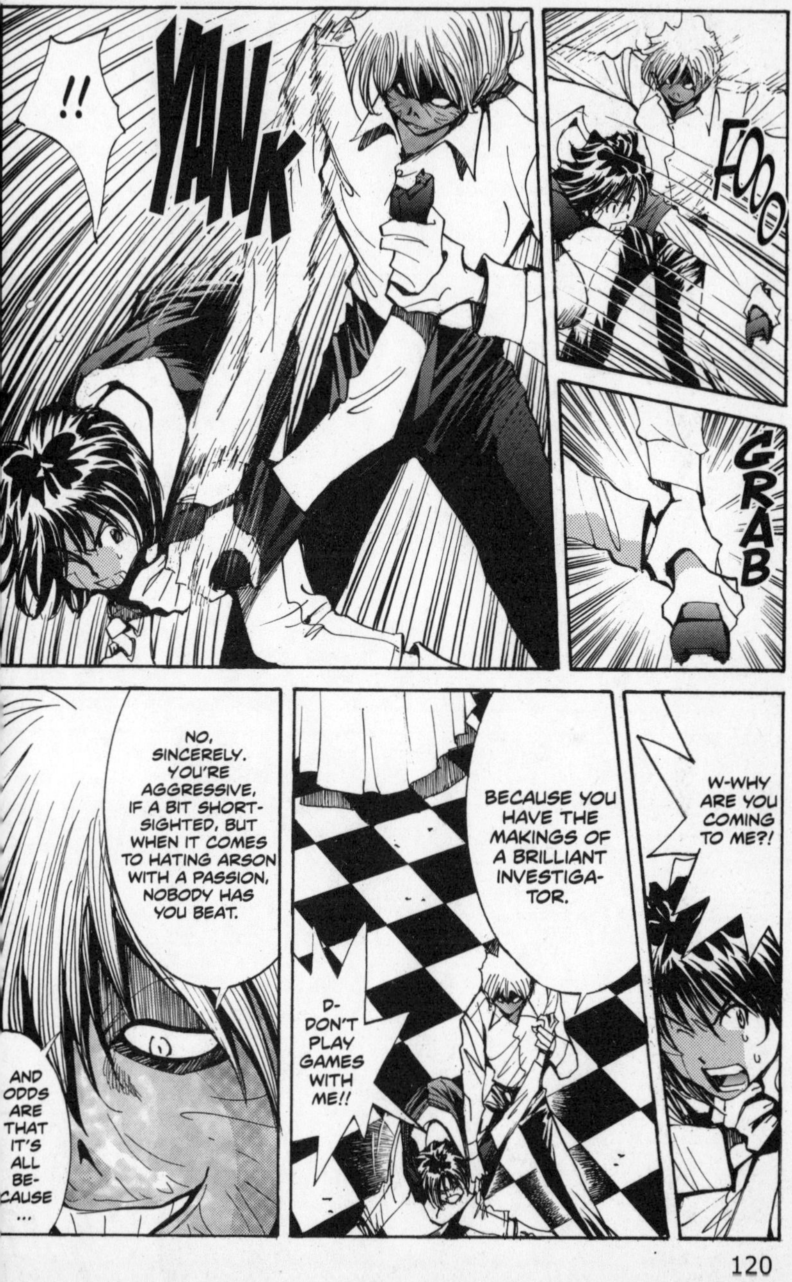
FOOO
GRAB
YANK
!!
W-WHY ARE YOU COMING TO ME?!
BECAUSE YOU HAVE THE MAKINGS OF A BRILLIANT INVESTIGATOR.
D-DON'T PLAY GAMES WITH ME!!
NO, SINCERELY. YOU'RE AGGRESSIVE, IF A BIT SHORT-SIGHTED, BUT WHEN IT COMES TO HATING ARSON WITH A PASSION, NOBODY HAS YOU BEAT.
AND ODDS ARE THAT IT'S ALL BECAUSE...

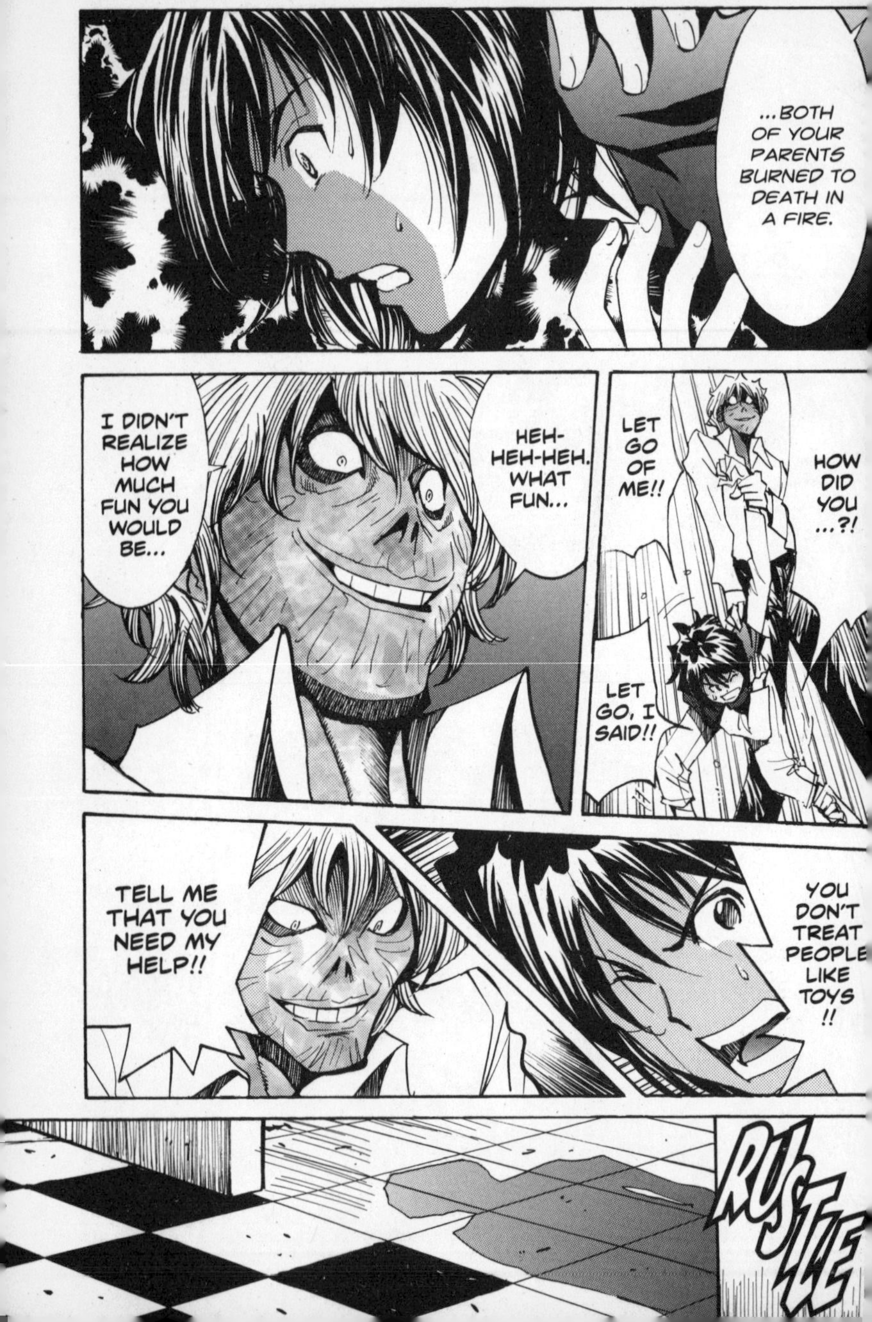
...BOTH OF YOUR PARENTS BURNED TO DEATH IN A FIRE.
HOW DID YOU ...?!
LET GO OF ME!!
LET GO, I SAID!!
HEH-HEH-HEH. WHAT FUN...
I DIDN'T REALIZE HOW MUCH FUN YOU WOULD BE...
YOU DON'T TREAT PEOPLE LIKE TOYS !!
TELL ME THAT YOU NEED MY HELP!!
RUSTLE

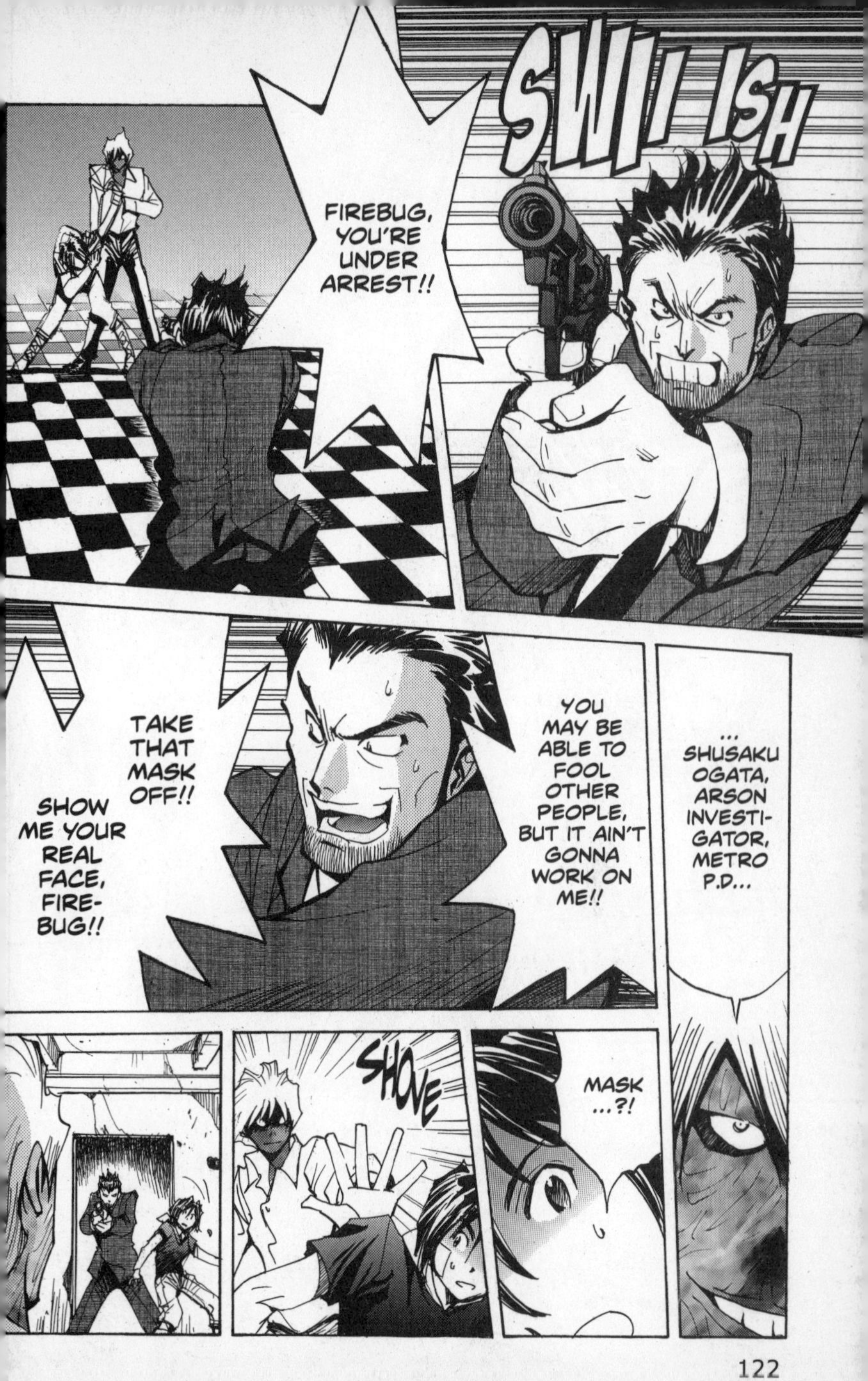
SWIISH
FIREBUG, YOU'RE UNDER ARREST!!
... SHUSAKU OGATA, ARSON INVESTI-GATOR, METRO P.D...
YOU MAY BE ABLE TO FOOL OTHER PEOPLE, BUT IT AIN'T GONNA WORK ON ME!!
TAKE THAT MASK OFF!!
SHOW ME YOUR REAL FACE, FIRE-BUG!!
MASK ...?!
SHOVE

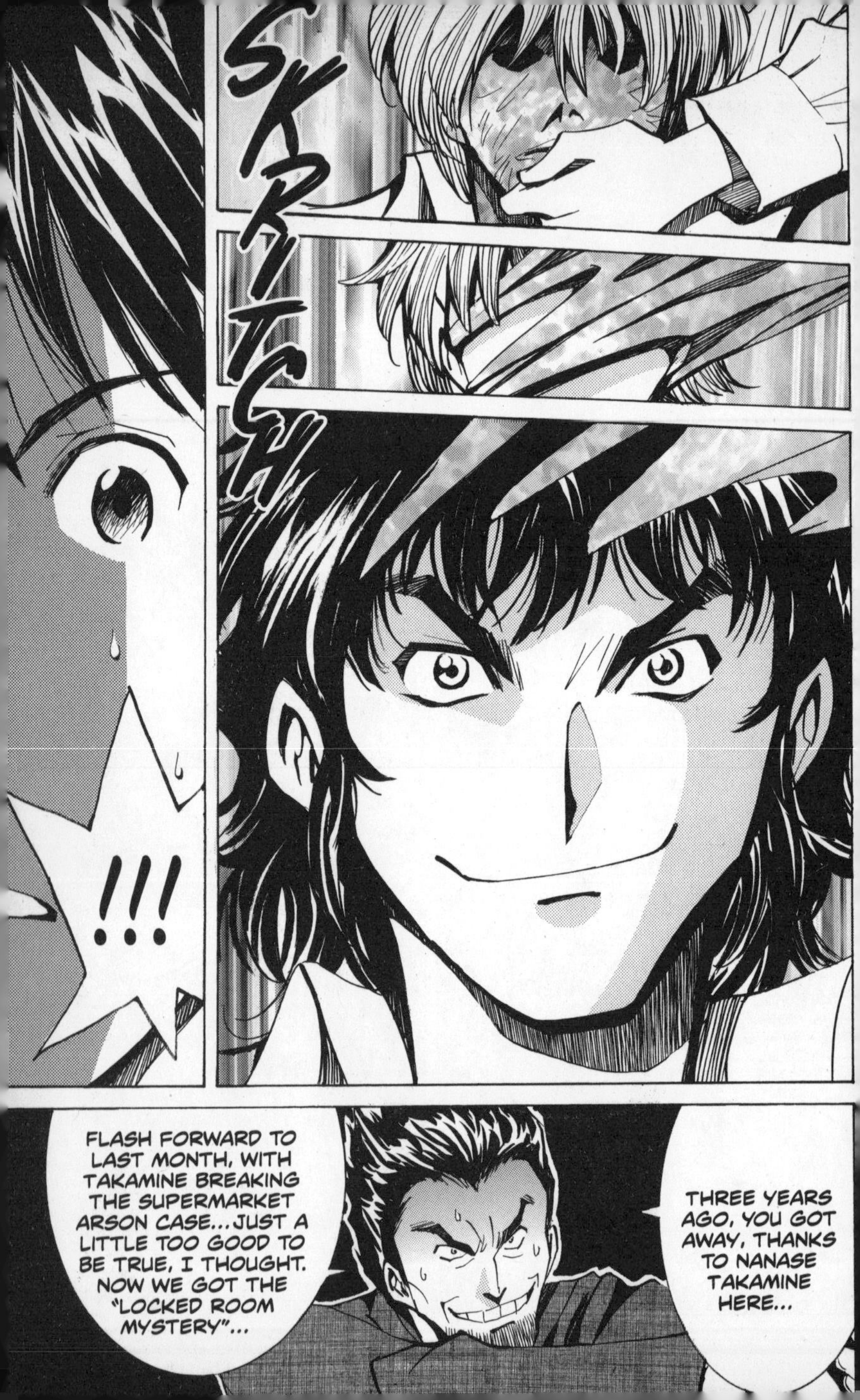
SKRITCH!
!!!
THREE YEARS AGO, YOU GOT AWAY, THANKS TO NANASE TAKAMINE HERE...
FLASH FORWARD TO LAST MONTH, WITH TAKAMINE BREAKING THE SUPERMARKET ARSON CASE...JUST A LITTLE TOO GOOD TO BE TRUE, I THOUGHT. NOW WE GOT THE "LOCKED ROOM MYSTERY"...

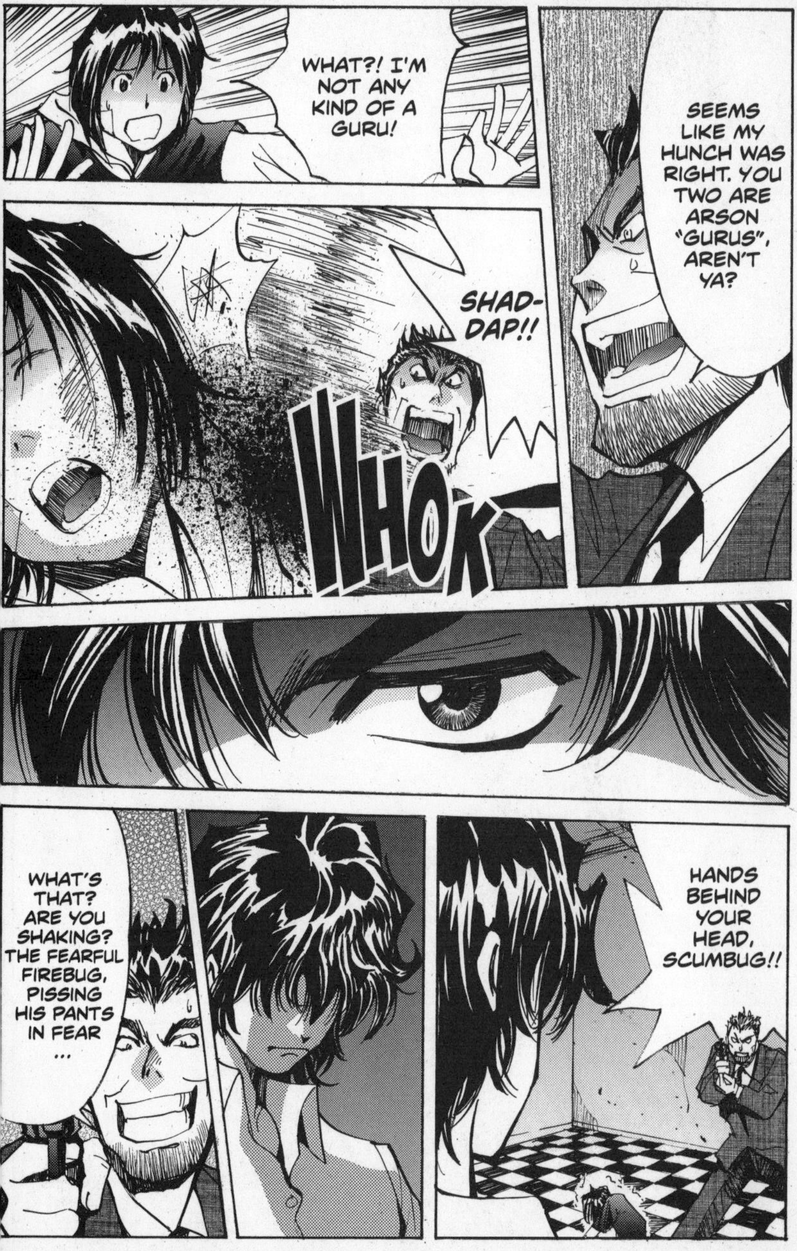
SEEMS LIKE MY HUNCH WAS RIGHT. YOU TWO ARE ARSON "GURUS", AREN'T YA?
WHAT?! I'M NOT ANY KIND OF A GURU!
SHAD-DAP!!
WHOK
HANDS BEHIND YOUR HEAD, SCUMBUG!!
WHAT'S THAT? ARE YOU SHAKING? THE FEARFUL FIREBUG, PISSING HIS PANTS IN FEAR ...

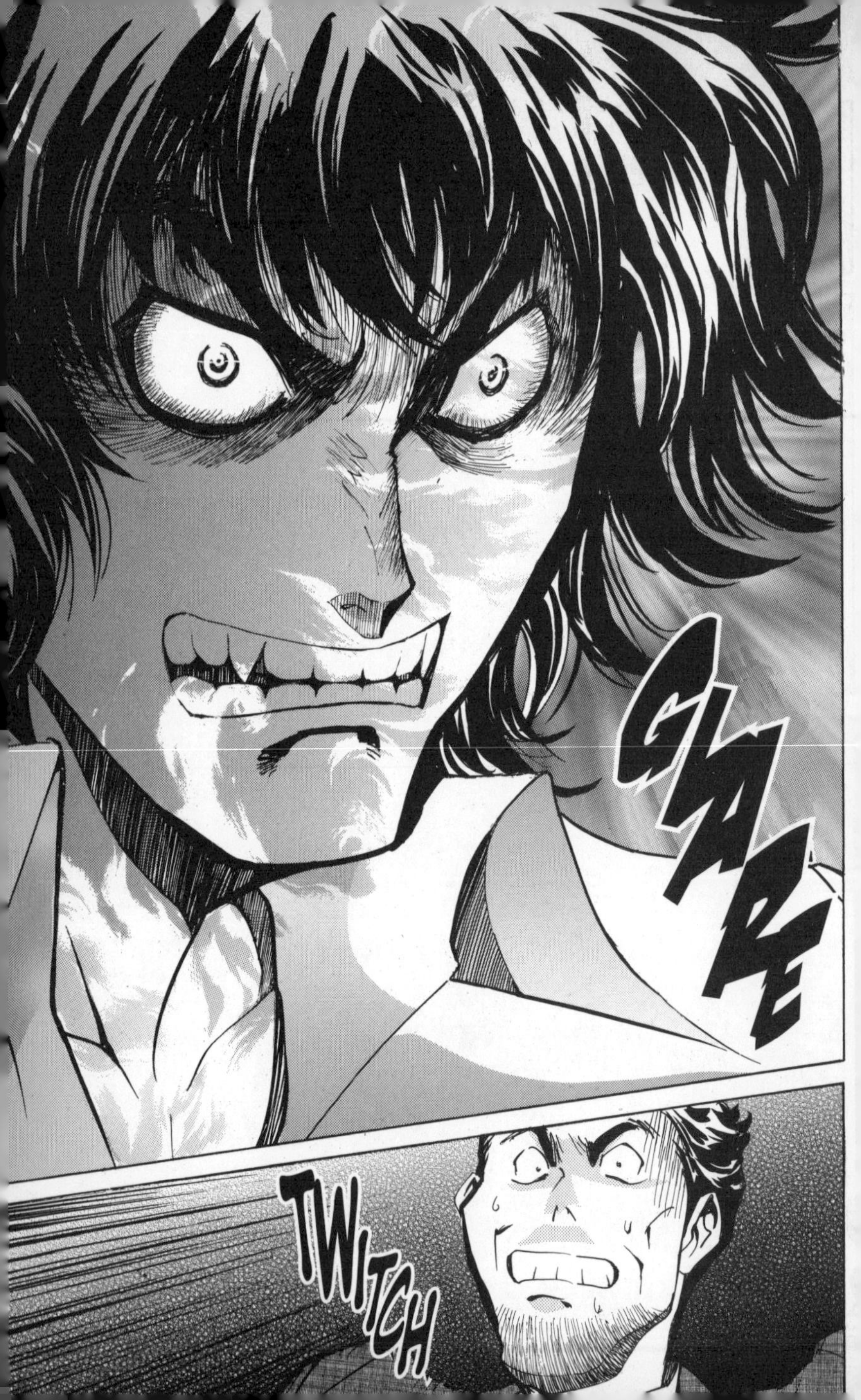
GLARE
TWITCH

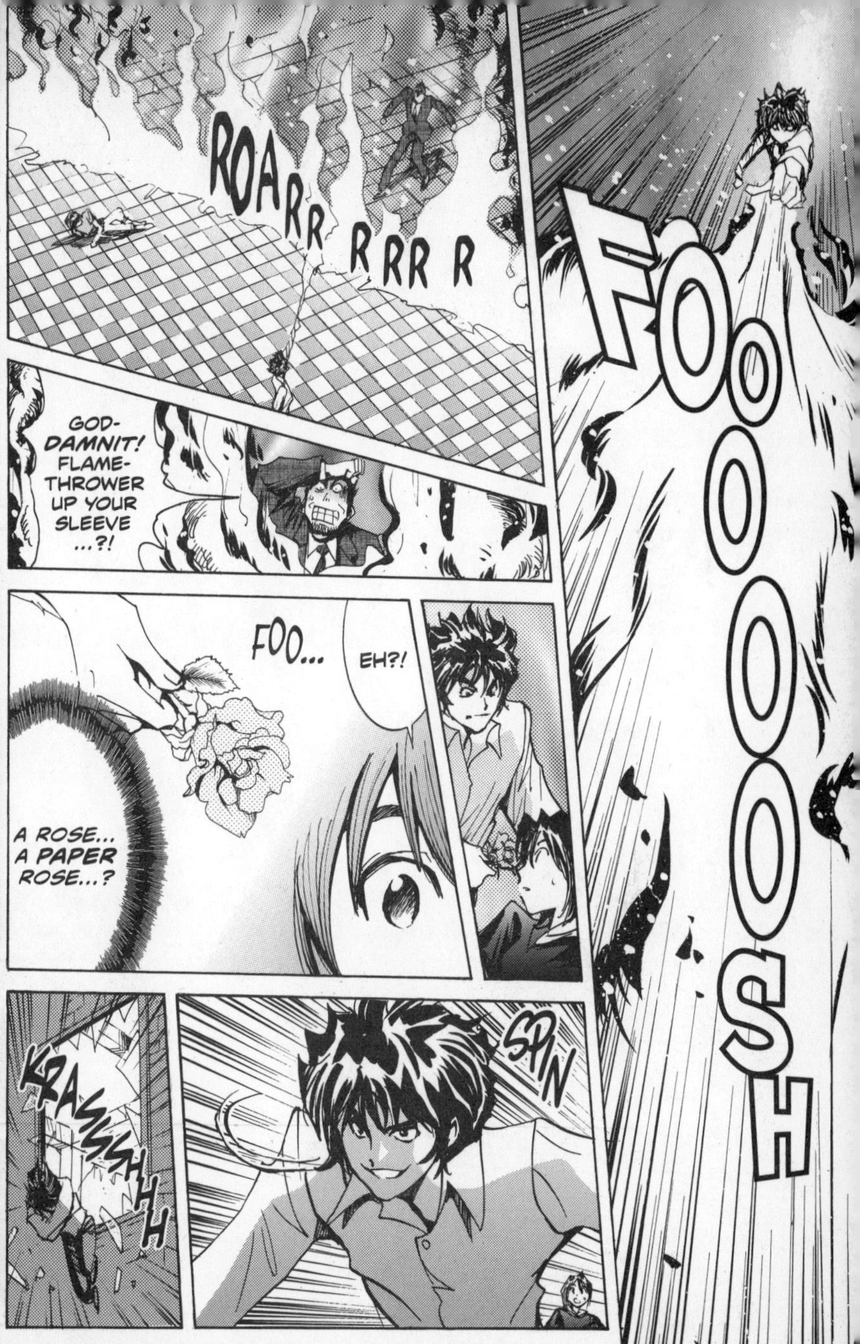
FOOOOOOOSH
ROARRRRRR
GOD-DAMNIT! FLAME-THROWER UP YOUR SLEEVE ...?!
FOO...
EH?!
A ROSE... A PAPER ROSE...?
SPIN
KRASSSHHH

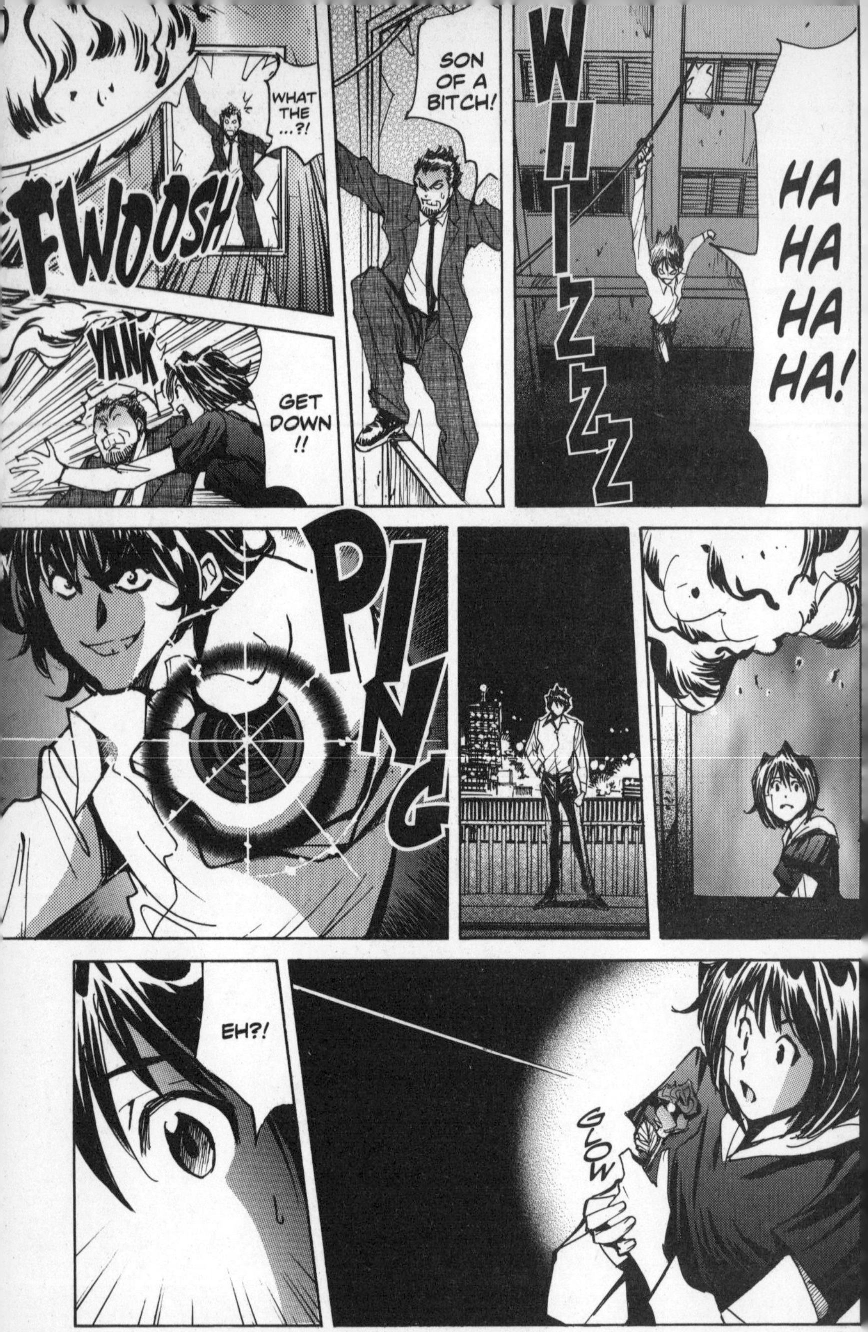
HA HA HA HA HA HA HA!
WHIZZZ
SON OF A BITCH!
WHAT THE ...?!
FWOOSH
YANK
GET DOWN !!
PING
GLOW
EH?!

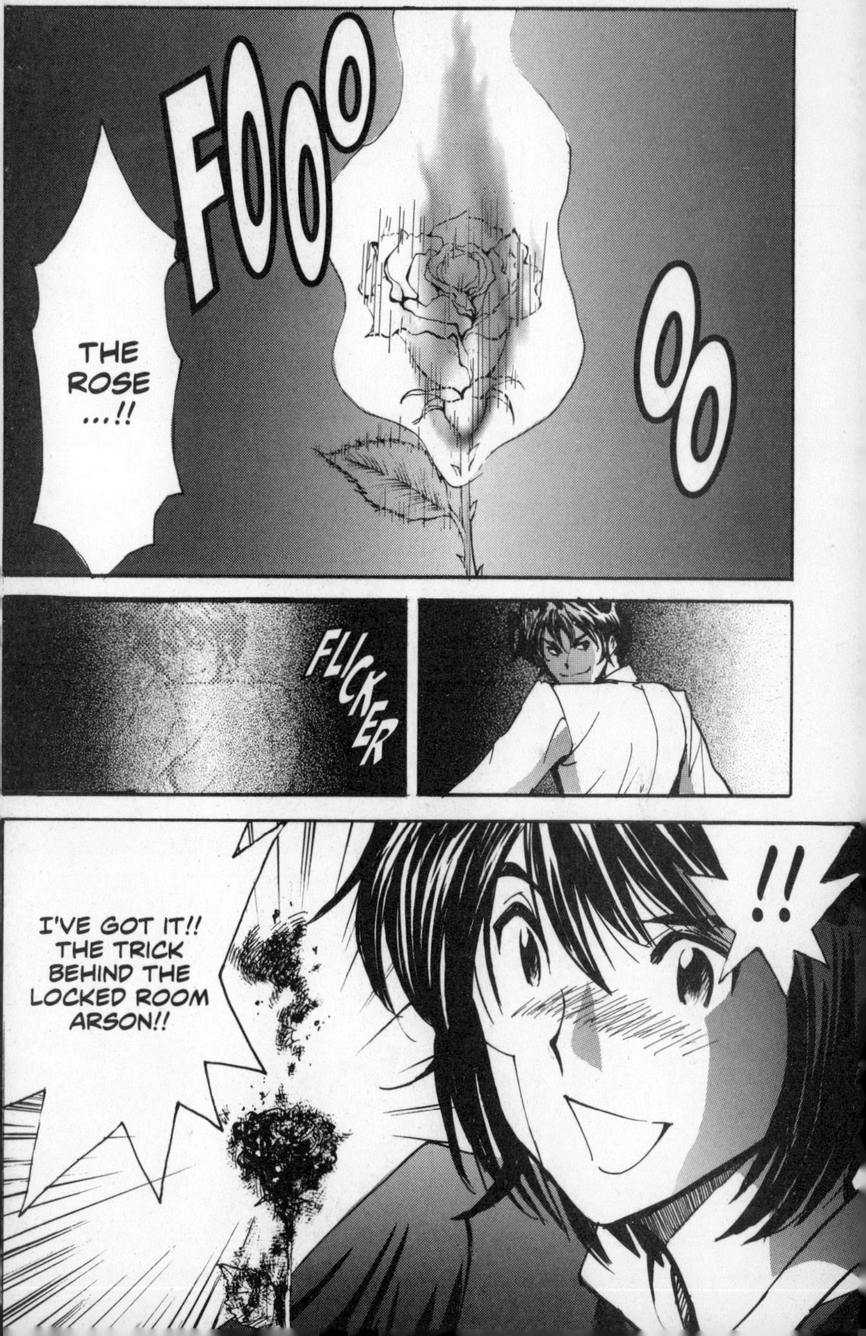
FOOO
OO
THE ROSE ...!!
FLICKER
!!
I'VE GOT IT!! THE TRICK BEHIND THE LOCKED ROOM ARSON!!

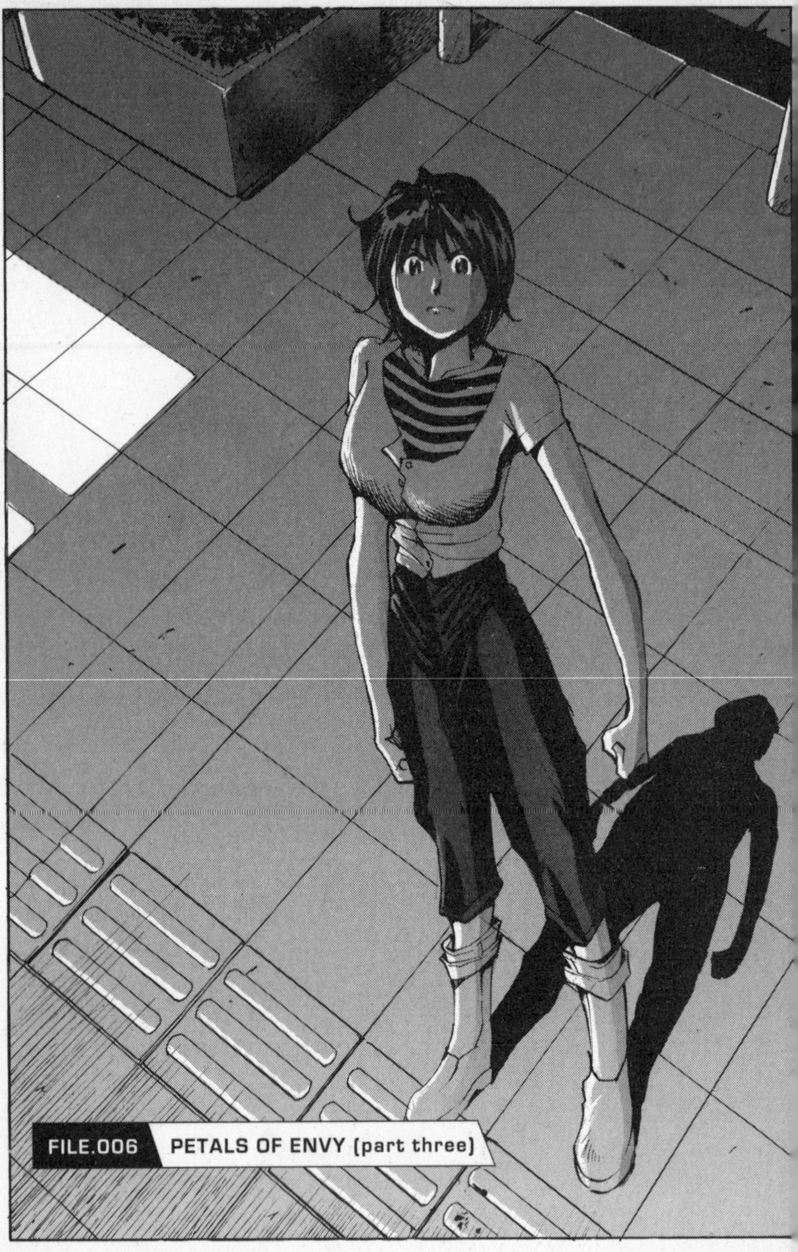
FILE.006
PETALS OF ENVY (part three)

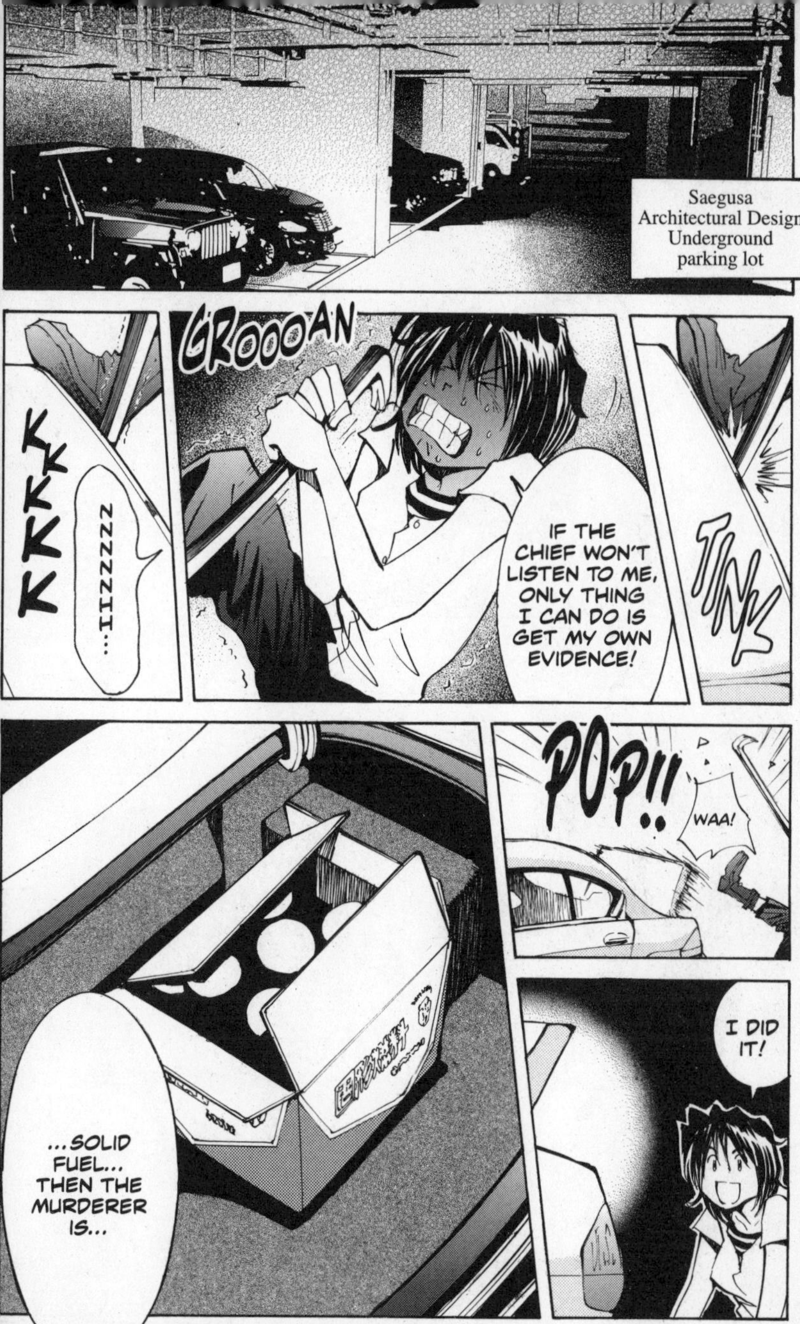
Saegusa Architectural Design Underground parking lot
TINK
GROOOAN
IF THE CHIEF WON'T LISTEN TO ME, ONLY THING I CAN DO IS GET MY OWN EVIDENCE!
KKKKKK
...IIZZZZZ
POP!!
WAA!
I DID IT!
...SOLID FUEL... THEN THE MURDERER IS...

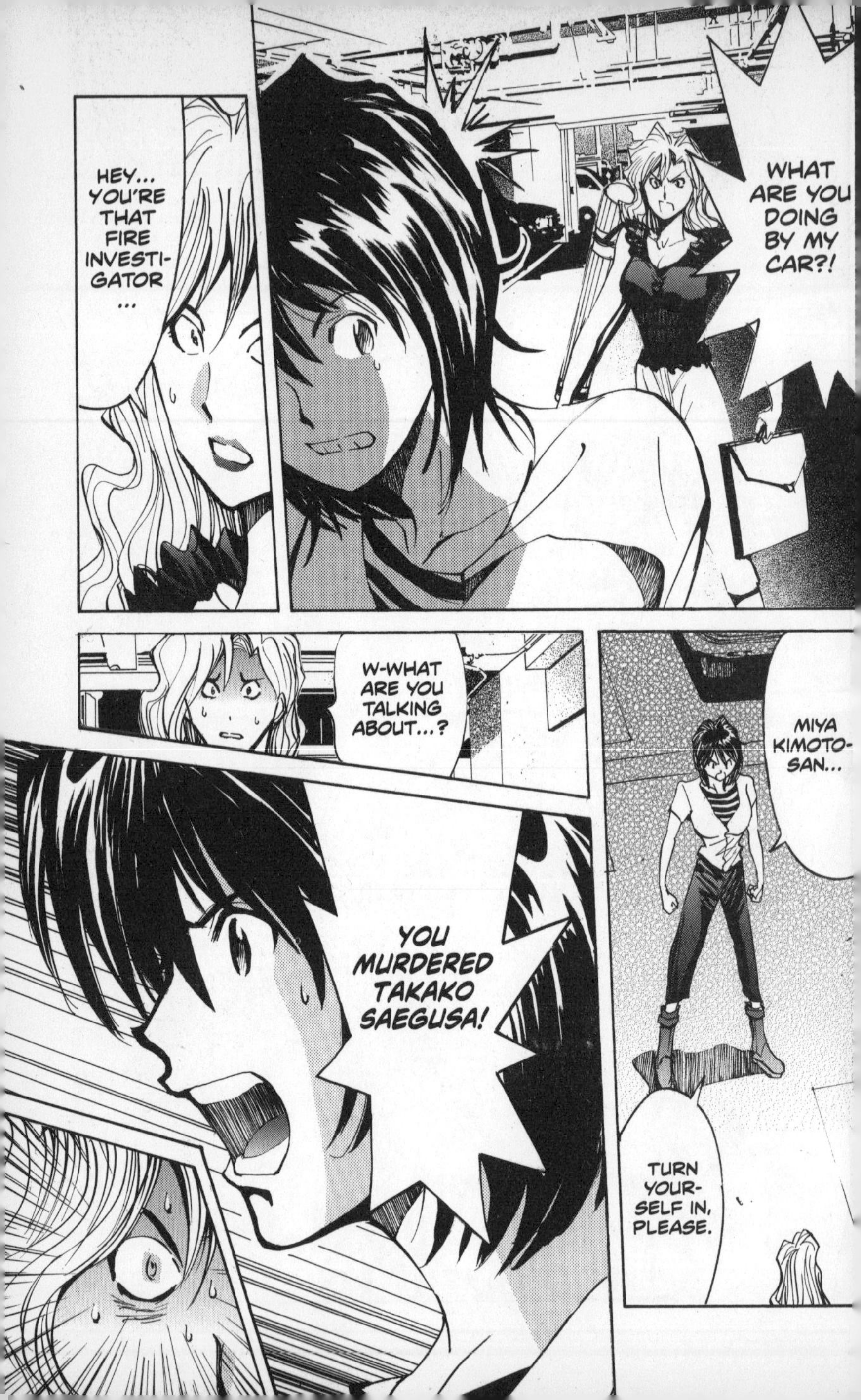
WHAT ARE YOU DOING BY MY CAR?!
HEY... YOU'RE THAT FIRE INVESTIGATOR...
MIYA KIMOTO-SAN...
TURN YOURSELF IN, PLEASE.
W-WHAT ARE YOU TALKING ABOUT...?
YOU MURDERED TAKAKO SAEGUSA!

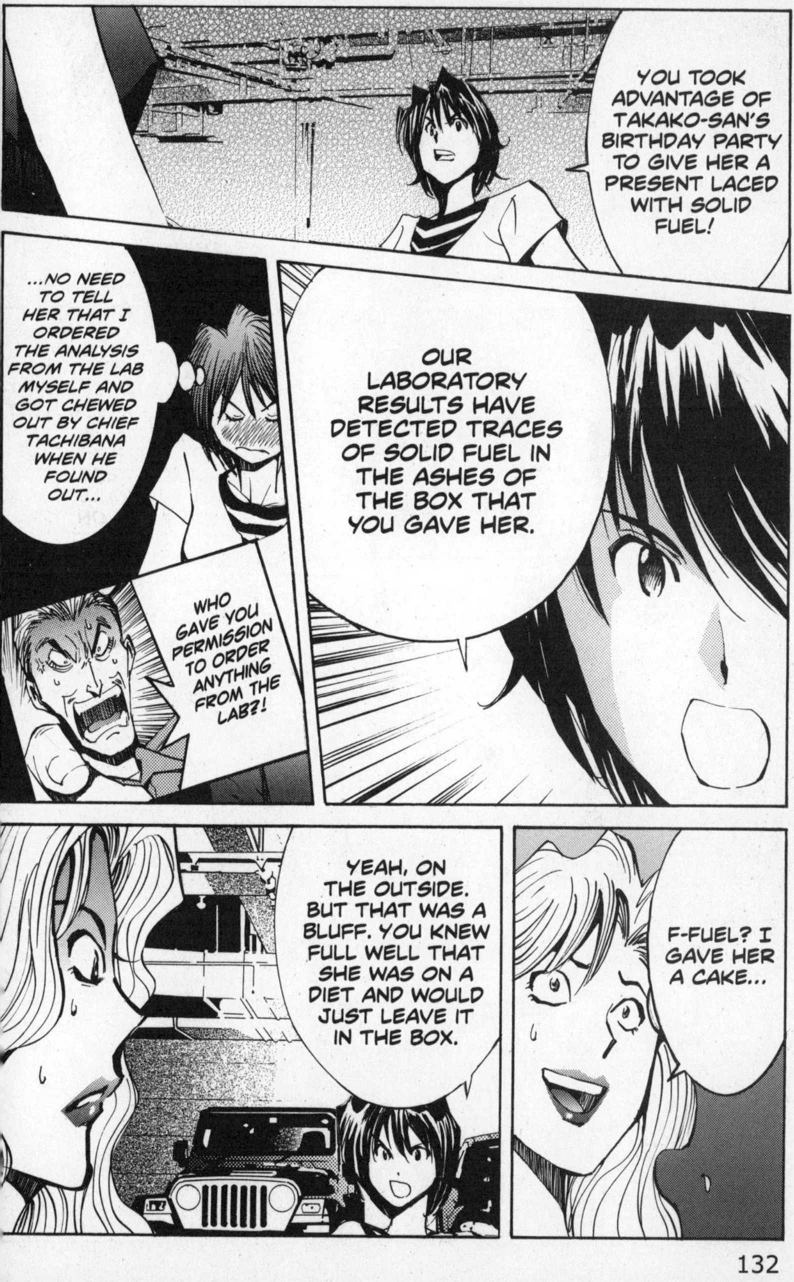
YOU TOOK ADVANTAGE OF TAKAKO-SAN'S BIRTHDAY PARTY TO GIVE HER A PRESENT LACED WITH SOLID FUEL!
OUR LABORATORY RESULTS HAVE DETECTED TRACES OF SOLID FUEL IN THE ASHES OF THE BOX THAT YOU GAVE HER.
...NO NEED TO TELL HER THAT I ORDERED THE ANALYSIS FROM THE LAB MYSELF AND GOT CHEWED OUT BY CHIEF TACHIBANA WHEN HE FOUND OUT...
WHO GAVE YOU PERMISSION TO ORDER ANYTHING FROM THE LAB?!
F-FUEL? I GAVE HER A CAKE...
YEAH, ON THE OUTSIDE. BUT THAT WAS A BLUFF. YOU KNEW FULL WELL THAT SHE WAS ON A DIET AND WOULD JUST LEAVE IT IN THE BOX.

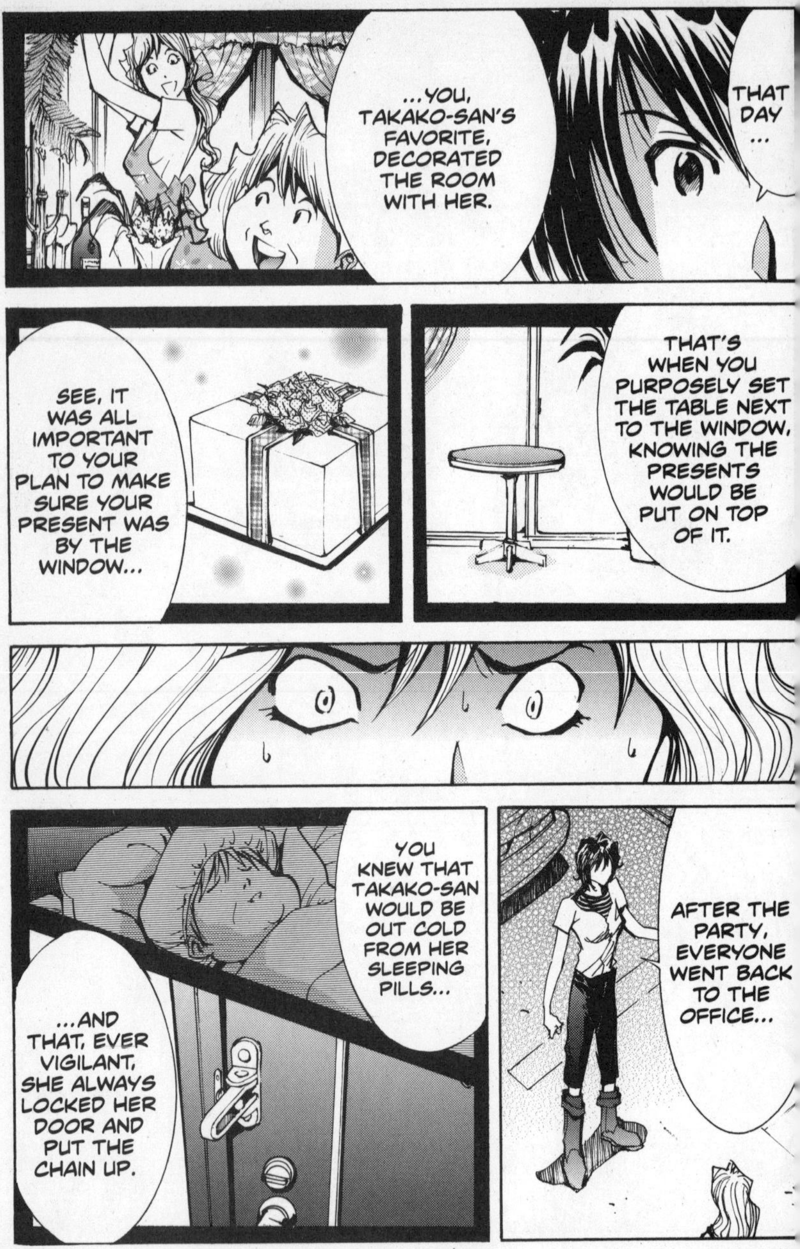
THAT DAY ...
...YOU, TAKAKO-SAN'S FAVORITE, DECORATED THE ROOM WITH HER.
THAT'S WHEN YOU PURPOSELY SET THE TABLE NEXT TO THE WINDOW, KNOWING THE PRESENTS WOULD BE PUT ON TOP OF IT.
SEE, IT WAS ALL IMPORTANT TO YOUR PLAN TO MAKE SURE YOUR PRESENT WAS BY THE WINDOW...
AFTER THE PARTY, EVERYONE WENT BACK TO THE OFFICE...
YOU KNEW THAT TAKAKO-SAN WOULD BE OUT COLD FROM HER SLEEPING PILLS...
...AND THAT, EVER VIGILANT, SHE ALWAYS LOCKED HER DOOR AND PUT THE CHAIN UP.

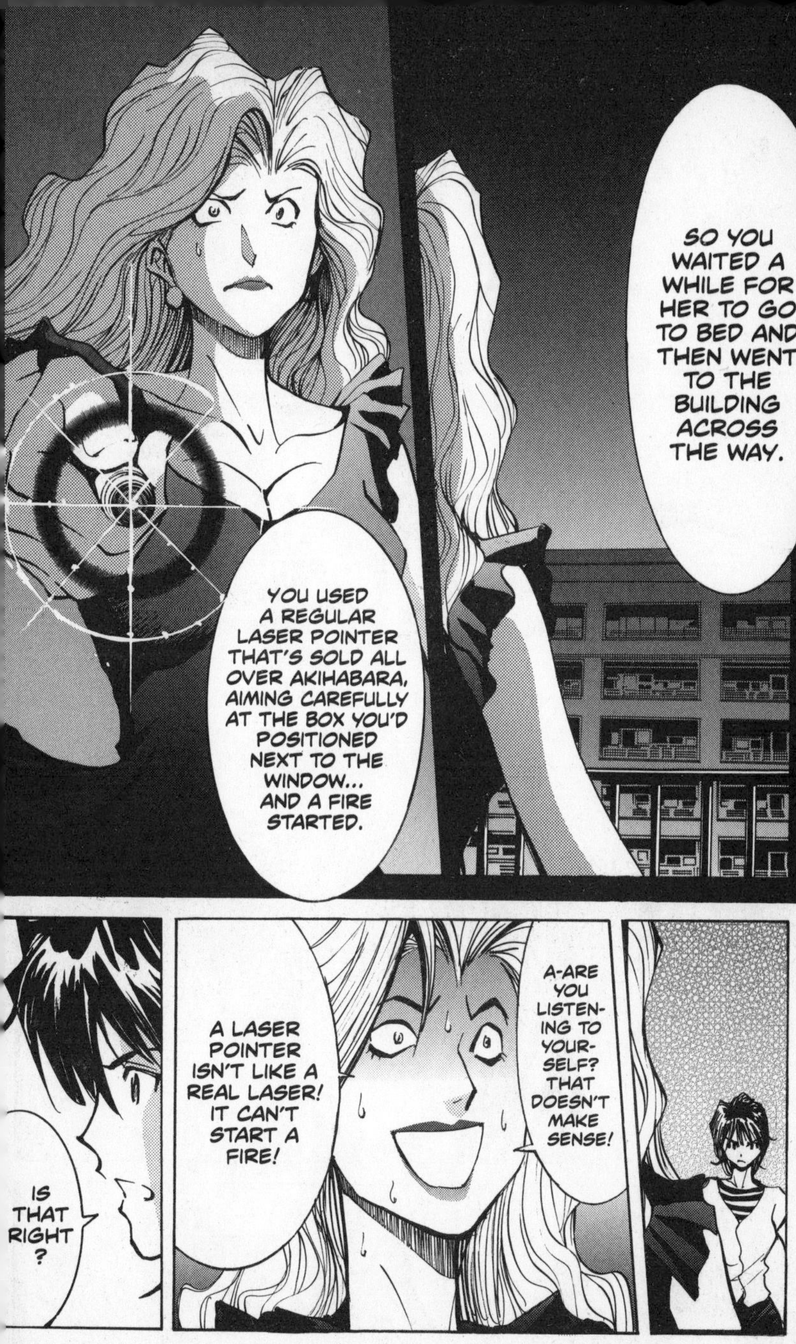
SO YOU WAITED A WHILE FOR HER TO GO TO BED AND THEN WENT TO THE BUILDING ACROSS THE WAY.
YOU USED A REGULAR LASER POINTER THAT'S SOLD ALL OVER AKIHABARA, AIMING CAREFULLY AT THE BOX YOU'D POSITIONED NEXT TO THE WINDOW... AND A FIRE STARTED.
A-ARE YOU LISTEN-ING TO YOUR-SELF? THAT DOESN'T MAKE SENSE!
A LASER POINTER ISN'T LIKE A REAL LASER! IT CAN'T START A FIRE!
IS THAT RIGHT?

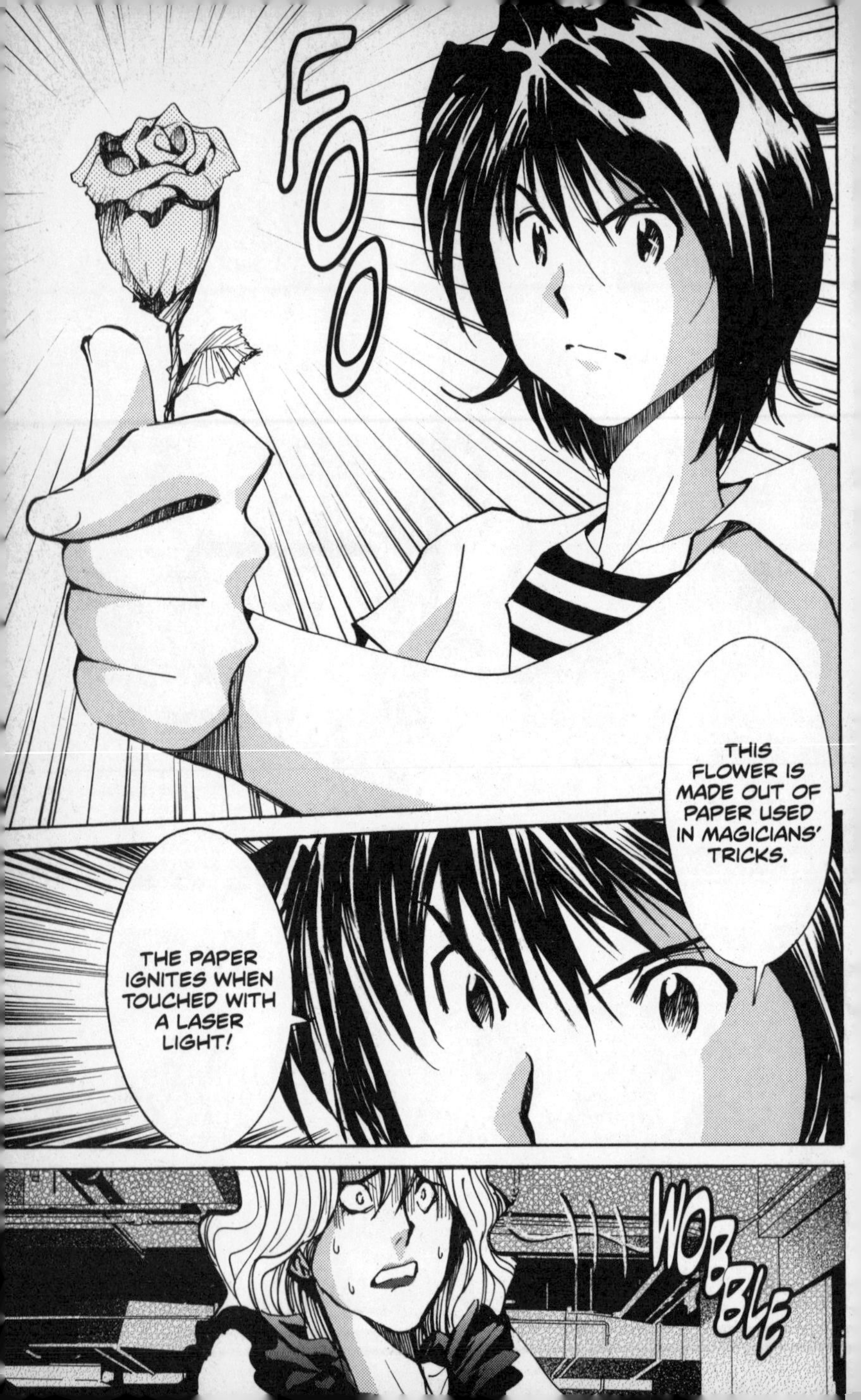
FOOO
THIS FLOWER IS MADE OUT OF PAPER USED IN MAGICIANS' TRICKS.
THE PAPER IGNITES WHEN TOUCHED WITH A LASER LIGHT!
WOBBLE

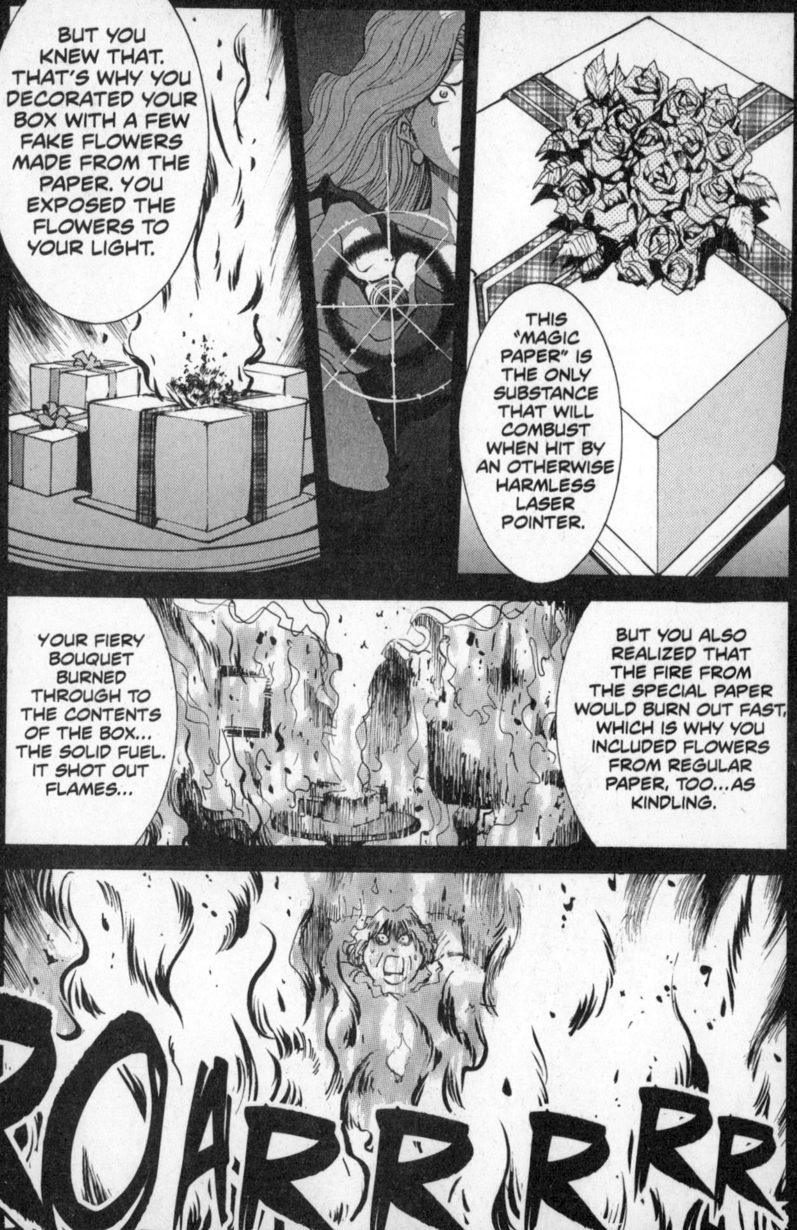
THIS "MAGIC PAPER" IS THE ONLY SUBSTANCE THAT WILL COMBUST WHEN HIT BY AN OTHERWISE HARMLESS LASER POINTER.
BUT YOU KNEW THAT. THAT'S WHY YOU DECORATED YOUR BOX WITH A FEW FAKE FLOWERS MADE FROM THE PAPER. YOU EXPOSED THE FLOWERS TO YOUR LIGHT.
BUT YOU ALSO REALIZED THAT THE FIRE FROM THE SPECIAL PAPER WOULD BURN OUT FAST, WHICH IS WHY YOU INCLUDED FLOWERS FROM REGULAR PAPER, TOO...AS KINDLING.
YOUR FIERY BOUQUET BURNED THROUGH TO THE CONTENTS OF THE BOX... THE SOLID FUEL. IT SHOT OUT FLAMES...
ROARRRRR

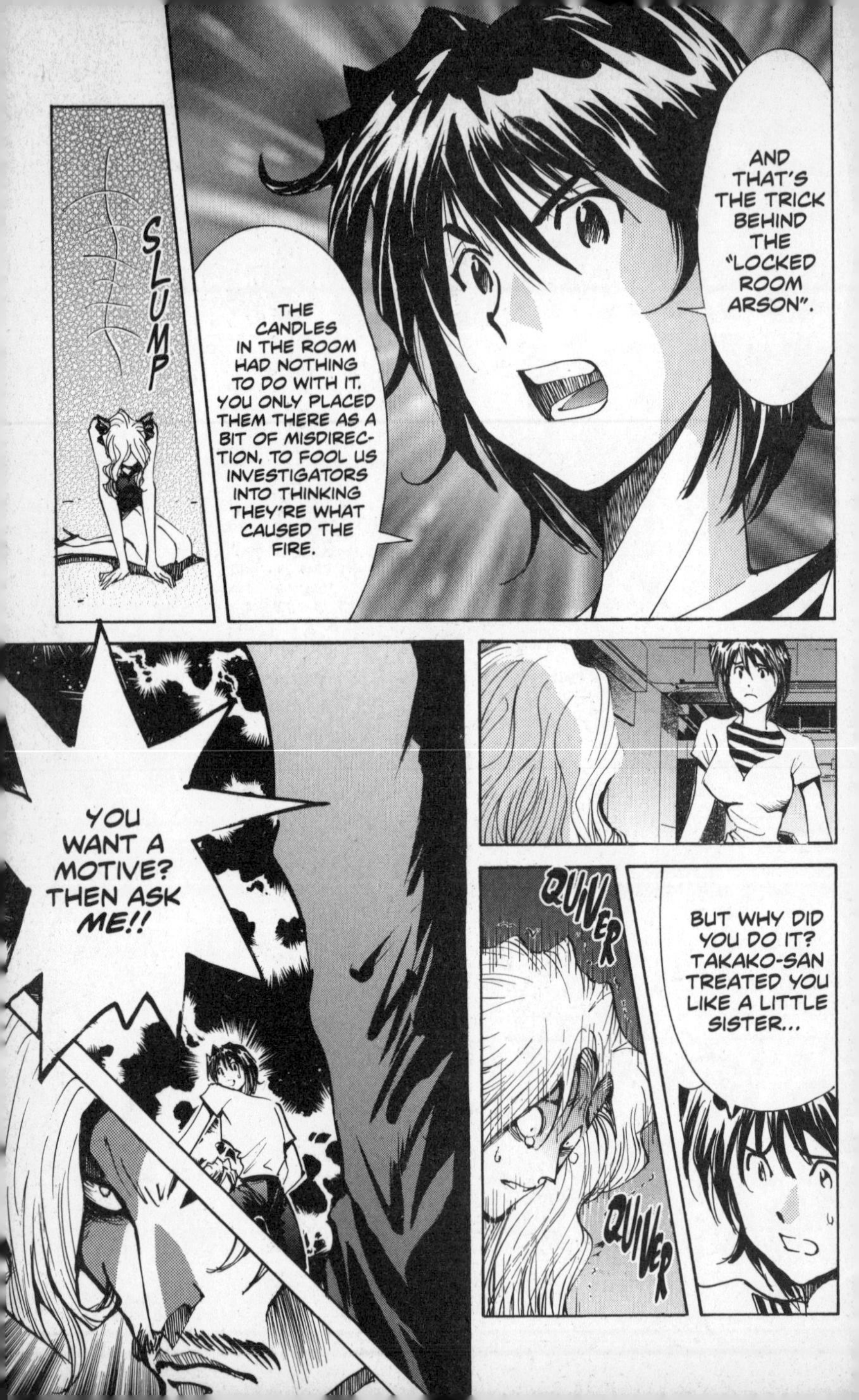
AND THAT'S THE TRICK BEHIND THE "LOCKED ROOM ARSON".
THE CANDLES IN THE ROOM HAD NOTHING TO DO WITH IT. YOU ONLY PLACED THEM THERE AS A BIT OF MISDIREC-TION, TO FOOL US INVESTIGATORS INTO THINKING THEY'RE WHAT CAUSED THE FIRE.
SLUMP
BUT WHY DID YOU DO IT? TAKAKO-SAN TREATED YOU LIKE A LITTLE SISTER...
QUIVER
QUIVER
YOU WANT A MOTIVE? THEN ASK ME!!

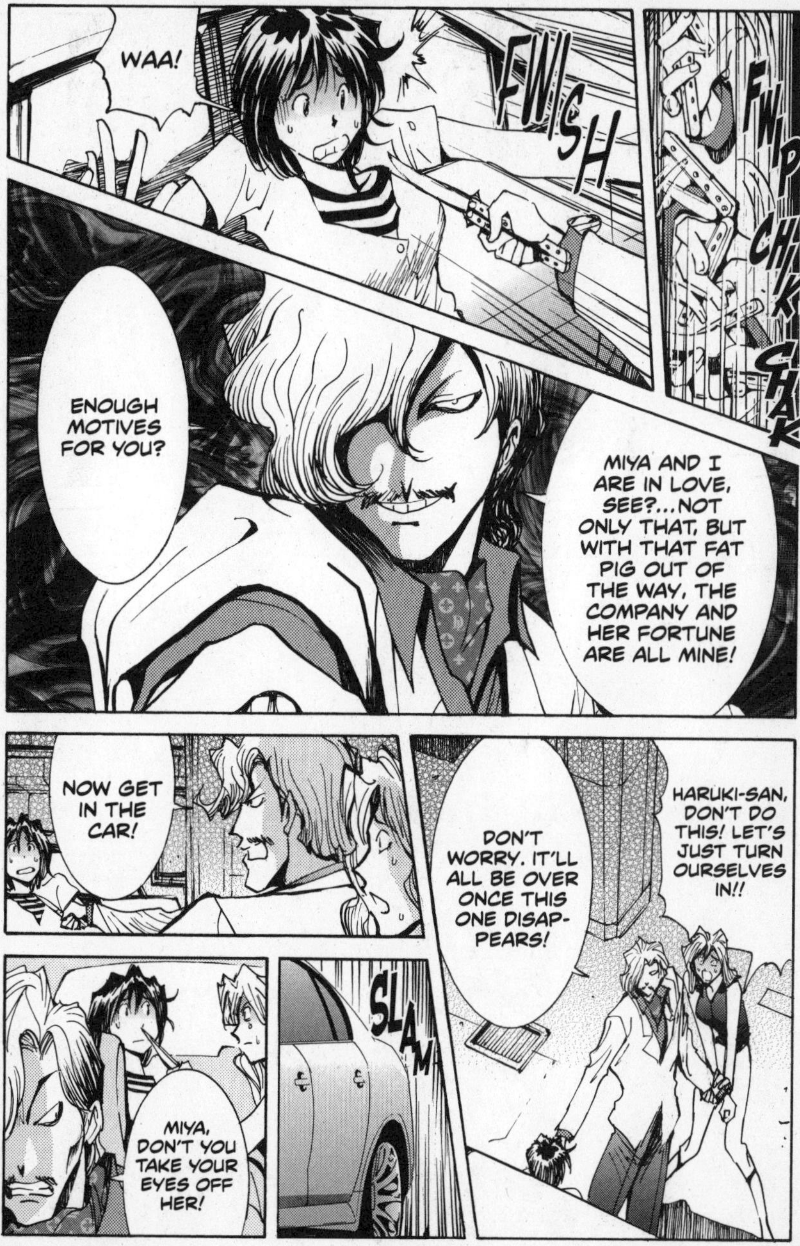
FWIP
CHIK
CHAK
WAA!
FWISH
MIYA AND I ARE IN LOVE, SEE?...NOT ONLY THAT, BUT WITH THAT FAT PIG OUT OF THE WAY, THE COMPANY AND HER FORTUNE ARE ALL MINE!
ENOUGH MOTIVES FOR YOU?
HARUKI-SAN, DON'T DO THIS! LET'S JUST TURN OURSELVES IN!!
DON'T WORRY. IT'LL ALL BE OVER ONCE THIS ONE DISAP-PEARS!
NOW GET IN THE CAR!
SLAM
MIYA, DON'T YOU TAKE YOUR EYES OFF HER!

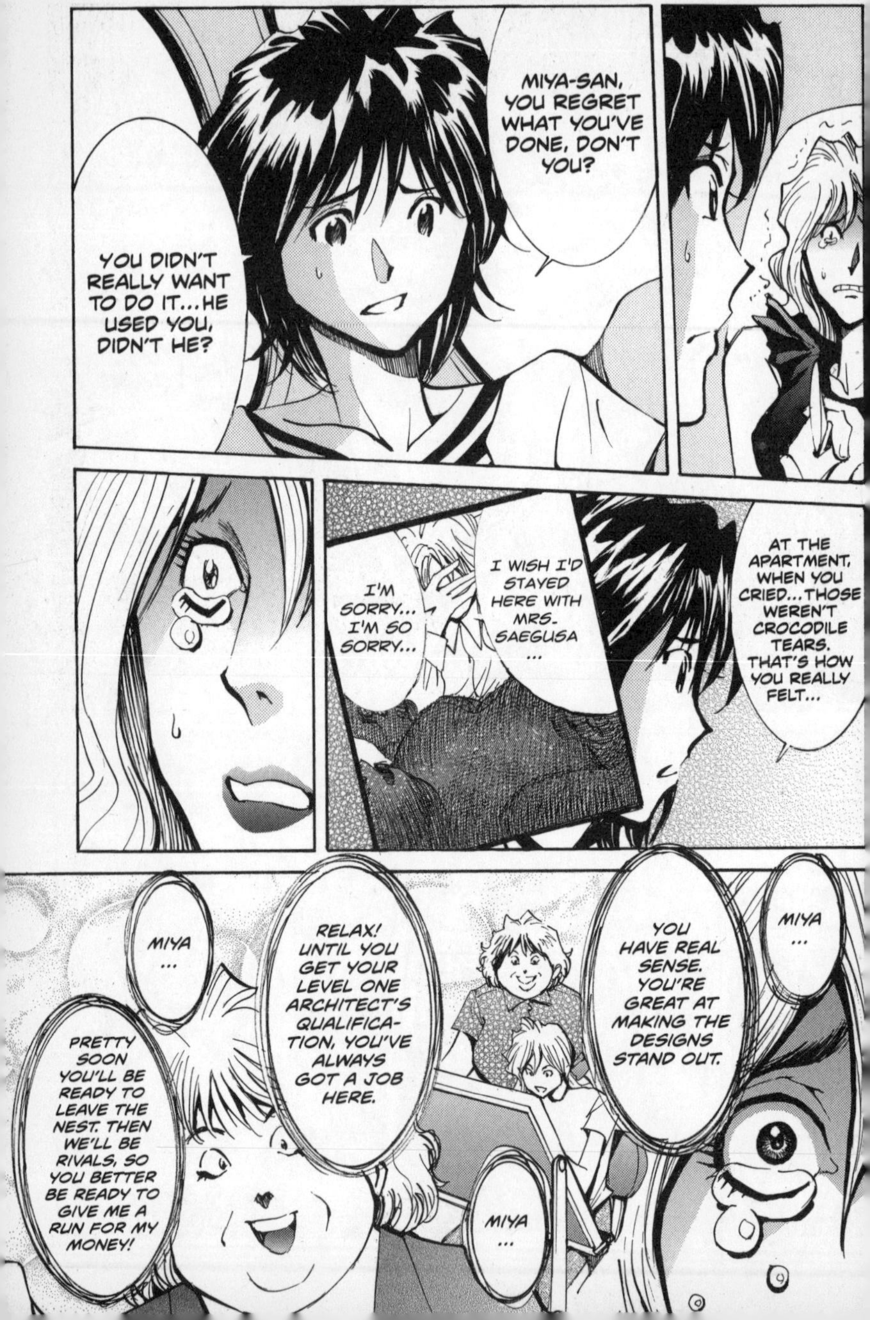
MIYA-SAN, YOU REGRET WHAT YOU'VE DONE, DON'T YOU?
YOU DIDN'T REALLY WANT TO DO IT...HE USED YOU, DIDN'T HE?
AT THE APARTMENT, WHEN YOU CRIED...THOSE WEREN'T CROCODILE TEARS. THAT'S HOW YOU REALLY FELT...
I WISH I'D STAYED HERE WITH MRS. SAEGUSA ...
I'M SORRY... I'M SO SORRY...
MIYA ...
YOU HAVE REAL SENSE. YOU'RE GREAT AT MAKING THE DESIGNS STAND OUT.
RELAX! UNTIL YOU GET YOUR LEVEL ONE ARCHITECT'S QUALIFICA-TION, YOU'VE ALWAYS GOT A JOB HERE.
MIYA ...
PRETTY SOON YOU'LL BE READY TO LEAVE THE NEST. THEN WE'LL BE RIVALS, SO YOU BETTER BE READY TO GIVE ME A RUN FOR MY MONEY!
MIYA ...

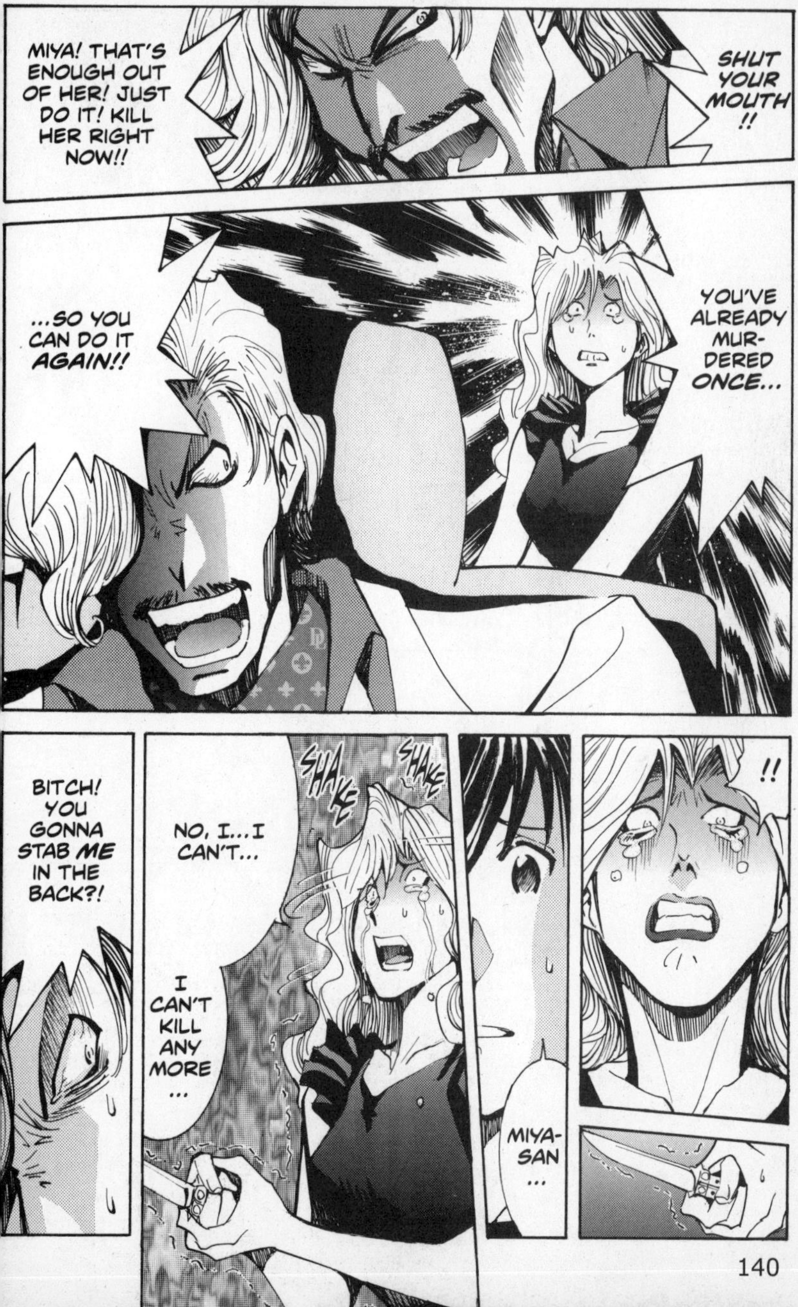
SHUT YOUR MOUTH !!
MIYA! THAT'S ENOUGH OUT OF HER! JUST DO IT! KILL HER RIGHT NOW!!
YOU'VE ALREADY MUR-DERED ONCE...
...SO YOU CAN DO IT AGAIN!!
!!
MIYA-SAN ...
SHAKE SHAKE
NO, I...I CAN'T...
I CAN'T KILL ANY MORE ...
BITCH! YOU GONNA STAB ME IN THE BACK?!

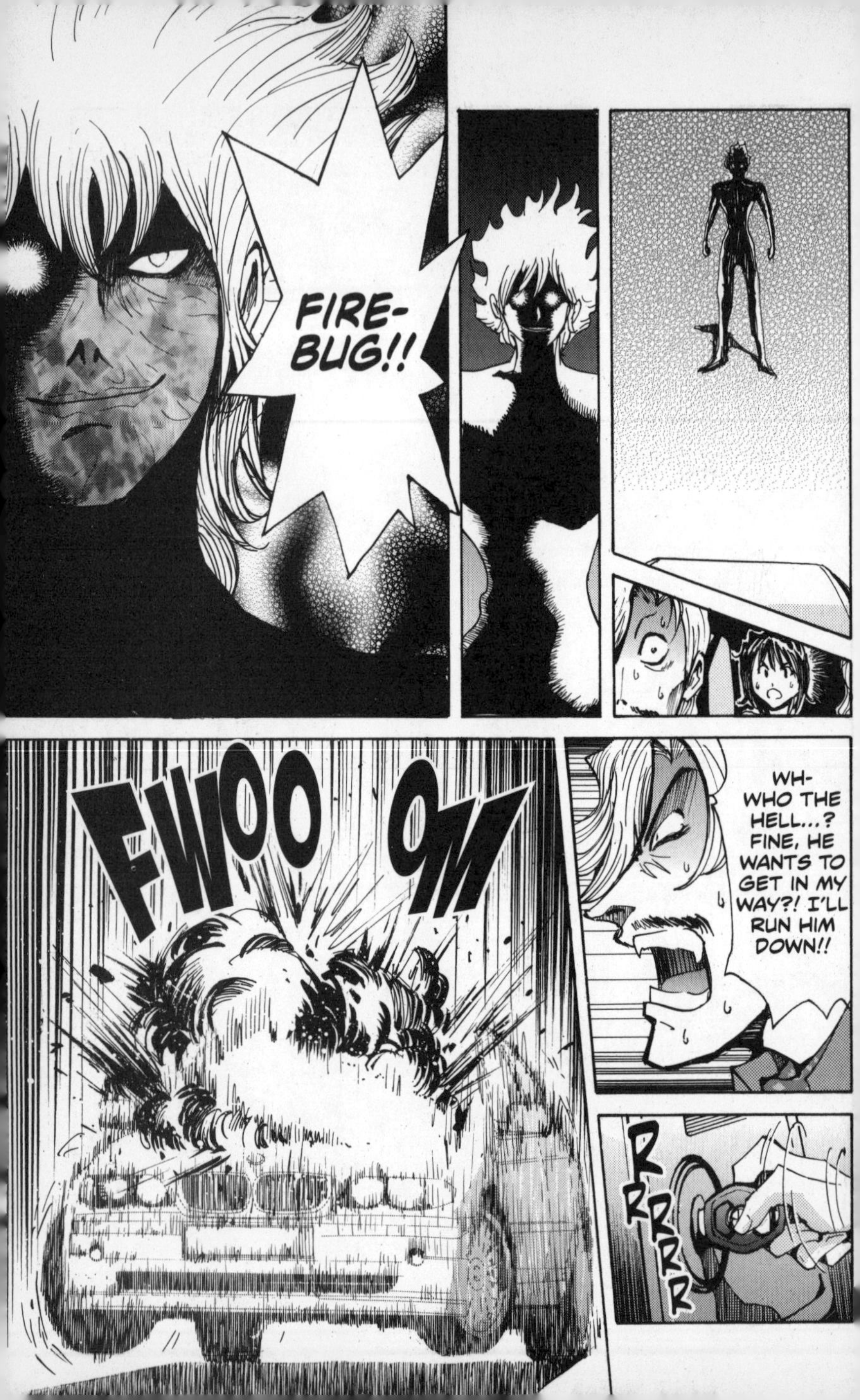
FIRE-BUG!!
WH- WHO THE HELL...? FINE, HE WANTS TO GET IN MY WAY?! I'LL RUN HIM DOWN!!
RRRRRR
FWOOOM

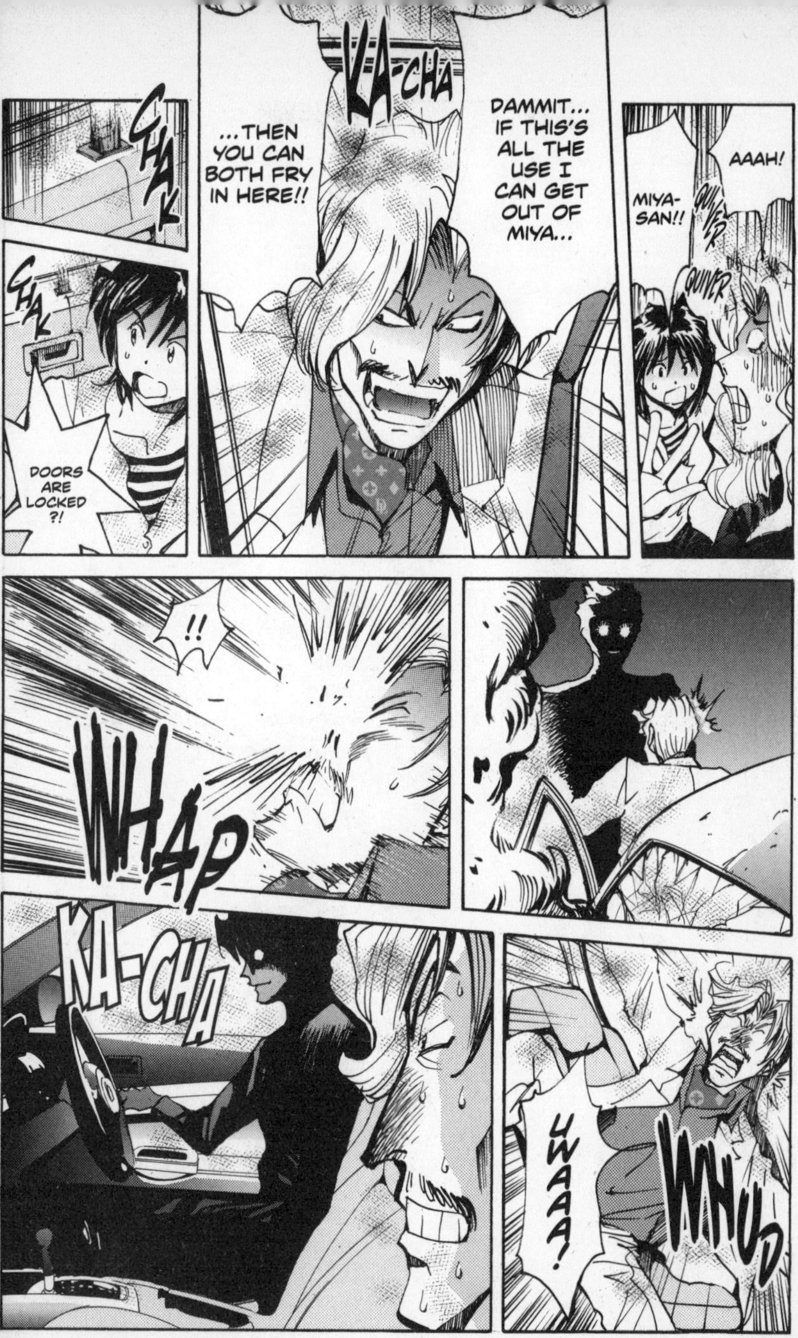
AAAH!
MIYA-SAN!!
QUIVER
QUIVER
KA-CHA
DAMMIT... IF THIS'S ALL THE USE I CAN GET OUT OF MIYA...
...THEN YOU CAN BOTH FRY IN HERE!!
CHAK
CHAK
DOORS ARE LOCKED ?!
!!
WHAP
WHUD
UWAAAA?
KA-CHA

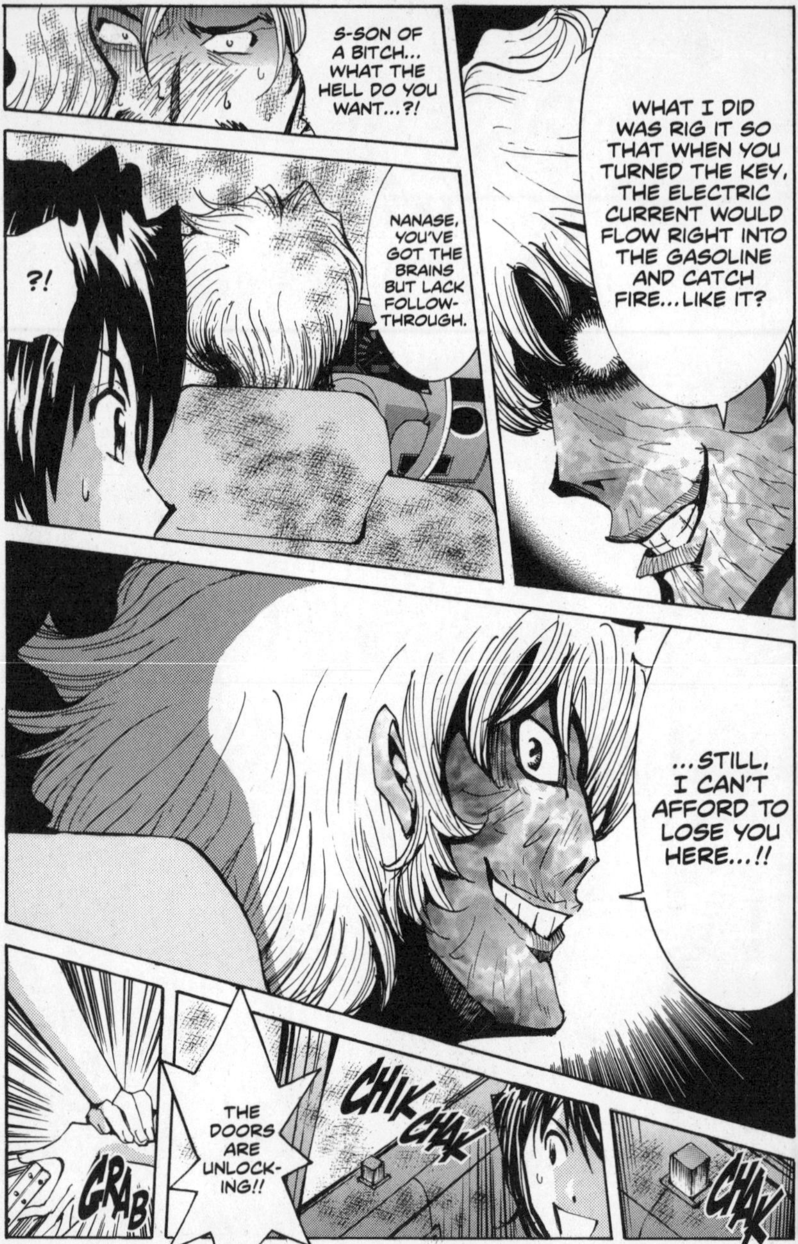
WHAT I DID WAS RIG IT SO THAT WHEN YOU TURNED THE KEY, THE ELECTRIC CURRENT WOULD FLOW RIGHT INTO THE GASOLINE AND CATCH FIRE...LIKE IT?
S-SON OF A BITCH... WHAT THE HELL DO YOU WANT...?!
NANASE, YOU'VE GOT THE BRAINS BUT LACK FOLLOW-THROUGH.
?!
...STILL, I CAN'T AFFORD TO LOSE YOU HERE...!!
CHAK
CHIK CHAK
THE DOORS ARE UNLOCK-ING!!
GRAB

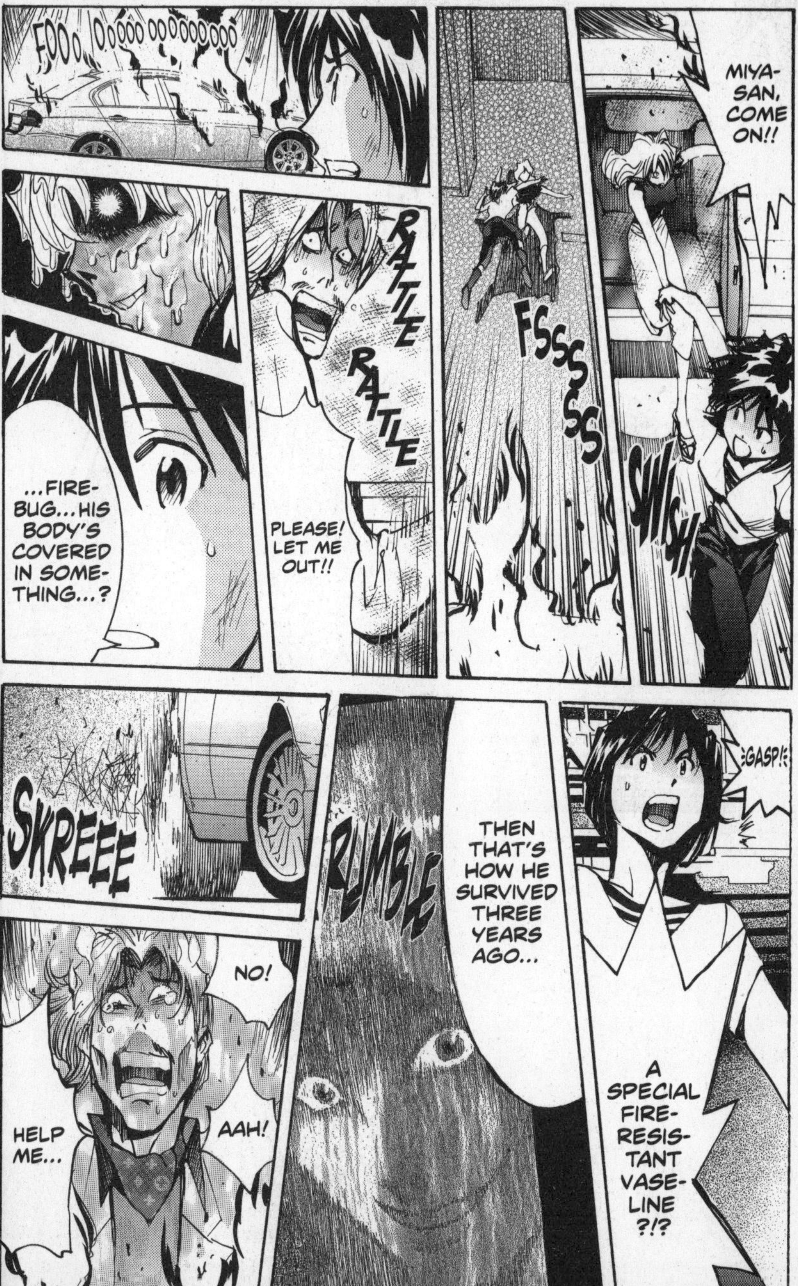
MIYA-SAN, COME ON!!
SWISH
FSSSSSS
FOOOOOOOO OOOOOOOOO
RATTLE RATTLE
PLEASE! LET ME OUT!!
...FIRE-BUG...HIS BODY'S COVERED IN SOME-THING...?
GASP!
THEN THAT'S HOW HE SURVIVED THREE YEARS AGO...
A SPECIAL FIRE-RESIS-TANT VASE-LINE ?!?
RUMBLE
SKREEE
NO!
AAH!
HELP ME...

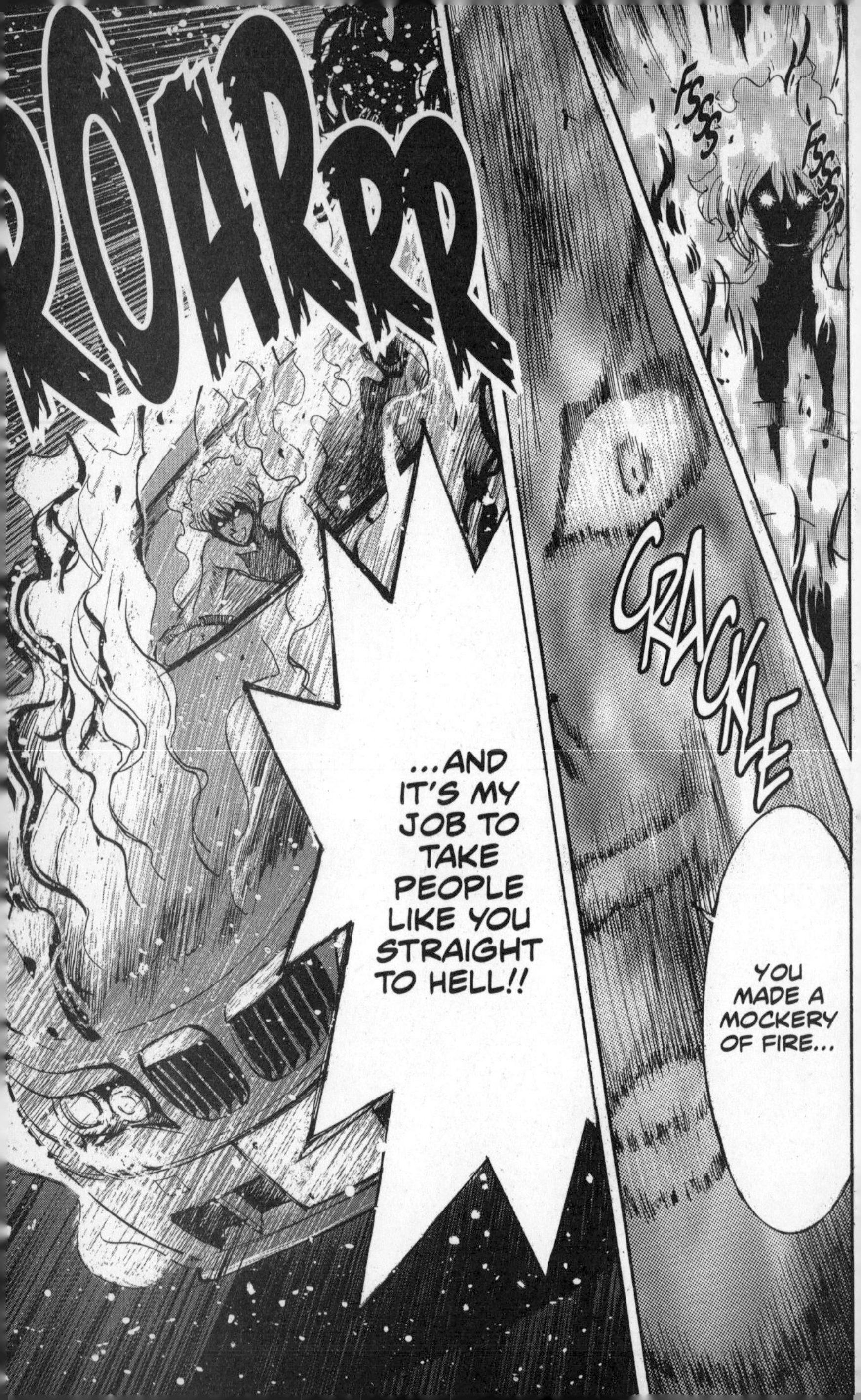
FSSS
FSSS
CRACKLE
YOU MADE A MOCKERY OF FIRE...
ROARRR
...AND IT'S MY JOB TO TAKE PEOPLE LIKE YOU STRAIGHT TO HELL!!

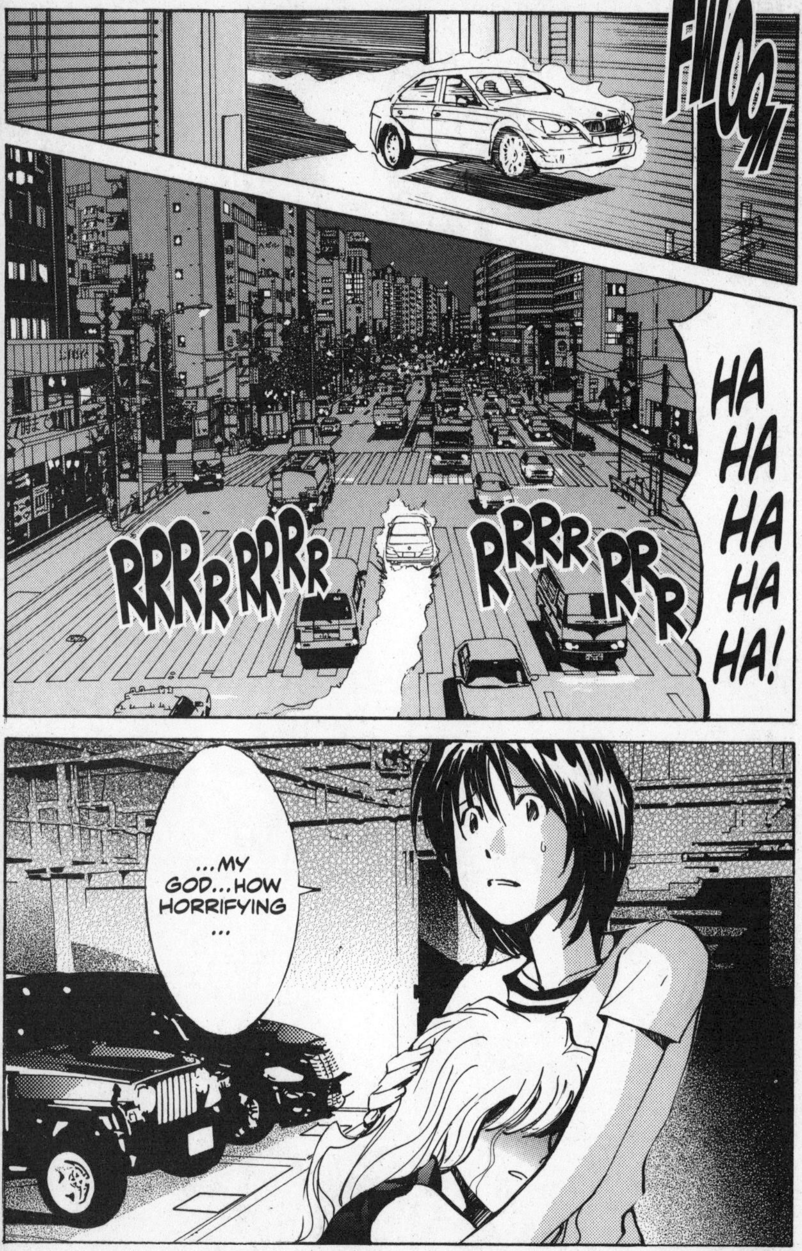
FWOOM
HA HA HA HA HA HA!
RRRR RRRR
RRRR RRR
...MY GOD...HOW HORRIFYING ...

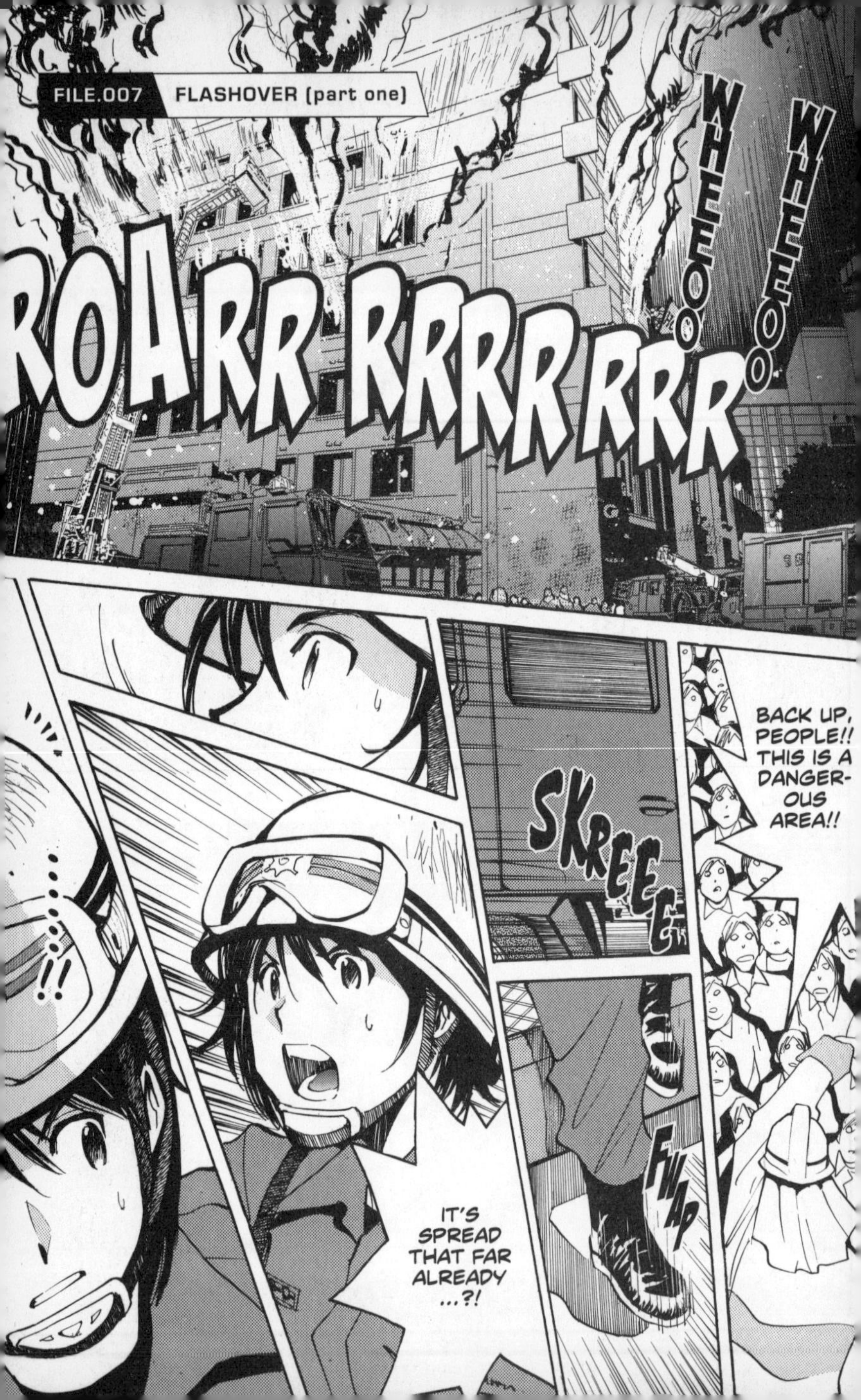
FILE.007 FLASHOVER (part one)
ROARR RRRRRRR
WHEEOO
WHEEOO
BACK UP, PEOPLE!! THIS IS A DANGER-OUS AREA!!
SKREEEE
FWAP
IT'S SPREAD THAT FAR ALREADY ...?!
......!!

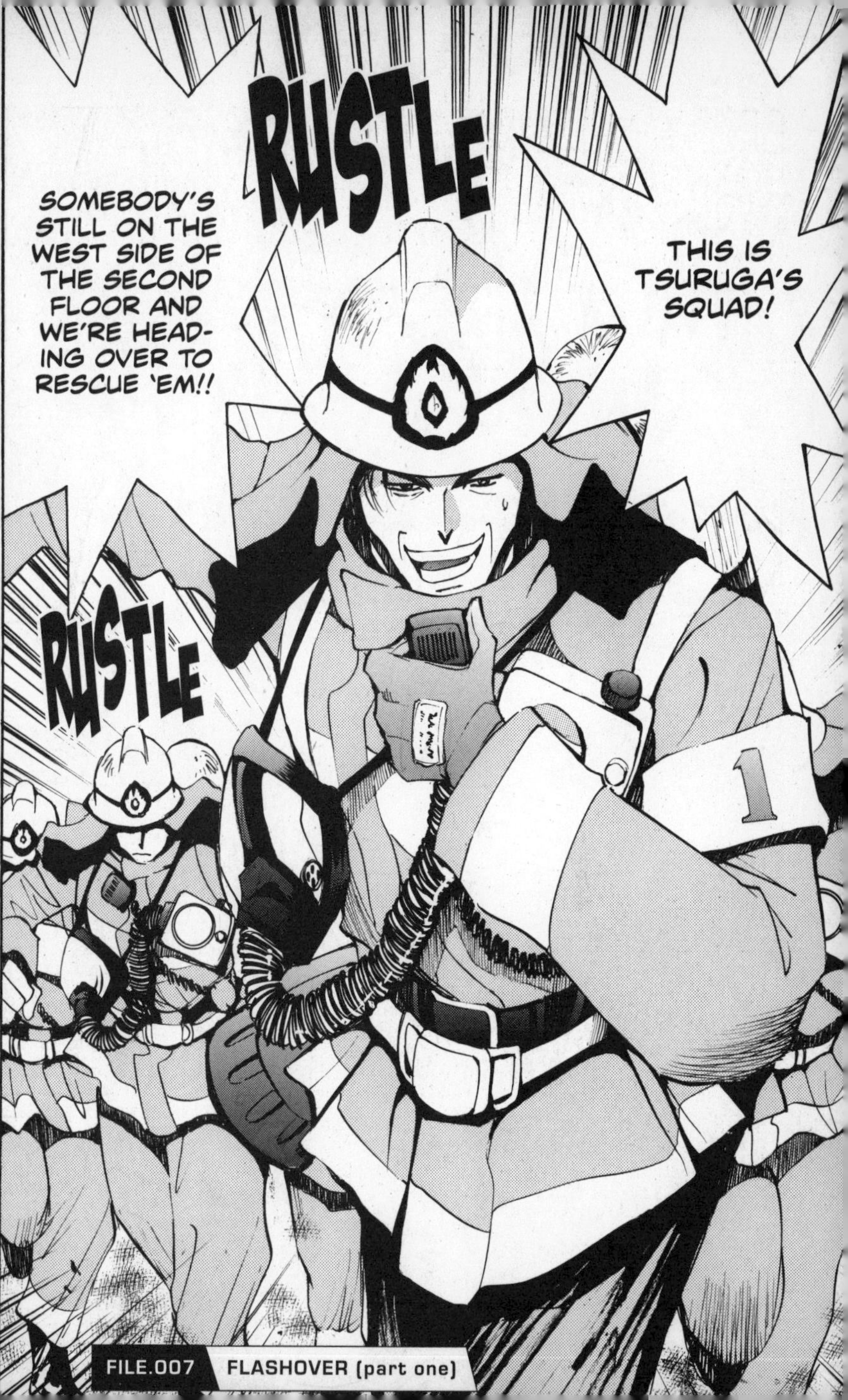
RUSTLE
THIS IS TSURUGA'S SQUAD!
SOMEBODY'S STILL ON THE WEST SIDE OF THE SECOND FLOOR AND WE'RE HEADING OVER TO RESCUE 'EM!!
RUSTLE
1

FILE.007 FLASHOVER (part one)

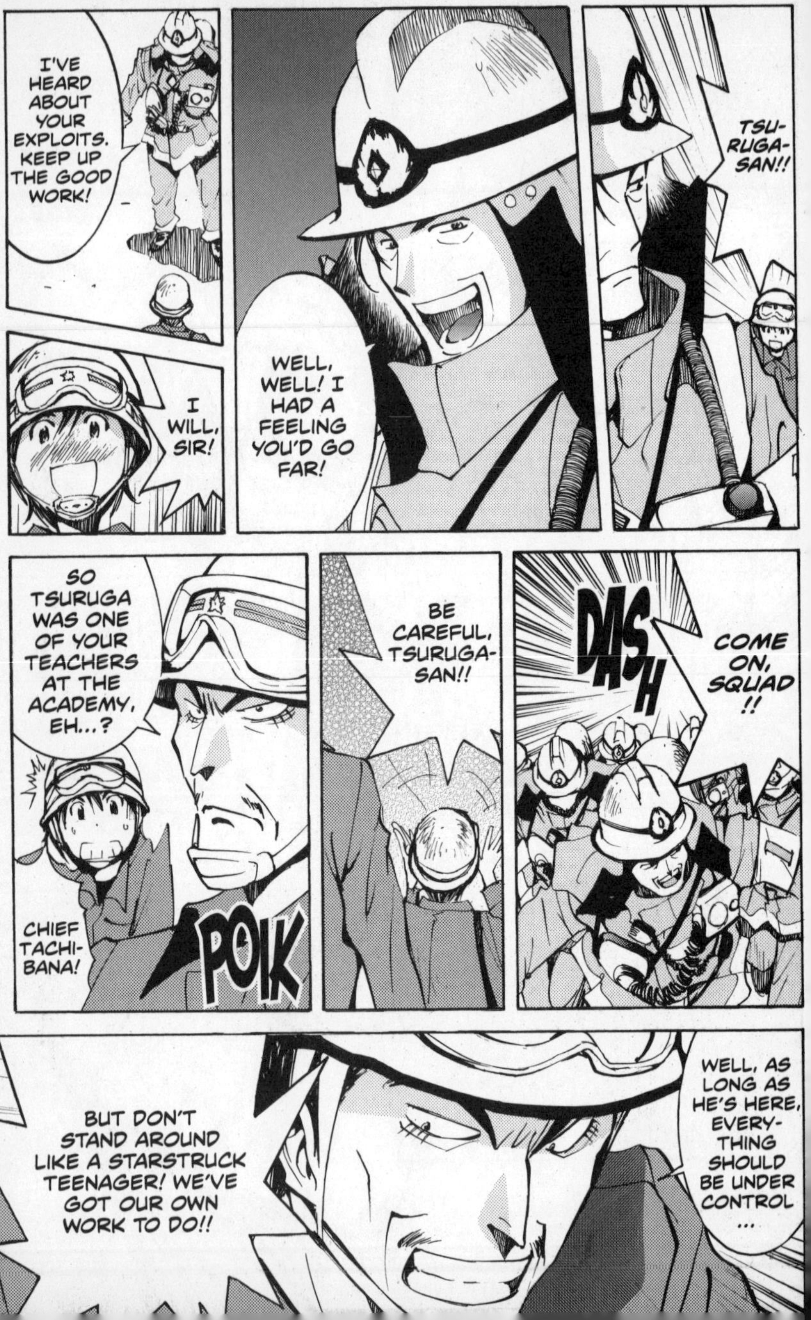
TSU-RUGA-SAN!!
WELL, WELL! I HAD A FEELING YOU'D GO FAR!
I'VE HEARD ABOUT YOUR EXPLOITS. KEEP UP THE GOOD WORK!
I WILL, SIR!
DASH
COME ON, SQUAD!!
BE CAREFUL, TSURUGA-SAN!!
SO TSURUGA WAS ONE OF YOUR TEACHERS AT THE ACADEMY, EH...?
POIK
CHIEF TACHI-BANA!
WELL, AS LONG AS HE'S HERE, EVERY-THING SHOULD BE UNDER CONTROL ...
BUT DON'T STAND AROUND LIKE A STARSTRUCK TEENAGER! WE'VE GOT OUR OWN WORK TO DO!!

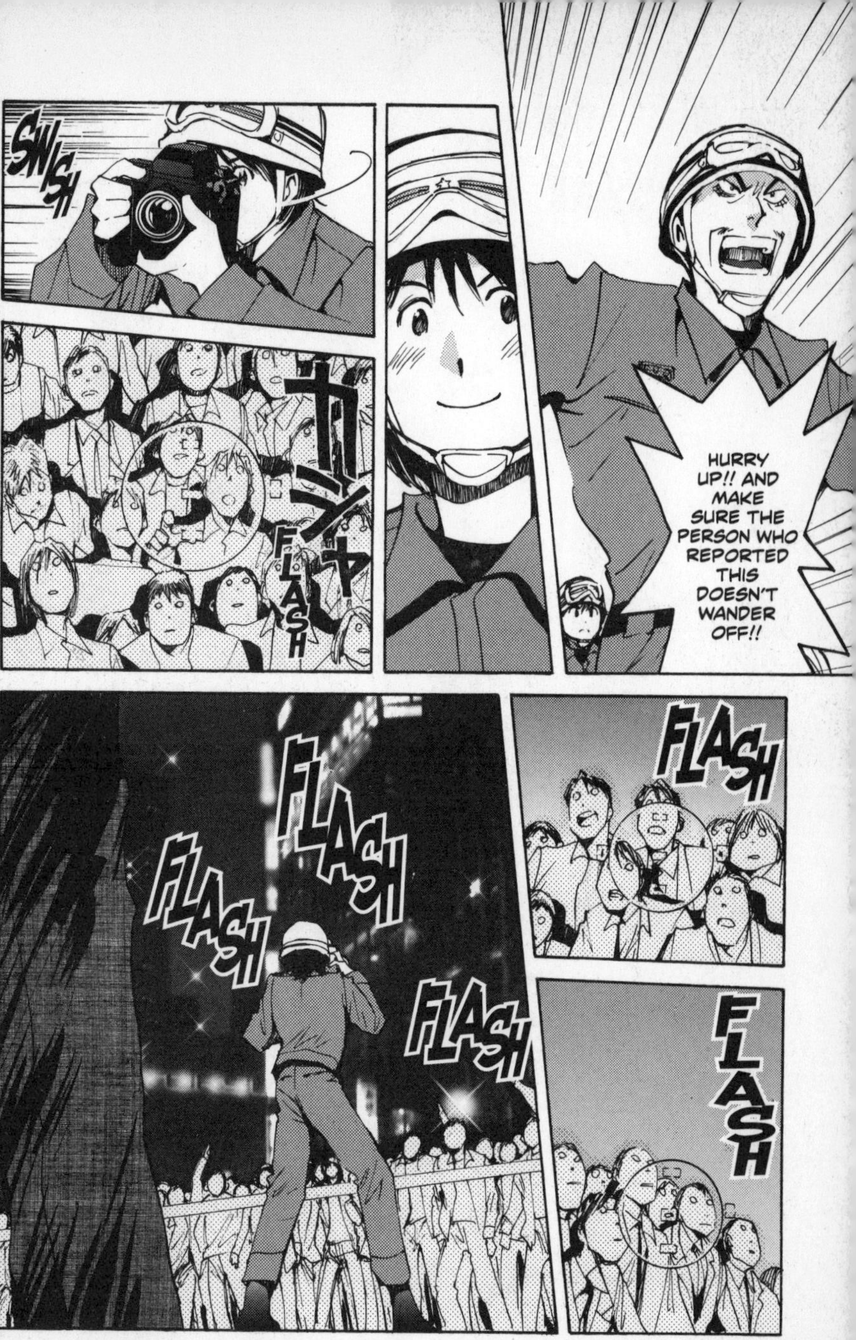
HURRY UP!! AND MAKE SURE THE PERSON WHO REPORTED THIS DOESN'T WANDER OFF!!
SWISH
ガシャ
FLASH
FLASH
FLASH
FLASH
FLASH
FLASH

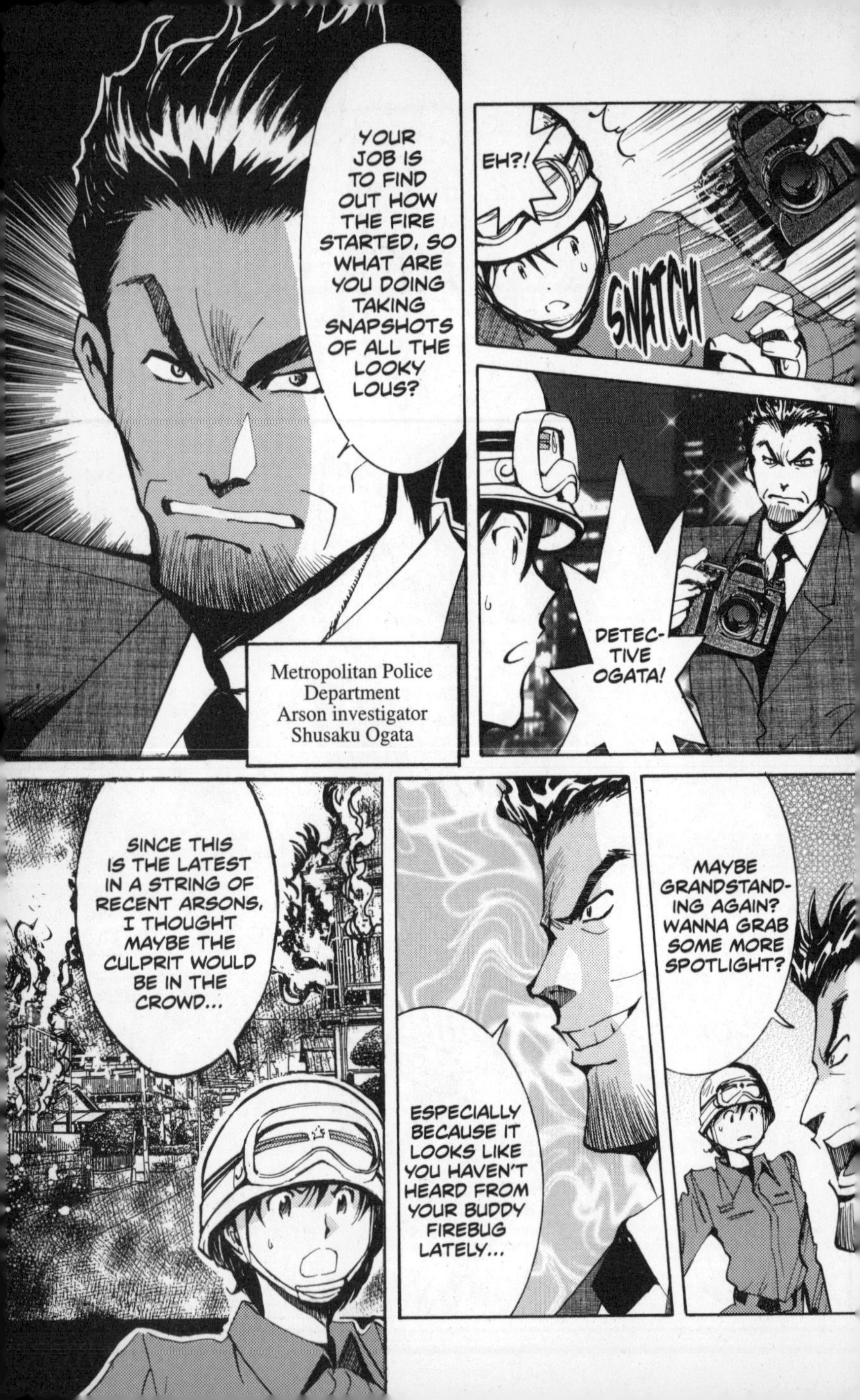
EH?!
SNATCH
DETEC-TIVE OGATA!
YOUR JOB IS TO FIND OUT HOW THE FIRE STARTED, SO WHAT ARE YOU DOING TAKING SNAPSHOTS OF ALL THE LOOKY LOUS?
Metropolitan Police Department Arson investigator Shusaku Ogata
MAYBE GRANDSTANDING AGAIN? WANNA GRAB SOME MORE SPOTLIGHT?
ESPECIALLY BECAUSE IT LOOKS LIKE YOU HAVEN'T HEARD FROM YOUR BUDDY FIREBUG LATELY...
SINCE THIS IS THE LATEST IN A STRING OF RECENT ARSONS, I THOUGHT MAYBE THE CULPRIT WOULD BE IN THE CROWD...

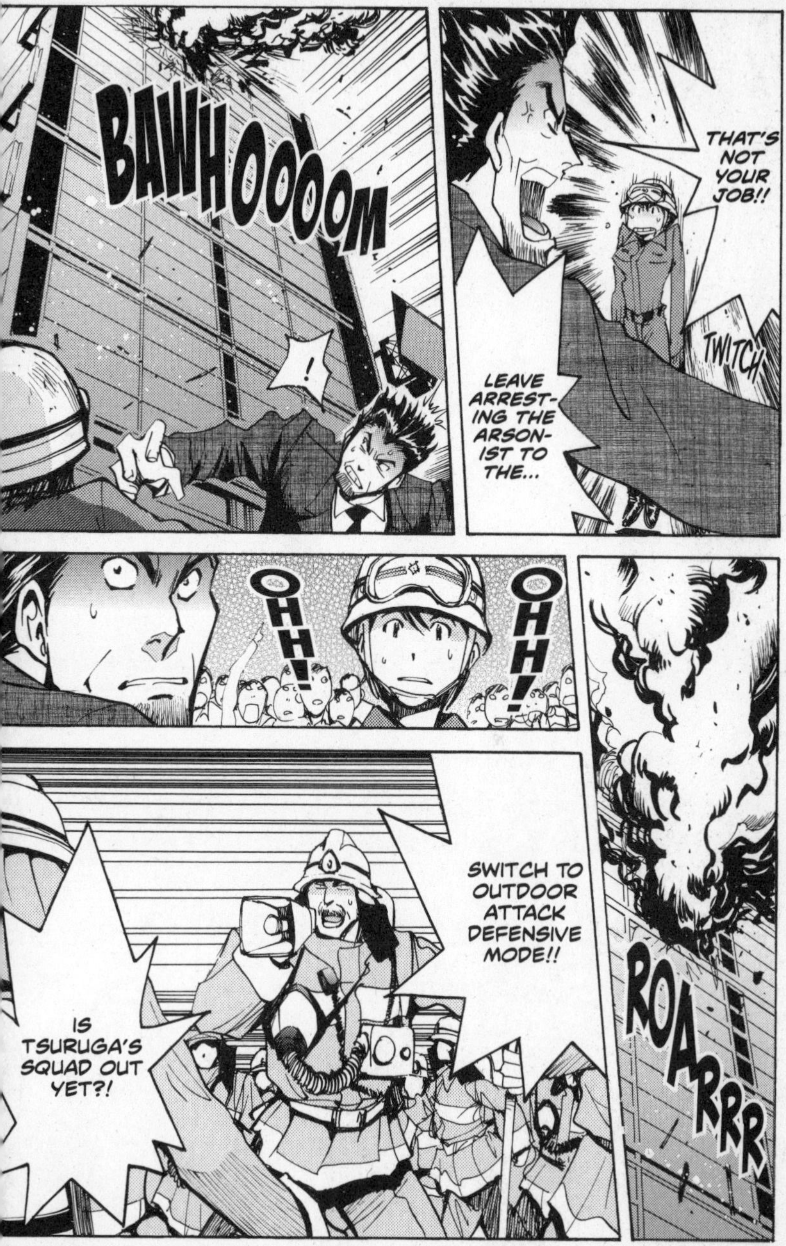
THAT'S NOT YOUR JOB!!
TWITCH
LEAVE ARREST-ING THE ARSON-IST TO THE...
BAWHOOOOM
!
ROARRR
OHH!!
OHH!!
SWITCH TO OUTDOOR ATTACK DEFENSIVE MODE!!
IS TSURUGA'S SQUAD OUT YET?!

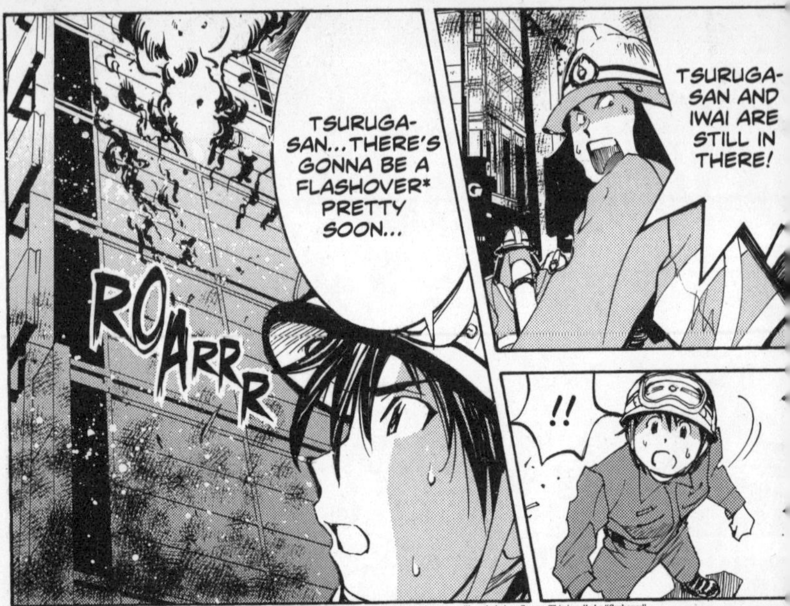
TSURUGA-SAN AND IWAI ARE STILL IN THERE!
!!
TSURUGA-SAN...THERE'S GONNA BE A FLASHOVER* PRETTY SOON...
ROARRR

* In a fire, when all released combustible gas accumulates and a certain temperature is surpassed, everything in the room will explode into flames. This is called a "flashover".

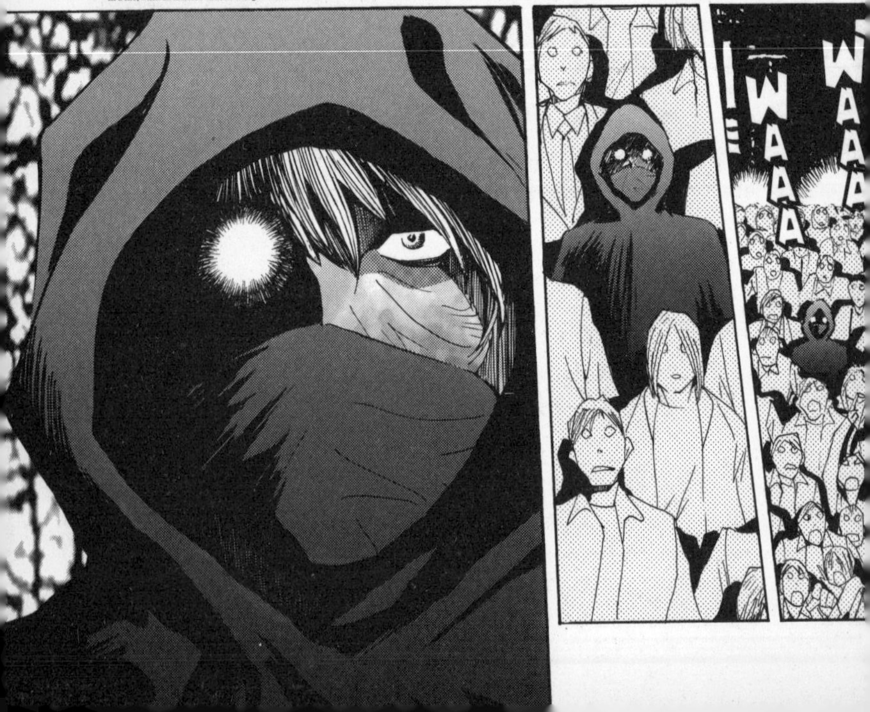
WAAAA
IWAAAA

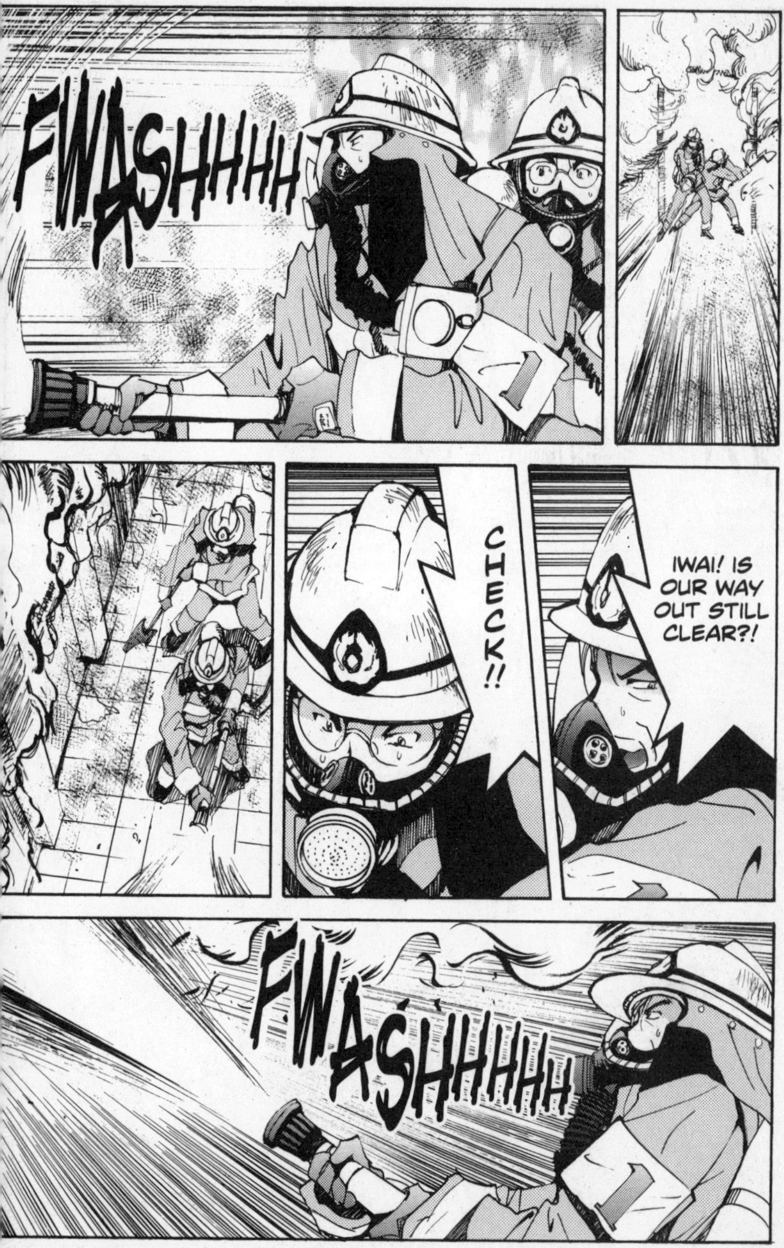
FWASHHHH
IWAI! IS OUR WAY OUT STILL CLEAR?!
CHECK!!
FWASHHHHH

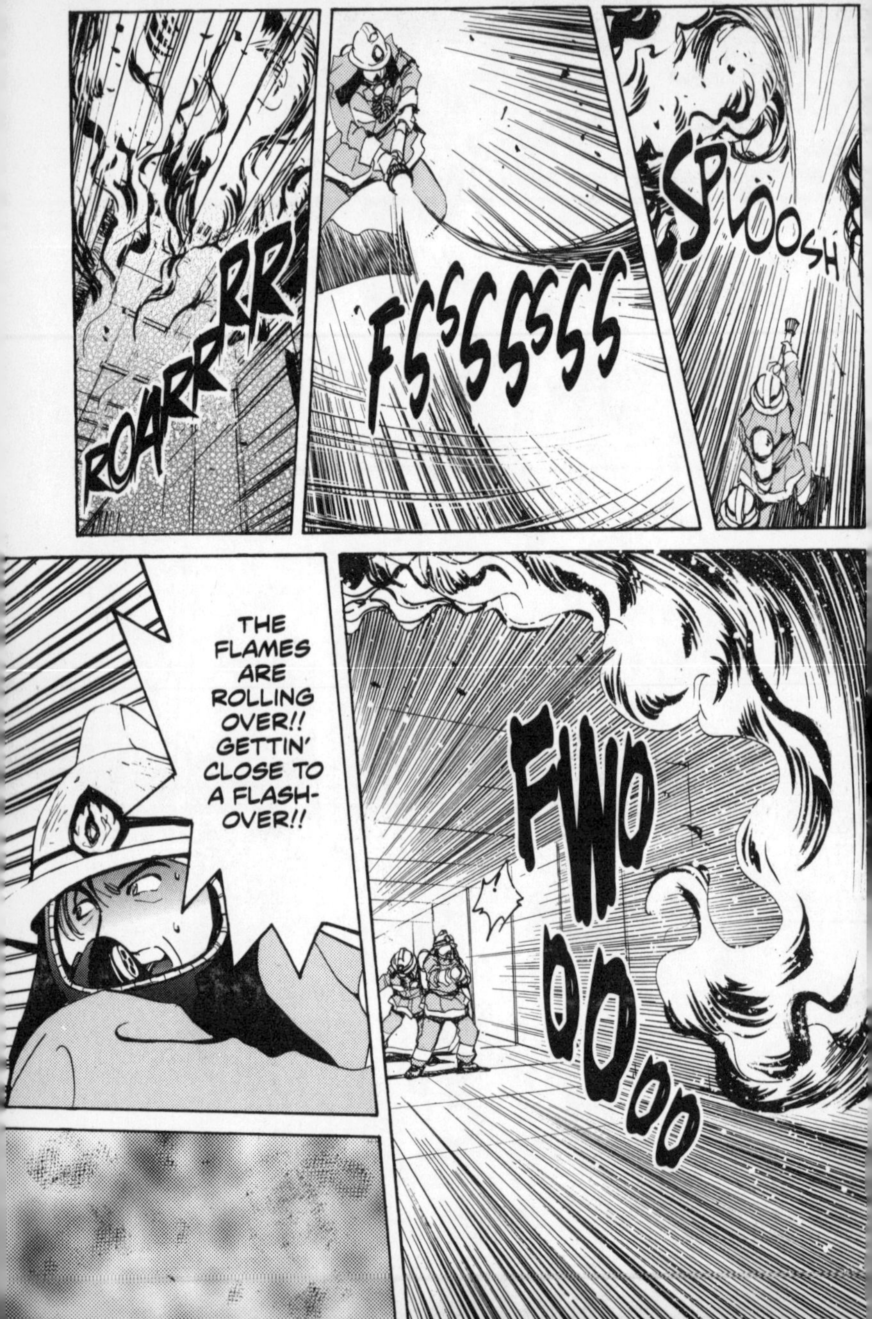
SPLOOSH
FSSSSSS
ROARRRRR
FWOOOOOOO
!?
THE FLAMES ARE ROLLING OVER!! GETTIN' CLOSE TO A FLASH-OVER!!

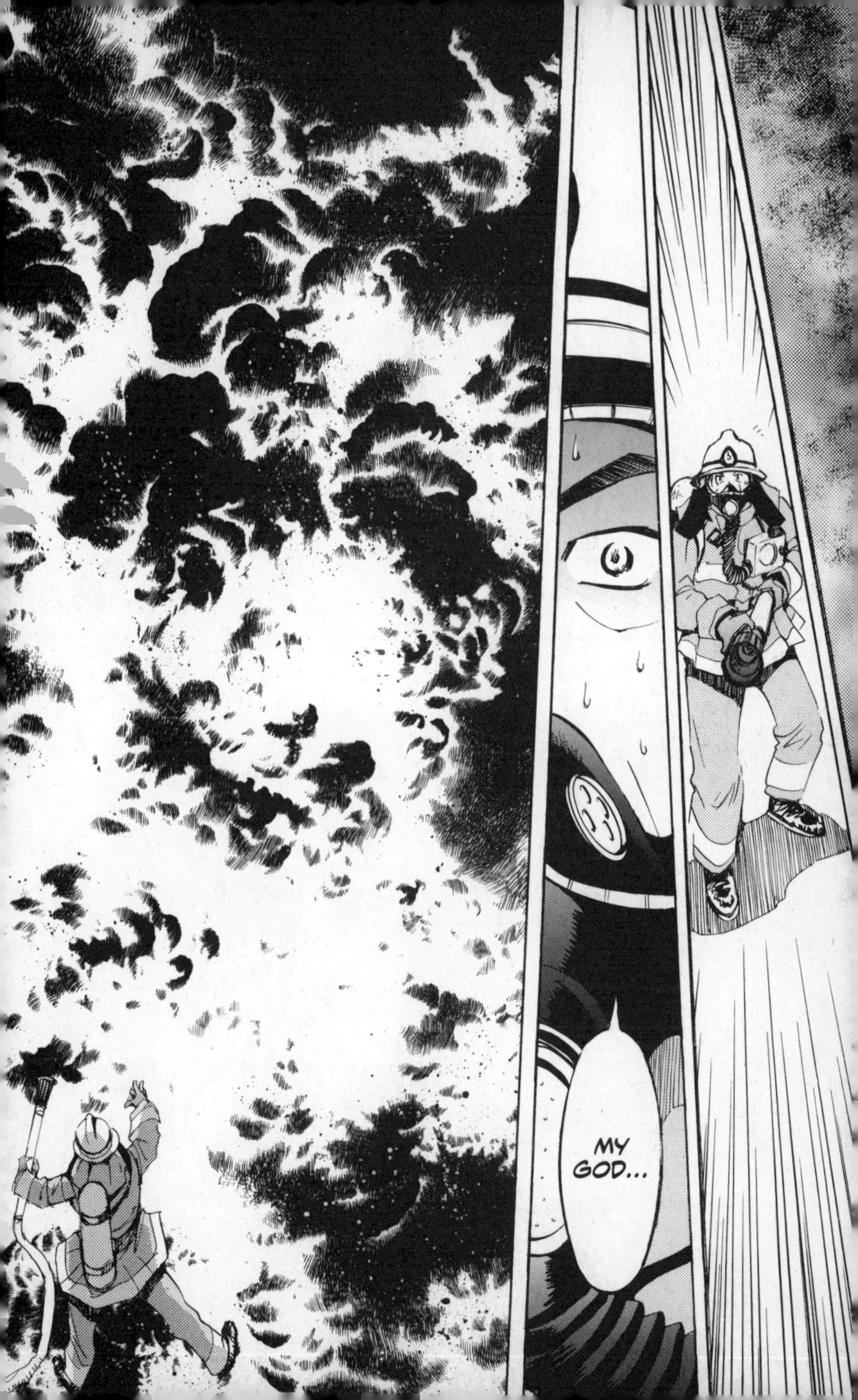
MY GOD...

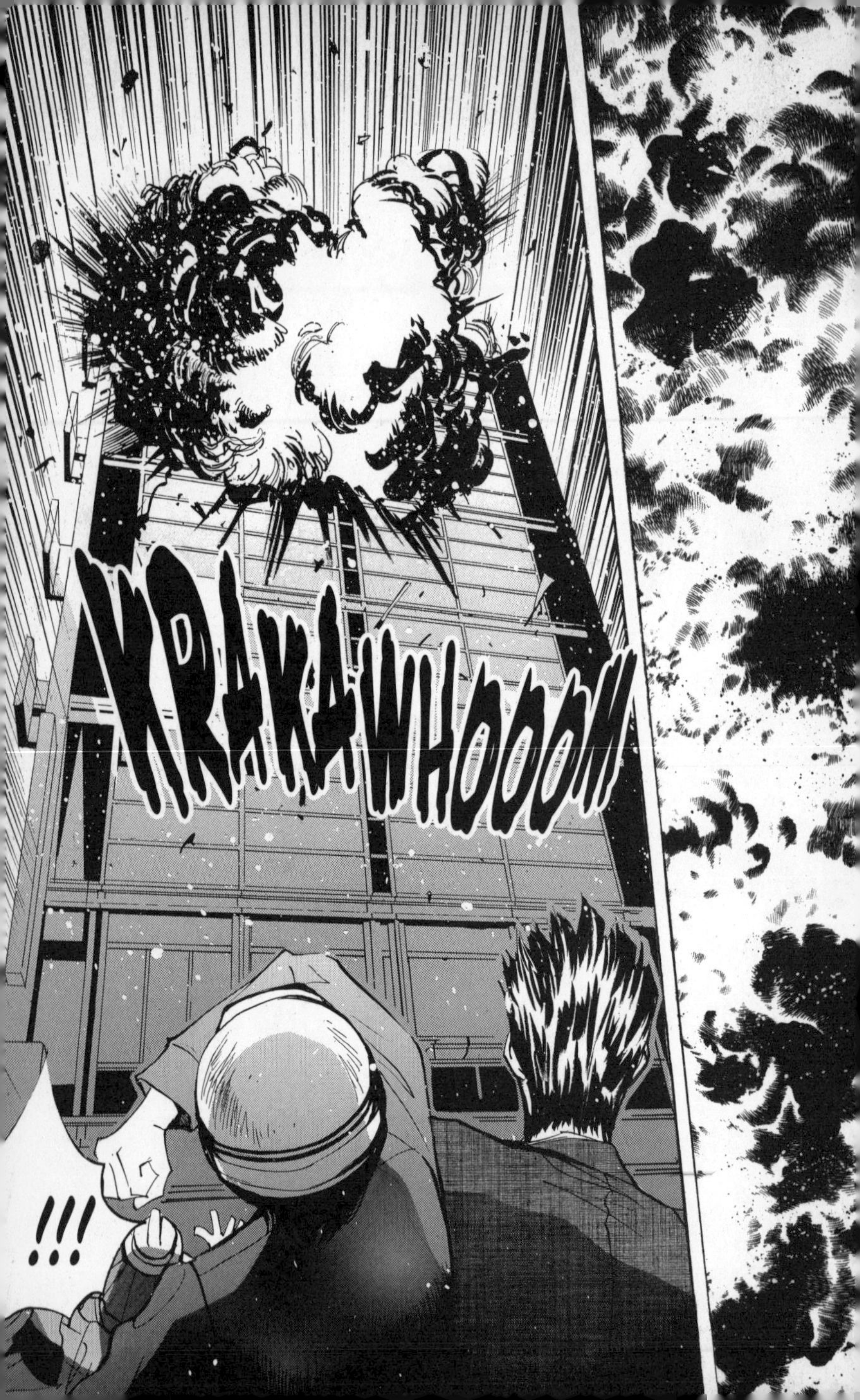
KRAKAWHOOOM
!!!

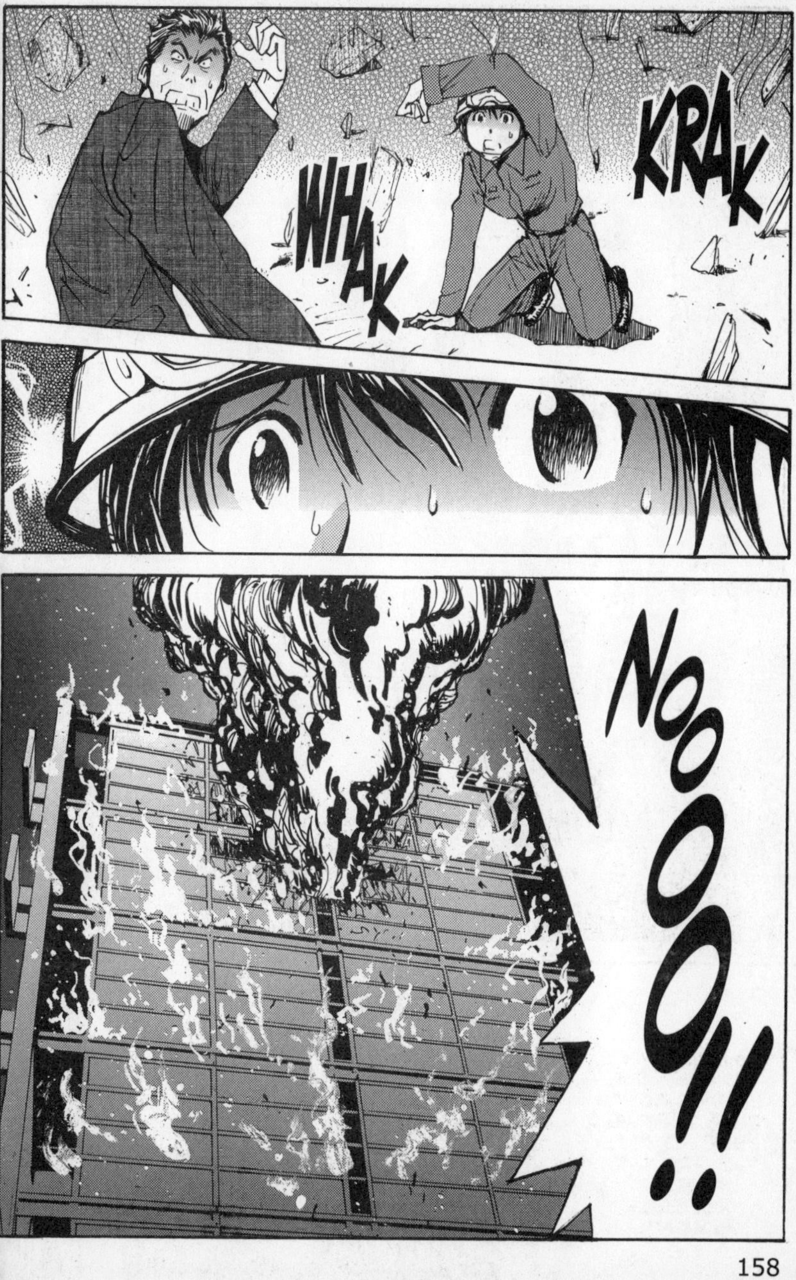
KRAK
WHAK
NOOOO!!

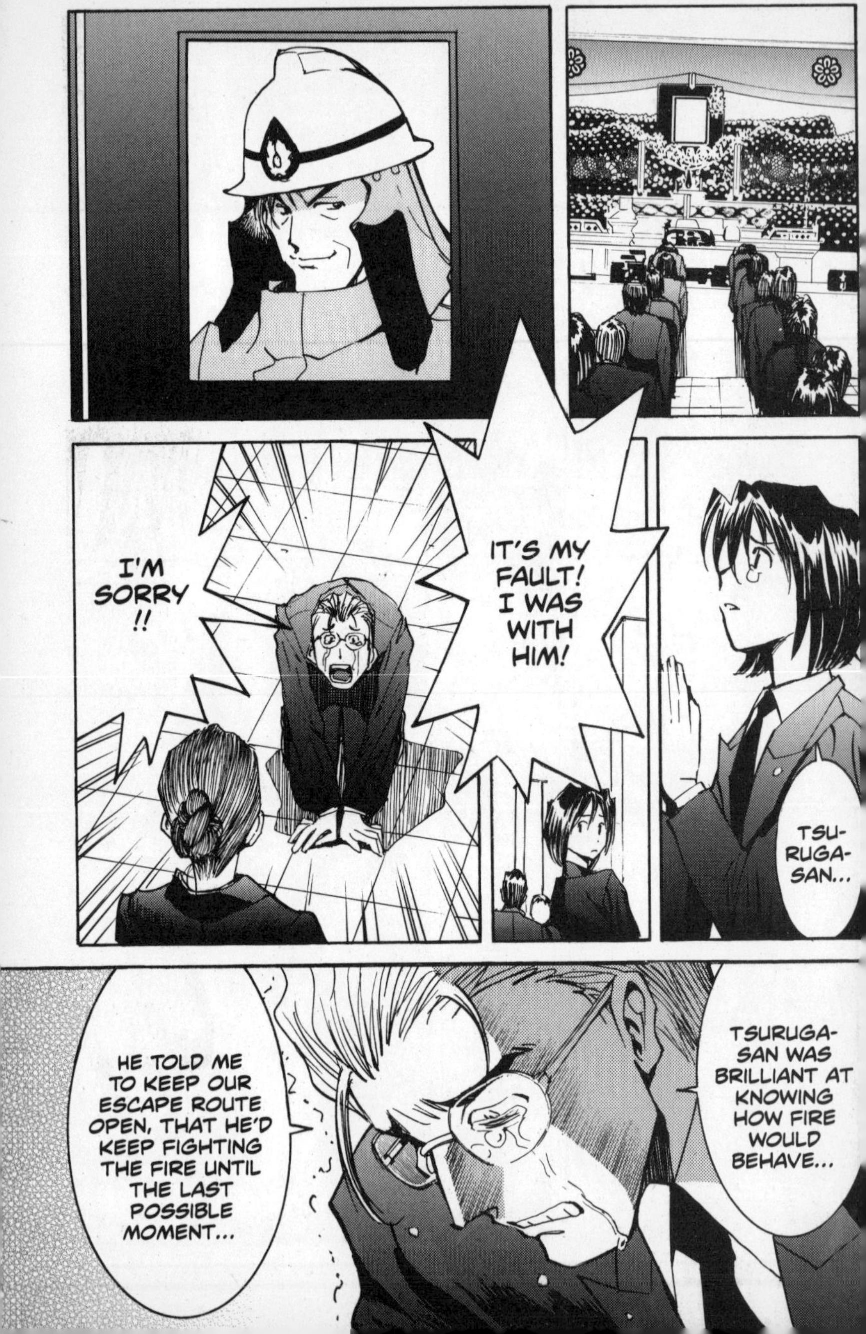
TSU-RUGA-SAN...
IT'S MY FAULT! I WAS WITH HIM!
I'M SORRY !!
TSURUGA-SAN WAS BRILLIANT AT KNOWING HOW FIRE WOULD BEHAVE...
HE TOLD ME TO KEEP OUR ESCAPE ROUTE OPEN, THAT HE'D KEEP FIGHTING THE FIRE UNTIL THE LAST POSSIBLE MOMENT...

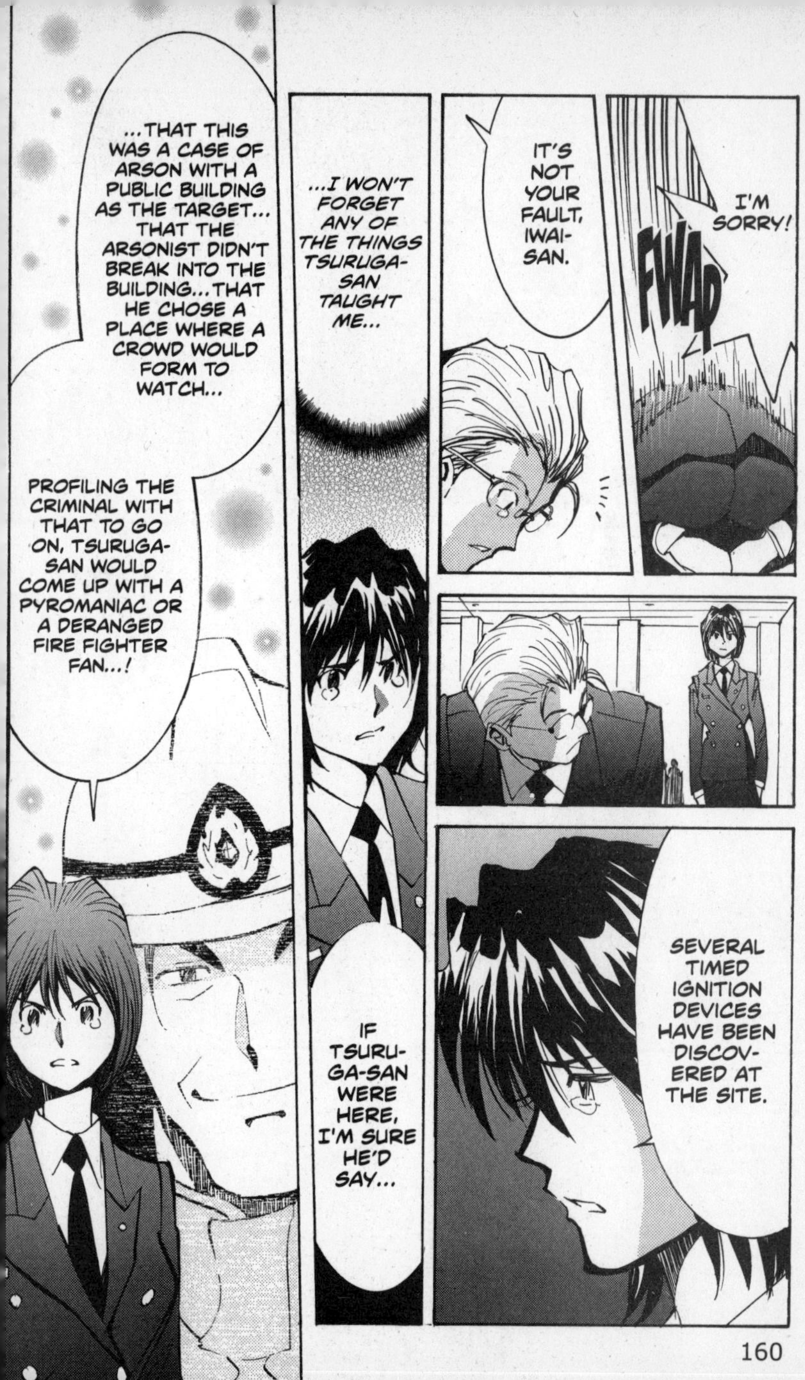
I'M SORRY!
FWAP
IT'S NOT YOUR FAULT, IWAI-SAN.
SEVERAL TIMED IGNITION DEVICES HAVE BEEN DISCOVERED AT THE SITE.
...I WON'T FORGET ANY OF THE THINGS TSURUGA-SAN TAUGHT ME...
IF TSURUGA-SAN WERE HERE, I'M SURE HE'D SAY...
...THAT THIS WAS A CASE OF ARSON WITH A PUBLIC BUILDING AS THE TARGET... THAT THE ARSONIST DIDN'T BREAK INTO THE BUILDING... THAT HE CHOSE A PLACE WHERE A CROWD WOULD FORM TO WATCH...
PROFILING THE CRIMINAL WITH THAT TO GO ON, TSURUGA-SAN WOULD COME UP WITH A PYROMANIAC OR A DERANGED FIRE FIGHTER FAN...!

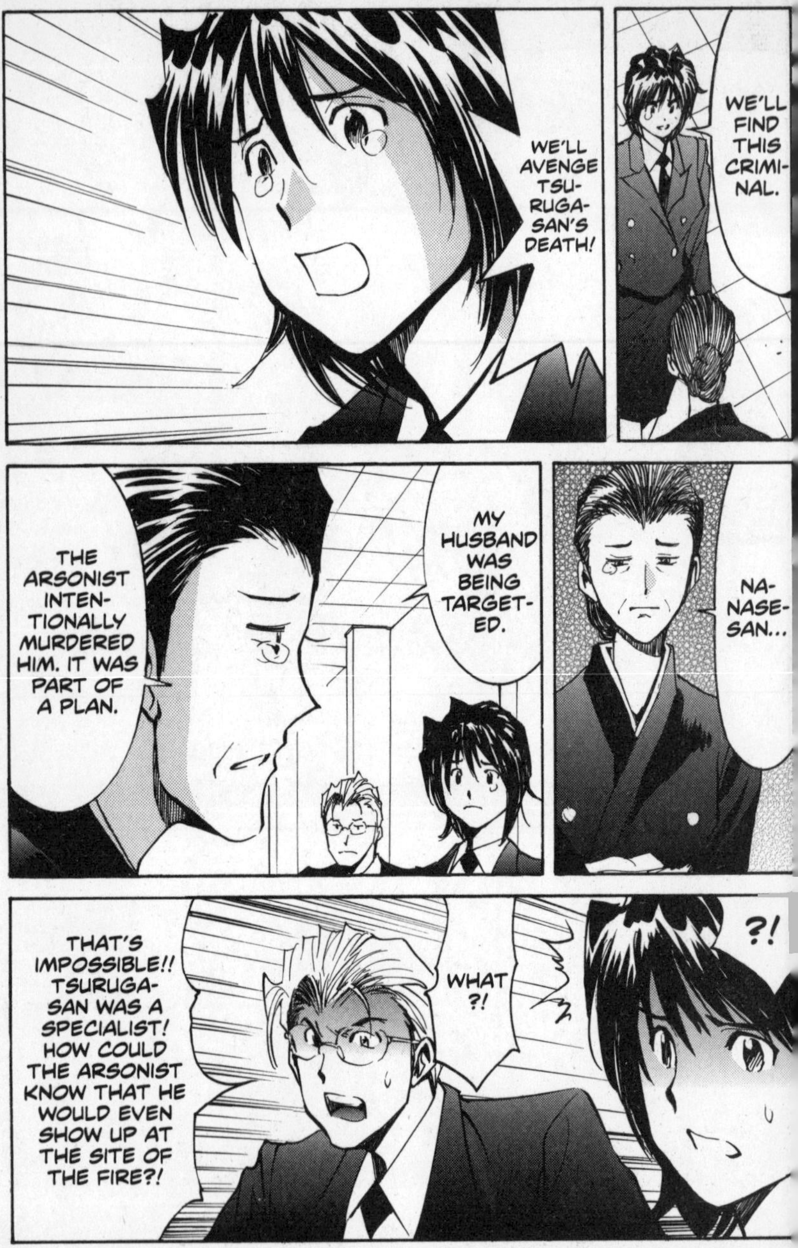
WE'LL FIND THIS CRIMI-NAL.
WE'LL AVENGE TSU-RUGA-SAN'S DEATH!
NA-NASE-SAN...
MY HUSBAND WAS BEING TARGET-ED.
THE ARSONIST INTEN-TIONALLY MURDERED HIM. IT WAS PART OF A PLAN.
?!
WHAT ?!
THAT'S IMPOSSIBLE!! TSURUGA-SAN WAS A SPECIALIST! HOW COULD THE ARSONIST KNOW THAT HE WOULD EVEN SHOW UP AT THE SITE OF THE FIRE?!

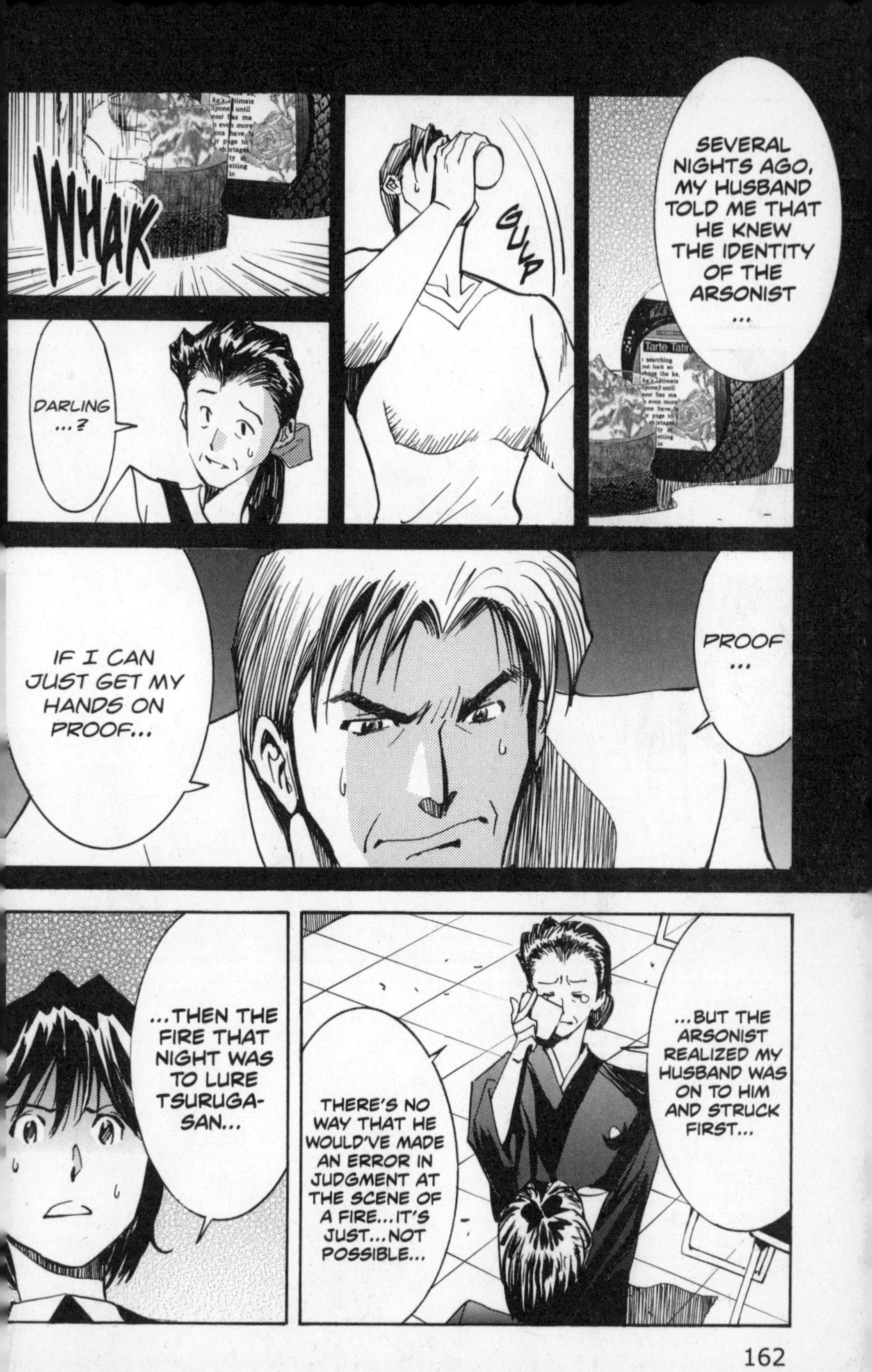
SEVERAL NIGHTS AGO, MY HUSBAND TOLD ME THAT HE KNEW THE IDENTITY OF THE ARSONIST ...
Tarte Tatin
GULP
WHAK
DARLING ...?
PROOF ...
IF I CAN JUST GET MY HANDS ON PROOF...
...BUT THE ARSONIST REALIZED MY HUSBAND WAS ON TO HIM AND STRUCK FIRST...
THERE'S NO WAY THAT HE WOULD'VE MADE AN ERROR IN JUDGMENT AT THE SCENE OF A FIRE...IT'S JUST...NOT POSSIBLE...
...THEN THE FIRE THAT NIGHT WAS TO LURE TSURUGA-SAN...

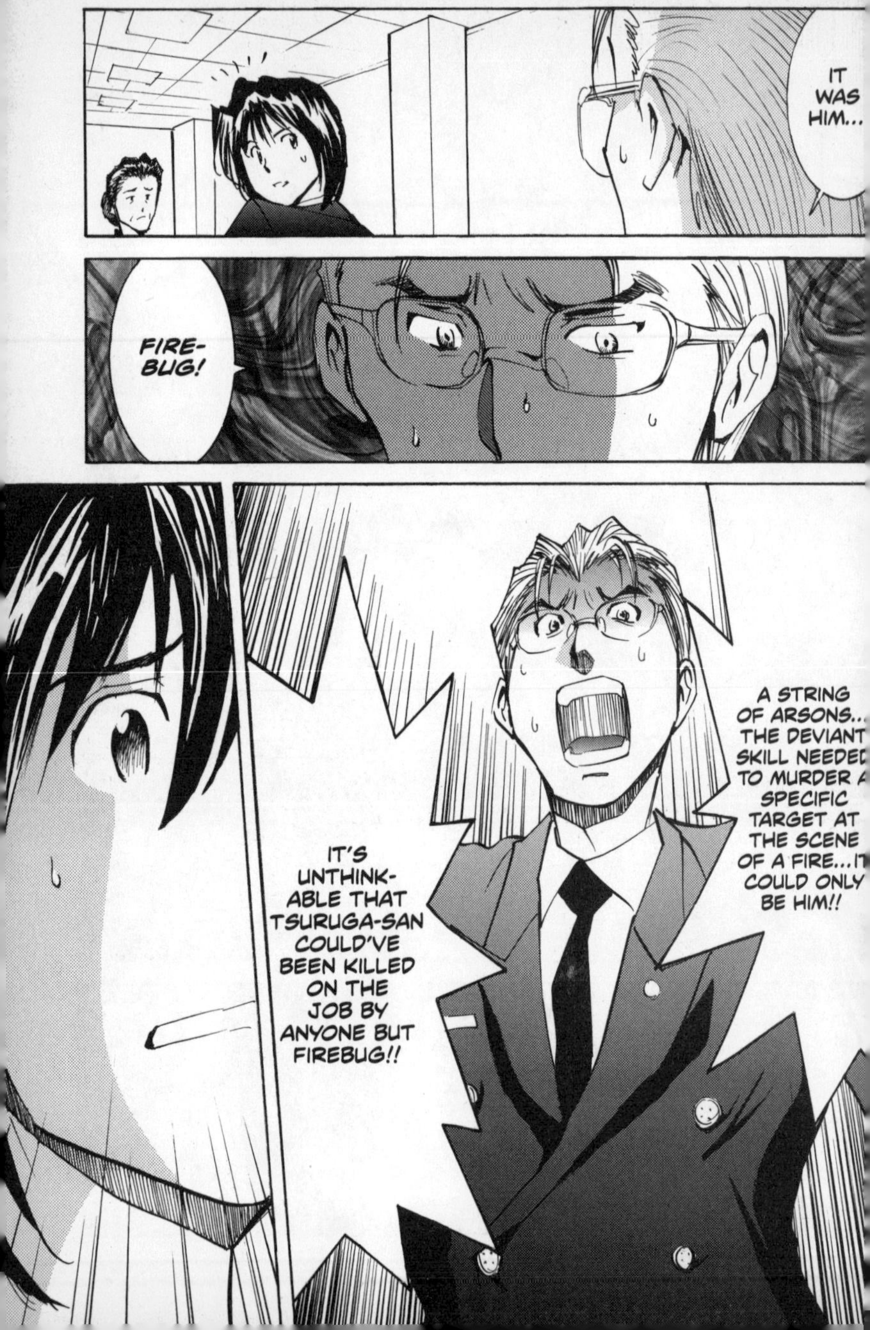
IT WAS HIM...
FIRE-BUG!
A STRING OF ARSONS... THE DEVIANT SKILL NEEDED TO MURDER A SPECIFIC TARGET AT THE SCENE OF A FIRE...IT COULD ONLY BE HIM!!
IT'S UNTHINK-ABLE THAT TSURUGA-SAN COULD'VE BEEN KILLED ON THE JOB BY ANYONE BUT FIREBUG!!

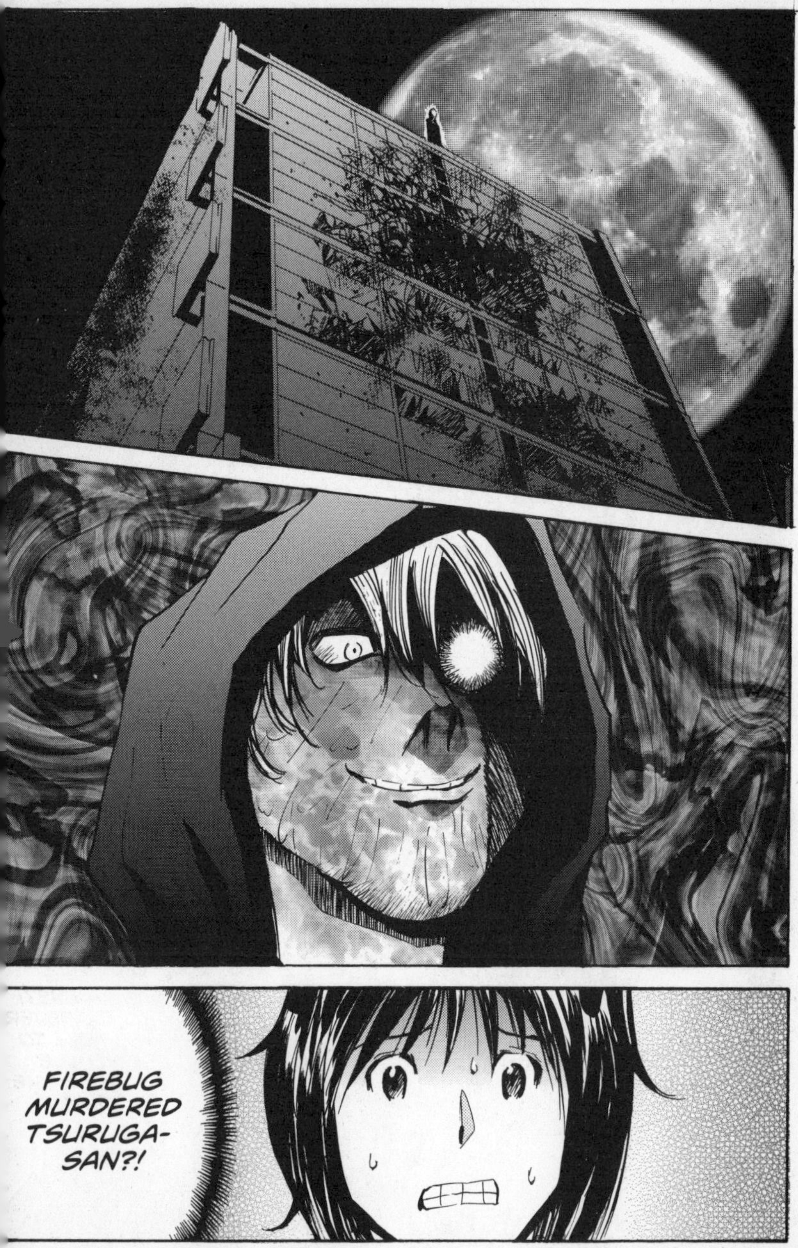
FIREBUG MURDERED TSURUGA-SAN?!

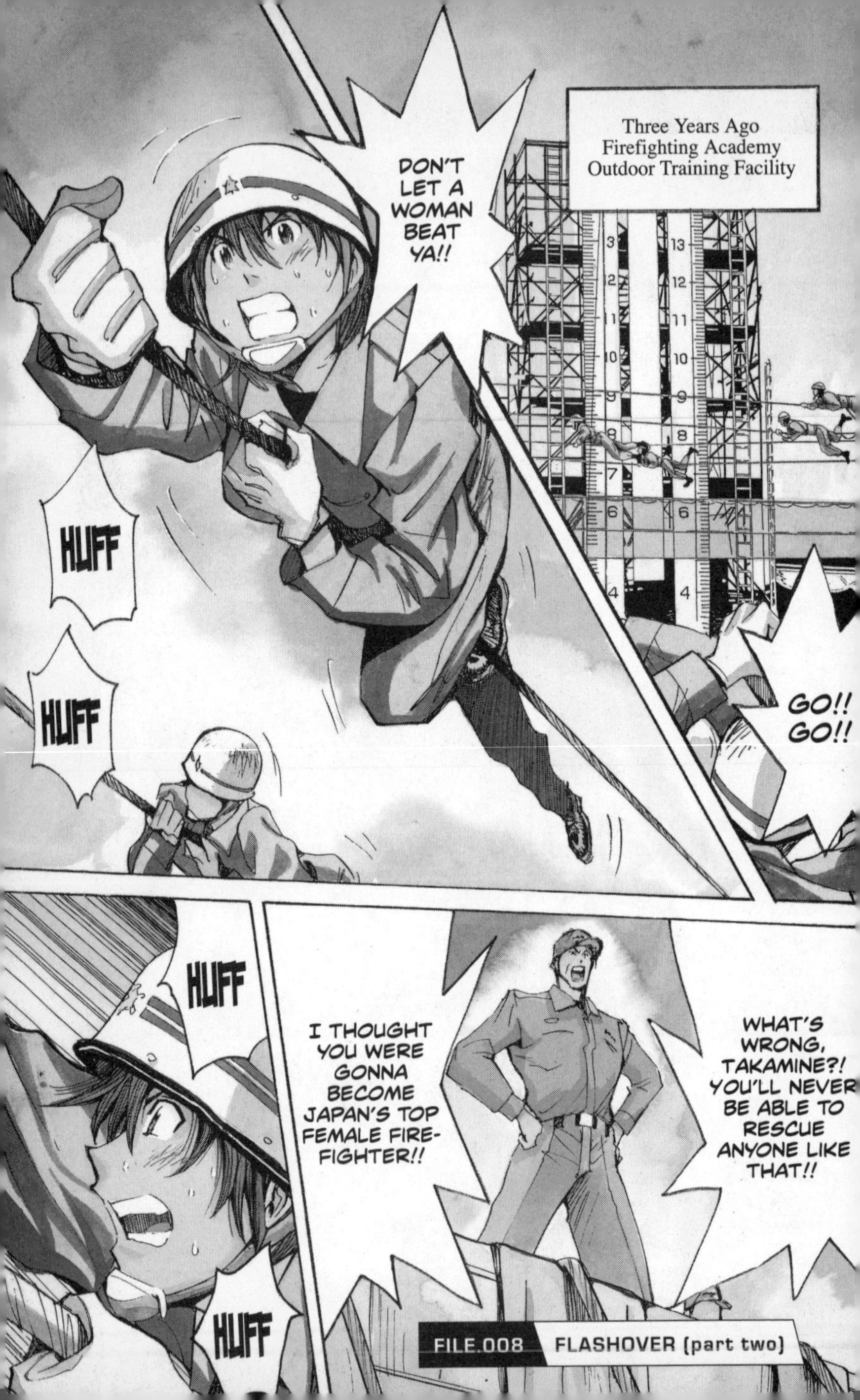
Three Years Ago
Firefighting Academy
Outdoor Training Facility
DON'T LET A WOMAN BEAT YA!!
HUFF
HUFF
GO!! GO!!
WHAT'S WRONG, TAKAMINE?! YOU'LL NEVER BE ABLE TO RESCUE ANYONE LIKE THAT!!
I THOUGHT YOU WERE GONNA BECOME JAPAN'S TOP FEMALE FIRE-FIGHTER!!
HUFF
HUFF
FILE.008 FLASHOVER (part two)

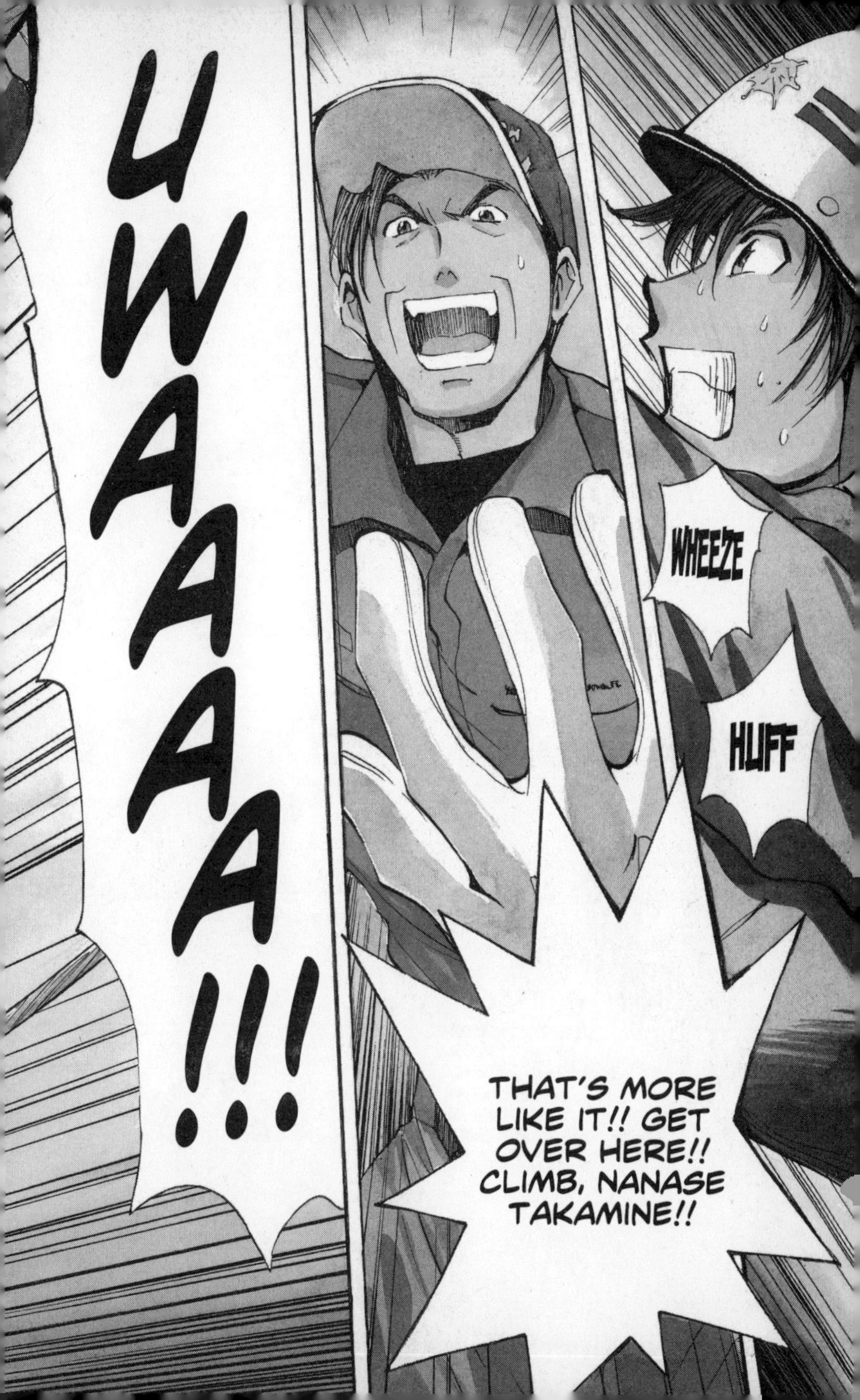
WHEEZE
HUFF
THAT'S MORE LIKE IT!! GET OVER HERE!! CLIMB, NANASE TAKAMINE!!
UWAAAAA!!!

FILE.008 FLASHOVER (part two)

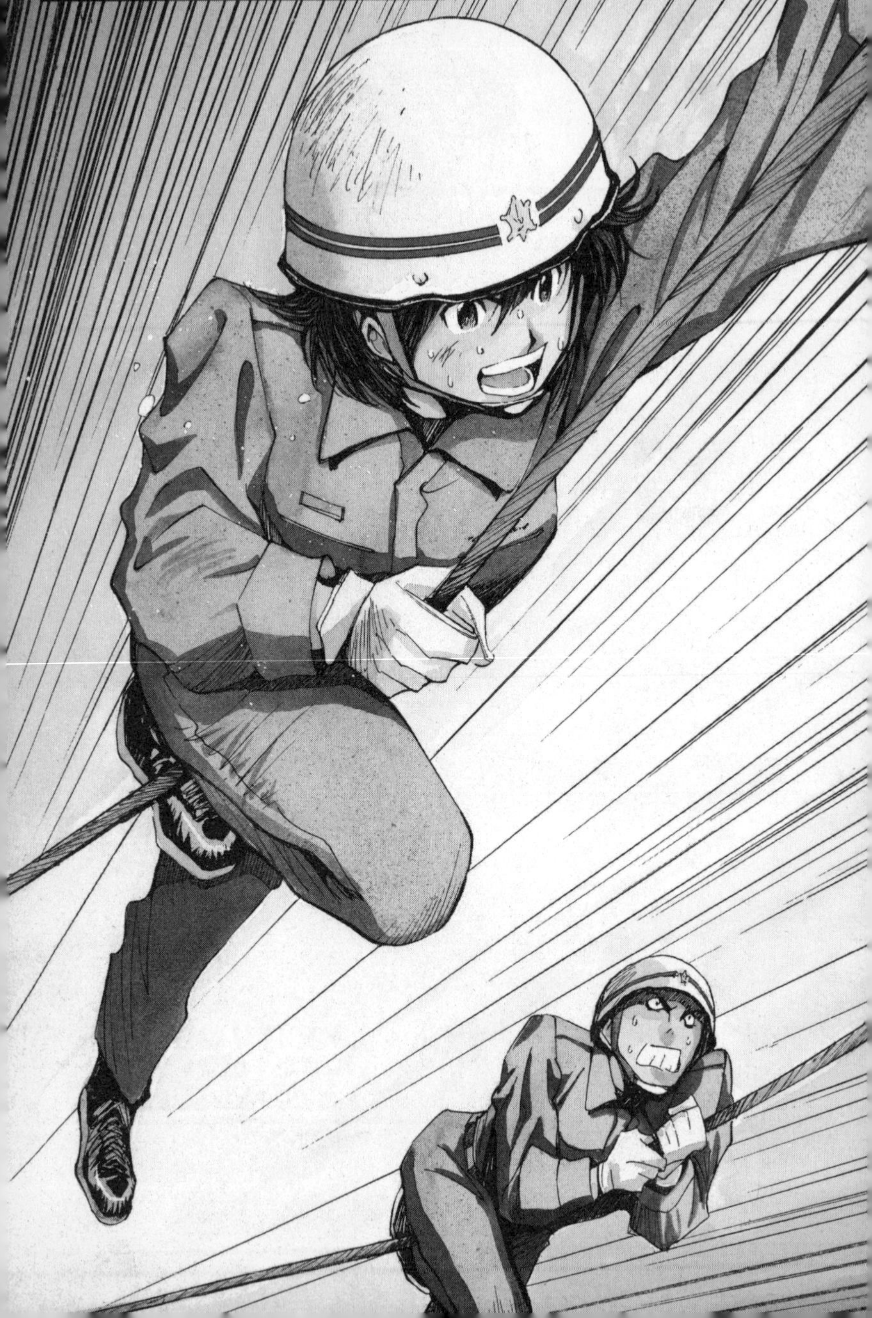

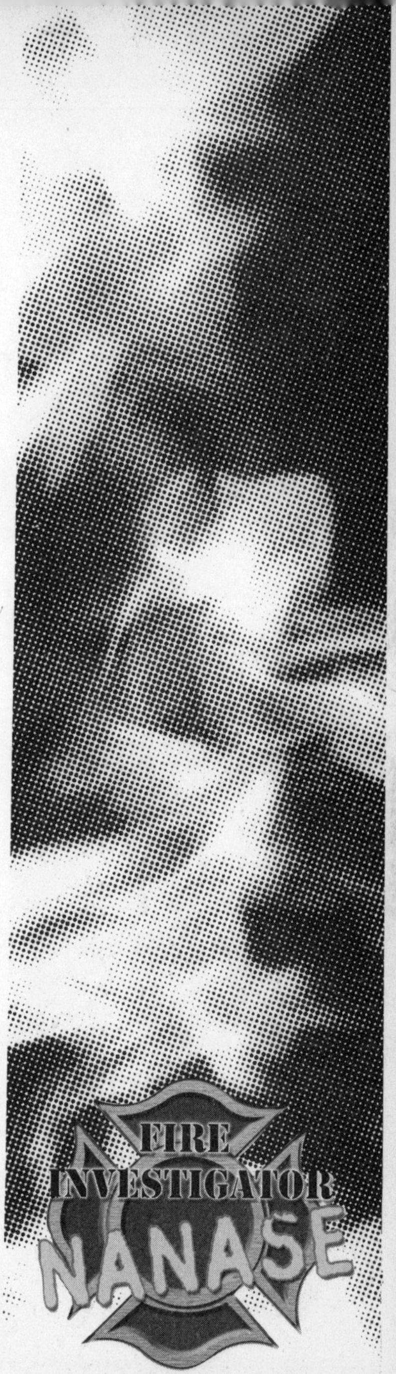
FIRE
INVESTIGATOR
NANASE

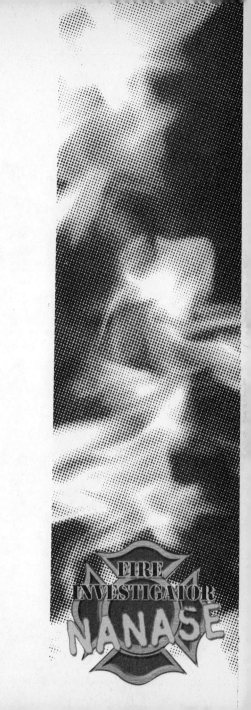

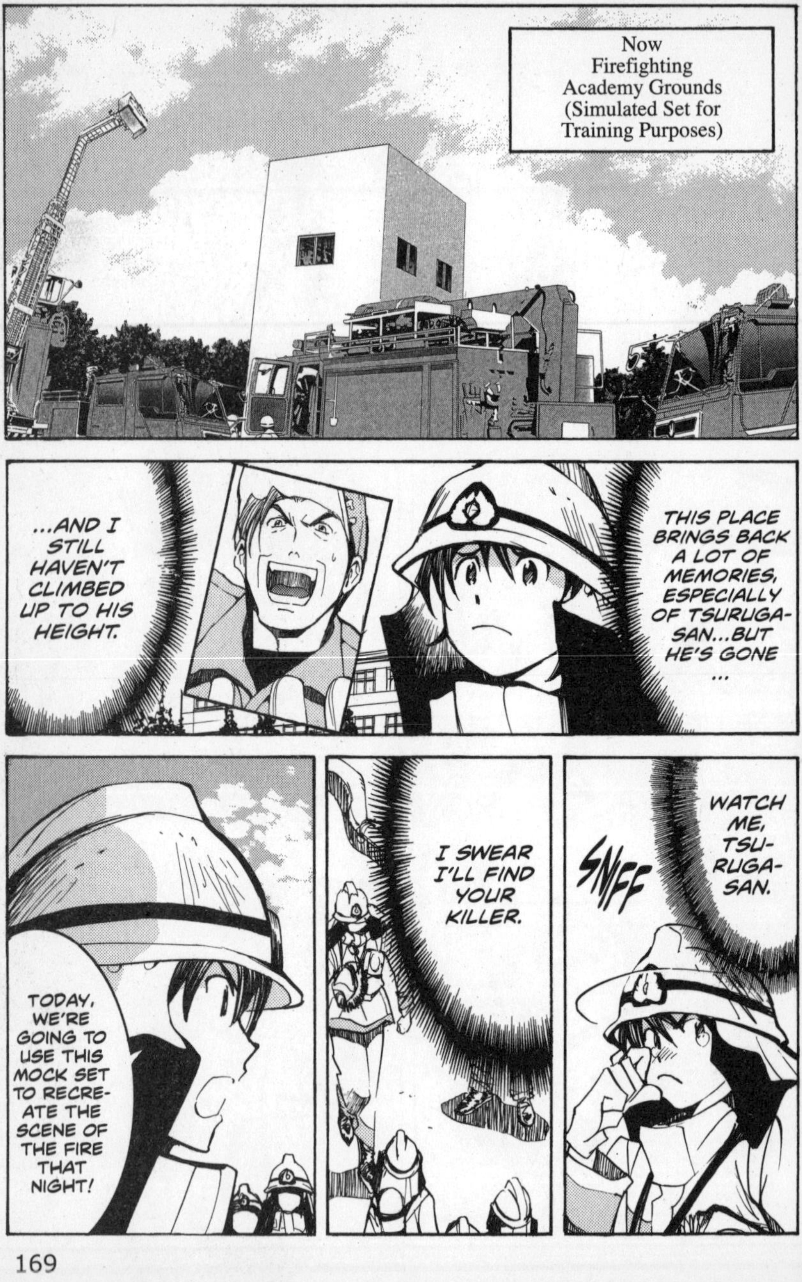
Now Firefighting Academy Grounds (Simulated Set for Training Purposes)
THIS PLACE BRINGS BACK A LOT OF MEMORIES, ESPECIALLY OF TSURUGA-SAN...BUT HE'S GONE ...
...AND I STILL HAVEN'T CLIMBED UP TO HIS HEIGHT.
WATCH ME, TSU-RUGA-SAN.
SNIFF
I SWEAR I'LL FIND YOUR KILLER.
TODAY, WE'RE GOING TO USE THIS MOCK SET TO RECRE-ATE THE SCENE OF THE FIRE THAT NIGHT!

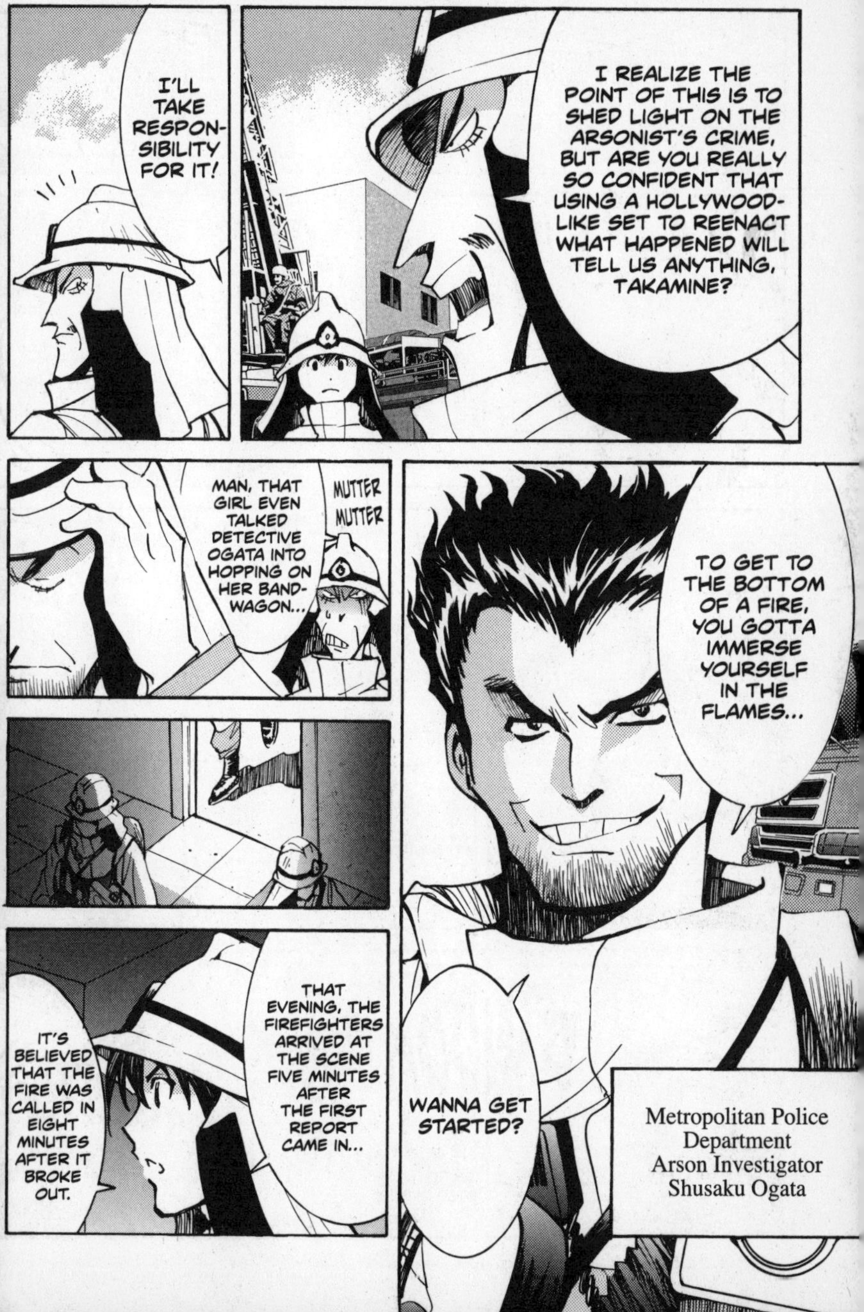
I REALIZE THE POINT OF THIS IS TO SHED LIGHT ON THE ARSONIST'S CRIME, BUT ARE YOU REALLY SO CONFIDENT THAT USING A HOLLYWOOD-LIKE SET TO REENACT WHAT HAPPENED WILL TELL US ANYTHING, TAKAMINE?
I'LL TAKE RESPONSIBILITY FOR IT!
TO GET TO THE BOTTOM OF A FIRE, YOU GOTTA IMMERSE YOURSELF IN THE FLAMES...
WANNA GET STARTED?
Metropolitan Police Department Arson Investigator Shusaku Ogata
MUTTER MUTTER
MAN, THAT GIRL EVEN TALKED DETECTIVE OGATA INTO HOPPING ON HER BANDWAGON...
THAT EVENING, THE FIREFIGHTERS ARRIVED AT THE SCENE FIVE MINUTES AFTER THE FIRST REPORT CAME IN...
IT'S BELIEVED THAT THE FIRE WAS CALLED IN EIGHT MINUTES AFTER IT BROKE OUT.

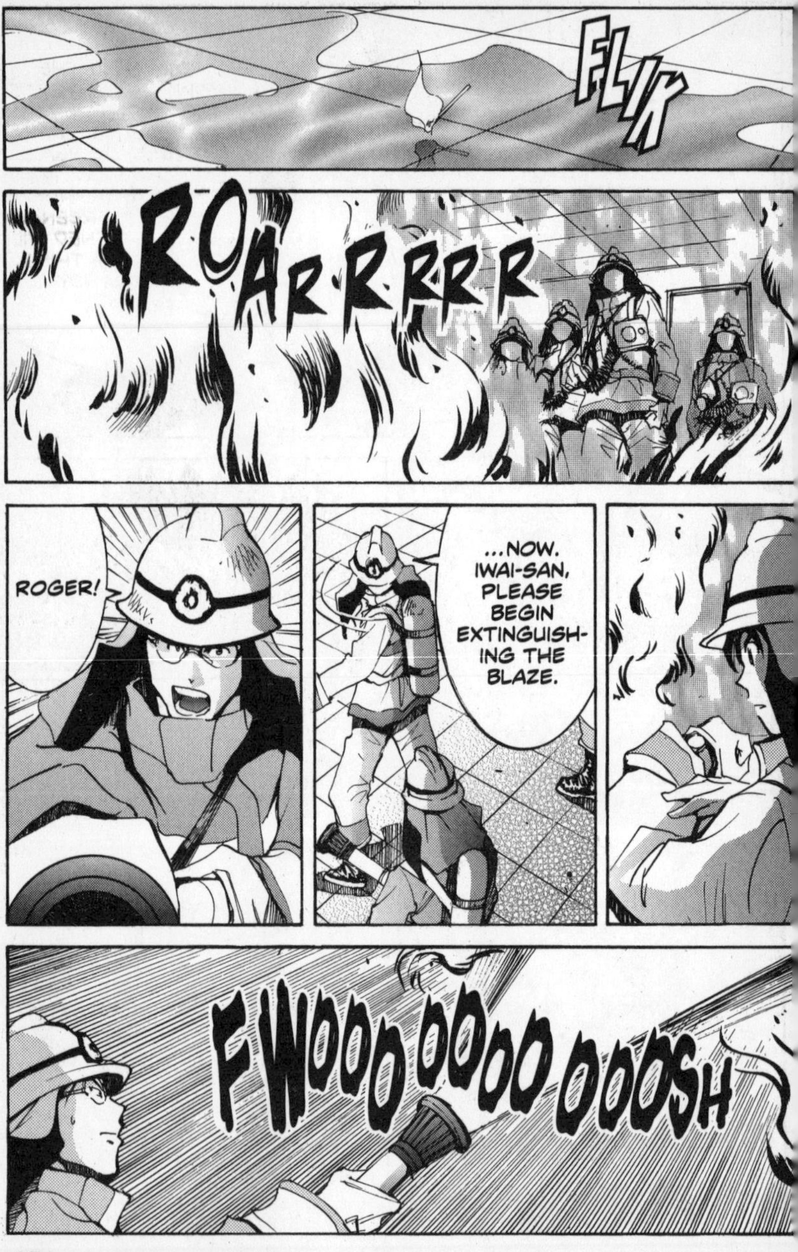
FLIK
ROARRRRR
...NOW. IWAI-SAN, PLEASE BEGIN EXTINGUISHING THE BLAZE.
ROGER!
FWOOOOOOOOOOSH

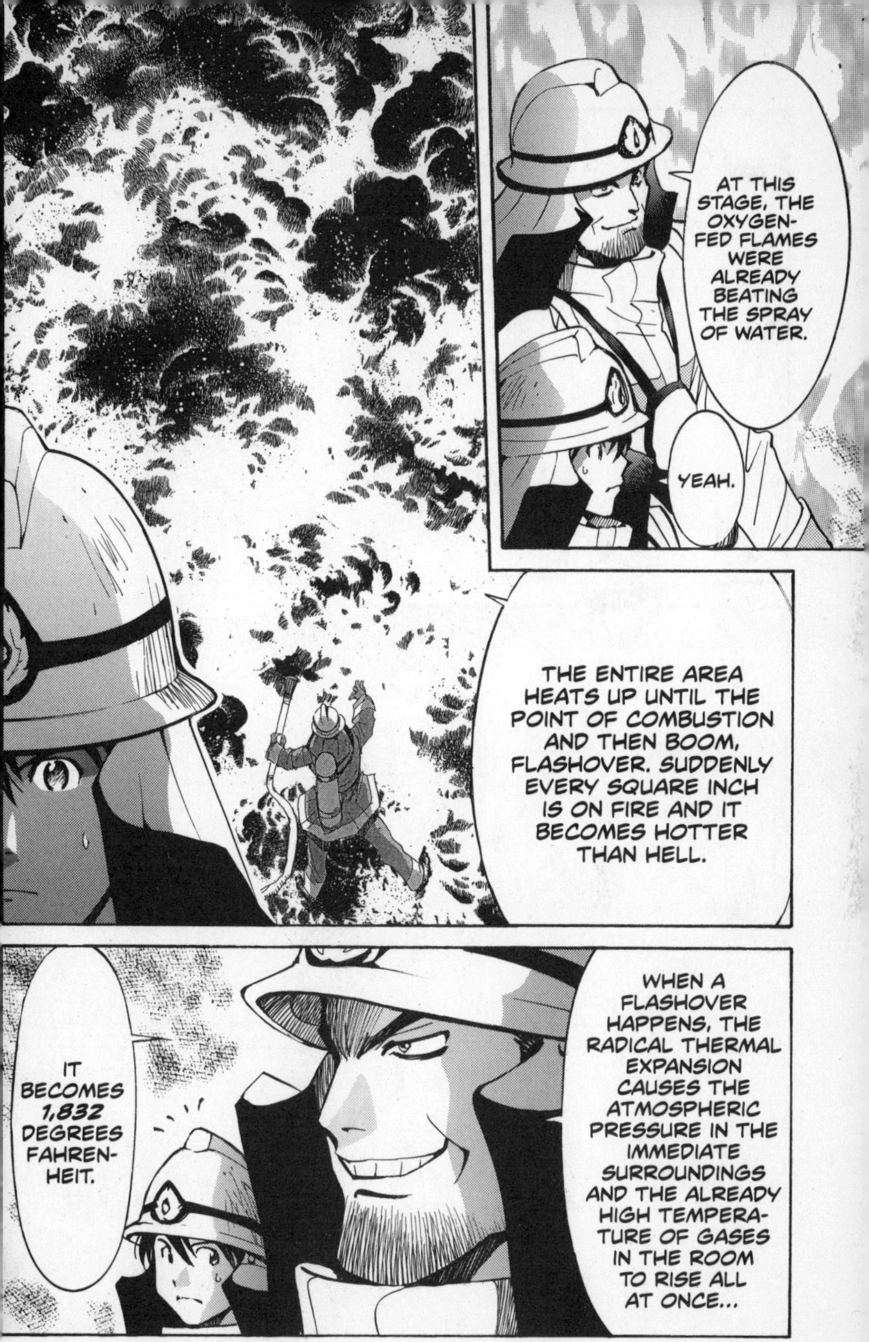
AT THIS STAGE, THE OXYGEN-FED FLAMES WERE ALREADY BEATING THE SPRAY OF WATER.
YEAH.
THE ENTIRE AREA HEATS UP UNTIL THE POINT OF COMBUSTION AND THEN BOOM, FLASHOVER. SUDDENLY EVERY SQUARE INCH IS ON FIRE AND IT BECOMES HOTTER THAN HELL.
WHEN A FLASHOVER HAPPENS, THE RADICAL THERMAL EXPANSION CAUSES THE ATMOSPHERIC PRESSURE IN THE IMMEDIATE SURROUNDINGS AND THE ALREADY HIGH TEMPERATURE OF GASES IN THE ROOM TO RISE ALL AT ONCE...
IT BECOMES 1,832 DEGREES FAHRENHEIT.

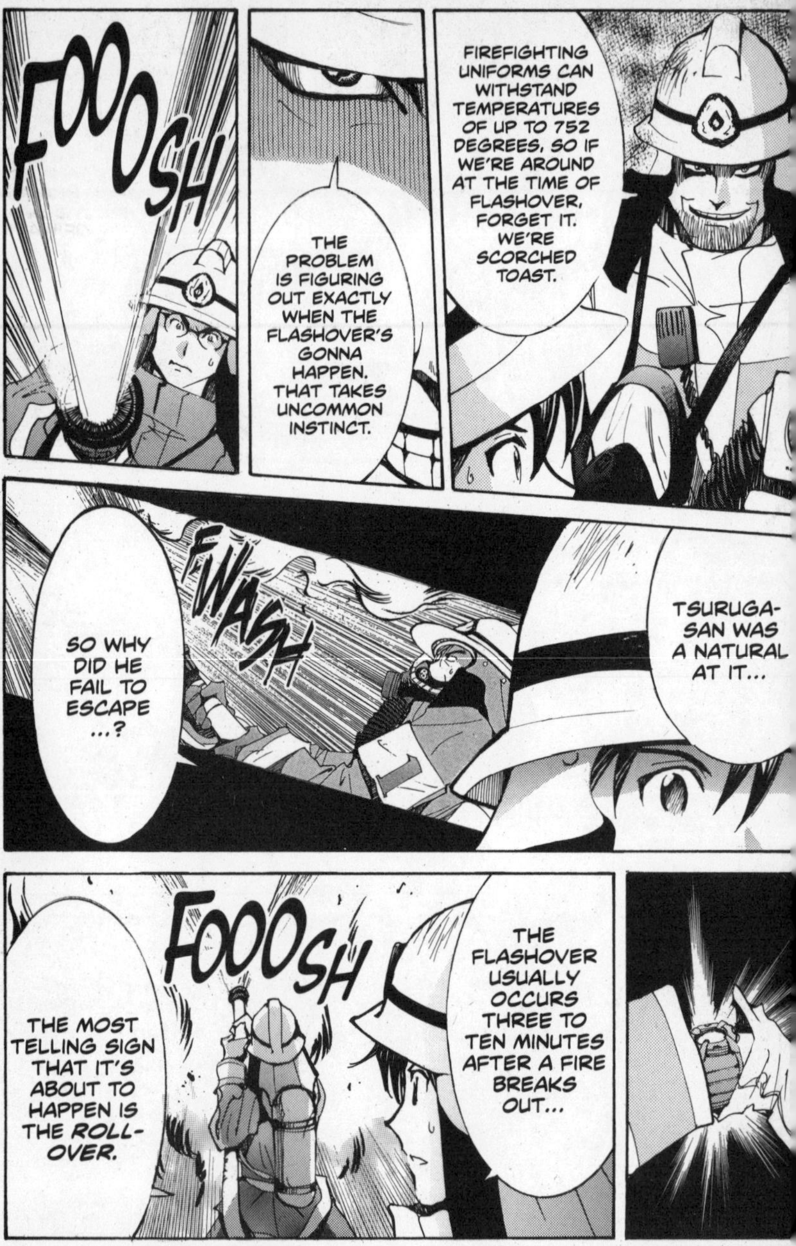
FIREFIGHTING UNIFORMS CAN WITHSTAND TEMPERATURES OF UP TO 752 DEGREES, SO IF WE'RE AROUND AT THE TIME OF FLASHOVER, FORGET IT. WE'RE SCORCHED TOAST.
THE PROBLEM IS FIGURING OUT EXACTLY WHEN THE FLASHOVER'S GONNA HAPPEN. THAT TAKES UNCOMMON INSTINCT.
FOOOSH
TSURUGA-SAN WAS A NATURAL AT IT...
FWASH
SO WHY DID HE FAIL TO ESCAPE ...?
THE FLASHOVER USUALLY OCCURS THREE TO TEN MINUTES AFTER A FIRE BREAKS OUT...
FOOOSH
THE MOST TELLING SIGN THAT IT'S ABOUT TO HAPPEN IS THE *ROLL-OVER.*

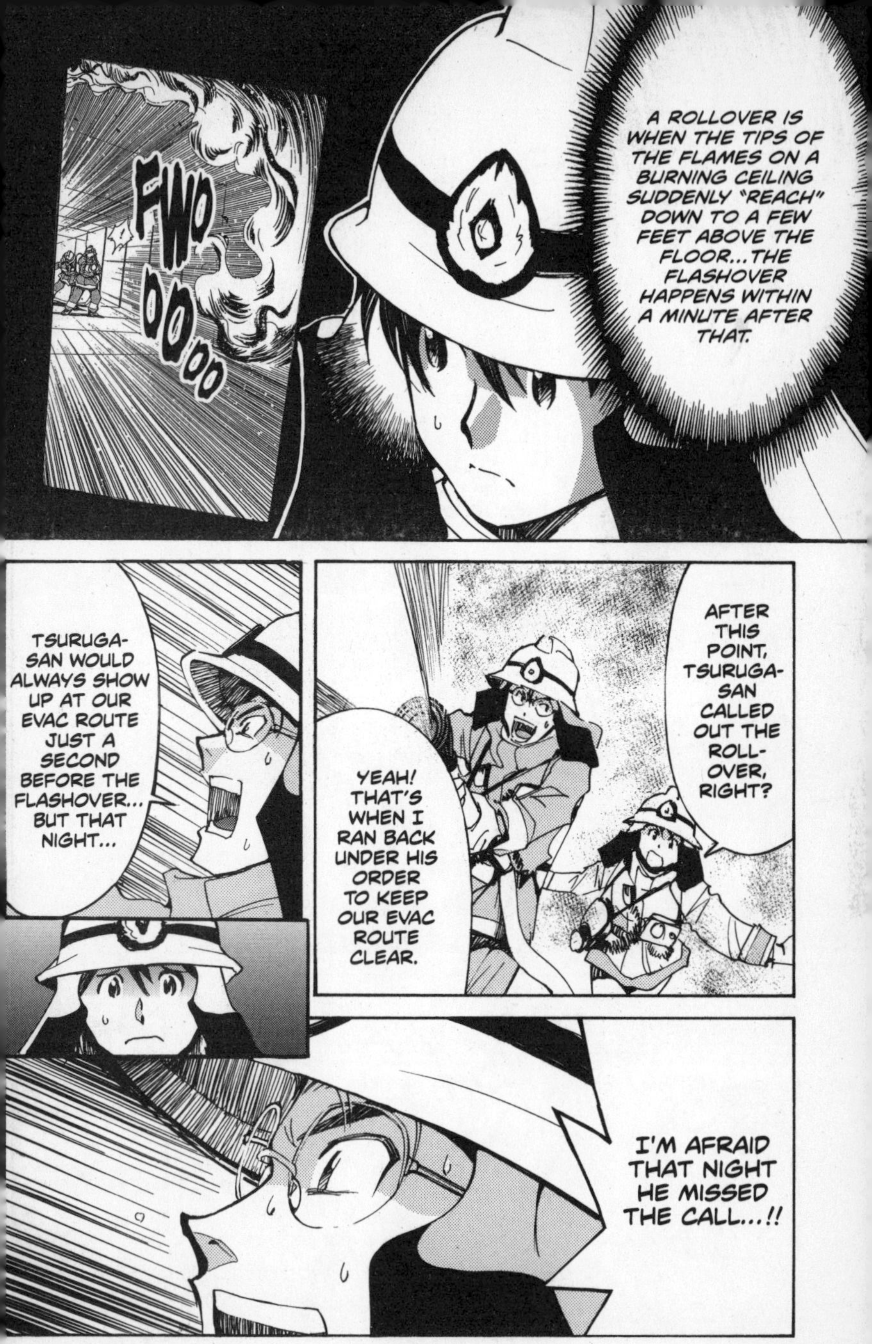
A ROLLOVER IS WHEN THE TIPS OF THE FLAMES ON A BURNING CEILING SUDDENLY "REACH" DOWN TO A FEW FEET ABOVE THE FLOOR...THE FLASHOVER HAPPENS WITHIN A MINUTE AFTER THAT.
FWOOOOOO
AFTER THIS POINT, TSURUGA-SAN CALLED OUT THE ROLL-OVER, RIGHT?
YEAH! THAT'S WHEN I RAN BACK UNDER HIS ORDER TO KEEP OUR EVAC ROUTE CLEAR.
TSURUGA-SAN WOULD ALWAYS SHOW UP AT OUR EVAC ROUTE JUST A SECOND BEFORE THE FLASHOVER... BUT THAT NIGHT...
I'M AFRAID THAT NIGHT HE MISSED THE CALL...!!

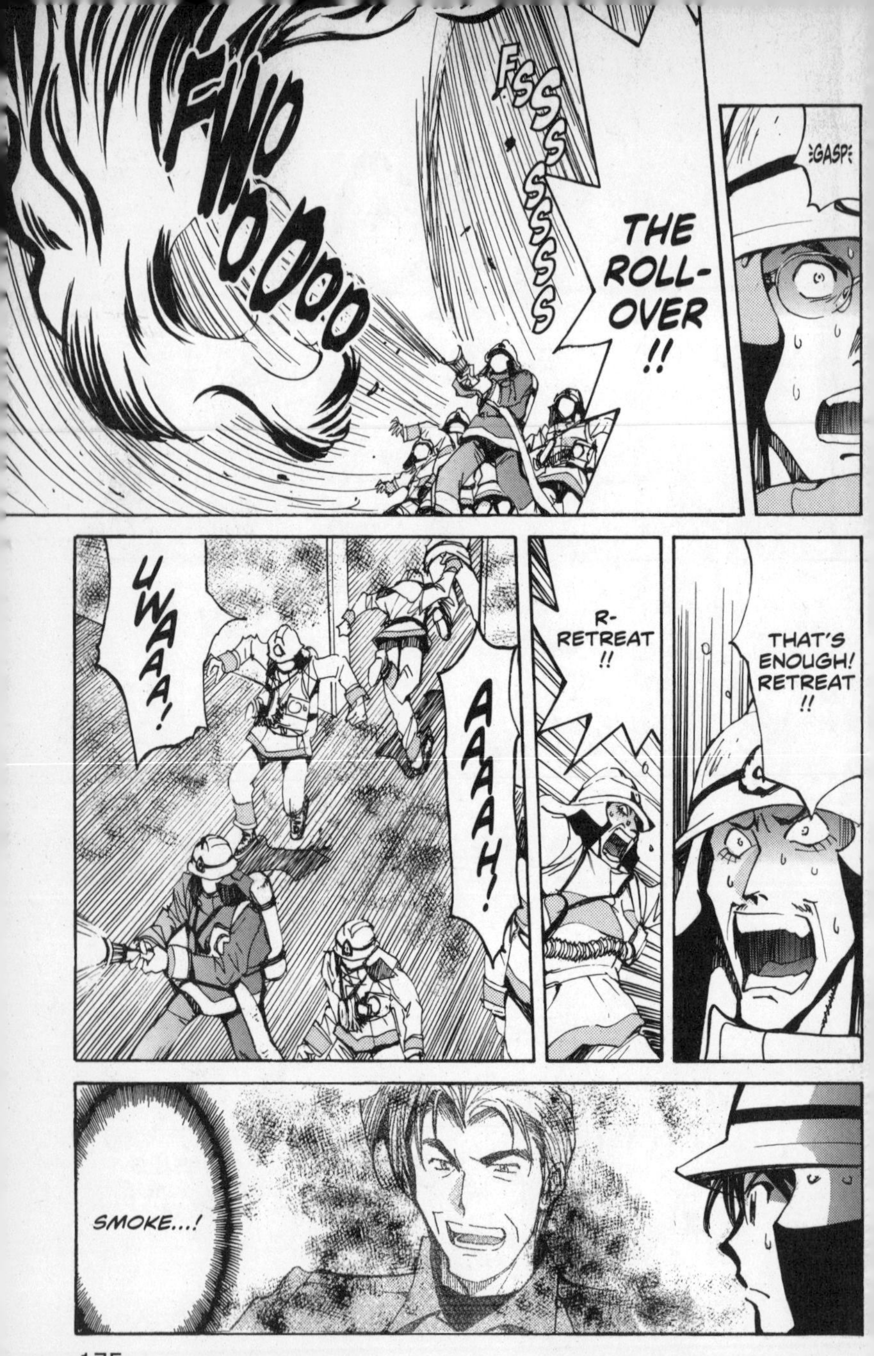
GASP
THE ROLL-OVER!!
FSSSSSSSS
FWOOOOO
THAT'S ENOUGH! RETREAT!!
R-RETREAT!!
AAAAAH!
UWAAAA!
SMOKE...!

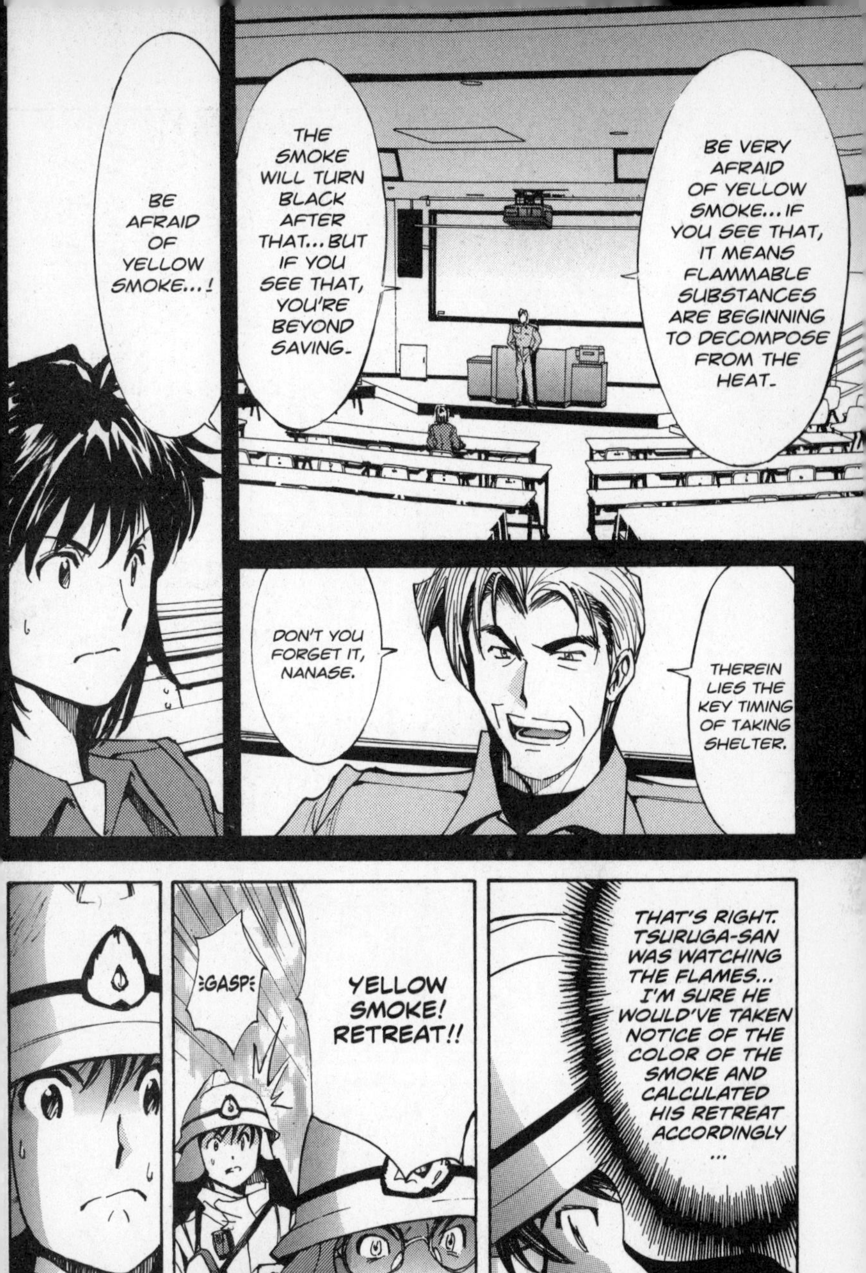
BE VERY AFRAID OF YELLOW SMOKE... IF YOU SEE THAT, IT MEANS FLAMMABLE SUBSTANCES ARE BEGINNING TO DECOMPOSE FROM THE HEAT.
THE SMOKE WILL TURN BLACK AFTER THAT... BUT IF YOU SEE THAT, YOU'RE BEYOND SAVING.
THEREIN LIES THE KEY TIMING OF TAKING SHELTER.
DON'T YOU FORGET IT, NANASE.
BE AFRAID OF YELLOW SMOKE...!
THAT'S RIGHT. TSURUGA-SAN WAS WATCHING THE FLAMES... I'M SURE HE WOULD'VE TAKEN NOTICE OF THE COLOR OF THE SMOKE AND CALCULATED HIS RETREAT ACCORDINGLY...
YELLOW SMOKE! RETREAT!!
GASP

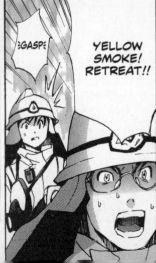

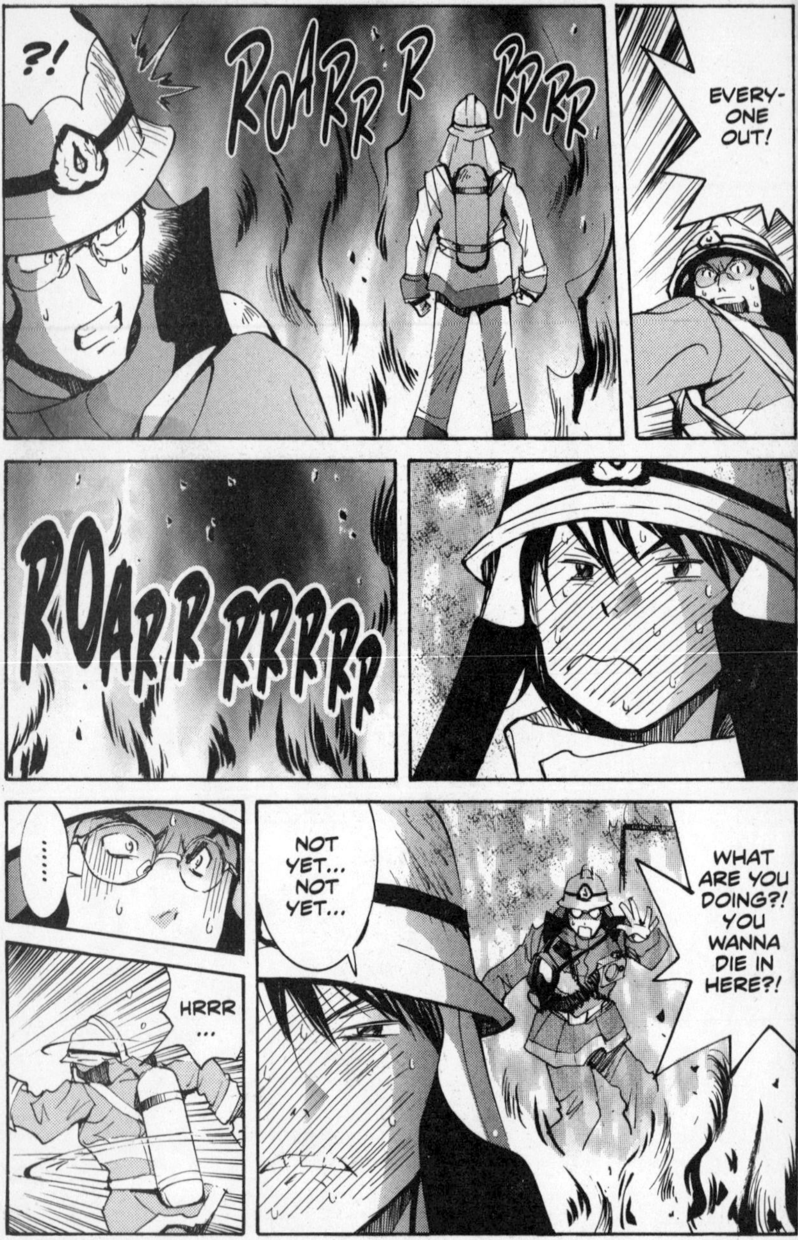
EVERY-ONE OUT!
?!
ROARRR RRRRR
ROARR RRRRRR
WHAT ARE YOU DOING?! YOU WANNA DIE IN HERE?!
NOT YET... NOT YET...
......
HRRR ...

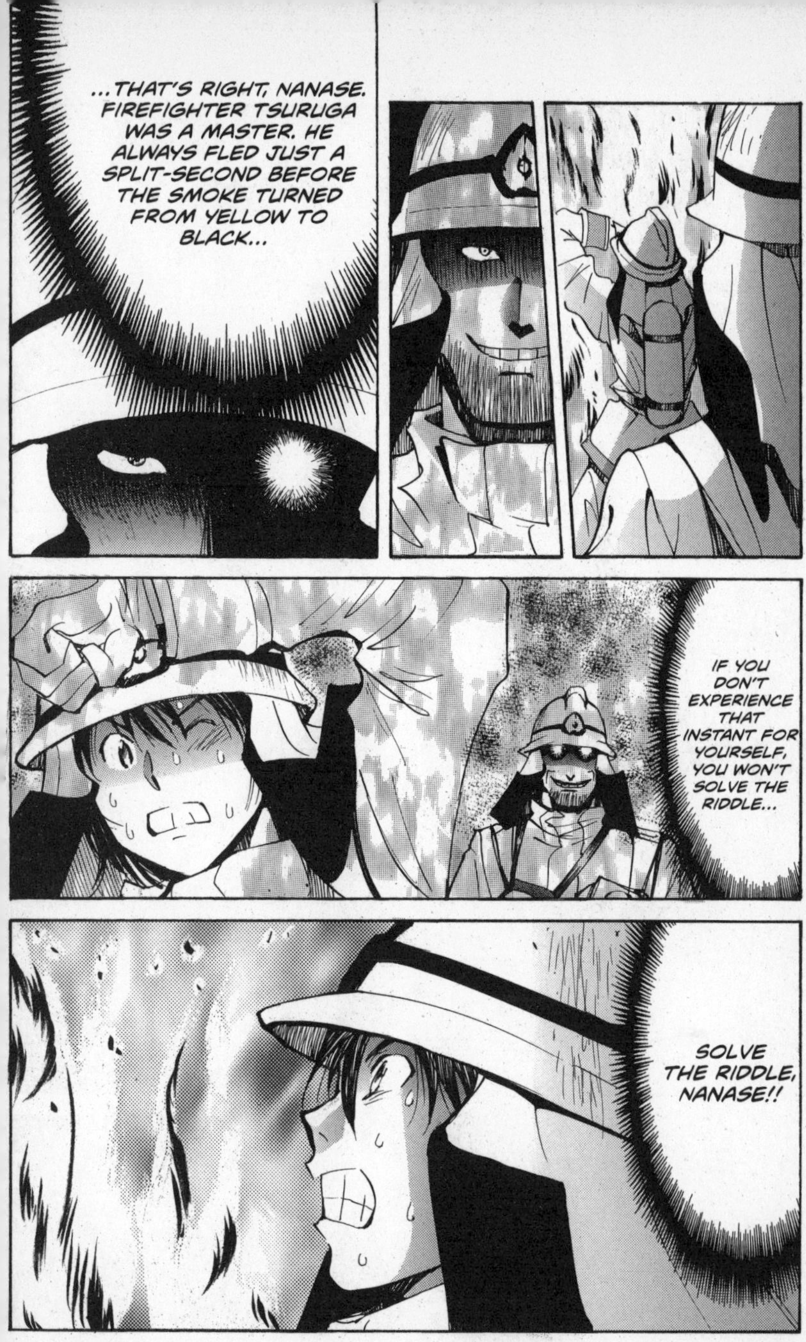
...THAT'S RIGHT, NANASE. FIREFIGHTER TSURUGA WAS A MASTER. HE ALWAYS FLED JUST A SPLIT-SECOND BEFORE THE SMOKE TURNED FROM YELLOW TO BLACK...
IF YOU DON'T EXPERIENCE THAT INSTANT FOR YOURSELF, YOU WON'T SOLVE THE RIDDLE...
SOLVE THE RIDDLE, NANASE!!

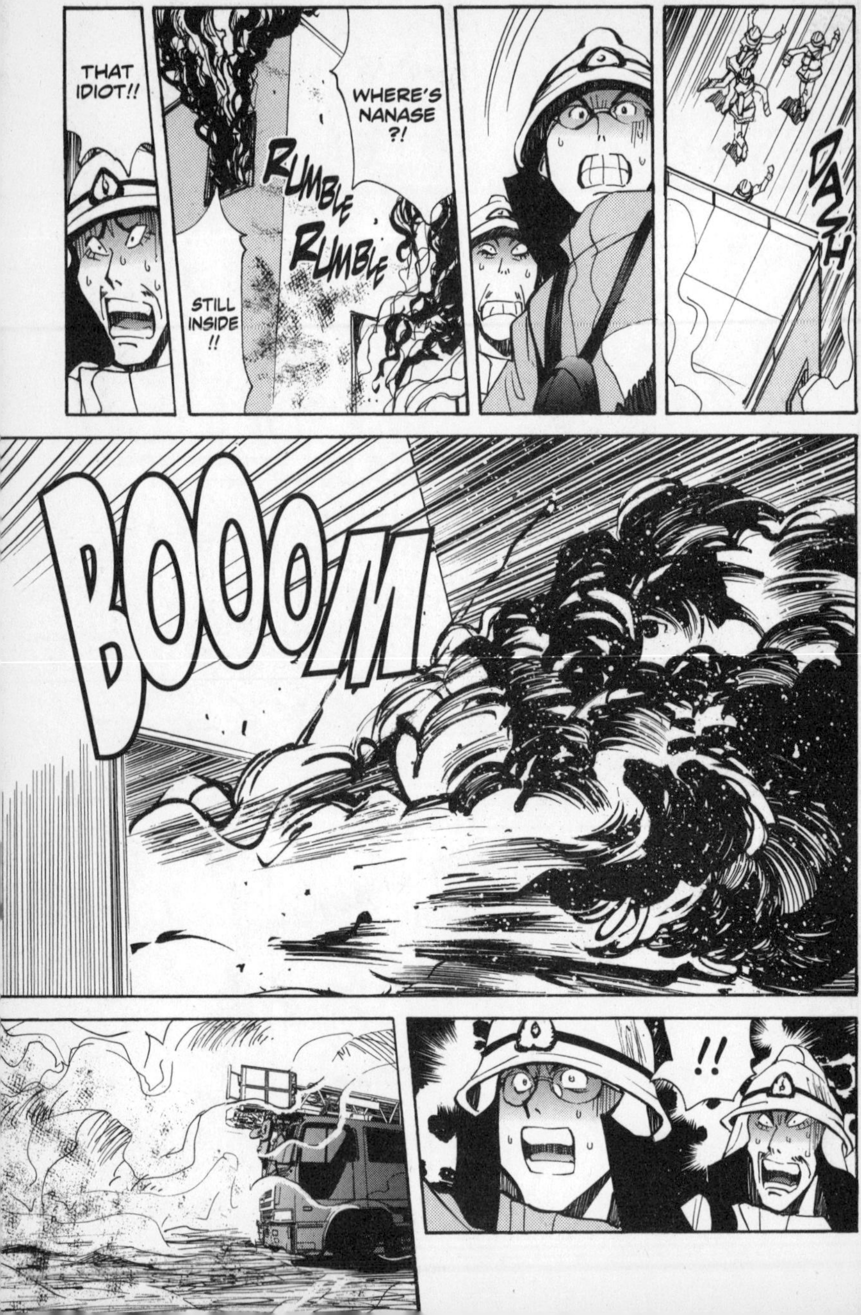
DASH
WHERE'S NANASE ?!
RUMBLE RUMBLE
STILL INSIDE !!
THAT IDIOT!!
BOOOM
!!

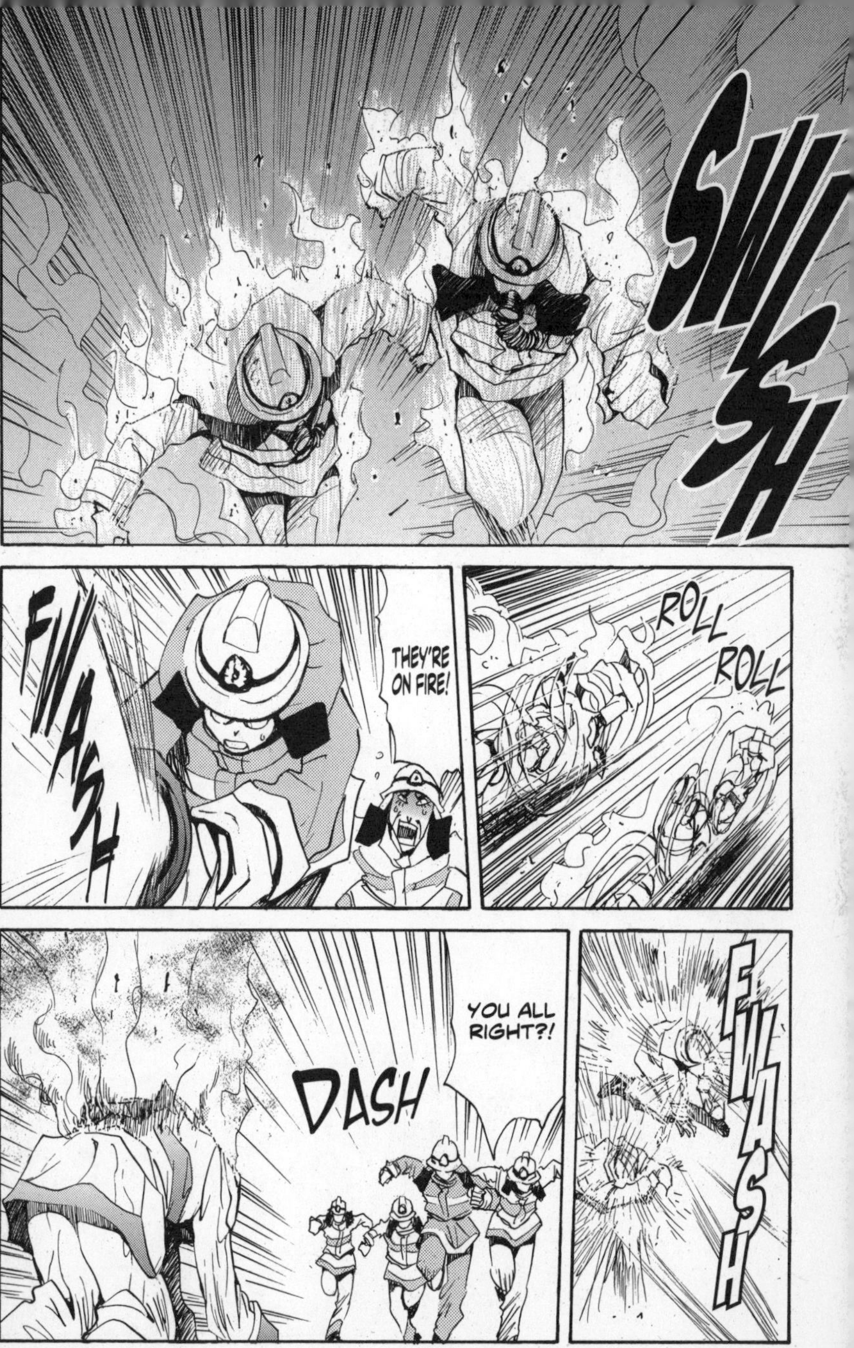
SWISH
ROLL
ROLL
FWASH
THEY'RE ON FIRE!
FWASH
YOU ALL RIGHT?!
DASH

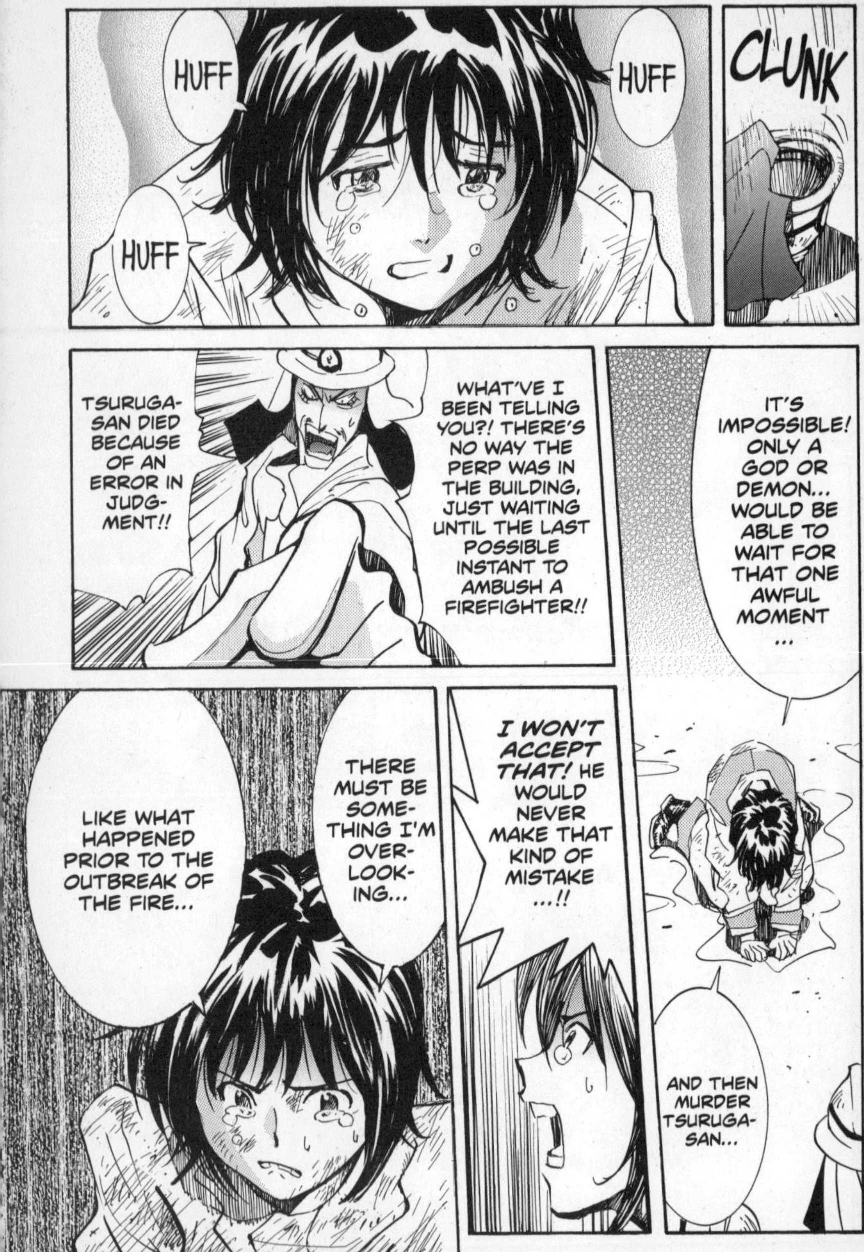
CLUNK
HUFF
HUFF
HUFF
IT'S IMPOSSIBLE! ONLY A GOD OR DEMON... WOULD BE ABLE TO WAIT FOR THAT ONE AWFUL MOMENT ...
AND THEN MURDER TSURUGA-SAN...
WHAT'VE I BEEN TELLING YOU?! THERE'S NO WAY THE PERP WAS IN THE BUILDING, JUST WAITING UNTIL THE LAST POSSIBLE INSTANT TO AMBUSH A FIREFIGHTER!!
TSURUGA-SAN DIED BECAUSE OF AN ERROR IN JUDGMENT!!
I WON'T ACCEPT THAT! HE WOULD NEVER MAKE THAT KIND OF MISTAKE ...!!
THERE MUST BE SOMETHING I'M OVERLOOKING...
LIKE WHAT HAPPENED PRIOR TO THE OUTBREAK OF THE FIRE...

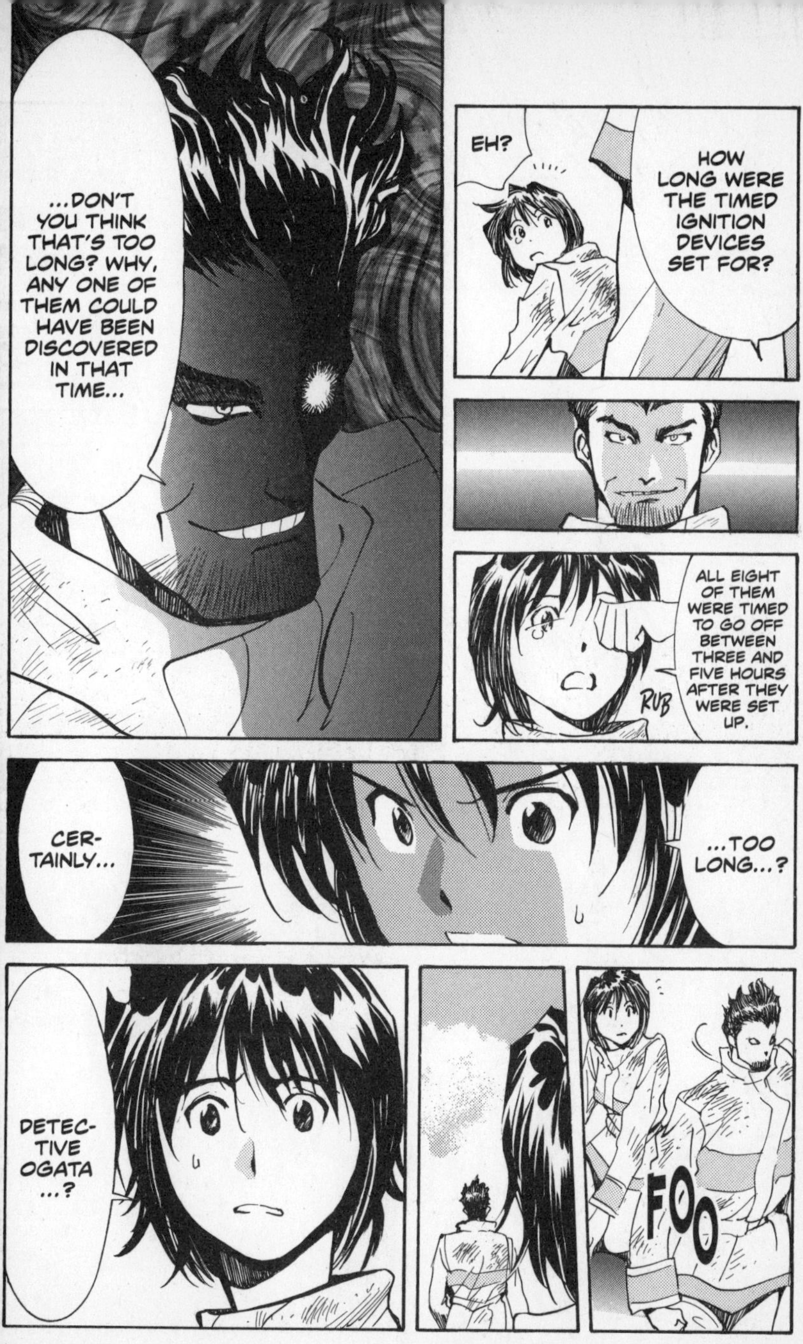
HOW LONG WERE THE TIMED IGNITION DEVICES SET FOR?
EH?
ALL EIGHT OF THEM WERE TIMED TO GO OFF BETWEEN THREE AND FIVE HOURS AFTER THEY WERE SET UP.
RUB
...DON'T YOU THINK THAT'S TOO LONG? WHY, ANY ONE OF THEM COULD HAVE BEEN DISCOVERED IN THAT TIME...
...TOO LONG...?
CER-TAINLY...
FOO
DETEC-TIVE OGATA ...?

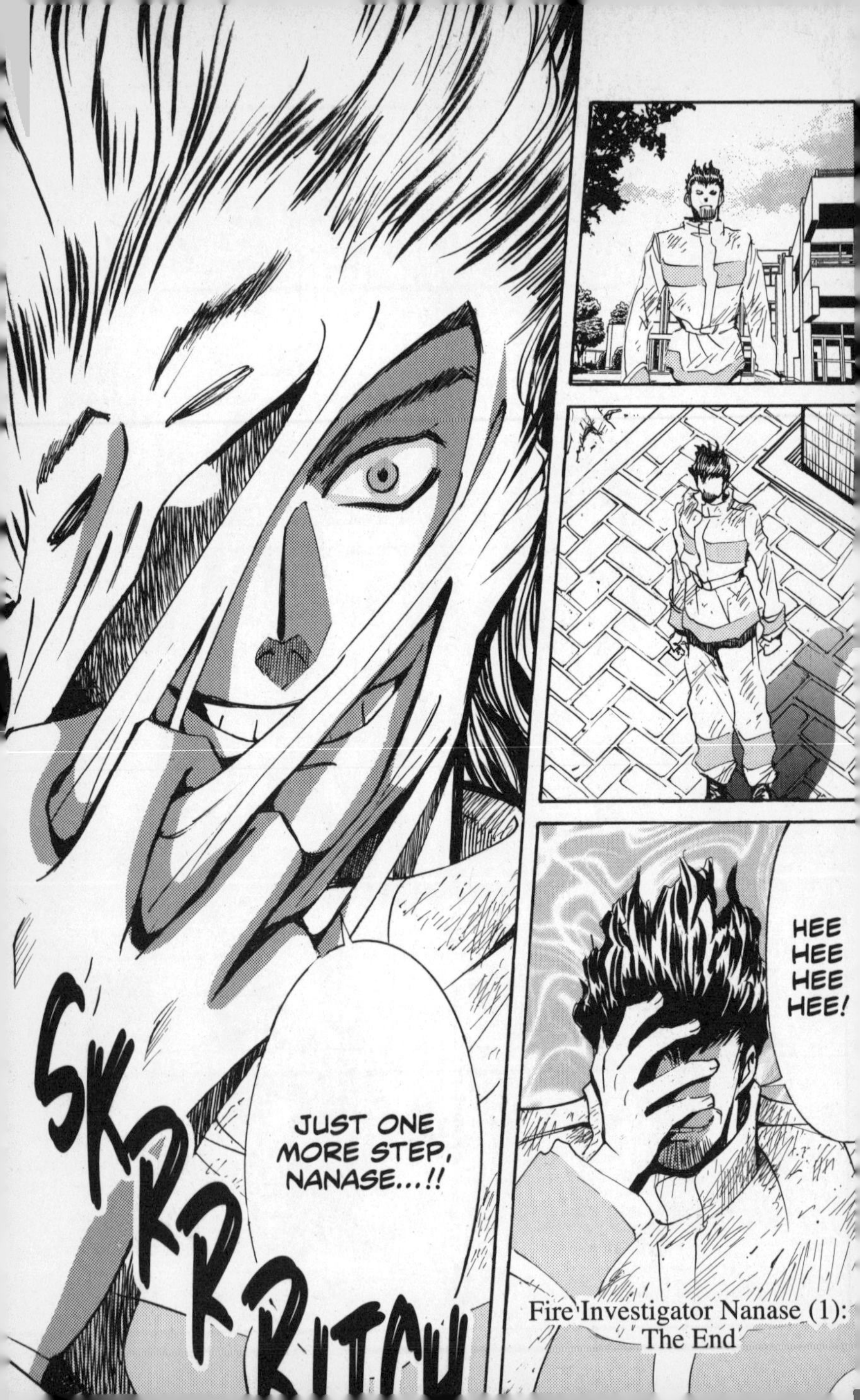
HEE HEE HEE HEE!
JUST ONE MORE STEP, NANASE...!!
SKRRRITCH
Fire Investigator Nanase (1): The End

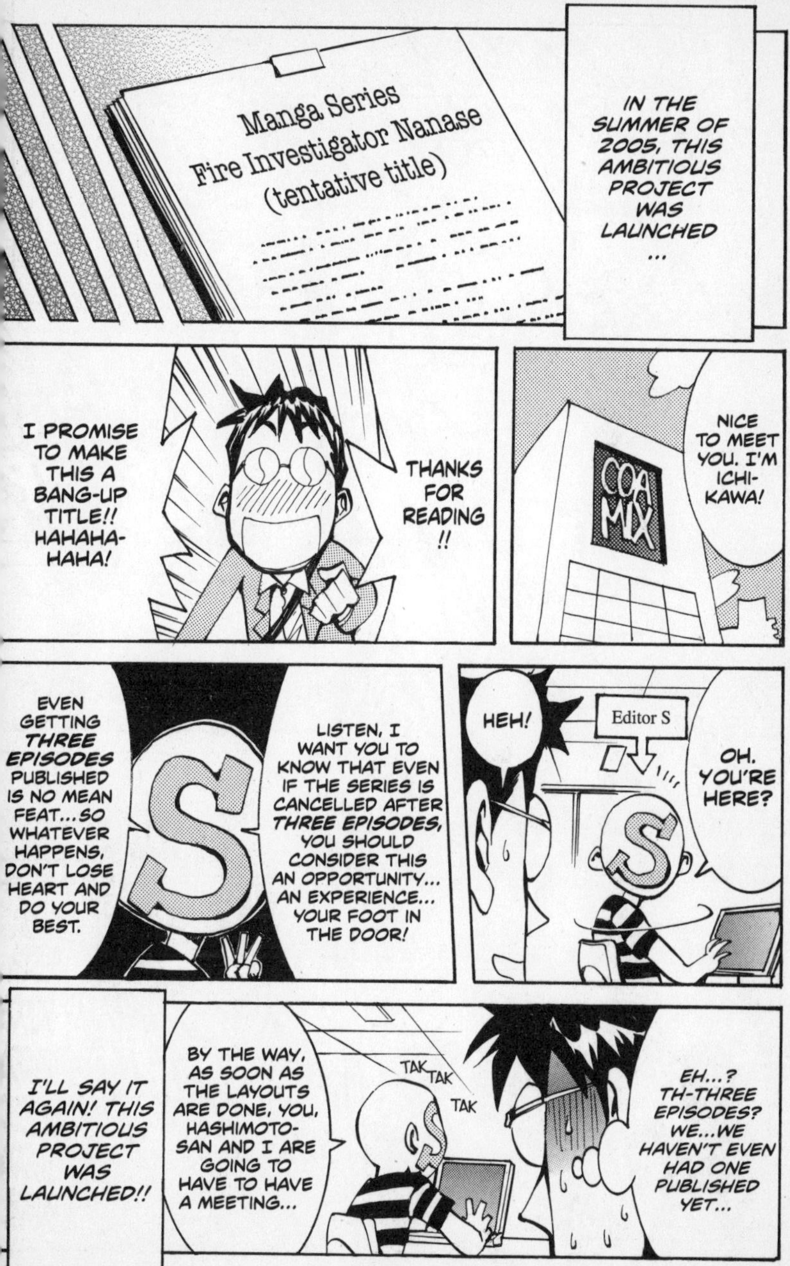
IN THE SUMMER OF 2005, THIS AMBITIOUS PROJECT WAS LAUNCHED ...
Manga Series
Fire Investigator Nanase
(tentative title)
NICE TO MEET YOU. I'M ICHI-KAWA!
COA MIX
THANKS FOR READING !!
I PROMISE TO MAKE THIS A BANG-UP TITLE!! HAHAHA-HAHA!
OH. YOU'RE HERE?
Editor S
HEH!
LISTEN, I WANT YOU TO KNOW THAT EVEN IF THE SERIES IS CANCELLED AFTER THREE EPISODES, YOU SHOULD CONSIDER THIS AN OPPORTUNITY... AN EXPERIENCE... YOUR FOOT IN THE DOOR!
EVEN GETTING THREE EPISODES PUBLISHED IS NO MEAN FEAT... SO WHATEVER HAPPENS, DON'T LOSE HEART AND DO YOUR BEST.
EH...? TH-THREE EPISODES? WE...WE HAVEN'T EVEN HAD ONE PUBLISHED YET...
TAK TAK TAK
BY THE WAY, AS SOON AS THE LAYOUTS ARE DONE, YOU, HASHIMOTO-SAN AND I ARE GOING TO HAVE TO HAVE A MEETING...
I'LL SAY IT AGAIN! THIS AMBITIOUS PROJECT WAS LAUNCHED!!

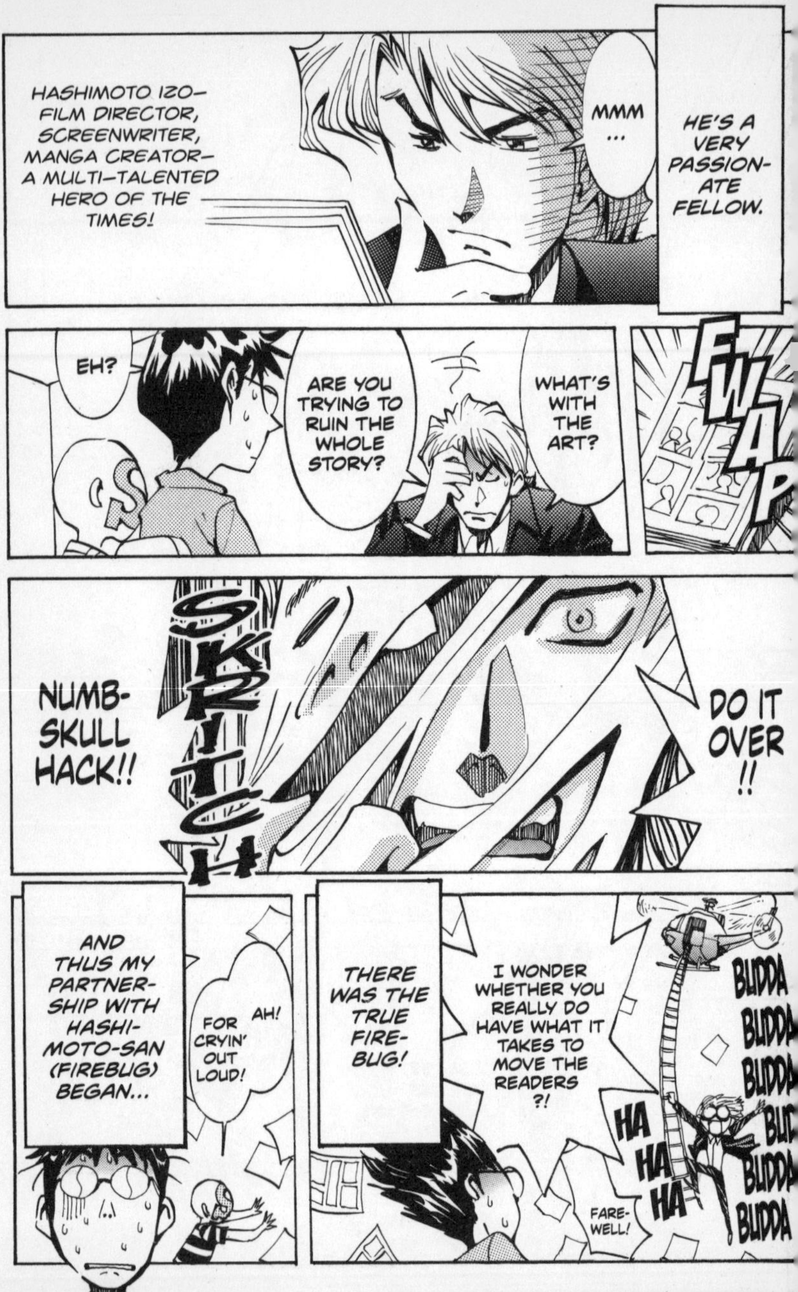
HE'S A VERY PASSION-ATE FELLOW.
MMM ...
HASHIMOTO IZO—FILM DIRECTOR, SCREENWRITER, MANGA CREATOR—A MULTI-TALENTED HERO OF THE TIMES!
FWAP
WHAT'S WITH THE ART?
ARE YOU TRYING TO RUIN THE WHOLE STORY?
EH?
DO IT OVER!!
SKRITCH
NUMB-SKULL HACK!!
BUDDA BUDDA BUDDA BUD BUDDA BUDDA
I WONDER WHETHER YOU REALLY DO HAVE WHAT IT TAKES TO MOVE THE READERS ?!
HA HA HA
FARE-WELL!
THERE WAS THE TRUE FIRE-BUG!
AND THUS MY PARTNER-SHIP WITH HASHI-MOTO-SAN (FIREBUG) BEGAN...
AH!
FOR CRYIN' OUT LOUD!

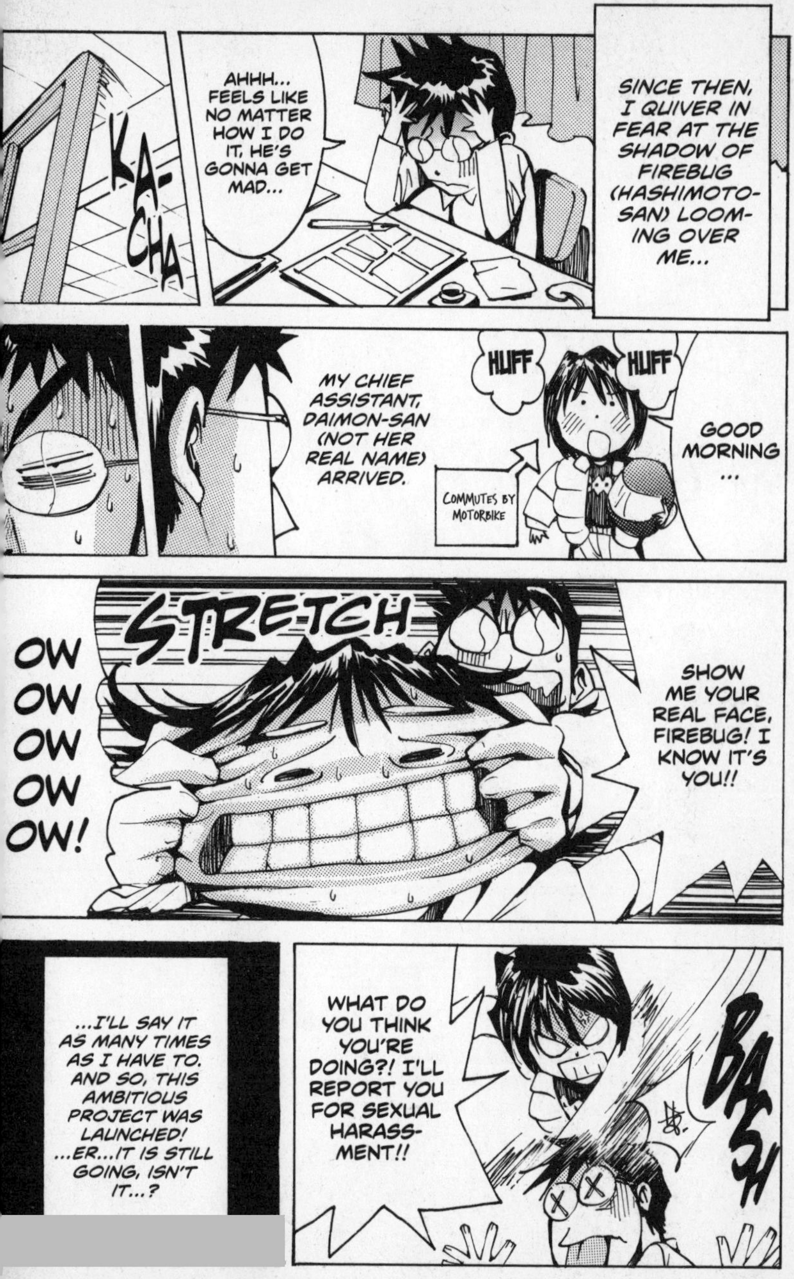
SINCE THEN, I QUIVER IN FEAR AT THE SHADOW OF FIREBUG (HASHIMOTO-SAN) LOOMING OVER ME...
AHHH... FEELS LIKE NO MATTER HOW I DO IT, HE'S GONNA GET MAD...
KA-CHA
HUFF
HUFF
GOOD MORNING ...
MY CHIEF ASSISTANT, DAIMON-SAN (NOT HER REAL NAME) ARRIVED.
COMMUTES BY MOTORBIKE
SHOW ME YOUR REAL FACE, FIREBUG! I KNOW IT'S YOU!!
STRETCH
OW OW OW OW OW!
BASH
WHAT DO YOU THINK YOU'RE DOING?! I'LL REPORT YOU FOR SEXUAL HARASSMENT!!
...I'LL SAY IT AS MANY TIMES AS I HAVE TO. AND SO, THIS AMBITIOUS PROJECT WAS LAUNCHED! ...ER...IT IS STILL GOING, ISN'T IT...?

MORE FIERY ADVENTURES IN MAY!

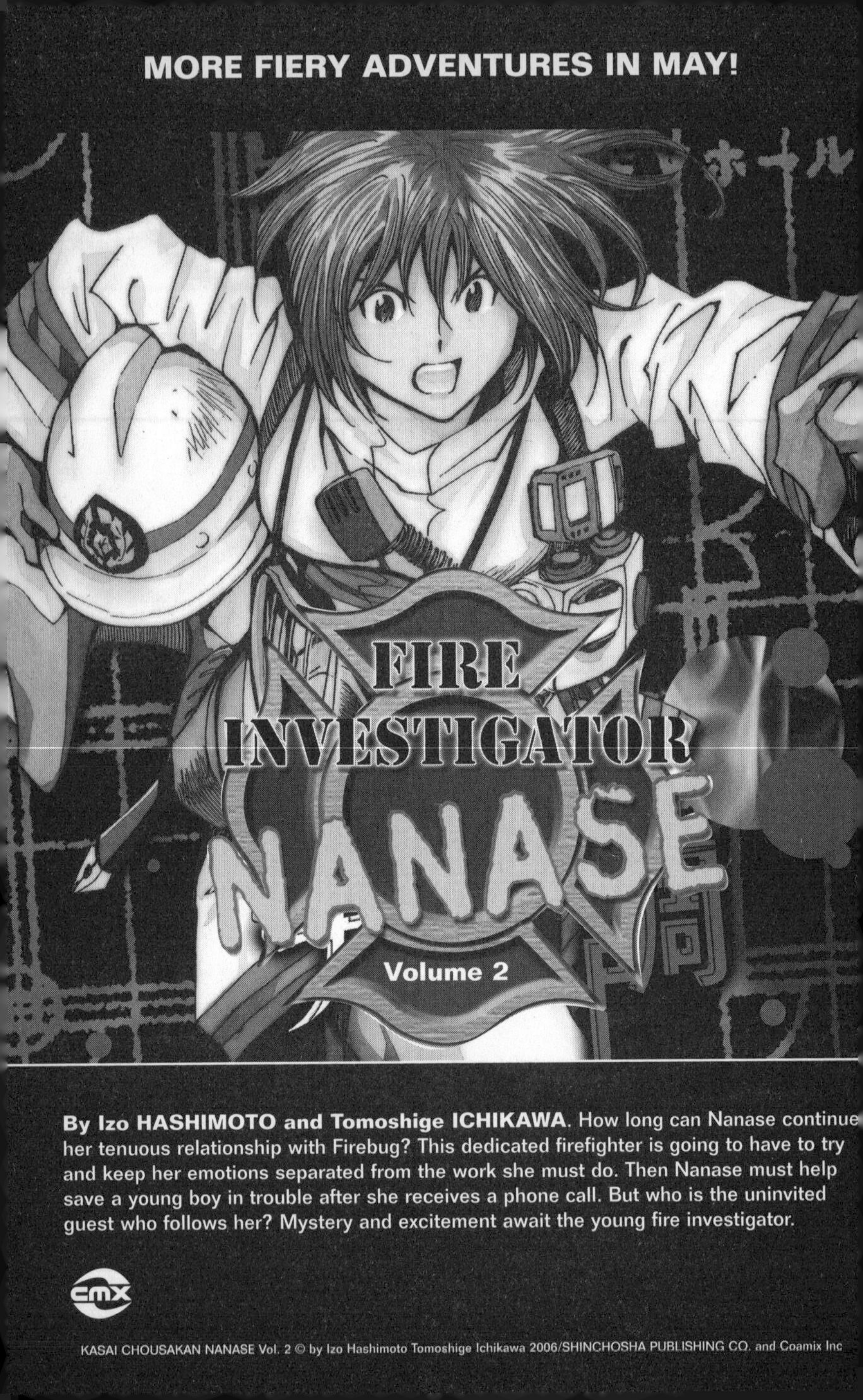
FIRE INVESTIGATOR
NANASE
Volume 2

By Izo HASHIMOTO and Tomoshige ICHIKAWA. How long can Nanase continue her tenuous relationship with Firebug? This dedicated firefighter is going to have to try and keep her emotions separated from the work she must do. Then Nanase must help save a young boy in trouble after she receives a phone call. But who is the uninvited guest who follows her? Mystery and excitement await the young fire investigator.

IT'S THE LAST CALL FOR EVERYONE'S FAVORITE DINOSAUR! ON SALE NOW!

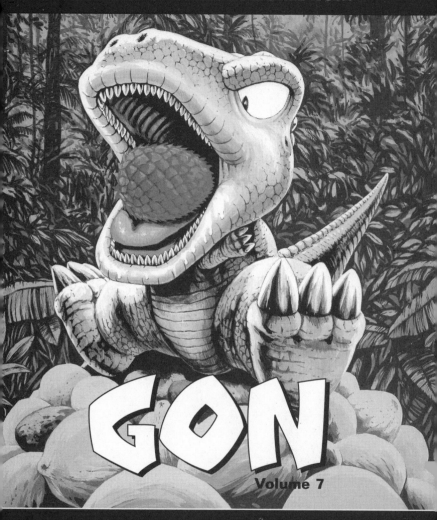

GON

Volume 7

By Masashi Tanaka. Join Gon for the final volume of this classic series. It's Gon doing what he does best—helping the targets of predators and having a little fun along the way. This time it's about families, as Gon befriends both a mother bird and her babies and an orangutan and her brood. But will the little guy's big appetite get himself and his friends in trouble? A craving for honey and a massive beehive form a potentially deadly combination, but Gon's never been known to avoid trouble, especially when he's hungry. Is he about to get stung in his final adventure?

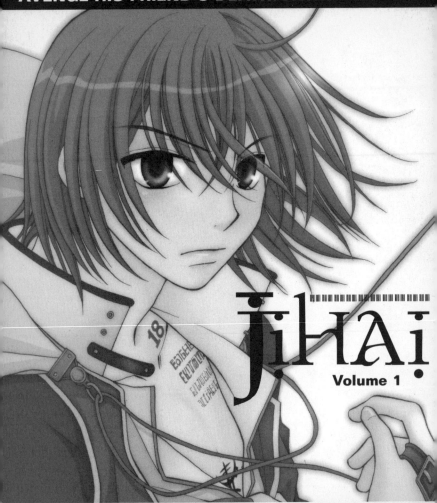

By Toshimi Nigoshi. Aoi is a courier who traverses long distances in impossibly short periods of time, by crossing through the Jihai (wasteland), where supposedly nothing can live. When a delivery goes awry and the recipient tries to kill him, Aoi is rescued and taken to an orphanage that isn't at all what it seems. Most of the kids there have some special, super-human ability. Will these children be allies in Aoi's search for vengeance…or an even greater threat?

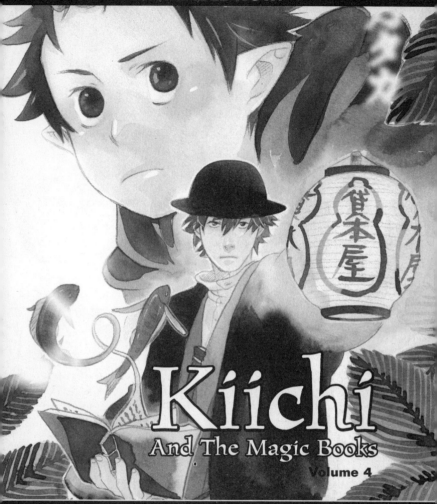

Jim Lee
    Editorial Director
Hank Kanalz
    VP—General Manager, WildStorm
Paul Levitz
    President & Publisher
Georg Brewer
    VP—Design & DC Direct Creative
Richard Bruning
    Senior VP—Creative Director
Patrick Caldon
    Executive VP—Finance & Operations
Chris Caramalis
    VP—Finance
John Cunningham
    VP—Marketing
Terri Cunningham
    VP—Managing Editor
Amy Genkins
    Senior VP—Business & Legal Affairs
Alison Gill
    VP—Manufacturing
David Hyde
    VP—Publicity
Gregory Noveck
    Senior VP—Creative Affairs
Sue Pohja
    VP—Book Trade Sales
Steve Rotterdam
    Senior VP—Sales & Marketing
Cheryl Rubin
    Senior VP—Brand Management
Jeff Trojan
    VP—Business Development, DC Direct
Bob Wayne
    VP—Sales

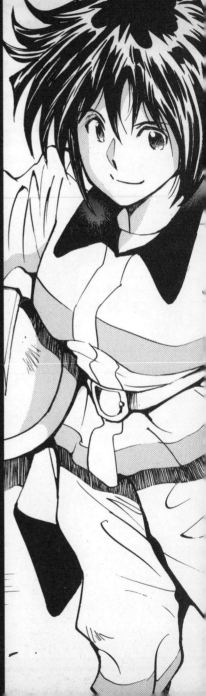

KASAI CHOUSAKAN NANASE © by Izo HASHIMOTO
Tomoshige ICHIKAWA 2006. All rights reserved. First
published in Japan in 2006 by SHINCHOSHA PUBLISHING
CO. and Coamix Inc., Tokyo.

FIRE INVESTIGATOR NANASE Volume 1, published by
WildStorm Productions, an imprint of DC Comics, 888
Prospect St. #240, La Jolla, CA 92037. English Translation
© 2009. All Rights Reserved. English translation rights in
USA and Canada arranged with SHINCHOSHA PUBLISH-
ING CO. and Coamix Inc. through Tuttle-Mori Agency. Inc.,
Tokyo. CMX is a trademark of DC Comics. The stories,
characters, and incidents mentioned in this magazine are
entirely fictional. Printed on recyclable paper. WildStorm
does not read or accept unsolicited submissions of ideas,
stories or artwork. Printed in Canada.

DC Comics, a Warner Bros. Entertainment Company.

Sheldon Drzka – Translation and Adaptation

AndWorld Design – Lettering

Larry Berry – Design

Jim Chadwick – Editor

 ISBN: 978-1-4012-2043-3

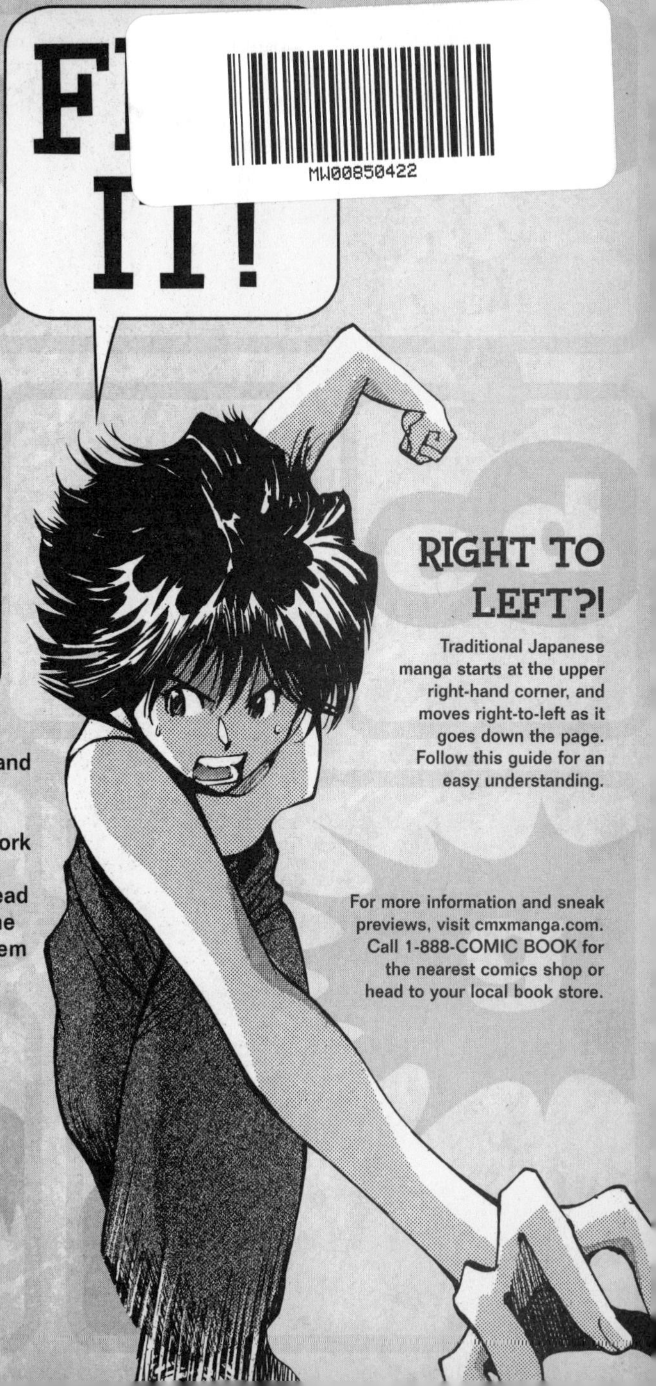
F
IT!

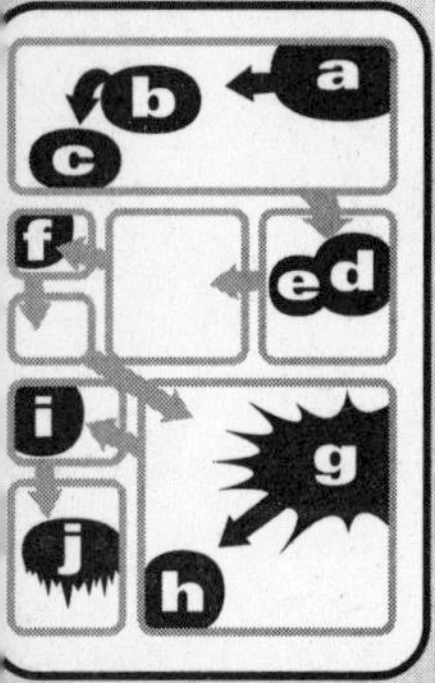
a
b
c
ed
f
g
i
h
j

All the pages in this book were created—and are printed here—in Japanese RIGHT-to-LEFT format. No artwork has been reversed or altered, so you can read the stories the way the creators meant for them to be read.

RIGHT TO LEFT?!

Traditional Japanese manga starts at the upper right-hand corner, and moves right-to-left as it goes down the page. Follow this guide for an easy understanding.